The Future of Values

Since September 1997, UNESCO's Division of Foresight, Philosophy and Human Sciences has organized a series of '21st-Century Talks' as a contribution to a global debate on some of the key challenges of our time. Each session brings together two or three leading scientists, intellectuals, artists or decision-makers from all parts of the world in a spirit of forward-looking interdisciplinary enquiry.

This volume constitutes an anthology of the contributions made to these future-oriented discussions, from the tenth up to and including the twentieth session of the 'Talks' held on 19 September 2001. Following the events of 11 September, the Division of Foresight, Philosophy and Human Sciences also staged a second '21st-Century Dialogues' session, on 8 December 2001, at which the topic of 'The Future of Values' was debated in the same spirit by an international panel of some twenty participants.

We wish to thank the authors whose generous contributions to the '21st-Century Talks' and 'Dialogues' have made this publication possible.

THE FUTURE OF VALUES
21st-Century Talks

Edited by
Jérôme Bindé

With a preface by
Koïchiro Matsuura
Director-General of UNESCO

Translator for the English edition
John Corbett
*(and Brian Verity for
Jacques Derrida's contribution)*

Berghahn Books
NEW YORK · OXFORD

UNESCO Publishing
PARIS

Published in 2004 jointly by the
United Nations Educational, Scientific and Cultural Organization
and **Berghahn Books**

© 2004 UNESCO

All rights reserved.
No part of this publication may be reproduced in any form or by any means
without the written permission of UNESCO and Berghahn Books.

Library of Congress Cataloging-in-Publication Data

The future of values : 21st-century talks / edited by Jérôme Bindé ; with
a preface by Koïchiro Matsuura ; translator for the English edition, John
Corbett and Brian Verity for Jacque Derrida's contribution.
    p. cm.
Includes bibliographical references.
    ISBN 1-57181-442-6 (alk. paper) — ISBN 1-57181-443-4 (pbk. : alk. paper)
    1. Ethics. 2. Values. I. Bindé, Jérôme.

BJ1012.F88 2004
121'.8—dc22

2004048528

ISBN UNESCO: 92-3-103946-6

Library of Congress Cataloguing in Publication Data

A catalogue record for this book is available from the British Library.

*The ideas and the opinions expressed in this work are those of the authors and do not
necessarily reflect the view of UNESCO. The designations employed and the presentation
of material throughout this publication do not imply the expression of any opinion what-
soever on the part of UNESCO concerning the legal status of any country, territory, city
or area or of its authorities, or concerning the delimitation of its frontiers or boundaries.*

Contents

List of Abbreviations	viii
Preface *Koïchiro Matsuura, Director-General of UNESCO*	ix
Introduction *Jérôme Binde*	xi

Part I
The Future of Values

Introduction *Aziza Bennani*	3
Twilight, Clash or Hybridization of Values?	5
Towards a Twilight of Values? *Gianni Vattimo*	7
Tactical Humanism *Arjun Appadurai*	13
From the Universal to the Singular: The Violence of the Global *Jean Baudrillard*	19
Values and the Challenge of the Inhuman	25
The Culture of the Inhuman *Hélé Béji*	27
The Devil's Advocate, between the Ethical and the Systemic *Peter Sloterdijk*	34
Serious Values or Frivolous Values?	41
The Ethics of Complexity and the Problem of Values in the Twenty-First Century *Edgar Morin*	43
For a Subversive Genesis of Values *Mohammed Arkoun*	47
Towards a Frivolousness of Values? *Jean-Joseph Goux*	55
Beyond the Aestheticization of Values?	62
Art Beyond Aestheticism *Wolfgang Welsch*	64
Towards a Postmodern Ethic of the Aesthetic *Michel Maffesoli*	69
The Soul of Values *Victor Massuh*	73
Towards the Reinterpretation of Values?	76
Values and the Construction of Subjectivity *Candido Mendes*	78
Towards a Feminizing of Values? *Julia Kristeva*	80
The Rise of Associations and New Forms of Solidarity *Roger Sue*	86
Universal Project, Multiple Heritages *Paul Ricoeur*	89
Towards the Century of the Spirit?	94
The Emergence of Cognitive Civilization *Thierry Gaudin*	95

Religion and the Challenge of the Spiritual in the
   Twenty-First Century *Souleymane Bachir Diagne* 98

Part II
Globalization, New Technologies and Culture

Globalization and the 'Third Industrial Revolution' 105
Globalization and its Discontents *Paul Kennedy* 107
Globalization, Peace and Cosmopolitics *Jacques Derrida* 110
Science, Technology and Globalization *Francisco Sagasti* 123

The New Technologies and Culture 127
The Age of Access *Jeremy Rifkin* 129
Is Culture Threatened? *Michel Serres* 142

Cultural Globalization and the Preservation of Diversity 147
A Tamed Schizophrenia? *Daryush Shayegan* 149
Reconstructing Culture *Alain Touraine* 154

The Future of Languages 159
Colonization, Globalization and the Future of Languages
   Salikoko S. Mufwene 161
The Life, Death and Resurrection of Languages *Claude Hagège* 166

Part III
Towards New Social Contracts?

The New Social Contract and Lifelong Education for All 179
Towards Lifelong Education for All *Jacques Delors* 181
Education and Citizenship in the Twenty-First Century *Jeliou Jelev* 187
Women and the Future of Education *Fay Chung* 191

A Natural Contract and the Future of Development 196
The Natural Contract and Development in the Twenty-First Century
   Jérôme Bindé 198
The Future of Biodiversity *Thomas Odhiambo* 204
Environment and Development in the Approaches to 2020
   Mostafa Tolba 210

Framing a Cultural Contract for the Twenty-First Century 215
The Case for a Cultural Contract *Alain Touraine* 217
What Future for Cultural Pluralism? *Hélé Béji* 220
Culture in the Twenty-First Century: Cloning or Hybridization?
   Eduardo Portella 228

Towards an Ethical Contract? 233
Bioethics and the Future of Living Things *Ryuichi Ida* 235
Future Ethics and Politics *Edgar Morin* 241
Development in the Twenty-First Century? *Lord Meghnad Desai* 245
Shaping a Universal Consciousness *Luc Montagnier* 248

Part IV
Science, Knowledge and Foresight

The Human Impact of the Genetic Revolution — 253
Does Natural Selection Still Drive Evolution? *Edward Wilson* — 255
From Genetic Mystification to Molecular Policing *Jacques Testart* — 260
The Political Challenge of Genetic Engineering *Gianni Vattimo* — 270

The New Faces of Racism — 273
Racism, Globalization and the Genetic Revolution
   Pierre Sané and Jérôme Bindé — 276
The New Aspects of Racism in the Age of Globalization
   and the Gene Revolution *Nadine Gordimer* — 280
Genism, Racism and the Prospect of Genetic Genocide
   George Annas — 284
The Genome, Biology and Racism *Axel Kahn* — 289
The Imaginative Roots of Racism *Achille Mbembe* — 293
The Changing Face of Racism *Elikia M'Bokolo* — 298

Self-Knowledge: Anticipating and Preventing Sickness of the Soul — 301
The New Maladies of the Soul *Julia Kristeva* — 303
The Compression of Time and Sickness of the Soul
   Denise Bombardier — 309
Exclusion and Sickness of the Soul *Adalberto Barreto* — 312

Human Beings and the Future of the Universe — 318
The Future of the Universe: Big Bang or Big Crunch?
   Trinh Xuan Thuan — 320
Cosmologies of the Future *Nicolas Prantzos* — 324
Scientific Enquiry: Doubts and Certainties *André Brahic* — 330

Conclusion: In Search of Lost Time—towards an Ethics
   of the Future? *Jérôme Bindé* — 341

Select Bibliography — 347

Abbreviations

UNDP	United Nations Development Programme
UNESCO	United Nations Educational, Scientific and Cultural Organization
NGO	Non-governmental organization
EHESS	Ecole des Hautes Etudes en Sciences Sociales
UNFPA	United Nations Population Fund
CNRS	Centre National de la Recherche Scientifique
WTO	World Trade Organization
FAO	Food and Agriculture Organization
R&D	Research and Development
GATT	General Agreement on Tariffs and Trade
GMO	Genetically modified organism
DNA	Deoxyribonucleic acid
PGD	Pre-implementation genetic diagnosis
IMF	International Monetary Fund

Preface

Our age is widely held to be experiencing a crisis of values. Many observers, fearing the collapse of all that gives meaning to our actions and our very existence, attribute this disquiet to the rise of globalization. Exclusively geared to technological progress, globalization is seen as soullessly materialistic, incapable of guiding our actions and indifferent to values. How have we come to this? Since the dawn of modernity, with its origins in the Renaissance and the Enlightenment, two fundamental ethical ideas have prepared the way for globalization as the emphasis has alternately been placed, with universalism, on the absolute of ideals and, with pluralism, on the diversity of practices. Together they have served as a kind of ethical compass. However, having reached the confines of a globalized world, we find ourselves lacking the means to explore it in all its complexity. For globalization has confronted us with a wholly new territory that renders our old navigation tools obsolete.

Does this mean that we are moving towards a world without ethics? I do not think so. Values are always present. I would even say that there have never been so many values in contention in the history of humanity. One of the first effects of globalization is arguably to reveal a plurality of cultures and a pluralism of values of which we were previously quite unaware. The strangeness of the phenomenon of globalization does not then lie in an illusory, rhetorical disappearance of values. It may even be that there are too many values today. For the crisis we are experiencing suggests that we have lost our ethical bearings and are unable to discern a horizon towards which to move. What we are facing is not so much a crisis of values but rather a crisis concerning the very meaning of values and our capacity for self-governance. The urgent question is thus how to orient ourselves among values.

The ethical upheaval through which we are living cannot therefore be said to be a moral disaster. After all, crisis is a time for critical appraisal, for calling things into question. All cultures are equal in dignity, and therefore of equal worth, since each can be seen as embodying an aspect of human totality. It follows that all cultures must be respected. But crimes against humanity, xenophobia and intentional destruction of the cultural heritage highlight the fact that all values are not equivalent. People have often sought to identify cultures with the values found in them, whereas each culture, from the moment it distinguishes between what is just and unjust, itself proceeds to sift between values deemed contradictory. Values are thus subject to re-evaluation. The shortcoming of universalism and relativism alike is to overlook the fact not only that values evolve but, more importantly, that they can be shaped in common and debated and negotiated between actors that are often very different All cultures have the same value and the same dignity, but all values are not equal.

We thus arrive at a conclusion that is more in the nature of a maxim concerning the creative diversity of human cultures. The challenge today is that the ethical effort must be mainly focused on a global community. Our hopes for a new ethical approach can be founded on the idea of a dialogue of cultures. Such a dialogue would start from the premise that cultures must be respected but also that values can be reassessed jointly. This ethic is distinctive in consisting of values that have been examined in common and that will be respected rather than imposed. UNESCO's role is to promote and serve as a forum for ethical discussion of this kind, which sets out to redefine and anticipate tomorrow's values. It is in this spirit that we have pondered the question of the "future of values". The key question is indeed in what direction these values may lead humanity. Ethical enquiry is a delicate exercise since it calls for a sense of anticipation. Its aim, rather than seeking to describe values, should be to understand the way in which they may be transformed—and may transform us.

Koïchiro Matsuura
Director-General of UNESCO

Introduction

The talk today is of nihilism, 'loss of meaning' and the 'disappearance of values', of the 'clash of civilizations' and supposedly irreconcilable values. The question of nihilism, and hence of values, has been central to philosophical enquiry in the twentieth century. At the end of the nineteenth century, Nietzsche prophetically identified history with the process of nihilism, which he summed up in the formula: 'the devaluing of the highest values'. The 'death of God' in his view entailed the death of Man:[1] Nietzsche thus prefigured Michel Foucault in *The Order of Things*. For Heidegger, nihilism is the movement whereby Being is forgotten and is wholly transformed into value. Beyond the differences of approach between Nietzsche and Heidegger, some philosophers—Gianni Vattimo in particular[2]—have seen an affinity between their two definitions of nihilism, namely 'the reduction of being to exchange value'. In this view, it is paradoxically because the 'highest values' have declined that the notion of value has been liberated in all its bewildering potential. Values could then display themselves 'in their true nature [...] as possessing the capacity for convertibility', as part of the 'movement of generalization of exchange value'.[3]

At the dawn of the twenty-first century, at a time when attempts to reappropriate values seem to have foundered—whether in relation to revolutionary schemes of political emancipation or ventures in the realm of philosophical, spiritual, ideological or political renewal; when certain prophets of doom are proclaiming the advent of a 'post-humanity', not to say of the inhuman; when tragic events leave us disoriented and discredit the hypothesis of the 'end of History'; and when societies are mobilized in the search for new ethical codes, UNESCO could not fail to address the question of the future of values from a forward-looking philosophical standpoint.

Voltaire, in the century of Enlightenment, still had no doubt: 'There is only one morality just as there is only one geometry'. But this universalist

---

1. As cogently argued by Gilles Deleuze.
2. Gianni Vattimo, *The End of Modernity*, Baltimore, The Johns Hopkins University Press, 1988.
3. Ibid.

certainty has long since crumbled with the denunciation of the all-too-human origins of morality. Suspicions as to the historical and cultural relativity of values, together with attempts to debunk them as ideological trappings masking power drives, have shaken philosophical, religious and artistic faith in absolute Truth, Goodness and Beauty. This great crisis of values, which has shaken the last two centuries to the core, has resulted in myriad uncertainties. What is the significance of the absence of any transcendent foundation that enables eternal values to be anchored in an unchanging firmament or received as a final and irrefutable revelation. Does it mean the twilight of values? Or, in a world where cultures encounter one another on a planetary scale, should we anticipate virulent antagonisms, potentially violent clashes between opposing values? Alternatively, will we witness new and unexpected hybridizations between value systems that are currently alien in origin and orientation?

The twentieth century has painfully called into question all our certainties concerning society, history and humankind. The contemporary crisis of values affects not only the traditional moral frameworks transmitted by the great religious faiths but also the secular values that succeeded them (science, progress, the emancipation of peoples, and humanist ideals of solidarity). The spectre of monstrous evil, which left its mark on the twentieth century, seems once again to loom over us. Is there not a risk that technological development—a crucial, unpredictable and uncontrollable factor of change—could render humanity unrecognizable, leading to what some have already disturbingly called a 'post-humanity'? Could the outcome of the genetic revolution not be a form of self-domestication of the human species? In a universe characterized by radical innovations and discontinuities, which will rapidly impact on the human species as a whole and will alter geopolitical balances, how can history continue to be conceived in terms of continuity, and how can the desirable utopia of a better life for the majority be sustained? Can we hold to the vision of a universal project compatible with the multiplicity of our heritages and enriched by their interwoven histories?

Paul Valéry presciently pointed out that, in a world dominated by speculation, our conception of moral or ethical values was increasingly influenced by the model of the stock market. There is no longer any fixed standard of value, any stable and absolute measure, but rather all values fluctuate in a vast market, their quotations rising and falling according to wholly subjective crazes, panics and wagers. The value 'mind', he joked, was no different to the value 'wheat' or 'gold', and it was continuing to fall.... In this way, the phenomenon of fashion, which was previously restricted to those sectors governed by arbitrariness and convention, is permeating our whole conception of values. We live in the realm of the ephemeral, accelerated obsolescence and subjective whim, as if the most sacred values, deprived of any foundation, could enter the great securities market and float in their turn. This speculative view of values as relative to a particular moment and circumstance applies to a great many ethical and aesthetic phenomena in the contemporary world. The role of information and the media reinforce this tendency since the logic of the stock-exchange model of values, like that of fashion and short-term trends, implies taking account of a whole series of ephemeral 'indicators', to be seized immediately, instantaneous information replacing a sense of history and recognition of its henceforth indiscernible long-term patterns.

In a context that overwhelmingly seems to privilege a view of values as frivolous,[4] how can we still think of them as *serious?* How can the crucial question of education find its rightful place in a fluctuating and malleable world subject to the emotional and intellectual influence of ephemeral images? The twenty-first century could find itself caught in a strange contradiction: never has such value been placed on the ephemeral; yet the emergence of knowledge societies, which are tending to make lifelong education for all not simply a dream but a practical proposition, seems to prefigure the development of a new tool for shaping long-term values that are simultaneously serious, recreational and juvenile.[5] At a time when the boundaries between the three stages of life are becoming blurred, new values—both cognitive and future-oriented—seem to be emerging. They are not so much inherited as invented, not so much reproduced as created, not so much received as transmitted.

Are we then moving towards an aestheticization of values, since the main concern is with their creation? Has aesthetics become the culmination of economics and ethics? Today, the antagonism between the artist and the bourgeois, between 'aesthetics and political economy' (in the words of Mallarmé), has disappeared. Not only is the artist fully recognized and lauded, but he has possibly never been placed on such a pedestal, never been made the very model of activity productive of meaning and novelty as he currently is. 'Creation' is all about us. We are all—or aspire to be—'creators'. All forms of production, enterprise and action are conceived on the model of artistic creation. In our personal lives, in the absence of stable and enduring frames of reference, each of us is obliged to resort to creation, if only of our own existence: we have to invent a 'lifestyle'. In economic life, innovation is recognized to be the engine of development; market forces place a premium on the seductiveness of the product, on the limitless proliferation of consumer appetites, which can only be sustained through a perpetual dynamic of alluring creations. This

---

4. See Jean-Joseph Goux, *Frivolité de la valeur*, Paris, Blusson, 2000. The author wishes to thank Jean-Joseph Goux for his valuable contribution to setting the terms of the UNESCO debate on the future of values on the occasion of the '21st-Century Dialogues' session organized at UNESCO Headquarters on 8 December 2001.

5. Jérôme Bindé, 'Demain, de plus en plus jeunes ?', introductory presentation to the 15th session of the '21st-Century Talks', Paris, UNESCO, 26 September 2000, published in the *Revue des deux mondes*, October–November 2002.

pervasive aestheticization affects not only society as spectacle (the media, the advertising world and the visual/aural environment) but the very core of ethical principle and of the business dynamic.

May we therefore predict the creation of new values? The twentieth century has seen a massive decline in many regions of the world in allegiance to traditional religious dogmas, but also an extraordinary diversification of personal or community quests of a spiritual nature. Are these minority insights a potential source of strong values that could prove essential for the future? Similarly, while the social cement has been weakened by the rise of an increasingly radical individualism that destroys inherited links and established identities, it is paralleled by an unprecedented growth of new forms of association and the birth of new forms of solidarity. What values will stem from these new networks of affinity, alliance and communication (furthered by technological innovation)? In a world increasingly ruled by economic motives and the materialistic and narcissistic values of consumption, hedonism and short-term satisfaction, can we discern the emergence of alternative values that could be described as 'post-materialist'? These questions are linked to the collapse of patriarchal structures (with their ethical, institutional, cultural and metaphysical dimensions), representing a considerable break with the past and leading to a feminizing of values with far-reaching consequences whose scope is still hard to gauge but which will affect all aspects of the century ahead.

The questioning of values is a symptom of the profound changes that our societies are experiencing under the combined influence of the major phenomena of globalization and the new technologies. Globalization, contrary to what one too often hears, is not reducible to the neoliberal integration of the markets or the emergence of global thinking. Globalization, understood as a sense of belonging to the world, has a long history that reaches back over the centuries. Was it not under the Roman Empire that philosophers first thought of the concept of cosmopolitanism? As Edgar Morin has pointed out, the history of the first phase of mobilization, that of the explorers, the great discoveries and colonization, which saw the prevalence of all kinds of hegemonies and all forms of domination, whether political, economic or cultural, should not make us lose sight of the existence of a second phase of globalization, that of the human conscience, which from Las Casas and Montaigne through NGOs to contemporary global civic movements, informed by the idea of our common humanity and a forward-looking vision of an earth citizenship, has been a political, philosophical and spiritual phenomenon as well as a cultural one. Does this lend support to the possibility of harmonious coexistence between cultures, prophesied by those subscribing to an irenic view of globalization? Here, though, we must point to the persistence of flagrant inequalities globally and nationally. Mention must also be made of the role of the new technologies and of the 'information revolution' as adjuncts of globalization. For there is a great risk that the changes taking place will deepen the digital, economic and social divide, which no longer coincides exactly with the North/South split. More than ever, we need to consider how knowledge can be universally shared and how genuine exchanges between cultures can take place.

From this standpoint, questions concerning the plurality of cultures cannot be restricted to the debate on values and the problem of relativism. In the age of globalization and new technologies, the new challenge is: How can cultural diversity be preserved? For the threats hanging over the diversity of cultures cannot be underestimated. The question of the future of languages illustrates the point. The number of languages spoken in the world—5,000 to 6,000 at the present time—could be halved by the end of the century. And the absence of a genuine multilingualism on the Internet can only accentuate this phenomenon of the extinction and erosion of languages. Before we start to discuss what is required to preserve cultural diversity, it is clear that we have to diagnose the dangers that threaten it.

New challenges call for new responses. This is a measure of how far the new world taking shape before us compels us to rethink totally the social contracts that underpin our societies. The global changes described above argue the need for a project of global social and political renewal, which UNESCO has tentatively suggested might be centred on the idea of four contracts.[6] A new social contract founded on lifelong education for all, a natural contract, a cultural contract and an ethical contract constitute its main thrusts in a global society where the challenges are planetary. Without the provision of lifelong education for all, how is absolute poverty to be eradicated, how are democratic values to be effectively promoted and how are genuine knowledge societies to be built? Without a natural contract under which humankind would be not the 'master and possessor' but the steward of nature, how can we put an end to the excessive exploitation of existing resources, which could irreparably jeopardize the possibilities of sustainable development and hence the prospects of future generations? Without a cultural contract, problematic as this may be, what recourse would we have against the dwindling of cultural diversity? Without redefining the ethical requirements that underpin the very ideal of human rights and provide a framework for human security, how can we lay the bases for a forward-looking democracy and a global citizenship? This is a measure of the scale of the task before us.

An appreciation of the value of a future-oriented approach is important to carrying such a project. Machiavelli said that 'prudent princes have to

---

6. See the UNESCO world futures report *The World Ahead: Our Future in the Making*, London, UNESCO Publishing/Zed Books, 2001. See also *Keys to the 21st Century*, New York and Oxford, UNESCO Publishing/Berghahn Books, 2001.

regard not only present troubles, but also future ones ... because, when foreseen, it is easy to remedy them; but if you wait until they approach, the medicine is no longer in time because the malady has become incurable'.[7] UNESCO's role is to be a forward-looking organization, drawing on the talent of leading scientists, researchers, thinkers, creators and international public figures to bring about the marriage of politics with prudent foresight. We now know that science itself, so long as its creativity is not curbed, must also observe the principle of foresight. The consequences of the genetic revolution in particular need to be questioned, both from an ethical standpoint and also from the point of view of the social preferences and discriminatory practices that it has not managed to eradicate. For in the wake of the possible self-domestication of the human species, old ghosts and old demons could return to haunt us.

Is there not a risk that too much questioning will induce a kind of disorientation and cause us to diagnose over-hastily this loss of meaning we referred to initially in terms of nihilism? Certainly, loss of meaning is the recurrent context of many of the issues confronting us today. One has only to look at the different forms of modern psychopathologies to see that contemporary societies, having lost touch with time, are also set to lose touch with the soul. It is as if, in the age of short-term returns, we had succumbed to the cult of stress and the tyranny of urgency. Is this not, in the words of Jean Baudrillard, a heavy price to pay for 'the ideal of self-maximalization, the social blackmail of performance, the unconditional realization of the human being as a programme'?

But the loss of meaning is perhaps no more than an illusion—a product of melancholy. In pondering the question of the future of meaning, we confine ourselves to a gloomy and partial response if we dwell on its loss. What we should rather be talking about is shifts in meaning and the creation of new meanings. Let us end with a wager: what if the renewal to which we aspire were to spring from knowledge and the spread of knowledge? What if knowledge societies were to take the place of value-based societies? For knowledge cannot be reduced to the questioning of received wisdom and the production of doubt, inherent in the scientific approach. Knowledge is also creation, renewal and gearing ourselves mentally to change. There could be no more admirable goal for UNESCO than to point the way to this new ethic.

Jérôme Bindé

---

7. Machiavelli, *The Prince*, chap. 3.

PART I

The Future of Values

Aziza Bennani

Introduction

Today's world has placed a premium on material development, sacrificing many moral and spiritual values on the altar of material progress. Economic, political, social, cultural and educational realities have evolved and changed in significant ways, with the result that our worldview, values and outdated schemes of thought do not always allow us to devise appropriate solutions to crucial problems. Nor have we always succeeded in preventing our values and cultures from becoming detached from the global economy, the rules of the market and the highly useful but invasive new technologies. This has led to a divorce between the twin poles of our existence. As a result, cultural allegiances and religious ideologies—often distorted from their true meaning—have increasingly imposed themselves as an exclusive response. Hence the need to strengthen our system of values, 'to try to build a society of minds, having set up a society of nations', as Jérôme Bindé wrote in *Keys to the 21st Century*.

The danger facing us today is not—as has been claimed—the clash of civilizations but rather the absence of shared values. The attacks of 11 September, along with their repercussions and the numerous questions they raise, call for searching analysis. Our thinking today must therefore be situated in a context that is both general and topical. It is more necessary than ever to subscribe to an ethic based on values conducive to a world of greater justice and solidarity, a world open to all in which freedom, equality, peace and non-discrimination prevail alongside respect for diversity and recognition of the richness of all civilizations. Diversity, in the words of Javier Pérez de Cuéllar, is 'creative'.

Reaffirming our attachment to such values, making them the basis of our actions and our coexistence with others, is therefore an essential and urgent task. In the present international context, the values central to UNESCO's mission are among the foremost priorities. They must be translated more effectively into practice, avoiding ritual slogans. This means educating individuals from the earliest possible age, giving each and everyone the chance to cultivate their differences, to develop and fulfil themselves in a context of peace.

None should impose on others their vision of the world, their culture, their way of thinking, their moral code. Accepting diversity, integrating it in the universal without succumbing to relativism, is undoubtedly the best approach. In the past, al-Andalus demonstrated—notably in the golden age of the Caliphate of Cordoba—the possibility of basing a splendid culture on a plural identity. 'Thanks to that great adventure of the spirit', in the words of Jorge Luis Borges, 'thanks to that unique meeting of minds' to quote Hamza Rami, thanks also to the values shared by the different elements making up that society, values very close to those identified today as characteristic of modernity, the most varied sensibilities found expression and the different cultural traditions profited from the contributions of others, without compromising their own identity. We should look closely at this example, at a time when we are questioning the values that govern our age. The memory of the different peoples contains many examples of this kind, which could serve as an inspiration for restructuring the relations between individuals and communities. They need to be highlighted, not of course in a nostalgic way but for the purpose of shaping a future project based on shared universal values and giving the greatest possible scope to the human being. The great moments of history have always been those that gave pride of place to humanity. The main concern of our time should be, while respecting differences, to give meaning to our shared humanity in the context of a renewed humanist project.

* * * *

Minister of Culture of Morocco from 1994 to 1998 and Moroccan Ambassador to UNESCO, **Aziza Bennani** was chairperson of the Executive Board of UNESCO from 2001 to 2003. She is also a member of the permanent secretariat of the Forum de la Femme Méditerranéenne and a former representative of Morocco on UNESCO's World Heritage Committee.

Twilight, Clash or Hybridization of Values?

In the wake of 11 September 2001, is the clash of values unavoidable? In a globalized world, it is true values seem to have lost something of their universality and moral certainties something of their force. Yet the violence of contemporary conflicts and expressions of grievance would suggest that the idea of the relativity of values, which has gradually come to dominate our thinking, is no longer a satisfactory way of approaching the question. Are we moving towards a twilight of values? Or shall we see a hybridization of values stemming from different traditions? In that case, we need to think about ways of establishing a constructive model for values.

Gianni Vattimo takes up the idea of a 'civilization of decline', traditionally associated with the West, and extends it to the relationship between values and the postmodern individual. He sets out in this way to sketch a third way intermediate between the violence of fanatical expressions of grievance and that simplistic form of Eurocentrism that tends to impose a Western model on the rest of the world: the shaping of a 'civilization of decline', incorporating recognition of the relativity of values and the need for a commitment to negotiation.

Arjun Appadurai also argues the case for negotiation as the touchstone of what he describes as a 'tactical humanism'. He does so in the context of the emergence of new forms of violence in the modern world, calling for an analysis based on a clear distinction between two types of organization: the old model of the nation-state and an emerging model reflecting the flows and networks arising from globalization, which excludes any possibility of taking universal values for granted.

Jean Baudrillard develops the hypothesis of an opposition between the global and the universal. By imposing dislocation and fragmentation, the forces of globalization effectively work in his view towards the destruction of the universal. From this standpoint, he interprets the revolt of singularities and its most extreme form, terrorism, as symptomatic of this lack of universality and as the ultimate stage of globalization.

* * * *

Gianni Vattimo, professor of philosophy at the University of Turin and a member of the European Parliament, is considered one of the leading figures of philosophical postmodernism. He has taught at various American universities, including Yale, UCLA and New York University. He is the author of *The End of Modernity* (1988), *Belief* (2000), *Dialogo con Nietzsche* (2001) and *Nichilismo ed emancipazione* (2003).

Born in India, **Arjun Appadurai** is an anthropologist, and currently rector of the New School University. He was previously professor at Yale University, where he directed the Initiative on Cities and Governance and taught in the departments of anthropology, political science and sociology. He is co-founding editor of *Public Culture* and the editor of *Globalization* (2001). His publications include *Worship and Conflict under Colonial Rule* (1981) and *Modernity at Large: Cultural Dimensions of Globalization* (1996). His research is particularly focused on ethnic violence and megacities in the context of globalization.

Sociologist, philosopher and writer, **Jean Baudrillard** taught at the University of Paris-X and has lectured at numerous universities throughout the world. His publications include *The Transparency of Evil: Essays on Extreme Phenomena* (1993), *Symbolic Exchange and Death* (1993), *The Illusion of the End* (1995), *The System of Objects* (1996), *The Perfect Crime* (1996), *The Consumer Society: Myths and Structures* (1998), *Impossible Exchange* (2001), *Spirit of Terrorism: A Requiem for the Twin Towers* (2002) and *Fragments* (2003). His recent publications in French include, with Edgar Morin, *La violence du monde* (2003).

Gianni Vattimo

Towards a Twilight of Values?

I hope I shall not be accused of taking up a familiar right-wing—not to say European fascist—theme if I begin by alluding to the title of a work published by Oswald Spengler in 1918: *Der Untergang des Abendlandes*, The Decline (literally 'Twilight') of the West. I propose to place a different political construction on Spengler's title while retaining some of its metaphorical implications. I shall lay particular stress on the link that he made between the decline of the West and imperialism. While I do not subscribe to the biologistic notion that our civilization is showing signs of old age, I observe the Western world to be displaying signs of maturity that characterize its calling, if not necessarily its destiny.

Nothing is easier than to develop these ideas in the aftermath of the events of 11 September, which some have been quick to term 'apocalyptic'. In my view, 11 September did not produce anything radically new since Wall Street's Twin Towers had already been attacked earlier by the same terrorists, thus enabling us to size up their intentions and their strike capability. Moreover, the economic recession in America did not begin on 11 September since it had been apparent since March 2001.

What is new is the unprecedented strength and cohesion of the 'Holy Alliance' that George Bush's presidency managed to put together in the fight against terror. Yet this mobilization would appear less and less sustainable as the war in Afghanistan nears its end, since questions are being asked about the methods that will then be adopted to destroy 'all' the terrorist bases in the world. The name originally given to this operation, 'Infinite Justice', of itself suggests that this will be an interminable task.

Vitalism versus secularization

While we are not witnessing a Huntington-style clash of civilizations, the unfolding of events in the Middle East and in the various theatres of terrorist activity can very well be described as an attack on a mature world—ours—that no longer has the enthusiasms and sometimes desperate violence of youth and of those ready to sacrifice themselves in the name of ethical and religious ideals. It is of course questionable whether all Al Qaida fighters are heroes or saints: alongside the fanatics who blow themselves up with their bombs or crash planes into the New York towers, there are certainly cynics who use religion as the 'opium of the people' and lukewarm believers who practise violence for very mundane and secular political motives. However, what is striking in the confrontation between fundamentalist Islam and the West is the fact that what is described as the asymmetry of war and terror also reflects a profound difference in spiritual attitude. If the press is to be believed, many people think—after and even before 11 September—that Western consumer society has become too sceptical to engage in a fight to the death, just as the Roman Empire in its declining years was unable to defend itself against the more primitive barbarians from the North, who were stronger, braver and above all 'younger', to employ Spengler's suspect biologistic terminology.

Although twentieth-century philosophy has invariably been marked by a kind of 'sociological impressionism', to borrow the expression used by Lucas with reference to Zimmel, it seems to me incontrovertible that one of the main aspects of the present conflict between the Western world and its enemies is the degree of secularization of the societies in contention. It is hard to point to the causes of this divergence, which we perceive almost exclusively from the Western standpoint: they include the mediaeval rivalry between the Papacy and the Empire, the Protestant Reformation, and the Enlightenment, to mention only some of the landmarks in the secularization of European societies. We should also add the technological revolution, one of its key developments in the nineteenth century being the emergence of the large city where, as shown by Baudelaire, Walter Benjamin and Simmel, the 'loss of centre', i.e., the dissolution of shared traditions and values, became a mass phenomenon. The attitude that Karl Mannheim identified in the 1930s as characteristic of intellectuals—a sort of sceptical dandyism that made of them the authentic 'classless class' capable of liberating themselves from ideologies—is now the dominant attitude among the mass consumers of goods and information in the industrialized world.

In 1874, in his second *Untimely Meditations*, Nietzsche described this attitude as typical of the nineteenth-century intellectual, overburdened with culture and historical information and strolling through the garden of history as though in a theatrical costumier's storeroom, able to choose at will what style to adopt, knowing that it can be changed from one moment to the next. This possibility robs the individual of all creative capacity and renders our civilization decadent. A surfeit of memory prevents us from creating new values. Nietzsche, in his mature writings, repudiated fairly explicitly this vitalist position of his earlier years, going so far as to write in an 'insane letter' sent from Turin in January 1889, that he felt as if he bore all the names in history. Madness or not (since it foreshadows in paradoxical mode the 'pathological' ideas of Nietzsche's maturity), it remains the case that this propensity for perpetual role-acting was, in Nietzsche's thinking, one of the characteristic features of the postmodern individual, and that we find traces of it no longer just among the intellectuals criticized by Karl Mannheim but among all the inhabitants of the megalopolis unified by the spread of television and the Internet.

The error, so to speak, of the young Nietzsche and later of Spengler in his *Decline of the West* was to think of the twilight in negative terms. I personally have no hesitation in considering their vitalism to be a reflection of the persistence of what Heidegger called 'metaphysics' and what a thinker like Derrida would call logocentrism or, more clearly, 'the domination of presence', or yet again 'the myth of presence', in the sense of plenitude of being as opposed to reminiscence or expectation of the future (the word 'twilight' signifying not only the setting of the sun but also the half-light before sunrise) or, in a word, any more spiritually elevated condition that claims to be truer than the truth that can be seen, touched and measured.

Beneficent decline

It is not hard to sense where this line of thought is leading us. Given that the West is in several respects experiencing a kind of decline, should we not take this decline seriously, to the extent of incorporating in it the idealization of presence, plenitude and all those things that seem to constitute 'real life' yet which reveal themselves as inseparable from the violence of any kind of imperious presence or the self-evident truth that precludes any subsequent discussion and so easily merges into authoritarianism, including that implicit in fundamental principles?

Nietzsche wrote that 'we are no longer material for a society', meaning that our degree of individualization renders us incapable of submitting to collective rules. This is not true however of the mass individual, since our societies are based, in the economic and social spheres, on the principle of uniformity of tastes, behaviour and values. As society has—fortunately—lost many of its traditional community-based characteristics, this uniformity turns out to be weak where values are concerned, to the point that it could be defined as a 'mass historicism' assuming the form of the intellectual dandyism referred to by Zimmel.

Is this weakness to be regarded as something negative? The question is inseparable from what, in philosophical terms, I called the persistence of metaphysics, in the sense in which it was used by Heidegger: metaphysics as a vitalist myth of fullness of presence (*energeia*), which is not simply the fact of being present but also the energy, muscle and decisionist resolve so dear to fascists of every stripe. According to Heidegger and Nietzsche, metaphysics does not undergo crisis for theoretical reasons, as if certain philosophers had discovered the error at its core, which is why the link with colonialism and imperialism is diametrically opposed in this case to that found in Spengler. Metaphysics does not reveal itself in the first instance as an error; it becomes impossible because of the social and political transformations that render obsolete a particular view of history that had previously legitimated metaphysics itself and imperialism. The peoples of the Third World revolt and gain their freedom—not in the realm of theory but as a realized fact—by changing the experiential context in which philosophy is formulated. We should not forget Napoleon on horseback at Jena, as observed by Hegel. The fall of metaphysics is not made possible but rather necessary by the liberation of the former colonial peoples.

The peoples of the Third World are cultures apart, and can no longer be accommodated within the Western mythology of a linear history. They are apart, not primitive pending accession to knowledge of the West's scientific 'truth' and recognition of the 'true' value of our declarations of principle. What is making the myth of presence untenable is the pluralism of cultures, since this myth implies the idea of a single truth, apprehended by a single method and meriting precedence over other points of view. If someone counts in a different way from me, I can never say definitively whether he/she is mistaken or whether, as Wittgenstein pointed out, he/she is applying a different mathematics. The difficulty is moreover even greater in the realm of values than in mathematics. Recognizing as much means apprehending values with an attitude of restricted belief, typical of the mass individual of postmodern civilization. Nietzsche did not take a negative view of this situation since he wrote, in *The Gay Science*, that 'one must continue to dream knowing that one is dreaming'. A superhuman capacity of this kind (*übermenschlich*) is what, apart from any racist ambiguity, characterizes Nietzsche's superman. Perhaps Nietzsche did not manage to define the superman in a non-contradictory way because he remained a prisoner of the metaphysical ideal of truth: a very strong self-belief—and hence the survival of a faith in truth—underlay the violent and imperious forms whereby the superman realized himself and on which Nietzsche also theorized in some of his writings.

The value of charity: The case for a civilization of decline

There is a good case for saying—transcending Nietzsche or perhaps returning to the hidden sources of his thought in Christianity—that if the superman does not wish to remain a prisoner of truth, he must open himself up to charity, i.e., to criteria of rationality based on respect for others, rather than to the idea of possessing a value that deserves to be asserted whatever the cost. Might this sceptical attitude towards values, this ability to espouse them without regarding them as absolute, not be one of the key factors in the decline of our civilization? In this view, we are moving from the twilight of values to the decline of (our) civilization. Could we not invert this latter expression and speak of a civilization of decline? We would have to tread carefully because we live in a world where it is the order of the day to speak of development. It is only recently that it has come to be qualified by the adjective 'sustainable'. Even in the economic sphere, the idea of unlimited development increasingly appears self-contradictory: every day we see examples of increases in the stock-market values of firms that reduce their staff, and very often their output. It is now clearly acknowledged that development cannot be pursued ad infinitum, in purely quantitative terms at least.

Transposing this thought to the realm of values, we come up once more against the theme of secularization, in particular the incomplete secularization of 'Third World' countries, where the terrorists that threaten us are said to originate—although it should be remembered that there are terrorists everywhere (like poets?), even at the heart of the developed world. Yet does this idea of an incomplete secularization not rest on the simplistic historicist myth that Third World societies still have some way to go in order to raise themselves to our level and cease to be a threat to us? Can we without hypocrisy refer to the Third World, scarred by numerous consequences of colonial domination, in terms of the failed emergence of a native middle class capable of taking over the government of newly independent countries after independence without adopting either the hidden Eurocentrism implicit in the notion of incomplete secularization or the universalist ideology of human rights defined once and for all by our international organizations?

Can we discover a third way between Eurocentrism and universalism? It could take the form of an explicit trade-off that respects the different traditions without betraying our own. We cannot impose our twilight approach to values on the countries of the Third World. We should first realize this approach ourselves so that we do not fall into the trap of thinking that the only way of preserving ourselves from attack by fundamentalist groups or societies is to become fundamentalist again ourselves. Yet this is the direction in which some would have us move, starting with the Church and certain left-wing democrat intellectuals who call on us, in the name of a tragic realism that sometimes harks back to Benjamin but more frequently to Carl Schmitt, to rediscover a 'genuine' passion for values. They would like, in other words, to subject us to a therapy of artificial rejuvenation, whereas that could only end up in a return to violence, or even to war.

It may be true that the novelty of the situation lies in the way in which we experience our values. Essentially, the wars of the past that pitted European countries against each other were symmetrical in terms of collective psychology. All the combatants shared the same degree of faith or non-belief in their values. Today, the strength and the weakness of the West lie in the fact that we 'no longer believe', whereas our adversaries are fanatics ready to die and, above all, to kill. Yielding to the temptation to become 'young' and violent again would signify *propter vivendi perdere causas*, surviving at the cost of giving up what constitutes our existence, not in the biological sense but biographically and ethically.

Incomplete secularization is thus something that concerns the West first and foremost. It does not mean that we should abandon any 'military' defence of our way of life, but it should make us aware that if weapons become the only solution then we no longer have any chance of saving ourselves. Insofar as we are placing our way of life in jeopardy from military defeat or the kind of permanent insecurity from which Israel suffers, we should shape for ourselves a civilization of decline, which is the only way to avoid encouraging the growth of mass terrorism. We must therefore give our development a less aggressive dimension by redefining it in terms of the quality of the relationships between individuals and societies. The way in which wealth is distributed among the different countries of the world requires that we adopt a genuine culture of restraint. The Director of the World Bank himself has called for such a transformation. It is the task of culture and education to foster, in the realm of the imagination and collective psychology, an outlook that leads the public to opt—on purely pragmatic grounds if nothing else—for this difficult approach.

Arjun Appadurai

Tactical Humanism

The crisis of names

We sense that something happened on 11 September 2001 that required our intuitions of crisis, emergency and rupture to help us. We needed to know what to call the world into which we entered on that date. Since that date, many terms and names have rushed in to answer this call. Terror is one of many of these names; civilization is another of them; and everywhere moral visions call for humanity to find names for its other.

The crisis of names and naming requires a response. Many of those who oppose the violence of 11 September are equally horrified by the violence of the United States' and British response. Samuel Huntington's model of 'the Clash of Civilizations' seems to have come even truer than he might have feared.

Yet this is not a clash of civilizations and the name will serve us badly. The reasons for this have been noted by many thinkers: the Muslim world is not unified. Al-Qaeda is as much opposed to many Arab regimes as it is to the United States. The Koran contains no mandate for generalized violence against civilians. Tolerance has always been abused by religions at war with each other.

Yet we all feel that this is a war of words and worlds. In my opinion this is a deep, not a shallow war. That is, it is war about a crisis that transcends its stated motives and even the nature of the particular actors and countries involved. It is a war about the future of the nation-state as a locus of civility, sovereignty, moral authority and as a monopolist of legitimate violence. The attack on the World Trade Towers was an act of war performed on gigantic scale by unseen and unknown actors. It named an enemy without naming a country as its author. In one stroke it inaugurated what we may call the Age of Authorless War. Such a war moves us beyond the question of just and unjust wars to an age of wars without the familiar maps of territory, sovereignty, borders and national interests. It is the military incarnation of the global financial economy, a borderless war, with ephemeral winners and losers, technically terrifying but not fully contained by traditional reasons or boundaries. Even more than the terrifying atomic assaults on Hiroshima and Nagasaki, the attack on the World Trade Towers was not merely an effort to kill civilians; it was an effort to end the idea of civilians.

The United States' response in regard to bombing Afghanistan (with the early bonus feature of dropping food packages) showed a new ambivalence between recognizing that the era of civilians was over and holding on to the idea that there were human tragedies to be somehow compensated.

Diagnostic wars

I have elsewhere argued that globalization has spawned special forms of uncertainty about group identity, which create new kinds of group violence in the name of ethnicity. In the large-scale ethnic wars of the 1980s and 1990s, cross-border movements of refugees, implosions of nationalist politics, fears of economic chaos and rumours of tyrannical autochthonies have produced large-scale ethnic violence involving extreme forms of bodily brutality. I have argued that such forms of violence are macabre forms of vivisectionist discovery, intended to 'discover' and uncover true identities behind false facades. These are monstrous versions of the methods of science.

In the terrifying attack on the World Trade Center (WTC) and in the continuing battering of the valleys, cities and caves of Afghanistan by the United States-led Alliance we see a state-led extension of these forms of vivisectionist violence which we may call 'diagnostic wars'. A diagnostic war is one in which major acts of violence are intended to both discover and decimate the enemy. They are part of a world in which violence is not about a known enemy but is an effort to find the enemy.

In the wake of 11 September, we have entered a world of diagnostic procedures, not just in the bombings and suicide attacks that continue, but also in the response of security states everywhere, which seek to document, classify, isolate and discover terrorists in their midst through various forms of violently invasive and randomized behaviour. The hunt for beards, names, accents, etc. is a pathetic and frightening index of the era of diagnostic wars and somatic inquisitions. We have entered a world where every face could be a mask. In this sense too, we may mourn the death of the civilian, if by civilians we mean persons who assume that their ordinary appearances are enough to assure that they are not seen as traitors or as enemies. Since almost no one, especially in the warring countries, is immune from the suspicion that they may be the enemy (whether or not they are terrorists), we can see why we experience new forms of anxiety in many parts of the world. It is no longer a world in which enemies produce wars, but one in which wars determine and diagnose enemies. Pakistan, for example, was forced to become an ally through diagnostic pressure. This is why the idea of a just war seems somewhat beside the point, since that debate presumes a routine causal link between reasons of state, enmity and acts of war.

The war of world systems

This is not a clash of civilizations but it is certainly a clash of world systems. I suggest that the best way to understand this clash is to contrast the 'vertebrate' world with the 'cellular' world. The vertebrate world is the world of the nation-state, defined in more or less realist terms. Also parts of this vertebrate world are the global, multinational corporations, which may and do cross frontiers and blur loyalties but still function substantially by co-opting, invading, leveraging or corrupting existing state forms. The capitalism that underwrites globalization is resolutely vertebrate insofar as its main actors, procedures and interests have clear links through various centralized structures, ranging from the United Nations and the Bretton-Woods institutions to WTO, GATT and other newer multilateral governance institutions, which aim to coordinate and control capital on a global basis in some synchrony (however contradictory) with the sovereignty of existing nation-states.

The cellular (or invertebrate) world is not just a world of flows and networks but also works through completely different forms of coordination and coherence. It functions by multiplication, isolation of functional units and action by imitation or sympathy rather than by command, and it relies on the infinite reproducibility of certain minimal principles, whether ideological or functional. The networks behind the attacks on the WTC (whether they are confined to Al-Qaeda or not) are excellent examples of this cellularity.

But we would be mistaken to assume that such cellularity is solely a feature of covert networks devoted to guerrilla terror. Cellularity is also a key aspect of many globalization movements, which function in very similar ways across national boundaries. Behind the high spirits of the globalization dramas of Seattle, Prague, Washington, Milan, etc.. is a great diversity of cellular organizations, connected by e-mail, dispersed financial assets, non-governmental sources of legitimacy and parastatal forms of communication and control. So-called global civil society thus often takes cellular form.

In some regards, the more mysterious parts of the corporate world, those that rely on quasi-criminal channels and resources, non-taxable off-shore havens, unofficial methods of money-transfer and large transactions based on personal ties rather than on official records, also have this cellular quality. The space where these corporate mechanisms meet the world of terrorist networks, to take just one example, is the mechanism of 'hawala' payments, a venerable way of transferring money without actually moving either money tokens or currencies, across large distances. Hawala financing is surely a big part of the terrorist world but it is also a big part of the grey world of finance and commerce in the era of globalization more generally.

In short, the clash we are witnessing is between the entire system of global governance informed by the principles of national sovereignty and international law, generated after the Treaty of Westphalia, and a newer world of global flows, alliances, allegiances, and mobilization that is cellular but also entirely global. In this sense, the technologies of cellular globalization (such as e-mail, open borders, visas for expert forms of labour, new forms of globally portable software, and highly transferable forms of wealth such as derivatives) constitute a virtually unbeatable threat to the nation-state as a classic envelope for sovereignty, territory and legitimate authority.

In an earlier period of industrial capitalism, there seemed to be neater division of labour between ruling classes, states and global capitalism. This relationship is now faced with myriad contradictions, including those between the 'vertebrate' and the 'cellular' dimensions of capital itself. Put another way, always ridden with contradictions, capitalism is now itself divided into its cellular dimension, which relies on stealth, criminality and cross-border mobility, and its vertebrate dimension, which still relies on state protection, bureaucratic instruments and nationally defined markets.

Many observers have stated their arguments and intuitions about the link between the attacks of 11 September and the general trend towards greater rage and frustration among the poorer regions and classes of the world, the world of the losers in the great game of globalization, especially after 1989. And yet many of these observers have also mentioned that the causal links between global dispossession and rage against the United States and its global allies in the world of capital are neither simple nor straightforward.

My own suggestion would be that the violence of 11 September, and the worldwide reshuffling of alliances that we have seen since then, is part of a more foundational struggle between cellular and vertebrate forms of globalization, in which the cellular forms have succeeded better, for the moment, in capturing the fear and rage about the United States that has long been active in most parts of the Southern world. The Islamic world is an excellent example of the relationship between indigenous tyrannies, excluded majorities, the United States presence and the frustrations of new kinds of Arab intelligentsia. But this formula could easily work in many other places, which is why this equation of terror with Islam, and of Islam with the Arab world alone, will not take us very far. As for the United States, it may be noted that the intense hatred of this country in many parts of the world seems to be related to its double personality: as the monopolist of dreams of the good life and as the perceived gate-keeper responsible for excluding many peoples and classes from access to this very good life, either by limiting immigration or by enforcing specific ideas of market, politics and development on poorer countries.

Tactical humanism

Even if we are careful to avoid the self-appointed apocalypticism of many experts in the media, the state machineries and public life in the West that accompanied the events of 11 September (that is, the tendency to see the world as having changed for ever because a major American building complex was demolished), we cannot but recognize that the new millennium, promised in the form of the chaos of Y2K, appeared by stealth as '9-11'.

And surely values are part of the carnage of the battles that have taken place since then, especially among the cities and mountains of Afghanistan. But how to think about this slaughterhouse of values, iconized by the statues of Bamiyan at one end and the imploded WTC buildings at the other?

The image of clash seems too weak because there are so many clashes, and the fault-line of civilizations is patently both simple and dangerous to describe these. The image of 'twilight' is perhaps better, if nothing else because it speaks of an eerie epistemological stress. Yes, we are seeing new secularisms arise in response to new fundamentalisms and hybrid deployments of the image of terror, and also hybrid mixes of allies both for and against the attacks of 11 September. New debates have come into view within the world of Islam as well as new debates about war and justice in different traditions. There has been much exchange between intellectuals and critics across borders (in hostile space such as India and Pakistan for example). In all these ways the inevitable work of hybridization goes on, powered by the technologies of global flow and flux.

I have already suggested that this is a clash between two kinds of globalized world systems, one cellular and one vertebrate. But what sort of values can guide us through this struggle, which has barely begun and has caught us largely unprepared? We know that simple Manichaeisms will not do, nor will a liberal faith that hybridization will always bring the best values to the fore. Even if this may be true in the long run, it is poor comfort in a world of emergency.

What is called for is some sort of tactical humanism, a humanism that is prepared to see universals as asymptotically approached goals, subject to endless negotiation, not based on prior axioms. This is not a recommendation in disguise for relativism, for tactical humanism does not believe in the equal claims of all possible moral worlds. It believes in producing values out of engaged debate, even while bombs fall and treason is a charge thrown around freely by the voices of an antique nationalism.

Such tactical humanism will need to recognize that we cannot rely any more on the moral certainties of the nation; that we have entered a period when the right to be civilian may have to be painstakingly rebuilt; that for the foreseeable future cellular networks may outpace other forms of global governance; and that we may see more diagnostic wars that seek the enemy, and their own justice, post factum. In such a world, we may need to cease to take universals for granted and begin to practise the art of constructing them one emergency at a time. This is a hard prospect but perhaps our best one: a humanism prepared to negotiate across borders unaccompanied by any non-negotiable universals.

Jean Baudrillard

From the Universal to the Singular: The Violence of the Global

There is a deceptive analogy between the terms 'global' and 'universal'. Universality relates to human rights, freedoms, culture and democracy, while globalization concerns technologies, markets, tourism and information. Globalization appears irreversible, whereas the universal would seem to be in the process of disappearing, at least as the constituent principle of a modern Western value system without parallel in any other culture. Any culture that becomes universal loses its singularity and dies. This is the case with those we have destroyed by coercive assimilation, but it is also the case with our own culture by virtue of its claim to universality. The difference is that the other cultures died as a result of their singularity, which may be accounted a good death, whereas we shall die from the loss of all singularity and the extinction of all our values, which is a bad death.

Globalization as destructive of the universal

We think that the destiny of every value is to be elevated to the level of the universal, without measuring the mortal danger that this elevation entails: it is more in the nature of a reduction, or indeed elevation, to absolute zero in the scale of values. From the time of the Enlightenment, universalization took the form of a progressive levelling up; today it takes the form of a levelling down, through a neutralization of values as a result of their proliferation and limitless expansion. Examples include human rights and democracy, whose expansion corresponds to their weakest definition and maximum entropy.

In fact, globalization is fatal to the universal. The dynamic of the universal as transcendence, an ideal goal or utopia, ceases to exist as such once it is achieved. The globalization of exchanges puts an end to the universality of values. It is the triumph of unipolar thought over universal thinking. What globalization involves first and foremost is the market, the promiscuity of all goods and exchanges, and the perpetual flow of money. Culturally, it represents the promiscuity of all signs and values, that is to say, pornography. For the succession and worldwide dissemination of indiscriminate material through the networks is none other than pornography. There is no need for sexual obscenity; this interactive copulation is sufficient. At the end of this process, there is no longer any difference between the global and the universal: the universal itself is globalized, and democracy and human rights circulate exactly like any other global product, such as petrol or financial capital. What happens, with the transition from the universal to the global, is a simultaneous homogenization and fragmentation of the system ad infinitum. The global interconnection of networks is coupled with a dislocation of the fragments. It is not the local that succeeds the central, but rather the dislocated; it is not the decentred that succeeds the concentric, but rather the eccentric. The result is thus a disintegration of the universal. Globalization is at one and the same time homogenization and growing discrimination. Relegation and exclusion are not an accidental consequence but are inscribed in the very logic of globalization—which, contrary to the universal, disaggregates existing structures the better to integrate them. Everywhere the gaps are opening up, often irremediably.

World order: Violence and disorder

The question then arises whether the universal has not already succumbed to its own critical mass and whether it ever had any real existence beyond the official rhetoric and moral posturing. In any case, the mirror of the universal is in our view shattered; we can indeed see in it something resembling the current state of the mirror of humankind. Yet it is perhaps a stroke of good fortune, since in the fragments of this broken mirror of the universal all singularities re-emerge. All those thought to be at risk survive, and those thought to have disappeared are reborn.

The situation changes and becomes more critical as universal values lose their authority and legitimacy. So long as they exerted a mediating influence, they succeeded to some extent in integrating singularities in the guise of differences within a universal culture of difference; but they are now no longer able to do so since the irresistible march of globalization sweeps aside all differences and values, inaugurating a culture or unculture of total indifference. Once the universal has disappeared, the all-powerful global technostructure is all that remains in the face of singularities that have reverted to nature and been left to their own devices. The universal had its historical opportunity, but today, confronted by a monolithic global order, an irreversible globalization process in which all are adrift, or the tenacious revolt of singularities, the concepts of freedom, democracy and human rights pale into insignificance, wraiths of a defunct universal. It is difficult to imagine that they can rise again from their ashes through the mere workings of politics, which is itself caught up in the same current of deregulation and today has little foundation other than moral and intellectual authority.

The universal was a culture of transcendence, of the reflexive subject and the concept, a three-dimensional culture of space, reality and representation. Virtual space is that of the screen, the network, immanence and the digital. Yet this fourth dimension is far from being simply additional to the others, since it eliminates them all. By creating a collision between all the other dimensions, the global screen creates a one-dimensional universe, or rather a non-dimensional space-time. We have yet to measure the full extent of the violence done to our representations by this forced immersion into this fourth dimension. The violence of networks and the virtual is viral: it is the violence of benign extermination, operating at the genetic and communicational level; a violence of consensus and forced togetherness that acts as a kind of cosmetic surgery in the social sphere; a seemingly innocuous violence, tending to root out evil and all forms of radical behaviour by prophylaxis and psychic regulation through the media; the violence of a system that pursues all forms of negativity and singularity, including the ultimate singularity that is death itself; the violence of a society in which negativity, conflict and death are virtually forbidden to us; a violence that puts an end so to speak to violence itself, but which works in any case towards the establishment of a world liberated from any natural order, whether of the body, sex, birth or death. Rather than of violence, we should speak of virulence: a viral violence in the sense that it does not operate head-on, but by contiguity, contagion and chain reaction, its aim being the loss of all our immunities. And also in the sense that, contrary to the historical violence of negation, this virus operates hyperpositively, like cancerous cells, through endless proliferation, excrescence and metastases. Between virtuality and virality, there is a kind of complicity. We must resist this viral violence of globalization—a violence wreaked on all singularities by the universal, on the universal by the global and on the species by genetic manipulation—by setting against it the radical singularity, the singular event, rather than the globalization of failing universal values.

The revolt of singularities

The triumph of globalization is not a foregone conclusion; the die is not cast. This dissolutive and homogenizing power finds itself confronted on all sides by an upsurge of heterogeneous forces that are not only different but antagonistic and irreducible. Behind this increasingly strong resistance to globalization, which in its social or political forms can seem like an archaic rejection of modernity, we should discern a reaction against the ascendancy of the universal, a kind of revisionism that breaks with all the acquisitions of modernity and with the idea of progress and history, the rejection not only of the famous global technostructure but of the mental structure that identifies all cultures and all continents in the name of the universal. This resurgence, not to say revolt, of singularity can take on violent, anomalous, irrational aspects from the standpoint of our enlightened thinking; its ethnic, religious or linguistic forms mask personality disorders or neurosis at the individual level. It would be a fundamental mistake to condemn these reactions as populist, archaic or even terrorist. All the events making the headlines today are carried out in opposition to this abstract universality, including the antagonism of Islam to Western values. It is because it represents the most vehement challenge to Western globalization that Islam is now public enemy n° 1.

What can arise from the fragmentation of the global system are singularities. These singularities are neither positive nor negative. They are not an alternative to the global order: they exist on another scale, they no longer conform to a value judgement, and they can therefore represent the best or the worst. The only absolute benefit they bring is to destroy the straitjacket of totality. They cannot be federated in some larger historical enterprise. They are the despair of any unipolar and hegemonic mode of thought; but they are not a single counter-ideology inasmuch as each invents its own game and the rules by which it is played.

A singularity may be subtle and non-violent, as with singularities of language, art and culture rightly understood; but there are other violent singularities, of which terrorism is one. It is a singularity because it brings into play death, which is doubtless the ultimate, radical singularity. In the New York terrorist attack, everything turns on death, not only through the intrusion of death 'live' on the screen, eclipsing in one sweep all the sham violence and death distilled for us in homeopathic doses, but through the intrusion of a larger-than-real symbolic and sacrificial death, the absolute and irrevocable event. Terrorism is the act that restores an irreducible singularity at the heart of a ubiquitous system of exchanges. All those singularities, whether at the level of species, the individual or cultures, that have paid with their death for the setting up of this global market governed by a single power are today exacting revenge through this terrorist inversion of situation.

It is the system itself that created the objective conditions for this brutal reaction. By monopolizing all the cards, it forces the other party to change the game and the rules by which it is played. The new rules of the game are ferocious, because the stakes are ferocious. Against a system whose excessive power poses an insoluble challenge, the terrorists respond with an act that excludes any possibility of exchange. It is terror against terror: terrorism against the terror of the system. Now, terror is not violence: it is not a real, determined, historical violence, one that has a cause and an end. Terror has no end; it is an extreme phenomenon—beyond ends, so to speak; it is more violent than violence. Today, any violence of the traditional kind regenerates the system, provided it has a sense. The only real threat to the system is symbolic violence—that which has no sense and embodies no ideological alternative. And it is obvious that terrorism does not embody any ideological or political alternative. This is what makes it headline news: it is not part of a real and continuing story but is rather in the nature of a pure event, one that cuts itself off from its causes and in the end has no consequences. The event does not form part of a continuous pattern of cause and effect, but is rather in the nature of a discontinuity. In this sense, every event meriting the name is a terrorist one. There is a special form of exultation associated with the transition to the symbolic act. Terrorism has no aim. This special exultation associated with the event and its violence, with the transition to symbolic action, is one that we never encounter in the real world or in the real order of things.

Thus terrorism has no objective and is not to be measured in terms of its real consequences. We should not therefore deplore the uselessness and absurdity of the terrorist act, for this is the price—the heavy price of suicide—that has to be paid for it to become transpolitical and exert a transpolitical effect of destabilization and embolism, triggering a chain reaction leading to the self-destruction of the system. This exultation is obviously very ambiguous, and it concerns death. The possibility of using a strategy whereby the adversary's power is hijacked and turned against him, while he is quite unable to respond in kind, can be seen as constituting the absolute superiority of terrorism in symbolic terms. It is not possible to hijack the terrorist's weapon or turn it against him, since the weapon in question is his own death. Even if it crushes the terrorist in a one-sided contest, the opposing power cannot escape from its own internal vulnerability, from the turning of its power against itself, a phenomenon that on the contrary increases with every seeming victory. It has no purchase on the death of the other, since the terrorist has already chosen and accepted his death. One cannot make the terrorist disappear, since he has in essence already disappeared. Whether Bin Laden exists or not, whether he is dead or alive, is of no importance. He exists only through the introjection of the *fatwah*, through the vulnerability of power contending with itself.

In this sense, terrorism is everywhere, like a virus, representing the ultimate stage of globalization. It is at heart of the very process of globalization and uses any medium and any actor, whether rumour in which we are all accomplices, or the panic linked to anthrax, or even natural disasters. Everyone has become photosensitive to terrorism. With the World Trade Center towers, a protective screen has finally collapsed and, in the fragments of this shattered mirror, we desperately seek our own likeness. There must be a deep-seated reason for this: what is unbearable is less the experience of unhappiness, suffering and poverty than the fact—and arrogance—of power itself. What is unbearable and unacceptable is the emergence of this wholly novel global power.

Values and the Challenge of the Inhuman

Inhumanity—'the worst of all vices' according to Voltaire—is all the more insidious in that it often springs from a humanist rhetoric. It represents a perversion of our cultural discourse to which we need to remain alert. In this connection, intellectuals have an important role to play in defending and renewing the concept of humanism and striking a proper balance between values and tradition.

Hélé Béji highlights the violence inherent in cultural claims and the brutal turn that traditionalist rhetoric is currently taking, supplanting what is sometimes known as the 'dialogue of cultures'. This tragic inversion of values is seen by her as revelatory of the inhuman face of modern humanism. If we wish to avoid the eclipse of the ethical by the ethnic, we must address the task of radically redefining the relationship of modernity with the idea of tradition.

Peter Sloterdijk also takes up the defence of the human, pointing to a more ancient distortion of our cultural discourse. He assumes the role of the devil's advocate, a modern devil's advocate whose task it is to relieve the individual of the immense burden of Christian sin and to plead ultimately in favour of egocentrism and revolt, making room in the humanist discourse for the principles of distance and difference.

* * * *

Writer, essayist and former professor at the Faculty of Tunis, **Hélé Béji** was the founder in 1998 of the International College of Tunis, of which she is the president. Her research is centred on the anthropology of decolonization. The author of numerous articles in *Le Débat* and *Esprit*, her published works include *Désenchantement national, essai sur la décolonisation* (1982), *Itinéraire de Paris à Tunis* (1992) and *L'Imposture culturelle* (1997).

Peter Sloterdijk is rector of the Hochschule für Gestaltung in Karlsruhe and professor of philosophy and aesthetics in Vienna. The lecture entitled 'Rules for the Human Park' that he delivered in 1999 at a symposium on Heidegger sparked an international debate on the possible 'end of humanism'. His publications include *Critique of Cynical Reason* (1983), *Thinker on Stage: Nietzsche's Materialism* (1989), *Regeln für den Menschenpark* (1999), *Sphären I—Blasen* (1998), *II—Globen* (1999), *III—Schäume* (2003)

Hélé Béji

The Culture of the Inhuman

My title—'the culture of the inhuman'—links two words that are in principle contradictory. Consciousness of culture as the basis or essence of our humanity has been raised to a supreme pitch in the modern world. We should not feel ourselves to be human without this tangible relationship with our culture, whichever it happens to be. Under the influence of European philosophy, decolonization ushered in a more inclusive concept of humanism, one postulating the equal worth of all cultures and entitling them all to universal recognition, in opposition to the hierarchical conception of civilization, too sullied by its dark colonial past. The dignity of every culture has been restored to confound the racial prejudice of the civilized man.

However, in the wake of the domestic triumphs of decolonization, this cultural humanism took a different turn. The pendulum swung the other way, and the decolonized peoples discovered a new kind of cultural pride in inverted colonial prejudice. Pluralism, diversity and difference, initially so productive, have become the seedbeds of a form of discrimination as virulent and intolerant as any racial ideology: culture having supplanted race, every culture, whether strong or weak, is today an apology for itself that is not amenable to rational criticism since each culture invokes its own rationality. No possibility of neutral arbitration exists any longer since every culture fixes its own rules of the game; no law is in a position to pass judgement since every culture prescribes its own rights in line with its own convictions.

The violence of cultural claims

The 'dialogue of cultures' rests, in my view, on a huge misunderstanding. All these cultural claims today embody a form of violence that is religious in nature; and I use the word 'religious' to connote tyranny of belief, as opposed to 'spiritual', connoting freedom of thought—one of the most inhuman signs of culture being *the dissociation of the religious from the spiritual*. The search for freedom, which was at the origin of human emancipation through culture, is being eclipsed by the search for identity.

This new mystique is perpetrating the disastrous fiction that the human being is reducible to cultural atavism, rather in the way that a coat of arms of the old nobility gave you a certain licence to inflict cruelty. Cultural origin is the new aristocratism of the masses. The emphasis on difference, which should in principle have made us more sensitive to the existence of others, has on the contrary merely served to sharpen our craving for identity. Every culture is arrogating to itself the right to be inhuman, and cultural rights are the prerogatives of the inhuman.

Yet is it not inevitable, in the face of the relentless encroachment of modernity, of this new face of necessity, of an impersonal world devoid of homeland, that we should all reconstitute the memory of an abode, a genealogy, a past, a historical being and a familiar horizon bestowing a sense of invulnerability in the face of a hostile world? When there opens up before us the abyss of a world without frontiers, an absence of pathways, the formless landscape of our own meanderings, are we not justified in giving the rights of tradition pride of place over the rights of progress?

When we consider the schemata of civilization (Science, Progress, Morality, the Republic and other 'capitalized concepts on the verge of collapse', to paraphrase Marcel Gauchet), it is clear that the modern individual is experiencing a psychological backlash in the form of that modern version of slavery known as *stress*. He is a victim of the illusion that he is master of his own destiny whereas he is in fact serving the obscure wishes of the masses, a casualty of the paradox whereby individualism has become a mass ideology as distinct from a creative singularity. When one recalls Freud's statement that it was to be feared that the price of civilization would be psychological abdication and existential despair, it is understandable why the quest for identity has usurped the quest for freedom.

It is all the more so in view of the dramatic split that has taken place between our internal time and external time. The most acute of modern ills is perhaps the loss of control over internal time and, as a result, a loss of the faculty of *contemplation*, of gazing attentively upon the world. Social time and internal time are dislocated. Psychoanalysis has been unable to reconcile them, no doubt because the spiritual is irreducible to the psychological—the confusion between them being at the origin of a great deal of unhappiness. In this respect, religion has perhaps become an illness insofar as it is more akin to a psychological symptom than a spiritual imperative.

It might have been hoped that these rights of tradition, in the face of a certain moral impoverishment inherent in progress, would lend an inner energy, a subjective savour or some human tenderness to our pangs of discontent. But, on the contrary, tradition is turning out to be a potentially brutal notion, a new form of stress, deficient in spirituality to the point that it is itself becoming one of the most ferocious scions of modernity.

Traditions have asserted the right to their own Renaissance, and this right is precious to the European mind since it recognizes the ancient to be a source of modernity. The decolonized peoples have brought about the renaissance of their traditions through a process of 're-orientation' ('to orient' etymologically means to design a building to face eastwards). This has given rise to such concepts as Negritude, Arabness, Jewishness and Islamity, which paradoxically illustrate an Enlightenment principle in the form of the right to self-government. There is thus something inherently ambiguous in this unitary radicalism, since it involves both identification with others and alienation from Europe.

The revival of traditions has involved their distortion, since the rights of tradition in decolonized countries are often enlisted in the cause not of equality and freedom but rather of submission, obedience and fear. It is too often forgotten that armed Islamism has taken a greater toll of Muslims themselves than of Christians (there have been over 100,000 deaths in Algeria). It follows that belonging to the same culture or the same religion is no guarantee of tolerance or political contentment. This is because the political link is civil rather than cultural in nature.

Another trait that makes cultural rights inhuman is that they place the Arab, Jewish, Muslim, Corsican, Basque, Serbian, American, Western or other cultural condition above the human condition. It is in this respect that the cultural illusion is most destructive: when one believes oneself to be human only by virtue of having a culture and not by nature, and when human dignity is circumscribed in terms of ethnic, religious, national or imperial origin. The word 'culture' is then no longer understood in the sense of autonomous self-realization but rather as the allegiance of conscience to a deterministic primacy. Let us not forget Hannah Arendt's admonition when she was accused, concerning her analysis of the Eichmann trial, of 'not loving the Jews', of not believing in them in an absolute manner: 'Does this people no longer believe in anything but itself? What good could come of that?' She went on to say that she felt no love for the Jewish people any more than for the Germans, the French, the Americans or the working class and that the only kind of love she believed in was that of individuals. 'Such a love of the Jews', she declared, ' would seem to me, being Jewish myself, somewhat suspect'.

The rights of tradition go astray, thirdly, in the very way in which they imagine themselves to be combating modernity—by espousing one of its worst aspects in the form of the mass propagation of new kinds of technologically enhanced idolatry. Fanaticism is manna to the media, which have notoriously usurped the right to think. If, with Condorcet, we define obscurantism as 'the tyranny exercised by cunning over ignorance', there is a form of obscurantism peculiar to the media, which like to set themselves up as public mentors. While they lead the way as information providers, they come last in terms of making the world intelligible. They foster the illusion of self-expression but not the faculty of mutual understanding. The media extend the scope of the unintelligible whereas the main role of a viable culture is to make the world intelligible to us—in other words, to borrow the title of a minor work by Kant, to make it possible to 'orient oneself in thought'. The disorientation at work in the media results from the competitive exploitation of culture to pander to public opinion. A religious object can become an advertising slogan just as an advertising slogan can become a religious object. Intolerance is never better served than by the instrument that was supposed to overcome it.

The archaic is hypermodern since it combines its prophetic paraphernalia with unprecedented lighting effects in the form of the audio-visual media and attunes itself to a mass audience that is at once apathetic and fascinated, cynical and terrorized. The disinherited of the earth employ the same devices to exist as its privileged do to dominate. Where we imagine ourselves to be combating uniformity by stimulating our sense of belonging, we are merely serving to demonstrate the power of the media—'financed by the strong to preach the cause of the weak', in Rousseau's telling phrase.

Just as the mystique of tradition is much better adapted than we think to global communication processes, so tribalism is not simply a relic of tradition. Modern society is tribal in its instincts of defence and survival. Can the West not be seen, in the last analysis, as a huge and very complex tribe whose raison d'être is rooted in that same cultural consciousness rehabilitated by ethnology (everyone having the right to extol their historical being), meaning, in the case of the West, its Promethean energy, its taste for exploration and its voracious technical appetite, even where these are detrimental to those who unwittingly serve as cogs in this huge and limitlessly powerful machine? Who indeed can prevent some cultures from claiming to pursue a global mission by virtue of the right of all to develop their cultural genius?

Humanism with an inhuman face

Modern culture is thus characterized by the fact that human rights of all kinds are turned into inhuman codes. *Sovereignty*, which is the authority exercised over self, is replaced by *supremacy*, which is the authority exercised over others. Tolerance, which is the rejection of the intolerable, has become the right to practise the intolerable. Voltaire said: 'the right to be intolerant is absurd and barbaric'. Democracy has become a slogan in support of hegemony or theocracy. The media, instead of furthering understanding, are propagating the unintelligible. Cultural differences, which were supposed to diversify peacefully, are converging in an identical practice of violence. *Humanitarian action*, which professes to be on the side of the weak, comes with a providential superpower backing that transforms it into a 'providential inhumanity'. Antiracism has become as intolerant as racism; and anticolonialism has become as fascist as colonialism. Individualism has served to increase our inner maladies rather than cure them. Antisexism develops an obsession with sex. The rights of the weakest are modelled on the abuses of the rights of the strongest, with the result that that the rights of victims are turning into a morality of cruelty. In the words of Catherine Labrusse-Riou, a law professor at the University of Paris-I, human rights have been reduced to the level of 'vague principles, interpreted in terms of individualistic and arbitrary ideologies without regard to the idea of right as the establishment of human relationships, which are predicated on rights and responsibilities rather than the exaltation of an isolated individual whose undefined freedoms amount to powers exercised over others and hence to an impingement on their freedom or dignity'.[1]

One of the subtlest challenges posed by the inhuman is thus rooted in humanism itself, insofar as unconstrained cultural rights become covert power drives. Humanism suffered its initial betrayal when Europeans, in the name of civilization, invented the first cultural right in the form of the crime of colonization. It did so a second time when the decolonized peoples ceased to be the oppressed and became the oppressors in the name of their cultural tradition. A third betrayal of humanism occurred when, confronted by the fascism of the weak, the West once more took up the banner of its civilizing mission, with the same military justifications, in order to pacify the 'savages'.

It follows that the inhuman is not man's violence or animality (this is a-human) but rather the civilized or cultural language of hatred used to justify cruelty intellectually or culturally by cloaking it in an apparel dignifying it with the title of cultural right. In the name of cultural diversity, we have become so frightened of the notion of race that we have forgotten the only race that merits consideration—the human race. The human being has become, dare I say so, an *object of racial hatred*.

Among the welter of cultural icons in the contemporary world, what is lacking is any representation of the human. The image of the human is absent from culture. Culture no longer offers access to our humanity, and

---

[1] Catherine Labrusse-Riou, 'Droits de la personalité et de la famille', in Mireille Delmas-Marty and Claude Lucas de Leyssac (eds.), *Libertés et droits fondamentaux*, Paris, Seuil, 1996.

this is perhaps what abstract painting is telling us when it goes beyond figuration in order to portray the density and pulse of the inner life of contemporary man. The cultural criterion no longer provides the foundation for an ethic of recognition. Ethnic consciousness has liquidated ethical awareness. Ensconced behind the cultural mask, we have lost touch with the 'natural light' of reason, that Rousseauesque ability to withdraw into oneself in order to listen to 'the voice of conscience amid the silence of the passions'.

The purpose of any genuine culture is to distinguish the human from the inhuman. The predilection for difference has been taken so far that the differences inherent in the human have been obscured. Man no longer wishes to resemble man. The old criteria of human identity no longer interest anyone. So long as we stand out from the crowd, we are happy to attach another name to ourselves—such as 'monster', for example. We are cultivating the image of the monster (from *monstro, -are*, to show, show oneself; or from *moneo*, which gave *monstrum*, a prodigious phenomenon outside nature). People are no longer so attached to their nature; they are settling for an inhuman culture in order to assert their difference. The monster is no longer concerned about belonging to the realm of human; it wants to belong to some other species and even claims a philosophical right to be a monster, i.e., someone who is insensitive not only to the sufferings of others but to his own sufferings as well.

A problematic relationship between modernity and tradition

Terror is simply the most dramatic expression of an evil already at work in our time: the bankruptcy of human identity and the loss of any yardstick of our common humanity. In the face of this humanist deficit, decolonization also has failed to live up to the promise inherent in its cultural potential—that of creating a more viable model of civilization. Decolonization has similarly failed in its attempt to set itself up as an alternative to modernity, of which it is but a negative epiphenomenon. The confrontation between modernity and tradition has deprived both of inspiration: it has stimulated them ideologically but discredited them morally. They converge in terms of the shadows—not the light—that they cast, of the destruction, not the creation that they produce. In this respect, terrorist attacks can be seen as a desire to enter modernity, albeit by way of destruction rather than creation.

Modernity cannot ignore the question of the past, which concerns not only the divorce between internal and external time but also the past time inscribed in each of us—whose importance has been encapsulated for the modern mind in the Proustian parable of time lost and regained. What is termed *otherness* could indeed be understood as one's own *anteriority* in time: the buried strata of the soul emerge ahead of us and the idea of progress is behind us; but the old and the new, the fixed past and the arrow of the future, have not found their human meeting point. The current ills associated with the term globality are the expression of this crisis of temporality, of this elusive synchrony of the resurgence of God with the death of God, of science with superstition, of the archaic with the technological, of the hypertrophy of memory with loss of memory. It is a matter in each case of our age having lost its 'bearings'—that is to say, a sense of the present.

Just as progress that was no more than an episode in a chronicle of oblivion would have no future, so memory that sought to monopolize the whole of meaning would destroy its own past. In both cases—the slavery of the new or the tyranny of the old—we lose our bearings in time. Our humanity drains away between illusions of memory and a disbelief in progress. It is lost in the void between the absence of homeland, or rootlessness, and an excess of homeland, or fanaticism. World culture is the expression of the impotence of time trapped between a hegemonic model and a sectarian or fanatical one. Globality can thus be seen as modernity's failed relationship with tradition, and vice versa. Modernity has been unable to harness its genius for power to the rhythms of consciousness, and no cultural tradition has succeeded in transforming its presence in the world into work upon the world.

Yet globality transcends any form of imperialism or empire. Empire belongs to the order of politics, whereas the global is an order beyond the political. The global is what cannot be governed, whether we are talking of order or disorder. Consequently, it is no longer we who govern the world, but the world that governs us. In the global order, the hegemonic instinct of every culture allows itself free rein. Everything that aspires to globality and communication secretly tends towards domination.

Like Jean Baudrillard, I hold that the global is not the same as the universal. The universal postulates the existence of a place other than the global, where the most vital exchanges of our time doubtless take place. The global is only an infinitesimal portion of the universal. It is by claiming to embody the whole of human exchanges that any culture claiming to be global becomes inhuman.

If there were only one world, it would be unbearable. A human universe requires the existence of at least two worlds: a battlefield and a shelter, an outward and a return journey, a past and a future, an earth and a heaven, velocity and slowness, sunrise and sunset, east and west, a point of departure and a port of destination, an origin and a horizon. If our lives are strained exclusively towards the future, we fall apart; and if we exist only in the recollection of the past, we become fixed. A dual time is needed to humanize the world. A near and far, a here and elsewhere, are necessary to establish a home and give the world a local habitation. Our imagination needs two worlds if we are not to be exiled and banished from the world, just as we need the world's full presence in order to dream of conceiving another.

Peter Sloterdijk

The Devil's Advocate, between the Ethical and the Systemic

I wish to allude here to the figure of the devil's advocate with the aim of setting the current state of moral philosophy within a perspective offered by the history of moral thought and metaphysics, or more precisely a history of theologically determined constructions of the image of the world. These constructions were certainly interrupted, but in no way terminated, with the advent of modernity. Their significance was—I shall argue—to prevent the problem of evil in the world being assigned to the realm of divine first causes, by overemphasizing human freedom and thereby placing an excessive moral burden on the human being.

The main problem of moral philosophy at the present time is the liberation of the egotism of the Other. This phenomenon goes by the name of 'human rights propaganda', a formula that has the advantage of being widely acceptable but also the disadvantage of masking the profound meaning, systemically speaking, of the egotism of the Other.

The wretched of the earth, or those who have yet to accede to the delights of this egoistic form of life, deserve the benefit of an advocate to assist them in their self-serving demands. Since such egoism has always been the chief enemy of Western moral philosophy, the person pleading the cause of the selfish needs of the other is necessarily a modern form of what has traditionally been called the 'devil's advocate'.

The role of the devil's advocate

As we know, the expression 'devil's advocate' derives from the language of the Roman Curia, or more precisely from its popularization. The *advocatus diaboli* is a figure transposed into popular language from the process of canonization or beatification that takes place before the Sacred

Congregation of Rites in the Vatican. He has as his model the so-called *promotor fidei*, whose role was to test the strength of the arguments in favour of the canonization of a deceased person—a function whose ironic side was more keenly apparent to theologically untrained observers in the streets and squares of Rome than to the various protagonists in the process, wrapped up in the gravity of the proceedings. Outside observers were no less ironic about the role of the person pleading the case for the defence as *advocatus Dei*. If we add to this what we know of popular opinion concerning the legal profession, we can form a good idea of the overtones likely to attach to their titles.

It is obvious that the devil has a vested interest in preventing any new accessions to the *communio sanctorum* for, from the standpoint of the Contradictor, the legion of those to whose corruption he can no longer in any way contribute is already too large. For him, any new admission to the nimbus of witnesses assembled above his head constitutes not only a source of irritation but also an irresistible pretext for attempted subversion. It is the devil who wishes to prove, always with sound reasons, that prospective saints are not true saints. His interest in doing so is not devoid of irony since the agent of hell, with his negations and subversions, in the last analysis always plays the game of the Adversary. He is condemned to fulfil that role so long as he obeys the injunction not to take the process to absurd lengths, which would abolish the true saints at the same time as the saints apparent.

We may perhaps conclude that the devil is in the end no less pious than the priest who plays his own particular role in the process. The irony of this position in the dispute has to do with the fact that the aforementioned promoter of the faith, whose role is that of detractor, has to be a particularly tried and trusted theologian—an essential condition if the procedure aimed at verifying a candidate's saintliness or beatific worth is to lead to a result that is valid in canon law. This is moreover an early and typical form of proof for what would today be known as the 'constraint without constraint' exercised by the best argument, in which it is even more clearly discernible than in the modern version of the problem that the argument considered the best is invariably the one that contributes most effectively to the realization of the desired consensus. Here again, the consensus is always a sacred one and rests on the injection, touched by grace, of a higher rationality into earthly proceedings.

This rationality always involves the pretence of having heard the arguments of the other parties as if they were of equal value and as if the consensus were the result of reliable processes of truth production. The piety of the procedure in question gives the lie to any faith in the processes as mechanisms of choice, functioning without flaw or failing. In them, it is the logos itself that makes the choice (nor indeed could it be otherwise, since the canonical process necessarily determines the outcome given that the human outcome is already consummated). And the Holy Spirit, on each occasion, condescends to blow upon the result of a process as if it were no longer blowing where it list but rather where procedure allowed. Thus it would seem that the procedural filter guarantees that no candidate having only the appearance of saintliness ever gains access to the *communio sanctorum* and that we are therefore spared diabolical simulacra, in just the same way as in communications obeying Habermas's rules of the games one can be certain that, after the final elimination, no theoretician of dissent, no pluralist, no constructivist and above all no artist could ever be found in the circle of those who communicate in a truly rational manner.[1]

It is moreover clear that the figure of the devil's advocate emancipated itself from Romanist procedures at the start of the Modern Age and became an emblem pure and simple of useful negativity. Just as in the canonization process, the *advocatus diaboli's* sole mission was to lend lustre to the final affirmative verdict, so the modern avatar of the negative had necessarily to prove itself as part of that force fully employed in Germany until recent times, which forever wills Evil and forever does Good. This logic so recommended itself to a contemporary German Franciscan father that he requested in 1960, during the Sacred Congregation of Rites at the Holy See, that procedures be initiated for the canonization of Judas Iscariot, without whose faithful betrayal the Passion would never have come to pass. It is not clear what became of this request. This wish could only have been favourably received in Rome if Hegel, Schelling or Soloviev had been elected official philosophers of the Vatican, and thus the modern assistants of Saint Thomas Aquinas. However, as we know, the Holy See opted in favour of Husserl.

The human being on trial

No great effort is needed to commend the reason why I am now going to uproot the model of the devil's advocate from its historical context in order to redefine it and assign it a role in a complex of problems described in another manner, historically and substantively. I am talking of the opposite of the procedures of canonization, namely, of the procedures of protracted accusation against the lineage of Adam in its entirety, procedures in which the adepts of this problematic genre have always been pushed into the position of overburdened defendants. The process in question in the history of ideas within Western Christendom is quite simply that which the Christianity of Saint Paul

---

1. Cf. Niklas Luhmann, ‚Ich sehe nicht, was du nicht siehst', *Soziologische Aufklärung*, 5, *Konstruktive Perspektiven*, Opladen, 1993. Luhmann highlights the structural intolerance of critical theory, and the forced consensualism it implies, linked as it is with the absolute notion of a single truth.

and especially of Saint Augustine used against man and his transcendental corrupter, the devil, by describing the human species as a line of creatures that had succumbed at an early stage of their history to the yoke of the *peccatum originale*.

I should underline that it is the adjective that is of prime importance in the expression *peccatum originale,* for the fact that human beings are fallible creatures or, if you like, that they have a predisposition to sin and to go astray or rebel would be a trite remark if one were not to add, with the word *originale*, that there must be from the outset a hereditary, not to say metaphysical, burden weighing upon the human condition. Since the time of Saint Augustine, anthropodicy is characterized by a strong tendency to overburden the human being with guilt. And if one was to add a less familiar but very apposite reason to all the usual justifications for modernity's break with the old Europe, it would undoubtedly be the fact that the Enlightenment, so-called since the eighteenth century, endeavoured to organize a permanent referendum in favour of ridding human beings of their sense of guilt or that it was at least at the origin of an intergenerational petition demanding a fresh vote on the fundamental guilt of the human being, a petition of which we today have a glimpse in the form of a library of the moral criticism deriving from the modern tradition, including contributions from thinkers as diverse as Montaigne and Cioran, Bacon and Luhmann.

Given the basic structure of reasoning in the old Europe, it was not so much the devil that needed to be represented by the advocate in the course of the procedure but rather human beings, weighed down by the immense burden of guilt heaped on their shoulders by Christian thinkers from Saint Paul and Saint Augustine to Pascal and Dostoyevsky, and more recently by the philosopher Levinas.

At this stage of the argument, it is useful to remind ourselves of the formulations employed by Saint Augustine to interpret and describe for all time the condition of fallen humanity. We shall discover there the first approaches to a problem that will not elicit a new response until we arrive at the high point of modernity, when the question will arise again as to whether egocentrism is good or bad for human beings and for the system.

Saint Augustine recognized the strategic importance of the concept of sin for the stabilization of the Catholic universe in the face of age-old scepticism; and he consequently undertook, with great perspicacity, an ontological deduction of what does not proceed from God and of what alienates from Him. In fact, it is not an easy task to discern, in a world created by God and characterized throughout by the fact of being well made, the point of departure for radical divergences. It is however obvious that the root of the separation in man, and in man alone, has to be found. It is just as obvious today that the repetition of the term sin, well worked by religious tradition, adds nothing new to the explanation of the state of affairs in question. The point is rather to understand under what conditions resistance to the divine law is possible and to identify in those conditions the initial metaphysical grounds for the sinful dissidence. Here the Augustinian analysis has a modern ring, since it arrives at a kind of in-depth diagnosis of the structures of the corrupted human subjectivity similar to what can be heard today in confirmative repetitions among philosophers of dialogue of Protestant, Catholic, Jewish or psychoanalytic persuasion and in the apologies for an anthropological psychiatry.

Analysis of a lapsed subjectivity

As the form of the lapsed subjectivity is prefigured in satanic subjectivity, it is sufficient to begin with the first negator and to observe him in his secession from the Divinity. It is here that we obtain the metaphysical deduction of exteriority. What is involved is a fragment of mythology in which the prelude to the beyond foreshadows the scenario of history in this world. Saint Augustine's Satan, who represents a kind of allegory of negation at a level below that of the principle, does not adduce—this is the only certainty—any external grounds for his revolt against the Origin. He finds all the necessary reasons for his revolt within himself, or more precisely in his capacity for freedom, his most important gift. Thanks to this, he can, parodying the *ex nihilo* divine creation, summon up his 'no' by an act of unmotivated will. One cannot therefore enquire as to the reason for or source of this ill will. Satan wills as he wills, and that is all there is to it. The will or, in more modern terms, the desire of the dissident is focused on itself and not on the Other who ontologically and morally confronts or precedes him. Satan begins with himself, free and unconstrained; and it is to him, him alone and for all time that the dissidence must therefore be imputed. The very fact of beginning with himself when he should have respected another more venerable beginning constitutes, from the standpoint of Saint Augustine and all the conservatives who followed him, the origin of sin and egotism. Sin is an inchoative operation in which originality and negativity are closely interwoven. Sin, in the last analysis, always consists in beginning where one should not, even when it seems no more than a continuation.[2]

Satan thus inaugurates the model of everything that has been denounced in Europe over the millennia as deplorable egocentrism and an irresistible temptation for mortals and has been conceived furthermore as their inborn vice. Augustine underlines the fact that one should not seek to explain the satanic preference in terms of external constraints

---

2. It thus has the character of an 'archi-action', to borrow the Fichtean terminology of schism and separation.

and, in particular, rival principles. The devil is not the vassal of an evil second god. He should not moreover plead that, because he has become autistic, he is entitled to suppose that his mother had failed him. The devil does not have to have had an unhappy childhood to become abysmally evil-minded. What matters to him is pure revolt. He wants to turn away or extricate himself, by means of a rotation, from the confrontation with the All-Powerful One. He wills the act as such. It is only on the basis of unmotivated freedom that he achieves his deviation from everything that the divine order and handicap represent. He determines himself in existence as the proprietor of his own stubbornness, and Evil thereby bodies forth in the shape of his dissident will. What in Platonic terms begins as a simple *malum privativum* condenses in the devil's ego in Christian terms to become a private domain of evil, of incurable autism. The circle of evil traced around him symbolizes systemic closure. In this way, the devil, master of the world, becomes the master of egocentrism.

With hindsight and arguably less ingenuously, it has to be added that this description conceals a premise that, had it been made explicit, would inevitably have destroyed the totality of the arrangement. I refer to the devastating paradox whereby freedom remains linked to a strict expectation of ordination and subordination, so that neither man nor his mythical protector Satan could have employed their freedom without committing a fault, unless they had decided not to employ it. To employ one's freedom, conversely, amounts to placing oneself in a state of insurrection and opting for one's own existential liberation—for distance and resistance, one might also say. From insurrection is born, according to this analysis, the distance that alone enables the unity between creator and creature to be observed externally.

For a satanic liberation of the human being

Distance accordingly becomes the problem child of classical metaphysics. So far, no theory of alienation has been able to get away from the theme of the guilt inherent in the act of distancing oneself from an acknowledged original unity. But when one thinks in these terms one loses sight of a simple reality: apartness, generally speaking, does not supervene upon a drama of separation. It is not consolidated in the traumatic memory traces of the event. Apartness is the initial state, natural and non-culpable, between individuals who have never and nowhere been united and who meet by chance. Only the metaphysical prejudice in favour of unity constrains us to think of apartness as alienation and thus to rob plurality of its ontological dignity and, correspondingly, its moral innocence.

To describe the inward rotation of the creature that liberates itself from its position in face of the creator, Augustine introduced a technical term equally instructive in kinetic and moral terms—the famous *incurvatio in se ipso* (curving in upon oneself), which is the charge levelled wherever human beings do not comply with the norm of extraversion (or direction of the self towards the object) and place themselves before their relations with others. This expression did not simply designate the immediate act of committing a sin—as we might speak today of communication being 'broken off' with someone seeking or requesting a conversation; it also referred to the result of an obdurately erroneous moral stance that the subject, with the best will in the world, could no longer amend. If Augustine, as a phenomenologist of self-healing, offers a sombre diagnosis of the postlapsarian human condition and if his assessment of human beings and their prospects of salvation leads him to a literally fatal conclusion, it is because he interprets the fall as a rotation, the 'having fallen' as an instance of 'having turned', seen as an erroneous and irreversible attitude. After the *lapsus*, the mortal descendants of Adam and Satan are fixed in their catastrophe and are no longer free to reverse their incurvature and restore by their own devices the broken contract with the great Whole and its personal principle, the offended god. They are inconvertibly perverted or 'coiled in upon themselves' and are therefore wholly dependent on the beneficence of the other side.

This beneficence manifested itself, throughout a whole historical era, in the form of 'grace'. This term provides a clue to the reversal of the incurvature that only the Other can accomplish. I therefore propose, as an essential intermediary on the path leading to access to the Other, the figure of the *advocatus diaboli* in the guise of the modern intellectual who, often unknowingly, offers his services as the advocate of the Other's as yet unemancipated and unliberated egotism. The task of this modern devil's advocate, then, would be to relieve man of the immense burden of Christian sin and to argue the case finally for egocentrism and revolt, making room for the principle of distance in the discussion of the human—which is the true dimension, ultimately, of the devil.

Serious Values or Frivolous Values?

Values are today under attack on all sides: they find themselves demystified, relativized, belittled and above all accused of being contingent, volatile and even frivolous. This notion of frivolity seems to deprive values of any foundation. And yet, paradoxically, the notion of value is becoming increasingly central to our rhetoric and, in appearance, increasingly charged with meaning. How can we reconcile these two divergent tendencies?

Introducing the theme, Edgar Morin argues the case for ethical complexification, underlining in this regard the need to recognize and take into account with respect to action the importance of the divergences not only between different value systems but also between such different realms as science, ethics and politics.

Mohammed Arkoun contends that it is inadmissible that this debate should be limited to the historical context of Western philosophical and moral thought. Preferring the idea of a subversive genesis of values to a specious distinction between serious values and frivolous values, he seeks to redefine the respective roles of religion and the social sciences in the constitution of our collective memories.

Finally, Jean-Joseph Goux throws light on the relativism currently influencing the concept of value by way of a comparison between Enlightenment man and the modern individual, who seeks to affirm his freedom through quasi-aesthetic creative gestures. He argues that this modern relation to values, which could arouse fears of a deep-seated instability and frivolity, is to be understood rather as one of the modes of our freedom.

* * * *

Sociologist and emeritus director of research at the CNRS (France), **Edgar Morin** is also president of the European Cultural Agency (UNESCO). He has been awarded many honours in recognition of his work, and his numerous publications include *Method: Towards a Study* *of Humankind: The Nature of Nature* (1992), *Introduction à une politique de l'homme* (1999), *L'Humanité de l'humanité: l'identité humaine* (2001) and, with Jean Baudrillard, *La violence du monde* (2003).

Born in Algeria, emeritus professor at the Sorbonne and fellow of the Institute for Advanced Studies in Princeton, **Mohammed Arkoun** is currently scientific director of the review *Arabica* and visiting professor at the Institute of Ismaili Studies in London. A member of France's National Ethics Committee for the life sciences and health (1990–1998) and of the Supreme Family and Population Council (1995–1998), he was the recipient in 2002 of the Giorgio Levi Della Vida Award in Islamic Studies. He is the author of *Rethinking Islam* (1994), *The Unthought in Contemporary Islamic Thought* (2002) and, with Joseph Maïla, *De Manhattan à Bagdad. Au-delà du Bien et du Mal* (2003).

Jean-Joseph Goux teaches philosophy at Rice University in Houston (Texas). He was course director at the College International de Philosophie (1989–1991) and associate research director at the Ecole des Hautes Etudes en Sciences Sociales (1988) and has taught at various American universities (Berkeley, San Diego, Duke, Brown). The founder of a new discipline, symbolic economics, his research is mainly centred on the links between economics, philosophy, psychoanalysis and aesthetics. His main publications are: *Les Iconoclastes* (1978), *Symbolic Economies: After Marx and Freud* (1990), *The Coiners of Language* (1994) and *Frivolité de la valeur* (2000).

Edgar Morin

The Ethics of Complexity and the Problem of Values in the Twenty-First Century

The problem of values in the twenty-first century will arise from ethical complexification. Until now the problem of the foundation of values was extremely simple: God had given us laws to enable us to do Good. The same was true within the secular context of closely knit societies, where ethical prescriptions were profoundly internalized. It was a self-evident truth that values must be observed and respected.

Matters naturally change with the growth of autonomy and individual responsibility, since the imperative no longer proceeds from God, religion, the state or society but from the individual himself, in accordance with the Kantian categorical imperative. This imperative has become insular, self-generating and self-justifying, and this situation must evolve through a recognition that the human being is not simply an individual, society or the human species, but rather an interdependent trinity comprising all three. From this standpoint, values relate not only to the individual, in terms of his sense of responsibility, dignity, virtue and honour, but also to the group and the species—particularly in a context of globalization. As it is difficult to observe these three overlapping requirements simultaneously, conflicts of duty frequently occur.

Formerly, the problem of the relationship between scientific knowledge and ethics did not arise since Western science was predicated on a rejection of any political, religious and ethical interference. 'Knowledge' was to be pursued regardless of the consequences. Their independence was not a matter of science being concerned with judgements of facts and ethics being concerned with judgements of value, but rather of judgements of fact being the supreme value in the scientific domain. Such a dissociation did not pose any problem until the twentieth century, when science started to develop enormous destructive and manipulative potential. The current proliferation of ethics committees is proof that the relationship between scientific knowledge and ethics has become crucial—particularly since the capacity of ethics to regulate science is far from established given the separation that exists between them. These spheres that should be united are thus completely disconnected.

An ecology of action

The inadequacy of pure morality stems from the fact that it is never concerned with consequences: it is persuaded that good intentions lead to good actions. Pascal, however, makes the following suggestion: 'Let us strive to think well, that is the basic principle of morality'. That does not mean that correct thinking necessarily leads to ethical behaviour, but rather that it is necessary to be aware of the context in which our actions are to be performed to know whether they will effectively promote the values they are supposed to further. Hence the emergence of an ecology of action that focuses on the circumstances in which well-intentioned actions in the service of values are to be carried out.

Pericles declared that the Athenians had the gift of combining boldness with prudence, whereas other peoples were either foolhardy or else cowards. His remark highlights the fact that effective action calls for daring, the acceptance of risk, but that it should nevertheless be tempered with its opposite.

The ecology of action also has to take account of the uncertainty inherent in the relationship between ends and means. We know that if we employ dishonourable means too long in pursuit of a noble goal the means eventually impair the end we are seeking, and even usurp it. Conversely, immoral actions can lead indirectly to essentially virtuous consequences. This is illustrated in Goethe's *Faust*: Faust seeks Margaret's happiness but only succeeds in bringing disaster upon her; whereas Mephistopheles, who seeks to ruin her, prompts the intervention of God and is thereby the cause of Margaret's salvation.

A strict ecology of action also implies taking account of the interplay of forces within the historical and social setting in which the action takes place, which embodies the risk that the action in question may rebound on and annihilate the person performing it. How many examples have we seen in the history of good intentions being thwarted in this way? One has only to point to the example of Gorbachev, who set in train salutary actions in the Soviet Union that led to the disintegration of his country.

There exists, then, an inescapable uncertainty principle, which should make us aware that everything we do is a wager. We cannot foresee the outcome of our actions in the long term since there exists a law of total unpredictability. Who can pronounce on the significance of the French Revolution, which caused so much blood to flow in the name of principles as fundamental as human rights and whose legacy still eludes any final assessment?

Contradictory imperatives

The existence of a 'polytheism of values', to borrow Max Weber's expression, frequently gives rise to conflicts between opposing ethical imperatives. Thus Antigone embodies piety as well as the sense of duty that binds her to her brother. Creon embodies politics and treachery to an enemy of the city whose burial he prohibits. Today, on the contrary, we have entered a world of ethical simplification unknown to civilizations that we consider backward. To the extent that we disregard principles as sacred as those of hospitality and the honouring of solemn promises, we are in many respects in a state of ethical underdevelopment. Militating in an association or party in defence of values as legitimate as they are abstract may, for example, cause us to neglect our family completely. Conversely, we may devote ourselves to those close to us and overlook the rest of humanity. On another level, we have seen major ethical conflicts arise in the interwar period concerning whether or not it was right to prefer one or other of the monstrous doctrines going by the name of Stalinism and Nazism. This uncertainty led, during the Second World War, to unnatural alliances between incompatible partners.

Ethical contradictions have always existed but they reappear today in the context of scientific developments that point up the antinomies inherent in medicine and more generally biology. Thus the Hippocratic imperative, which prescribes that the physician should combat death, finds itself confronted by a dilemma: is it right to prolong the life of a person who is brain dead but biologically still living, or should that person's organs be removed to save the life of someone else? The question of euthanasia poses a similar dilemma. And what of abortion, which contributes to the liberation of women but which conflicts with the right to life of the unborn child and the community's proscription on killing?

If one had to single out in the history of the planet a particularly cruel example of domination, it would have to be Europe's hegemony over the rest of the world from the sixteenth century onwards. In this connection, one has only to think of colonization and the slave trade. However, it so happens that the West, as well as being the hub of a system of domination, was also the source of potentially universal values that were adopted by the enslaved peoples in order to liberate themselves. The colonized were only able to decolonize themselves by turning to account the ethical notion of the rights of peoples and nations. This spread of Western values was such that the only regret we may have today is that the rights of man and of the citizen, together with women's rights, have not become sufficiently universal—always supposing that they correspond to the fundamental aspirations of those who are subject to domination. The Islamic countries are today divided between a tendency wishing to benefit from what is best in Western culture without sacrificing their identity and traditions and another tendency believing that Western values constitute a basic affront to Islamic virtue.

Complexifying ethics means trying to conceive and then establish a proper relationship between science, ethics and politics, in other words, 'de-insularizing' the problem of values; it means recognizing the conflicts between equally powerful ethical imperatives; it means acknowledging the ultimate uncertainty of the outcome of actions motivated by the best intentions and by respect for values.

Mohammed Arkoun

For a Subversive Genesis of Values

The mytho-historical categories constructed since the nineteenth century to signal the advances and superiority of the West over the rest of the world have continued to function in more or less cryptic form even in the wake of so-called decolonization. A study of the historical genealogy of 11 September, informed by a Nietzschean critical radicalism in the approach to values, would reveal the subterranean paths that led a composite group of ideologues lacking any territorial homeland, precise national affiliation or articulable historical memory and recognizing Ben Laden as their combatant guide, to carry out an apocalyptic act that ultimately turned on a question of values not yet properly posed by any of the mainstream intellectual traditions ranged in opposition on the question of 'true' and 'false' values. Exploited polemically and ideologically, but not—I repeat—from a philosophically subversive Nietzschean genealogical standpoint, this inadequately posed question of values is increasingly converted into a political issue designed to legitimize what the secular 'West' calls a 'just war' and what the ideological bubble of Ben Laden, striking an imaginative chord with much of Islam, calls *Jihad*. As I have demonstrated elsewhere, the two concepts overlap very precisely in respect both of their legitimation of warlike violence and in the historical genesis of their theological constructions, going back to Saint Augustine on the Christian side and to the theologian-jurists of the seventh to tenth centuries in the case of the Muslims.

Historical perspectives

I wish to take the debate on values beyond the Mediterranean world in which Christianity, Islam and latterly Judaism have for centuries fought in the name of 'values' whose stewardship has been left to the religious authorities in alliance with the political powers, and extend it to the world's cultures as a whole. I know that we cannot achieve everything at once in a domain in which questions relegated to the *unthinkable* and the *unthought* are more vital and crucial for the future than those polemically aired within the bounds of the thinkable tolerated by the stewards of the sacred or by the secular priests of Enlightenment reason, likewise allied from its earliest struggles with the new holders of political sovereignty. That is why the author of *Human, All Too Human, The Gay Science* and *Beyond Good and Evil* never ceased to strive for the establishment of a 'New Enlightenment'. The fate reserved for this Nietzschean project even by Western philosophical thought is a good illustration of the ideological mechanisms whereby selected 'thinkable' issues are promoted and subversive topics and quests aimed at escaping from intellectual impasses are relegated to the realm of the *unthinkable*. Enlightenment reason had promised us future values that would be more conducive to the emancipation of the human condition. In reality, it had simply dressed up in secular and scientific garb the main axioms, postulates and historico-transcendental themes of classical metaphysics, which had to await the interventions of the deconstructivists (Foucault, Derrida, Lévi-Strauss, etc.) before their idealistic, fanciful and above all misleading rhetoric was revealed. The American researcher Robert Kagan[1] has clearly shown how, in the geohistorical sphere of Europe/the West, states have employed a system of thought based on the use of a dual criterion: that of idealized political and moral values in the tradition of classical metaphysics coupled with military, scientific and technological power.

I have never subscribed to that current of thought in Islamic circles that continuously reminds Europe/the West of the historical debt owed to classical Islamic civilization with respect to its philosophical and scientific output from the seventh to the thirteenth century. This intellectual posture is at once radically apologetic and ideological: two major betrayals of critical reason when it comes to taking a position on the question of values. As a historian of Islamic thought, I would argue the need for a genealogical re-reading of values, extending the work of Nietzsche on Christianity and Greek thought to all those systems of thought and belief that have interpenetrated one another while defending, or imposing, their vocation to possess and teach the unique, true and insurmountable Truth, ontologically based either on revealed fact or on Enlightenment principles duly controlled by secular reason independent of any external dogma. The torrent of declarations on all sides since 11 September shows just how far we all, everywhere, remain prisoners of ancient categories of binary thought, dualistic oppositions and operations of sacralization,

---

1. 'The Americans are idealists, but they have never known how to promote their ideals without the help of their power ... Gary Cooper will defend the township whether the inhabitants like it or not...' (Robert Kagan, *Le Monde*, 28 July 2002).

transcendentalization, essentialization and substantialization, all inherited from medieval theologies and mediated by classical metaphysics (Platonism, Aristolelianism) and even today by the pragmatism, functionalism and empiricism of triumphant neoliberal thought.

Far be it from me, then, to applaud the return to religion or God and to celebrate the supremacy of the values preached by Islam—one must always ask which Islam?—over the 'materialistic' values of the West. I simply note the existence of powerful movements, political in essence and ideological (or even, in some cases, fantastical) in orientation, that claim to represent an Islamic faith in total discontinuity with its moments of emergence, geographical expansion and theological and mytho-historical construction up to the thirteenth century. The Islam brandished by militants of every rank and persuasion since the 1970s, even going back to the 1930s with the launching of the Muslim Brotherhood, is an essentially ideological dialectical product of three powerful factors: firstly, the pressures of an unassimilated modern tradition reinforced by runaway globalization since the proclamation of the 'end of history' in the United States after 1989/90; secondly, the policies of cultural and social regression imposed by a large number of so-called 'national' regimes, which are in fact totalitarian and predatory; thirdly, a demographic surge on an unprecedented scale in the history of human societies, never addressed by the predatory regimes, which have favoured the rise of a parasitical class and politico-financial mafias.

A subversive genesis of values

We should familiarize ourselves with the facts of history, with the sociology of languages, cultures and law and with anthropology as a critique of all cultures before engaging in philosophical speculation and political polemics on the future of so-called 'higher' values and 'dangerous' values. Values become dangerous in all cultures and in all contexts when they are used as a cloak for inadmissible and reprehensible ventures motivated by the desire to dominate, exploit and profit from those without whose help the powerful of this world would not enjoy the monopoly that they do. Values must be constantly recreated because of the actions of the very people who are supposed to be the stewards and protectors of so-called sacred, divine, humanist or universal values and who appropriate them for their own ends so long as they are shielded from the subversive criticism of non-conformist thinkers. The distinction between 'frivolous' values and 'serious' values itself requires justifications that contemporary ethical thinking would be hard pressed to formulate in a convincing manner.[2]

---

2. See Monique Canto-Sperber, *L'Inquiétude morale et la vie humaine*, Paris, PUF, 2001.

This is why I prefer to speak of a subversive genesis of values, just as linguists speak of a destructive genesis of meaning. The life of values is inseparable from the conditions of socialization of each human subject, who becomes a social actor in constant interaction and competition with other actors with varied and shifting motivations. To take account of the future of values, it is necessary to identify these parameters constantly.

This critical approach to values is at odds with the normative definitions of an invariant value system underpinned by Divine Commandments or the categorical imperatives of Kant's transcendental subject. But the postulates of dogmatic theology or of spiritualist metaphysics can only function in the framework of fundamentalist thought whose devastating effects when it invades the social and political realm are well known.

Islamic thought experienced a very fruitful period of receptivity to other cultures and particularly to the rational philosophical stance.[3] Much thought was given to values by comparing and contrasting their religious and philosophical foundations. This experience has been totally forgotten; reference to philosophical reason virtually ceased after the death of Averroes in 1198; and in the fundamentalist ideological climate that has prevailed over the last thirty years, the question of values has ceased to preoccupy religious clerics and 'thinkers' alike (very few of whom merit this name and status) and essayists of a secular persuasion. Ideological struggles pervade and pervert all fields of thought, creation and research. Societies live on scraps—deriving from the remnants of traditional cultures or from little understood and unequally distributed Western cultures, which are often violently rejected in the name of supposedly 'authentic' Islamic values subject in reality to the same forces of disintegration and patched together with varying degrees of success. The fierce denunciation of the West's 'cultural aggression' (*ghazw fikri*) serves as a dual token of political struggle and solidarity with a moralizing ethos that confers social recognition and grants access to political functions that have become, together with business, the main sources of status. Even the so-called religious functions have been affected by this transfer to the political and economic spheres of the mechanisms of 'status enhancement', which has less and less to do with ethical or spiritual values. This evolution of 'values' and of the processes and sources of status enhancement is not peculiar to Islamic contexts; it is likewise found in Western societies, where however intellectual, scientific, artistic and cultural creativity continues to be valued as a source of more lasting and gratifying status.

---

3. I have published a detailed study on Arab humanism from the fourth to the tenth century in Iran-Irak under the Buyid dynasty (*L'Humanisme arabe an IVe–Xe siècle*, Paris, Vrin, 1982).

The search for new values

In the light of what has been said concerning the subversive genesis of values, it seems to me urgent to reconsider the role of 'the revival of religion' in the production, or conversely perversion, of what are indiscriminately termed 'values' by all sections of society. It is certain that the current situations of religions in relation to their respective traditions, their political and cultural environments and their foreseeable future over the period 2010–2020 differ widely. Western European Christianity (Catholicism and Protestantism) have profited more from the positive and emancipating benefits of modernity than the Christianity of Eastern Europe, Islam or even Judaism (I leave aside the case of the major Asian religions). We know that the secular West congratulates itself on having successfully 'made its exit' from the Christian religion; but this exit makes it incapable today of devising and applying a modern policy in the religious domain that takes into account the expansion of non-Christian religions in Europe and America. There is here a new and historic field for the production of values attuned to the demands of pluralistic democratic societies. Yet we do not see the emergence of any relevant responses to these new demands for values. Western Christianity, more liberated than ever from the compromises inherent in the political management of public life, has the chance to propose and advance values that would ensure a better integration of the progress made as a result of the separation of the spiritual and temporal authorities. John Paul II has made many efforts in this direction; but he also speaks of re-Christianizing Europe and through it the world. And it is clear that such a project would run the risk of reactivating the mimetic rivalry with an Islamic faith that also talks of Islamizing the world and modernity, or a Judaism that defends its singularity with notorious political vehemence. Where are the values in question? Where are the creative minds and the works conveying values capable of transcending the loss of direction, confusion and systemic violence with which all societies, cultures and religions are contending at the present time? I shall limit myself to these questions, which are not rhetorical but programmatic. There are vast enterprises waiting to be undertaken, substantial gaps to be filled, new territories to be explored and radical rethinking to be carried out in our relationship with 'values'.

All these ventures are under way in Europe/the West, but two forms of expansion are needed. One is required within Western societies themselves to reverse the current total dominance of throwaway thought and populist culture, increasingly subject to the implacable laws of the neoliberal market. This is reflected in the reduction in the public outlets for critical thought in the human and social sciences. On the pretext of rooting out jargon, excessive erudition and abstract speculation (which is legitimate), you finish up by impoverishing the wide-scale transmission of the very real advances made by research in the social sciences, history, linguistics, semiotics, anthropology, criticism of political and legal thinking and ethical enquiry. The other form of expansion concerns the systematic application of the social sciences to the study of under-analysed societies, cultures that have been scandalously overlooked and very influential and even crucial systems of thought such as foundational thought—or the quest for foundations—and the fundamentalist imaginative world constructed with the help of mytho-historical and mytho-ideological representations. I am here employing a 'jargon' that even the editors of major newspapers, reviews and publishing houses claim not to understand. Why? Is it because the author loves to use jargon or because they themselves do not realize that no contemporary society—including those most rich in universities and scientific productions—can do without mytho-historical and mytho-ideological representations? The so-called cultivated public is the first to live, perceive and interpret on the basis of a postulate of rationality that ignores the influence of mytho-historical representations in so-called evolved societies. As for under-analysed societies, ravaged by all forms of populist culture, the term fundamentalist popularized by the media gives the measure of all the complexities nullified by the 'commonsense' terminology concerning this ideological monster constructed in the sole name of 'Islam', with a capital I since Khomeiny's Islamic revolution. Thus it is in the name of a 'commonsense' language immediately intelligible to all that the historian of Islamic thought is continuously censured in the West, which is loath to go beyond the confines of its imaginative universe on the subject of Islam, just as in Islamic contexts where the culture of the human and social sciences is desperately absent. Who can say whether the situation I have just denounced has a crucial and lasting negative impact on the current state of values? There is an urgent need to act along the lines of subverting the intellectual realm, practice in the social sciences and systems and channels not only of knowledge transmission but of ways of thinking of the world today, and to revisit the mytho-historic pasts that clutter up our collective memories, our social imaginations and our interpretations of the real world, to the point of unwittingly perverting the 'values' in whose name we embark on wars that are as implacable as they are pointless and at the same time destructive.

A philosophy of power

The crusade against 'terrorism' under way in the United States underlines the historical urgency of the forms of subversion I am advocating: there is a need to combat the *systemic violence* arising from the 'Western' manner of conceiving power and meaning and of making any proposition depend on a true, functional and reassuring meaning, on the existence of a 'nation', on the power of deterrence that can, at any moment, turn into strike power that ensures the total victory of one side against the enemy. At a time when wars were fought between adversaries commanding equal weapons and resources, this philosophy of meaning and power produced outcomes accepted, if not acceptable, as legitimate. But since the eighteenth century at least, humanity has entered the era of fundamentally unequal wars: scientific and technological advances have given the West an undeniable supremacy in all spheres of power. This is one of the factors that has forced recourse to resistance through guerrilla warfare and terrorism. The fact that this essential fact has hardly been taken into account in justifications of the 'holy war' against terrorism tells us something about the limits set to ethical questioning in present-day 'Western' thought. A new 'right to war' is necessary; but we know the resistance of the United States to any advance in this direction. Yet to negotiate a new right that would encompass all the problems posed by systemic violence from the colonial wars to the war against 'terrorism' would be the most radical way not of responding to each terrorist act by disproportionate reprisals but of breaking the infernal cycle of systemic violence institutionalized like the doctrine of an eye for an eye. It is clear that the systemic violence inseparable from the geopolitical strategies of Europe/the West has taken the place of the balance of terror during the Cold War; so long as this 'philosophy' of 'meaning' and power prevails, it would be pointless, misleading and unworthy of the human mind that retains a sense of its responsibilities to engage in discussions on values capable of being universalized for the first time in the history of the ethical imperative.

It is not surprising then that our concern with the future of values is confined to the historical context of Western philosophical and moral thought. Is this intellectually acceptable? Is it permissible from a scholarly standpoint? I have struggled and fought for thirty years to establish a consolidated history of the Mediterranean, because it is within this framework that it may be possible to create a sense of historical solidarity and to generate new values with the participation of all the peoples reduced to the state of remnants. I would note in this connection that the instrumentalization of Enlightenment reason has militated against the most elementary principles of humanism within Europe itself. Apart from the Second World War and the programmed historical tragedies it engendered, the deviations of Western reason are one of the direct sources of the events we have suffered: the Suez crisis, the Algerian war, the Six Day War, the Yom Kippur War, the Gulf War and the American campaign at the present time. It will remain thus so long as we have not created the intellectual conditions in which our history is shaped on the basis of human solidarity rather than on secret arrangements between states. For there are states that work against their people. The colonized peoples, who rightly argued that they had been victimized, have not managed to derive from the experience of colonization a liberating historical project, and we have witnessed some terrible ideological deviations inflicted by States on their peoples. Islam, rather than benefiting from the liberations of the 1960s and 1970s and starting to think again about its own past, i.e., subjecting it to a critical review as radical as the one we are carrying out in the West with regard to the values transmitted by Judeo-Christianity, has provoked a total divorce between contemporary Islamic reasoning and the classical age of Islamic thought from the seventh to the thirteenth centuries. Still today, Muslims do not know how to speak of this age, because Islamic historical research lags considerably behind. Incapable of understanding our heritage, we are likewise unable to dialogue on equal terms with Europeans with a view to creating new values, as I am nevertheless attempting to do in this presentation.

Contemporary Islam has also forgotten the scraps of modernity that Islamic intellectuals, particularly the Arabs, tried to integrate during the period that, in the nineteenth century, was termed 'Renaissance'. This oversight is explained in large measure by the fact that modernity has subsequently had a negative effect on the colonized peoples, since its benefits have been associated with cultural domination and denigration. In conclusion, I would insist on the need for all of us to create the conditions in which we can move from a history based on a hierarchy of peoples and cultures to a history based on solidarity in order to shape together those values of the future to which we all aspire.

Jean-Joseph Goux

Towards a Frivolousness of Values?

The fact that we are speculating on the future of values means that we have abandoned any attempt to ground them in unalterable commitments, fixed credos or absolute concepts of beauty, truth and goodness inscribed in tablets of stone. This uncertainty, which is also an immense responsibility, is very recent in the history of civilizations. Voltaire believed that there was 'only one morality' just as there was 'only one geometry', and Kant would probably not have dissented from this view.

Values on trial

The Age of Enlightenment, which remains the source of all that is best in us, was a century of questioning, dissent and revolution but not of nihilism. For, beyond the injustices, faulty laws and distorted or perverted theology, a Voltaire or a Rousseau still glimpsed a hidden universality. There existed in their view, transcending the deviations contingent upon evil societies, a natural and universal law that silently governs humanity throughout time and needs only to be rediscovered, still intact and resplendent, behind the distortions imposed by tyranny and ignorance.

What we find difficult or are unwilling to echo is doubtless the Enlightenment's invocation of this natural law—unwritten yet inscribed in the unchanging nature of human beings, beyond the reach of arbitrary and deceitful dogma. This is where, notwithstanding our so-called 'universal' values (Liberty, Equality, Human Rights, etc.), we part company with the Enlightenment emancipators. We have been exposed to the great tide of demystification and suspicion that has caused us to sacrifice in certainty and fervour what we have gained in lucidity, or perhaps cynicism. According to the great demystifiers, eternal laws identical for human beings everywhere and at all times do not exist, neither in heaven nor in the human heart. What we take for unconditioned, transcendent actions, originating in heaven or nature, are no more than human viewpoints, relative options, subjective choices, which reflect no more than an all-too-human perspective and which only a metaphysical optical illusion could induce us to take for absolute values.

This disabused interpretation claims to throw light on the obscure mechanisms governing the institution of values. Are not the notions of good and evil, the great moral imperatives, a mere idealist disguise, cloaking the basest and most materialistic instincts of possession and domination? Is not individual or collective self-interest the hidden spring of our actions? Does not the institution of values posing as universal in order to extend their empire have its obscure origins in the will of a particular class, group or nation to exercise political or economic power? This is the gnawing suspicion, eroding what seemed to be absolute and sacred, that obsessed the most iconoclastic and lucid of nineteenth-century thinkers.

It is at this point, moreover, that the notion of value becomes omnipresent. The right to challenge, overturn and transmute values is claimed; the main claim, however, concerns the creation of values, since the Promethean subjectivity of the human being is recognized as having a capacity previously attributed only to an all-powerful God—that of creation *ex nihilo*. The human being, or rather the individual, is creative and free: he raises himself up against the void to affirm what is good and what is evil, hazarding a wager in the absence of any absolute criterion. This is the unconditioned freedom of consciousness, which presupposes no attachment, either to nature, history or any form of celestial transcendence. It is the anguished freedom of a rootless being, an insular individual.

The aestheticization of values

When Sartre, the representative of atheistic existentialism, was criticized for the gratuitousness inherent in his conception of freedom emerging from nothingness to create values devoid of natural or transcendental foundation, he replied by citing the example of Picasso: 'When Picasso paints, he does not conform to any existing standard, any notion of the beautiful or any eternal ideal of pictorial art, and yet when we speak of a canvas by Picasso we never refer to it as gratuitous. He is not indiscriminate in the way he paints or in what he paints: he is demanding. Admittedly, he invents criteria specific to him, but he subordinates himself to those criteria until he achieves a result that is fully satisfying to him: he is a creator of values.'[1]

---

1. Jean-Paul Sartre, 'Existentialism is a Humanism', trans. Bernard Frechtman, reprinted as 'Existentialism' in *Existentialism and Human Emotions*, New York, Citadel Press, 1985.

It is significant that Sartre should have responded to the charge of gratuitousness with reference to the artist, in particular the initiator of the Cubist movement. The artist was in the process of becoming the supreme model of human activity—particularly the avant-garde artist, the one who breaks with established artistic canons to pursue boundless invention, even if this involves grossly distorting perceptible reality, bending it to the most unexpected subjective demands. And, since Nietzsche, what we have witnessed is precisely this aestheticization of the ethical. Foucault would speak of life as a work of art, and Deleuze of philosophy as the creation of concepts. What seems to be at work then, beyond knowledge and power, is an artist-operation and an artist-will bent on destroying any rationalist and normative attempt to establish overall explanatory notions or establish values.

This aestheticizing tendency is all the more disconcerting since contemporary art, while not lacking in minor inventions and provocations, appears to be experiencing a crisis of legitimacy, a period in which it is running out of inspiration, entailing the risk of gratuitousness. Paradoxically, references to art are omnipresent at a time when art itself is unable to find any firm foundation for its existence and is exploring, mostly in ironic vein, its own futility and disarray. Indeed, there are no more established aesthetic standards to revolt against, and almost a century has passed since Picasso distorted the *Weeping Woman*, Marcel Duchamp exhibited the urinal and Tristan Tzara wrote a poem composed of words drawn at random from a hat. Since then, these astonishing deconstructions have never stopped—as we see today in the realm of design with Starck's dwarfs.

The stock-exchange model of values

This risk of gratuitousness or futility has another consequence, which I would describe as the 'stock-exchange model' of values and which is in no way incompatible with the aestheticizing tendency of which I have spoken. Economic values are not of the same order as aesthetic, ethical or spiritual values. But it is above all in the economic sphere that the word value has taken on a precise meaning, and it is certainly in the economic and financial sphere that the process whereby value becomes something subjective and variable, rather than absolute and stable, began to emerge.

The classical economists believed, with Adam Smith, that *work*—the labour necessary for production—could provide the universal measure of the value of goods exchanged in a market. They thought that they had in their possession, in the work time expended on a product, a kind of universally applicable law that regulated more or less self-evidently the exchange of goods. But in the 1870s the shift to an exclusive concern with the real and verifiable price, as determined variably and at a particular moment in a given market through the unpredictable interplay of supply and demand, led to another conception of value. It is no longer supply but rather the subjective intensity of the need or desire for such and such a good, at a given moment, that determines its value.

To determine what goods are worth, the neoclassical economists tell us, it is the point of view of the self-gratifying consumer that counts and not that of the producer. The relevant standpoint is the *satisfaction* derived from consuming and not the labour involved in manufacturing. The market, in its pure form, characterized by the perfect competition referred to by the neoclassical economists, essentially resembles an auction or a stock market where multiple factors (subjective desires, passing whims, random wagers) determine an instantaneous price, through the process of supply and demand, without it being possible to identify any stable basis or universal and permanent law that could explain the determination of the price to which the partners in the exchange have agreed. The wildest fancy can weigh as heavily as the most concentrated reflection. A valuation deemed to be objective and impersonal, at least in terms of underlying value, is replaced by a value that is subjective, or intersubjective, and in any case transitory and momentary, which does not seem to correspond to any regulatory law transcending the permanent confrontation of supply and demand inherent in the operation of the market. Value no longer belongs to the realm of the norm but rather to that of the event. The hedonistic and subjective corner had been turned in economic theory, and the tendency has continued to dominate up to the present time.

Paul Valéry, an attentive reader of Léon Walras, the founder of neoclassical economics in France, had clearly discerned this turning point and its philosophical significance. In a text dating from the end of the 1930s (a decade marked by the most terrible crisis of financial values that the West has known and by profound disarray in the realm of moral and political values), Valéry borrowed the stock-market model of values to reflect on all human activities. In the moral and aesthetic realm, as in the economic domain, there is no absolute standard, no stable measure of values. Society with its material and spiritual productions, Valéry writes, is a great market where everything fluctuates according to stock-market principles. Values rise and fall over a short space of time. The value 'mind', he continues jokingly, is no different from that of 'petrol', 'wheat' or 'gold, and it unfortunately continues to fall.[2] The random, the subjective and the ephemeral replace any idea of foundation, transcendence and duration. The logic of fashion, which was dominated by the arbitrary and sanctioned by a passing unanimity

---

2. Paul Valéry, 'La liberté de l'Esprit', in *Regards sur le monde actuel et autres essais*, Paris, Gallimard, 1946.

or transgression but which concerned only subordinate aspects of existence, pervades everything.

Since the 1980s, and particularly today, we are in a better position to comprehend Valéry's insight. The non-convertibility of currency is emblematic of this situation. For some time now currency has ceased to be weighed: it is written, it is conveyed as information or token, it traverses the global electronic networks, passing through banks whose coffers have become empty. There used to be a world, that of commodity money and work value, where gold circulated as such; then came the circulation of signs, whose only value was to *represent* gold; what we have today is the inconvertible, floating money token, whose only value is the credence given to it, the more or less unanimous demand exerted or not upon it. All values, not only economic ones, seem driven by a kind of volatility, of relativism, and are subject to phenomena of inflation, overvaluation, collapse and depreciation.

This is the realm of the non-convertible sign (always in search of a constantly deferred real counterpart) and of stock-market values (dependent on unpredictable variations), which is perhaps tending to invade the whole of our culture, or at least to become its most visible and spectacular aspect. Information itself is caught up in this same snowball logic of inflation that can cause us to lose our sense of reality.

The informational and financial bubbles are linked. It is on the basis of a whole range of rapidly changing global indicators that stock-market wagers are made, with contagious effect. A slowly evolving history, embodying clear long-term tendencies, is giving way to a feverish, seismographic history, which has something chaotic and fractal about it.

The universe of finance and stock-market speculation is a world traversed by instantaneous signals, in which the fluctuations of a share quotation, the difference between a rise and fall in value, represent the outcome of myriad interlinked human activities. The enormous productive labour of enterprises throughout the world is, from this vantage point, reduced to a permanent game involving the most irrational of wagers, as if the seriousness of productive enterprises and outcomes was converted into the fever that grips the gambler in a casino: patience and effort at the base against the throw of the dice at the apex.

It is clear that a universe in which values are transformed into share quotations runs the risk of becoming one exhibiting frivolous and unstable values, essentially linked to conditions of superabundance and luxury or, more exactly, to the difference between richness and poverty—a universe lacking in universality. However, the feverish and chaotic spectacle of the stock exchange, the world of fashion and the media is perhaps no more than a shimmering surface effect, which for all its influence does not engage core historical and social phenomena.

Just as the distinction is often made between the speculative or virtual economy and the real economy (a distinction that incidentally deserves to be questioned), there is also an instability, an insubstantiality even, of aesthetic and ethical values that is perhaps no more than a froth bubble effect. When we are surprised by events of some gravity (the spectre of war or shortages of essential goods), our values fairly quickly reacquire a certain hierarchy that the speculative spectacle tends to dissipate, just as the real, long-term, non-fractal economy seems to 'correct' the so-called irrational exuberances of the market.

The complex relationship between freedom and frivolousness

Our Enlightenment philosophers had resources that we lack. They could appeal to a human nature that remained unchanging and eternal, beyond the variations arising from customs, the passions of the moment or commerce. This was how Helvetius, Condorcet or Voltaire thought of frivolity. It was the result of 'a modish turn of mind that is continually replacing one ridiculous thing by another'.[3] Our suspicion is today less easy to dispel. If, as Valéry suggests, the stock-market paradigm contaminates all values and becomes the general pattern for values in our world, whether in art, morality or politics, we thereby lose all possibility of appeal to the sometimes liberating standards provided by the ideas of human nature or natural law. Mode in the broad sense of the term (including media phenomena, the financial situation and all forms of instantaneous bidding and quotation) is no longer a surface effect but the unique form of being in a world marked by the commercial aestheticizing of values and moving towards the realm of the ephemeral and the frivolous.

It must however be recognized that this aestheticization and extension of the stock-market model, which seem to deprive values of any foundation, are the reflection and consequence of a great freedom, an emancipation that seems unlimited in a social regime that has democracy as its supreme principle and in which there is no imposed *a priori* as to the possible forms of human desire and creative innovation. The well-known dictum of Jean-Baptiste Say to the effect that 'supply precedes demand' ushers in a world, today's world, in which entrepreneurs as dishevelled as the most surrealistic of poets, the inventors of unpredictable novelties that reactivate consumer desire by means of shock, difference and surprise, who construe themselves on the model of artistic activity. The anthropological juvenilization of mainstream values, going beyond the ideology of 'youthism', feeds on this tendency.

We may conclude by noting a paradox illustrative of the tension commonly found in our value systems between two tendencies, one

---

3. Claude Adrian Helvetius, *De l'Esprit*, 'Discours II', chapter 19, Paris, Durand, 1758.

serious and the other frivolous. On the one hand, we attach—or should attach—increasing importance to the compact with nature, the link of reciprocity, as opposed to unilateral domination, that humanity wishes and ought to maintain with the planet; the recognition that we are a fragile part of the biosphere and that our survival as a species is no longer certain. There is, or ought then to be, a marriage between humankind and nature, in a new union that transcends the old fearful and sacralized relationship with Mother Nature and likewise the modern presumption that views nature as a resource to be exploited indefinitely. To this extent, in a confused and novel manner, we are reintegrating the notion of nature into our new equations. The very idea of earthly survival implies an intergenerational responsibility, a relationship with the future and our progeny rooted in the most immemorial and obscure of commitments. On the other hand there is the difficulty of escaping from the excessive and destructive futility of values based on short-term fluctuations, of giving our values a firm grounding in unwritten and unformulable laws, which would safeguard both our freedom and our self-belief.

Beyond the Aestheticization of Values?

How is the current aestheticizing tendency affecting values? In a world in which aesthetic quality has become a yardstick of value, one may ask what remains of the ethical dimension. The role of art itself in this context is no less uncertain: for some, it is a medium that mirrors the hesitations of the century, while for others it offers the opportunity for rearticulating human aspirations destabilized by the cacophony of modernity. Will the model it seems to offer provide a solution to the fragmentation of values?

Wolfgang Welsch attempts to define the position of art itself in this context of aestheticization. To prevent aestheticization leading to art's demise, he suggests that it should adopt a new stance, neither individual nor social but rather 'transhuman'. Through such a distinctive transcendence of the human, art could become the setting for a 'rational Buddhism', paving the way for a reinterpretation of values and of our relationship with the world.

Michel Maffesoli also finds in this aestheticizing trend the potential for a new, local ethic grounded in aesthetic experience. At a time when we are witnessing the end of universalism and a pervasive relativization of values, the phenomenon of communion centred on artistic images could provide the paradigm for a new ordering of knowledge.

For Victor Massuh, on the other hand, the universal values to which we aspire are to be sought elsewhere. In his view, the aestheticization of values, reinforced by the alliance between art and technology, is producing an 'aestheticizing colonization' of the world, which is undermining values and precipitating their decline by excluding any form of dialogue. We must therefore resist the fragmentation of modern values by trying to rediscover the voice of universal Truth in the midst of this cacophony.

* * * *

Wolfgang Welsch is professor of philosophy at the University of Jena in Germany. He taught at a number of German universities prior to being awarded the Max Planck Research Prize (1992) as well as numerous research fellowships in Austria and Japan. His research is currently focused on aesthetics, the theory of art and the philosophy of culture. His publications include *Unsere postmoderne Moderne* (1987), *Ästhetisches Denken* (1990), *Vernunft* (1995), *Grenzgänge der Ästhetik* (1996), *Undoing Aesthetics* (1997), *Aesthetics and Beyond* (2002).

Professor of sociology at the University of Paris V since 1981, **Michel Maffesoli** is director of the Centre d'Etudes sur l'Actuel et le Quotidien (CEAQ) and of the Centre de Recherche sur l'Imaginaire at the Maison des Sciences de l'Homme (MSH). His many published works include: *Au creux des apparences* (1990), *La Transfiguration du politique* (1992), *The Time of the Tribes* (1995), *Eloge de la raison sensible* (1996), *Du nomadisme* (1997), *Le Mystère de la conjonction* (1998), *L'Instant éternel* (2000) and *La Part du diable. Précis de subversion postmoderne* (2002). He is also director of the review *Sociétés* and *Cahiers de l'Imaginaire*, and vice-president of the International Institute of Sociology and a member of the Academia Scientiarum and Artium Europea.

The Argentinean philosopher and writer **Victor Massuh** is a former professor at the University of Buenos Aires, where he held the chairs of philosophy of history and philosophy of religion. He was also director of the department of philosophy in the same university. His main publications include: *El diálogo de las culturas* (1956), *El rito y el sagrado* (1965), *La libertad y la violencia* (1968), *Nietsche y el fin de la religión* (1969), *Nihilismo y experiencia extrema* (1975), *Agonia de la razón* (1994) and *¿Cara y contracara: una civilización a la deriva?* (1999). A former ambassador to UNESCO and Belgium, he was twice a member of UNESCO's Executive Board, which he also chaired.

Wolfgang Welsch

Art beyond Aestheticism

I am rather surprised by the ready equation made between values in the economic and the ethical sense, between cash value and moral value. Yet such a view might have a point given the wave of aestheticization we are experiencing today, when aesthetic distinctiveness has indeed become the guiding currency—at least in most Western countries (and the Western model is becoming increasingly prevalent throughout the world).

For or against aestheticization

There is no need to expand here on the manifestations of aestheticization: they are all too obvious and have been discussed at length for twenty-five years.[1] The question I want to address is how art positions itself with respect to the current aestheticization of the everyday. Broadly two options can be distinguished: one is collaborating with the trend and the other is resisting it.

Many artists—even some of the most renowned ones—have turned to helping embellish our everyday environment. One motive is certainly that the aestheticization boom provides great job opportunities, that beautifying the everyday is a business that pays. But, besides this economic motivation, there is also a specifically aesthetic one. It has long been a dream of aesthetics to redeem our world by beautifying it. Think of Schiller's proclamation that only by becoming aesthetic can we overcome modern fragmentation and restore the 'wholeness in our nature',[2] or Hegel's claim that aesthetics will bring about a new and perfect social unity, this even being considered the last and greatest work of humankind. Or think of the hopes of movements

---

1. See Wolfgang Welsch, *Undoing Aesthetics*, London, Sage Publications, 1997.
2. Friedrich Schiller, in the sixth of the *Letters on the Artistic Education of Man*, trans. Reginald Snell, Bristol, Thoemmes Press, 1994.

such as the Bauhaus to improve our world and society through aesthetic input. All of those movements were convinced that aestheticization would improve and even redeem our lives and the world.

Is this dream finally being realized? Of course not. The results clearly run counter to expectations. Total aestheticization results in its opposite: when everything becomes beautiful, nothing is beautiful any more. And the increasing shift from beautification to excitement does not help either: permanent stimulation leads in the end to indifference. Aestheticization eventually leads to anaesthetization: we no longer appreciate and notice the beauty that is pumped into everything; or we even experience it as disgusting and close our senses against the compulsoriness of the hyper-aestheticized environment.

Paradoxically, the complete aestheticization of the everyday makes art superfluous. In an over-embellished environment there simply is no need for art any more. It is even becoming impossible to distinguish what is, properly speaking, art, since everything is artistic. Aestheticization digs art's grave, as Jean Baudrillard aptly noted a quarter of a century ago in his work *Symbolic Exchange and Death*: 'art is everywhere, since artifice lies at the heart of reality. So reality is dead, since [...] reality itself [...] has become inseparable from its own image.'[3]

Given the extent of this failure, it is understandable that another group of artists should have taken the opposite stance by resolutely opposing aestheticization. They continue creating difficult, hermetic artworks that resist integration into the movement of aestheticization of the everyday. In so doing, they maintain the otherness of art in an attempt to secure its survival.

Although I am sympathetic to the latter stance, I do not think it is in step with contemporary conditions. Today's 'cultural machinery' requires and supports the creation of difference, which it needs as a stimulus to its continued existence. Hence the attitude of resistance is equivalent in the end to underpinning the cultural machinery. One cannot get away from the system by opposing it, for doing so complies precisely with its logic. For me, the most striking indication of this objective alliance was the case of Pollock. Even before he became popular in European art circles, Pollock was introduced to the European public by *Vogue*. In 1951, just one year after it was created, his (subsequently very famous) painting *Number 32* was used as a backdrop to the presentation of the most recent *haute couture* models. What was still rated as outrageous in the art world was welcomed and used in the fashion world.

It is clear, therefore, that both options (for and against aestheticization) lead nowhere. Aestheticization and the contemporary cultural machinery have rendered the concepts of artistic and aesthetic value effectively inoperative. Talk of the end of art thus has a point.

---

3. Jean Baudrillard, *Symbolic Exchange and Death*, London, Sage Publications, 1993.

Beyond the human

Yet there is another possibility—one that rejects conformity or resistance and adopts a stance that is neither individualistic nor societal nor human, but in a sense transhuman. History offers many examples of art seeking to transcend the human pale, and I should like to show that this tendency is present as a leitmotiv of twentieth-century art.

Apollinaire declared in 1913: 'Above all, artists are people who want to become inhuman. They painfully seek traces of inhumanity.'[4] Some ten years later, Ortega y Gasset diagnosed a 'dehumanization of art' as being typical of the modern tradition.[5] Merleau-Ponty considered Cézanne's painting as revelatory of the inhuman foundation of human nature.[6] And Adorno famously declared that art can be 'loyal to humanity only through inhumanity toward it'.[7] While Robinson Jeffers, the great Californian poet, writes:

> We must uncenter our minds from ourselves;
> We must unhumanize our views a little, and become confident
> As the rock and ocean that we were made from.[8]

Painters have also sought to produce, through art, the same dehumanization. Malevitch attempted to make us experience a cosmic dimension through his use, in particular, of black. For when you see black, then your gaze suddenly loses its hold and you are literally sucked up by infinity. I experienced this for the first time when I faced Malevitch's *Black Square* painted on a plaster board in an exhibition at the Centre Pompidou.

Dubuffet, for his part, attempted to reveal a terrestrial transhuman world, especially in his series *Topographies, Texturologies, Phénomènes* and *Matériologie* during the late 1950s and early 1960s. He wanted to create paintings, he said, 'based on the dehumanization of the subjects, of man and his gaze',[9] adopting a resolutely anti-cultural stance: 'Our culture is like clothing that does not fit—or in any case no longer fits'.[10]

Even decidedly geometrical works such as Walter de Maria's *The 2000 Sculpture* (my favourite example) produce the same effect. When you walk around the piece, you discover an amazing variety of perspectives,

---

4. Guillaume Apollinaire, 'Méditations esthétiques, les peintres cubistes', in *Oeuvres en proses complètes*, vol. 2, Paris, Gallimard, 1991.

5. José Ortega y Gasset, 'La deshumanizacion del arte', in *La deshumanizacion del arte e ideas sobre la novella*, 1925.

6. Maurice Merleau-Ponty, 'Cézanne's Doubt', in *Sense and Nonsense*, trans. Hubert L. Dreyfus and Patricia Allen Dreyfus, Evanston, Ill., Northwestern University Press, 1964.

7. Theodor W. Adorno, *Aesthetic Theory*, 1970.

8. Robinson Jeffers, 'Carmel Point', in *The Collected Poetry of Robinson Jeffers*, Stanford, 2001.

9. Jean Dubuffet, *Prospectus et tous écrits suivants*, Paris, Gallimard, 1967.

10. Jean Dubuffet, 'Positions anticulturelles', in *L'Homme du commun à l'ouvrage*, Paris, Gallimard, 1951.

with none of them being stable or distinguished as *the* perspective of the work. The flow of perspectives is all there is; and, despite its perfectly geometrical arrangement, the work gives you a strong sense of incomprehensibility. In the midst of your perception, something exceeding human expectation and comprehension arises.

The works of John Cage or Morton Feldman produce a similar effect: the sounds do not unfold according to the logic of a theme but seem rather to emerge by themselves, they come from nowhere. When listening to this evolvement of sounds, we are absorbed into their flow and finally move along with it, like elements and not observers of what we hear. We experience ourselves like beings welcomed and participating in a world that is not on a human scale.

A rational Buddhism

Works of this kind lead us beyond a closed human world, criticizing in the process the modern stance. For in modern times we have come to think of the world we refer to as basically constituted by the human mind and therefore in principle restricted to human understanding. The modern point of view is profoundly anthropocentric. 'Man', Diderot typically declared in 1755, 'is the unique concept from which we must start and to which we must refer everything back.'[11] A few years later Kant provided the modern stance with its perfect epistemological legitimation. Kant's basic thought—so seminal to all modern thinking—was that we can recognize only what we make. Hence our cognition of the world testifies to the world's character of not being a given but (in its fundamental structure at least) something produced by us. So Diderot's maxim and the modern standpoint are altogether right: we are indeed to take ourselves as the exclusive point of departure and reference. However, works of the type mentioned try to break open this modern cage of self-reference.

It is perhaps no coincidence that some of those artists named—Cage, Feldman, and Walter de Maria—felt close to Eastern art and thinking. Seeing the human as fundamentally not opposed to but participating in a greater-than-human world and advocating a transhuman view is far more natural to Eastern than Western thinking. While in a Western perspective, man is supposed to be primordially opposed to the world ('man against the rest of the world' being the prototypical formula of *modern* Western thinking at least)—Eastern consciousness is aware of our deep connectedness with the world.

The artworks I refer to have nothing to do with the aestheticization of the everyday. They rather seek to transcend the current framework of modernity. To understand ourselves in terms of connectedness with

---

11. Denis Diderot, *Encyclopédie*, vol. 3, Paris, Hermann, 1976.

a greater-than-human world is, it seems to me, the path we should look to for the future. Certain philosophical considerations that I have treated elsewhere,[12] and which I do not have space to develop here, argue in favour of such a transition. To put matters in a nutshell, the West needs to envisage a kind of 'rational Buddhism'.

That does not mean that it is sufficient to complement anthropocentric modernity with its nonhuman counterpole, as many thinkers have done against a background of religious inspiration. Plato and Aristotle appeal to our divine nature, Kant emphasizes our 'intelligible character', and certain philosophers such as Heidegger, Scheler or Lyotard speak of our transcending nature. In every case, human exclusivity remains the nub of the problem. It is simply that normal human intelligence seems too narrow and the attempt is made to complement it with its opposite.

If, on the contrary, we managed to develop a transhuman perspective—and I am sure that many artists will do so in the twenty-first century—what would this mean with respect to values?

Firstly, this new framework would require that we see values in a new way, as being embedded in a world that is not just of our making. The modern conception, in contrast, has understood values from a narrowly humanistic standpoint, considering man as the measure of all things.

Secondly, the new set of values will demand that we respect our connectedness with the world. It will be integrative rather than anthropocentric. This may sound like romantic or ecological thinking. But both romanticism and ecology derive from the anthropocentric model—the romantic approach by assuming the world to be intrinsically human-like, and the ecological approach by falling into the functionalistic and technological trap.

Thirdly, our habitual values, those of the modern set, are in need of reinterpretation according to the new framework. Autonomy, for example, could be assessed as a partial value within a larger evolutionary, not to say cosmic, frame.

Much more reflection along these lines will clearly be required, but it is worth noting that new approaches in the artistic sphere have already breached the barrier of modernity and are in the process of altering our perspectives.

---

12. 'Transcending the modern closure of the human mind', address by the author to the conference 'New Perspectives in Contemporary Philosophy', Universidade do Estado do Rio de Janeiro, 8–10 August 2001.

Michel Maffesoli

Towards a Postmodern Ethic of the Aesthetic

Max Weber encouraged us, in his essays on science and politics as a vocation, to 'measure up to the world in its everyday routine'. He also suggested, in his analysis of the origins of modernity, that it was important to 'understand the real on the basis of the unreal', that is, to reconcile the everyday and the imaginary. In the 1960s, we used to say that our ideas were in everybody's heads. I propose to bring these ideas together, which is the role of the intellectual, while endeavouring to pose the problems elegantly, as recommended in an Aristotelian dictum.

What distinguishes us as an animal species is the capacity for self-articulation. What we call culture or values is nothing more than the articulation of a mode of being. What is said includes those self-evident truths whereby we are, think, eat or love as we do. It is important to remember that there may be a surfeit of self-evident truths, as we see about us at the present time. There is a discrepancy between lived experience and what is thought about lived experience. This discussion, and the wealth of literature on which it draws, demonstrates on the contrary that there are no more self-evident truths. There is therefore an urgent need to analyse what is coming into being on the confines of the self-evident truth, which continues to exist through force of inertia, particularly in institutions such as ours. The university does not escape this tragic law whereby we continue to repeat what may in reality no longer exist.

The end of universalism

My obsession is to make us attentive to the relativization of values, which takes place in defiance of the intellectual *doxa*, namely universalism. Whatever we say, whatever we do, we remain obsessed by universalism, whereas our lived experience remains within the domain of relativism. It is not done to say one is a relativist, but I have no compunction in declaring myself a relativist in both theory and practice.

As Simmel has shown, theoretical relativism is not the incapacity to know, but rather the interrelation of different forms of knowledge. In this respect, it is important to note the dramatic rise of polyculturalism, which is nothing less than the transposition of relativism into the realm of lived experience.

Universalism, as Mohammed Arkoun has underlined, is a Western exception, since values forged in a small canton of the globe have been exported and extrapolated throughout the world. Modernity, in my view, did not begin in the sixteenth or the seventeenth century but well before, when Saint Augustine, crystallizing the Judeo-Christian heritage, performed the founding act. Did he not defend, in the *City of God*, a soteriological conception of the world, that is to say, one dedicated to the search for salvation and thus to something that is to come? This was the starting point for the development—culminating in the nineteenth-century ideologies militating in the cause of a perfect society to come—of an economy and history of salvation, which is the weft of what we call history. Saint Augustine was the point of departure for all the theories of emancipation that have shaped us: we must free ourselves from sin, imperfection and alienation. Does he not postulate that Evil has no existence in itself? That it is simply a *privatio boni*? It is on this basis, it seems to me, that we can understand how the logic of 'ought to be', i.e., moralism, took shape.

Georg Lukacs, in *History and Class Consciousness* (1923), showed that that which belongs to the realm of the everyday is deemed in our worldview to be infamous. He even went so far as to refer to the 'infamy of the existent'. The existent does not articulate itself; it exists only to be criticized. The Freudian perspective throws the stigmatization of the everyday into even sharper focus: the intellectual, according to the founder of psychoanalysis, is the 'knight of hatred', and we know the positive role he attached to that hatred. One similarly finds in Goethe a recurrent reference to the 'mind that always says no'. Through these different propositions we discern the outline of the logic of the Ought, which I for my part have called a 'logic of domination'. Self-mastery and mastery of the world are the foundation of the philosophy of the Enlightenment and the great social systems of the nineteenth century that flow from it. Thus futurism promised satisfaction in the world to come, which would be the result of working on oneself and the world but at the cost of the 'arraignment of the world' as described by Heidegger. It is this approach that still informs morality and geopolitics, just as it does the Kantian imperatives referred to by Edgar Morin. The *libido dominandi* is indissociable from the *libido sciendi*.

From the *libido dominandi* to the *libido sentiendi*

In my view, what is self-evident in our thought no longer corresponds with what is evident. To overcome this hiatus, I propose to take as my point of departure not the *libido dominandi*, exercising control over the self and the world, nor the *libido sciendi*, giving me knowledge of how to master myself and the world, but rather the *libido sentiendi*, the desire to feel. It should be stated at once that such an inversion of polarity gives rise to both the best and the worst, beginning with tribalism and a return to nomadism.

Should we speak, as we are spontaneously tempted to do, of a regression or involution? Perhaps, to be accurate, we should employ a term such as 'backtracking' to suggest the revisiting of archaic material, in the etymological sense of archaic (which is fundamental or primordial). We must recognize that the barbarians are among us and indeed within us. I would therefore set against political, abstract and universal morality something arguably belonging to the order of ethics. Ethics, indeed, is something different from morality: it is the cement that binds together values rooted in their local setting. This localism, I recognize, does not relate to the scheme of history. Nietzsche once said of a small German town: 'In this place, one could live here because one lives here.' He was referring to a kind of dynamic rootedness that is linked to localism. Nietzsche spoke of *amor fati* but one could go so far as to speak of *amor mundi* to describe the love of the world for what it is. This may be seen as a form of aestheticization, on the understanding that such an aesthetic, while immoral from the standpoint of universal morality, is ethical insofar as it cements on the basis of values lived with others in the here and now. We are no longer dealing with history but with a community of destiny or with histories.

There can also be an ethic of the aesthetic. I put forward the idea, two decades ago now, of a sociology of orgy (*orgè*: shared emotion), since I believe that such shared emotions are central to our time—for example, in sporting, musical, consumer and religious-type communions. 'Orgiasm', aesthetically speaking, is the loss of self in another, as opposed to the economy of self and the world. An empirical cult of the body has become the foundation of the body social since the exasperated individual body merges into a collective body, which is the efficient definition of hedonism.

Valéry ironically noted: 'Intellectuals are naturally *de profundis*.' They are indeed always seeking to delve deeper, while lamenting: '*De profundis clamavi ad te Domine*.' We should, on the contrary, endeavour to look at what is on the surface of things. Simmel, Weber and Nietzsche have all reminded us that at certain periods the profound is concealed within the surface of things. The profound in this case is hedonism, the cult of the body, what prompts the self-enclosed individual to yield to a community of local destiny, giving rise for better or worse to a specific ethic.

I observe, alongside our methodical individualism, communions centred on images. There exists today a social erotic that can no longer be interpreted in terms of categorical imperatives. Ortega y Gasset wrote that there was a need to institute 'atmospherical imperatives', that is to say, to understand climates not on the basis of morality and what ought to be, but on the basis of what actually is. Sporting, warlike or terrorist commotion, and the corresponding flare-ups around our cities, are aesthetics linked to this social erotic, that is to say, shared images or myths around which people cluster. We are dealing here with something that is no longer akin to economic consumption but rather to *consummation*: we lose ourselves in others, in what is foreign. One shifts in this way from a political morality to an ethic of the aesthetic. This emergence is no longer perceptible using our favoured tools of analysis—the self-mastering rational individual and the notion of the social, national or international contract. The challenge of the ethic of the aesthetic thus consists in reflecting on what might lie alongside or behind the democratic ideal as formulated by Hannah Arendt: a community ideal. Walter Benjamin said that 'each age dreams of the next', and I think that it is important for us to assume responsibility for what is in the process of being born, on pain of seeing the dream turn to nightmare.

Victor Massuh

The Soul of Values

From the start, humanity has aspired to values that are absolute, timeless and independent of history—values such as truth, goodness, holiness and beauty. In proclaiming the 'death of God', nihilism was instrumental in the dethroning of Truth. It was soon to find a close ally in ethical relativism, which challenged the notion of Goodness by arguing the case for the equivalence of all values. We then came to realize that the values to which we adhere cannot be any more than goals, given the subjective bias inherent in power relations, self-interest and resentment. The unity of moral values also disintegrates on occasion into a congeries of conventions protective of defensive corporatisms, reflecting the fact that ethical value, when reduced to the sole function of safeguarding social cohesion, loses sight of its true horizon, that of human universals.

Philosophical nihilism and ethical relativism have a great deal in common, in my view, with religious fundamentalism. When a value regarded as sacred, associated with a belief, demands the exclusion of denominational divergences, faith becomes a form of power. When this occurs, it loses its most secure foundation, namely the faculty of dialogue independent of all forms of power. The force of revelation has made way for the discourse of the doctors. The exaltation of the sacred as a justification for exclusion leads to its debasement. Secular society, subverted in this way, can then succumb to blind folly.

The dangers of aestheticization

Art expresses the value that is conventionally known as beauty. Can this value stand apart from history? Not if we are to believe Malraux in *The Imaginary Museum*: 'Art today bears witness, in all its forms, to a wide diversity of adventures that makes aesthetic contemplation, and above all feeling, difficult. The chaotic complexity of contemporary art makes the definition of art in terms of traditional values a doubtful enterprise and illustrates the crisis of our time, in search of modes of evaluation able to take account of the singular and unique value of its testimony.'[1]

Many see art as the lyrical expression of history. It has to be said that the chaos of our present age is not conducive to a celebration of the world. In fact, art is not simply celebration. Rilke realized as much when he wrote that 'the beautiful is no more than a terrible beginning'.[2] Yet I would argue that it is in the realm of art that creative freedom records its greatest victories over chaos. It is obvious, for example, that by incorporating scrap material in its assemblages of objects modern art testifies both to the disintegration of reality and to a profound metaphysical yearning for integration. This is the source of the ambiguity and disconcerting aspect of contemporary art. The drama of this art may also be said to arise from the fact that it is caught up in the blind onward rush of technological development. Art and technology are vying for supremacy in the spheres of innovation, the creation of plastic forms and the production and use of new materials. However, their approaches are essentially different: art is an end in itself, the ultimate expression of the human mind and spirit, whereas technology is no more than a practical means, even if it sometimes calls for genius.

It remains true that art is the major accomplice of the technological revolution through which we are living, since it uses the materials that technology discovers to embellish the productions of modernity. In a sense, art and technology have made themselves masters of the world by helping through their alliance to embellish it. It even seems that the attack on the twin towers of New York, which led to the destruction of many works of art, cannot jeopardize such an alliance, since the aestheticization of the world has already had an irreversible influence on the sensibility of the population at large by offering them new tastes, flavours and pleasures that have rapidly turned into needs.

Advertisements in the form of aestheticized images have invaded public spaces in defence of messages that are far from universal. Everywhere in the city, visual blandishments encourage the incessant consumption of goods. The mere announcement of a book, a fashion show, or the opening of a political campaign, even the inauguration of a factory, receives the cosmetic treatment. The bellicose news reporting of the media and the endless stream of images come in the end to seem like a perpetually renewed ritual in which aesthetic criteria predominate. In contemporary life, appearance takes precedence over reality; the spectacle of existence seems truer than life itself.

---

1. André Malraux, *Le musée imaginaire*, Paris, Gallimard, 1965.
2. Rainer Maria Rilke, *Duino Elegies*, trans. David Young, New York, W.W. Norton, 1993.

Art adds to the technological aestheticization of the world the power of artifice, marking the triumph of man over nature. Beauty, which according to Kant is 'purposefulness without purpose', is enlisted for the purpose of shaping a collective existence ordered like a stage performance. The media stage has thus acquired the status of the supreme tribunal of the real.

The aestheticizing colonization of the world by art and technology working in concert does not only affect the realm of values since we are confronted, under the convergent influence of philosophical realism and ethical relativism, by the notion of the gratuitous act. This culminates in the ritual and narcissistic reactivation of the aggressive and desperate fundamentalism we witness today.

The voice of truth

As Jean-Joseph Goux and Wolfgang Welsch point out, the omnipresent aestheticization of values, linked to economic structures, leads to their degradation or their takeover by substitute powers. The progress of specialization has led to the fragmentation of every value. In the philosophical domain, the boundaries between the different disciplines make dialogue unintelligible. The same phenomenon occurs in the domain of ethics and religion. We live in the realm of the fragmentary: the expression of different styles has become a cacophony.

Fragmentary values cannot give a direction to history, for they are in the service of subordinate goals. An ethical system consisting of isolated professional codes of conduct loses touch with human dignity. An aesthetic proud to participate in the expression of the world's chaos is not a good ally of beauty or of the world. The assembling of disparate fragments, strewn here or there, is a cultural endeavour that may make for good spectacle but will certainly not be productive of meaning. Amusement, rapid movement, high decibels, violent sensations and furtive ecstasy are typical forms of contemporary aestheticization. They deliver the world to us, but at the cost of our soul.

Rediscovering the soul of values involves recognizing that truth, goodness, beauty, holiness are the ultimate goals of human aspiration and that apprehending one of them affects all the others. These goals are inseparable, contrary to what aestheticization would have us believe. Ultimately, truth is one of the faces of beauty, an extension of human dignity and an intimation of the sacred.

A life of values today calls for no great resources, only reflection and silence. Beyond the allurements of aestheticization, we should be receptive—without recourse to media or intermediary—to the voice of truth, to the serenity deriving from righteous or heroic conduct, to the wonder attaching to beauty and to the transcendent allure of mystery.

Towards the Reinterpretation of Values?

The twentieth century saw shifts in traditional historical dynamics and frames of reference. In addition to the new networks, issues and priorities that accompanied and often reinforced these shifts, may we also speak of the emergence of new values? In the context of these changes, the search for criteria of value, both individual and collective, is a constant concern in our societies and dictates the need to reflect on the possibility of a renewal of values. This question is relevant to all aspects of our thinking on identity and culture.

Candido Mendes proposes first that we reflect on the very nature of the postmodern discourse and its implications, and the need to adopt a heuristics of the particular as a prerequisite to being able to conceive of the Other. Julia Kristeva sees in certain specifically feminine values a potential source of the renewal of values, involving a different relationship with time and the world.

Roger Sue seeks to derive from the present-day rise of associations a new model that will enable us to escape from the old prejudices of liberalism. Finally, Paul Ricoeur, denouncing the half-truths that pervade received wisdom on identity and values, argues the need to overcome these prejudices, which impede the revitalization of our constantly renewed heritages. He proposes a radical rethinking of our received ideas, reconciling, by way of translation as a paradigm for all exchanges, the search for a universal with the awareness of the multiplicity of our heritages.

* * * *

Candido Mendes has been rector of the University of Rio de Janeiro since 1963. A member of the Brazilian Academy of Letters and Secretary-General of the Academy of Latinity, he has also been president of the International Council of Social Sciences and president of the International Association of Political Sciences, a member of the Pontifical Commission Justice and Peace in Brazil, a member of the Council of the United

Nations University and a federal deputy in the Brazilian Parliament. His many published works include: *Beyond Populism* (1977), *Justice, faim de l'Eglise* (1977), and *Lula et l'autre Brésil* (2003).

Linguist, semiologist and psychoanalyst, **Julia Kristeva** is a professor at the Institut Universitaire de France and the University Paris-VII Denis Diderot and teaches regularly at Columbia University and the University of Toronto. As a writer, she has published *New Maladies of the Soul* (1995), *Feminine and the Sacred*, with Catherine Clément (2001), and *Female Genius: Hannah Arendt* (2001), *Melanie Klein* (2002) and *Colette* (2004).

Sociologist and professor at the Universities of Caen and Paris-V, **Roger Sue** was director of sociological studies at the SOFRES, deputy director of the information service of the Ministry of Town Planning and Housing and *chargé de mission* at the Commissariat général du Plan. His publications include *Vers une société du temps libre* (1982), *Temps et ordre social* (1994), *Vers une économie plurielle* (1997), *La richesse des hommes. Vers l'économie quaternaire* (1997), *Renouer le lien social. Liberté, égalité, association* (2001) and *La Société civile face au pouvoir* (2003).

A former professor of philosophy at the Universities of Strasbourg, Paris-Sorbonne and Paris-X Nanterre, **Paul Ricoeur** is, among other things, a member of the editorial board of the review *Esprit* and of a number of academies, notably the Académie Universelle des Cultures. He has been awarded many honours for his work and his numerous publications including *The Conflict of Interpretations* (1974), *Fallible Man: Philosophy of the Will* (1986), *Critique and Conviction* (1997), *Oneself as Another* (1994) and *Memory, History, Forgetting* (2004).

Candido Mendes

Values and the Construction of Subjectivity

The most problematic form of postmodern deconstruction is that of the axiological discourse. The construction of subjectivity is postmodern in that it attempts to free itself from the prison of the *logos*. How can we deconstruct the logos so as to be able to sense, perceive and experience values 'agonistically'—agonistics being understood as the tension between identity and difference? Despite the guarantees we hold, we are today witnessing a renewal of the reification process in such pernicious forms as simulacra, cultural prostheses and the persistent confusion between culture and civilization.

Jérôme Bindé has clearly defined what the creation of new values entails. Searching for an alternative in this domain presupposes that we have an agreed framework for contradiction. In fact, we are still floundering in postmodernist ambiguity, sleepwalking in the wake of a dysfunctional dialectic along paths where dissipation gains the upper hand, as evident in the worlds of commerce, fashion and entertainment.

The question I ask is this: are we speaking about new values or are we still engaged in a postmodern deconstruction of values? When I hear some people talk of negotiation, or when Arjun Appadurai speaks of diagnostic wars, it is for me a measure of the dialectical disjunction that has occurred with the advent of Gianni Vattimo's 'weak phase', which is reminiscent of Jean Baudrillard's allusion to 'hijacking'. In any event, we are dealing with a *praxis* intent on having us move beyond the tyranny of the dialectic.

'Agonistics' is an approach based on the idea that values are relative to the being-mode and are constructed in a relationship of equality and not of transcendence. There are submediations in the postmodern understanding of values, meaning principles whereby the race to the dialectic is finally broken. The problem of difference being related to that of reference and denotation, the submediation of the problem of identity is the absolute, namely the possible submediation of lack of being, inasmuch as being and the other, from whom difference springs, relate to the submediation of the spectacle. Axiological deconstruction thus leads us to these two fundamental elements of submediation: the absolute and the spectacle. And if it is true that 'agonistics' eludes the grip of the logos, reification reactivates it with a vengeance.

Identity is mediated by the simulacrum, whereas difference is mediated in major social processes by hegemony. Consequently, the simulacrum pursues the game of reification, resulting in a social reality reduced to the coexistence of tribes depending on an interjective culture, tattoo marks and recognition divorced from the concept of the universal. Have we already effected the reduction of the simulacrum, or are we still at the stage of what is known, in the concept of identity, as withdrawal into self?

As regards the all-too-common confusion between civilization and culture, I would underline that civilization is linked to the whole process of the reification of rationality, which—with technology and power as its vector—is infinitely exportable and creates the history of progress. Culture, on the other hand, is bound up with meaning, significance, singularity, lifestyles, representation and an overall understanding of the world. It seems to me very serious to be witnessing what Ricoeur calls 'the erosion of civilization', that is, the wounded grip of civilization on culture, whereas the dialogue between them should be taken up from the angle of cultural understanding. Without that, we shall end up with cultural prostheses such as 'Afro-American identity', whose vacuity is betrayed in its inability to counter American fundamentalism. The failed attempt to elevate Afro-American identity to civilizational status demonstrates that it is impossible to pass off elements indissolubly linked to culture as belonging to civilization.

We need to promote a heuristics of the particular, so as to avoid the *incurvatio in se ipsum* and be able to conceive the Other. To my mind, the fractal to which Jean Baudrillard referred can constitute a first step towards understanding.

We are in a situation where a failure to distinguish between the cultural and the civilizational is leading to a reversibility of fundamentalisms. How can one of the parties claim to be the sole player in the drama of civilized values? One of the combatants in Afghanistan remarked rather pertinently: 'Here come the crusaders of the West.' He was denouncing Western fundamentalism and its defence of the New Jerusalem of the virtual tomb and cybernetic redemption.

Julia Kristeva

Towards a Feminizing of Values?

The question posed by my title is not whether women, as a human group, are in the process of assuming their place in social, political and cultural life but whether those values on which we believe that life may be based can be given a feminine slant.

To take just one recent example, in the debate that took place in France on the issue of parity between men and women, many distinguished participants, including women, spoke out against the idea there could be any difference between men and women, particularly in terms of their moral, cultural and political choices. The concern with maintaining the universal link, with not succumbing to a new form of communitarianism rooted in a male/female division that could split humanity in two and lock us in a war of the sexes, seemed to guide the thinking of these opponents of parity, who accordingly did not hesitate to deny sexual difference itself. I for my part was, and remain, firmly on the side of parity.

At the stage we have reached, I think that our societies need to promote the integration of women in the different spheres of social life through incentive measures such as the law on parity. I believe that sexual difference implies psychological differences, and consequently cultural and ideological differences, that can modulate the universal link, making it more flexible and rich in content without jeopardizing it. In other words, a specifically woman's creativity is possible. It has manifested itself throughout history and has asserted itself more strongly, it seems to me, over the last century. This creativity would make humanity more highly differentiated and more complex. The question of whether values can be 'feminized' remains legitimate however; and I should like to express my own view on the subject, in reviewing the way this issue has evolved in the recent history of women's struggles for their rights.

The struggle for equality

Women's struggle for emancipation has gone through three stages in modern times. It began with a demand by the suffragettes for *political rights*; it was followed by an assertion of ontological *equality* with men (in opposition to the notion of 'equal but different'), which led Simone de Beauvoir[1] to demonstrate and predict a fraternity between men and women transcending their natural specificities. Finally, the third stage—following 1968 and taking a lead from psychoanalysis—took the form of a search for sexual differences as a potential source of an original form of feminine creativity, encompassing sexual experience and the whole range of social practices, from politics to writing. At all these stages, the aim was the liberation of women as a whole. To this extent, the feminists did not disown the totalizing ambitions of the libertarian movements deriving from the Enlightenment and, going back further, the determination to break up the religious continent, which the movements concerned were set on achieving through rebellious negativity and millenarist teleology.

We are all too familiar with the impasses of these total—not to say totalitarian—promises. Feminism itself, irrespective of its different currents in Europe and America, has not escaped these ambitions, and this tendency has finally become ossified in a dead-end militancy that, disregarding individuality, thinks that it can encompass all women—like the proletariat or the Third World—in a campaign as fierce as it is desperate.

It should however be acknowledged that the most celebrated figure to which the feminist movement looked for inspiration, Simone de Beauvoir, was far from underestimating the 'subject' or the 'individual' in woman, who in her view 'feels an infinite need to transcend herself'. Faithful to this view rooted in existentialist morality, to which she added an individual Marxist note, Simone de Beauvoir attempted to tear women away from the subordinate status of being the Other of man, who in his turn is deprived of both the right and the opportunity to be Other. Robbed of the possibility of personal transcendence, woman as constituted by the history of a male-dominated society is in this view fated to remain in a state of immanence, immobilized as an object, 'since her transcendence is perpetually transcended by another essential and sovereign consciousness', that of man. Woman therefore does not have the historical possibility of becoming that other consciousness.

Simone de Beauvoir's campaign was essentially targeted on the reduction of women to their biological nature. We all know the famous proposition: 'One is not born but becomes a woman'. This issue apart, it was against metaphysics that Simone de Beauvoir continued to rage, since it was metaphysics that imprisoned woman in the Other, placing

---

1. In *The Second Sex*, New York, Alfred A. Knopf, 1952.

her in a situation of *artificiality* and *immanence* and refusing her access to true humanity, which is that of autonomy and freedom. However, setting aside the problem of difference in favour of that of gender equality, Beauvoir stopped short, it seems to me, of carrying through the announced extension of her existentialist project, which should have led her to reflect on the condition of women in their plurality and on the chances of freedom for each of them as unique human beings—even if, as we all know, she spoke a great deal in *The Second Sex* of the different experiences of womanhood, from Saint Theresa to Colette through Mademoiselle de Gournay and Théroigne de Méricourt. Individuals form the fabric of *The Second Sex*, but the argument concerns all women and not each woman. Simone de Beauvoir no doubt came too early to defend feminine singularity, at a time when the social and economic status of women presented many obstacles to their emancipation. However, in an emerging postmodern era so wedded it would seem to conservative and archaic ideas and practices, a shift in the way in which the women's issue is posed has become necessary.

Embracing feminine singularity

It is not sure that the 'conflict' between the *condition of all* and the *free self-realization of each* can be resolved if one is concerned only with the 'condition' and neglects the 'individual'. I think that the time has come to pose the following questions. In what way is each woman singular? In what way, while experiencing a common condition, have we the right to espouse that singularity we referred to previously when speaking of a positive individualism? I am persuaded, listening to women today—those that express themselves in social movements and those who wish to be recognized in their singularity as persons and who are searching for a form of creativity and for specific and singular recognition—that we are entering a new stage in the demand for freedom.

The goal to which the rights of men and women ultimately tend is none other than attentiveness to the full realization of our singularity, a concern with the emergence of the 'who' within the 'any', with what Duns Scotus called the *ecceitas*, the singularity of each being. That is why, not wishing to produce a comprehensive study on woman in general but to focus on the budding of feminine singularities, I have devoted myself in recent years to a work on feminine genius, treating three particular twentieth-century trajectories: those of Hannah Arendt, Melanie Klein and Colette.

The provocative hyperbole of 'genius' has helped me, in this long undertaking, to elucidate the way in which these women transcended their situation in their respective areas of philosophy and politics, psychoanalysis and literature, with the aim of encouraging self-transcendence in all of us. Arendt, Klein and Colette did not wait for the 'condition of women' to ripen before realizing their freedom. Does genius not consist precisely in breaking through and beyond one's situation? Appealing to the genius of everyone is not to underestimate the weight of history but to try and liberate the condition of women, and humanity in general, from the constraints of biology, society or destiny, by placing the spotlight on the subject's conscious or unconscious negation of the programmed inertia of these various forms of determinism.

While dissociating myself from Simone de Beauvoir, who was interested in the condition rather than the singular subject, I want to stress that we cannot trace this breakthrough of the singular unless we take account of the condition, but this must be done without reducing woman to her condition alone, by trying to explain how, within that condition, the singularity of each woman is achieved. I appeal to each woman to assert her singularity, her creativity and her freedom while maintaining that this particularity springs from a common destiny, which is that historically constituted on the basis of sexual difference.

I should at this point say how I, as a psychoanalyst, conceive of the feminine psychosocial difference. Woman is shaped by a maturation process much more complex than in man. We observe in the psychoanalytic experience, in the development of each feminine subject, an initial link with the mother, a first version of the Oedipus, which remains very repressed and which governs what Freud calls an endogenous feminine homosexuality, that is to say, a very intense bond of complicity and rivalry with the other woman. This is followed by a second version of the Oedipus, in which the small girl—unlike the small boy who seeks his erotic object directly in the heterosexual choice of the mother figure—changes objects and abandons her mother to focus on the father, i.e., man, as a love object. One can imagine the psychosexual maturation that this change of object demands. And, as if that were not enough, in this choice of the masculine love object another split occurs: woman becomes the love object of man, but at the same time she identifies herself with masculine values inasmuch as they are symbolic values. She learns to speak, learns the language, thought and taboos and thereby enters the realm of Law and becomes part of the social universe. Very often, we have the impression that this process is accompanied by a feeling of strangeness: I am in this universe but I am not sure that I am part of it. I am perhaps excluded, perhaps elsewhere. Where else? In the realm of the senses, the ineffable, the maternal, the archaic? The feminine experience is tinged with this feeling of essential or absolute non-belonging. This leads men thinkers to ask this question, starting with Freud: what does a woman want? Hegel goes so far as to write: 'Women, eternal irony of the community.' The woman who feels herself a stranger to social values is more prone to melancholy, and we know to what extent women find themselves, in some situations, excluded from the social consensus and consequently develop an increasingly obvious depression. This can become, in the best cases, a form of revolt, a positive reaction to constraints.

Think of the demands of French policemen's wives: it is in the name of their dual function within the social order and as mothers and wives that they are calling for a more humane deal and greater recognition for their husbands. The problem is this: will this demand fuel narrow corporatist self-interest, not to say the confinement of men to the role of father, or will it promote recognition of the policeman not as a 'faceless member of the force' but as a complex human being who, provided he wishes to have and has his rights recognized, could perform his duties better? It must also be remembered that the policeman's wife is called Jean or Mary and, as well as being mother or wife, she is a teacher, a cashier or perhaps a painter in her spare time, and wishes to be recognized in her singularity. By demanding acknowledgement of their status, women are preparing the way for greater recognition of the specific. Is this a threat to the social bond, the universal link? Not necessarily.

Specifically feminine values

I would cite as evidence some examples from my three feminine geniuses. Whatever the differences between Klein, Colette and Arendt, they have at least three things in common. The first is that, unlike the great thinkers or great figures of twentieth-century Western culture, however specific their achievements, their value does not lie in the ego or in the solitude of the individual. All three place great emphasis on the social bond. One recalls Hannah Arendt's conflicts with Heidegger, to whom she declared herself faithful, but also unfaithful. This unfaithfulness manifested itself in particular in the fact that she did not consider the social bond as abjectly anonymous but on the contrary as something that could forged out of difference. The bond is experienced as difference, except where it is apprehended as an aesthetic judgement. It is possible, for example, to share the unique aesthetic feeling you have experienced at a concert.

The same is true of Melanie Klein: whereas Freud thought that early childhood was characterized by narcissism, she affirmed that as soon as the child is born it establishes a bond with the other, in the form of the maternal breast. Klein went on to try to construct a conception of the subject as already focused on an object relationship.

As for Colette, we know how strongly she was bound by the love relationship and how essential she considered this relationship to be, although she spent her time deconstructing the relationship of the couple to discover links beyond the couple with Being, the Cosmos, animals, children, and so forth.

The second feminine specificity lies in the notion of thought as life and carnal experience. The brilliant contributions of my male colleagues in this regard frequently prompt my admiration but likewise a certain regret at their high level of abstraction. The three women I have picked out, on the other hand, are expressive of a conception of thought as bliss. They consider that an involvement in ideas, in the Word, in psychoanalysis or in writing engages simultaneously the sensory, the instinctual and the sexual.

There is no metaphysical dichotomy between the concrete and the abstract, the physical and the mental. There is an involvement that one might call dialectical, even if the term is not wholly appropriate.

The third trait that leads me to think in terms of a feminine specificity is women's understanding of time. As we all know, time points to death. Without denying the role of death in our experience, Hannah Arendt, Melanie Klein and Colette placed great emphasis on birth, while not necessarily having children yet remaining attentive to what Colette referred to as 'burgeoning' or 'renewal'. Arendt puts forward an idea that one finds in Saint Augustine, but which she develops in an extraordinary way: the ontological foundation of freedom is to be found in birth. Freedom in this view is not transgression but the possibility of beginning as ephemeral strangers. Each child is very much an ephemeral stranger, fated to die and to be misunderstood; but he or she is above all an embodiment of renewal. It is this obsession with renewal that these three women attempted to apply to their different realms of experience.

The feminine experience is thus specific. However, far from wishing to reduce all women to this particular specificity, although it is their point of origin, I try to discern the way in which they are singular, despite belonging to this feminine continent. An interest in life, an interest in thought as a sensory experience and an interest in the burgeoning of time are characteristic of my three geniuses and doubtless of all women; but it is important to know how we react, as individuals, to these three singularities.

Perhaps one of the tricks of the history of the last century, which was so obsessed by sexual difference, lies in the fact that this difference should not be allowed to ossify into a duality: women on one side, men on the other. This trick, if such it was, should lead us beyond dichotomy to the singular. We are each of a different sex, and there are as many women's sexualities as there are individuals. We must therefore foster as a specific value that singularity for which the struggle of women will perhaps have prepared the way.

Roger Sue

The Rise of Associations and New Forms of Solidarity

I should like to begin by distinguishing between three sorts of values: values of principle, internalized values and values as practised. I believe that these three categories are fairly distinct and should not be confused.

Abstract values, or values of principle, were promoted by the Enlightenment, with its assertion of the values of the individual, freedom and equality. While these values are familiar, we have neglected—mistakenly in my view—the value of association, with which they remain inextricably linked. For a particular social bond, namely the association between individuals, is necessary if there is to be any chance of the other values proving viable.

The doctrines of the social contract, whether English or French, maintained that a valid contract presupposed the existence of this associative relationship. The history of ideas can be interpreted as the desire to establish the social contract on the basis either of greater equality or of greater freedom. The two main currents of liberalism and communitarianism come together here in their attempt to link up with source values by way of the concept of association. Indeed, what kind of contract would it be if there was no freedom and equality of the contracting parties? Modernity has had to confront this dilemma of the failure to translate abstract values into practice, which throws doubt on the reality of the social contract.

The internalization of values of principle

What seems to me to have changed today is that we have moved on from the stage of abstract universal values to that of internalized values. Although they have not yet become values actually practised, abstract source values have finally been humanized as a consequence of being believed and assimilated. This, then, is a great step forward, which explains why the associative model today figures much more prominently in relations between individuals.

Individualism, in the positive sense of the term, is one of the factors that has enabled abstract values to take root in everyday life. We have moved from individualism as a release from community-based values, implying a withdrawal into self and one's immediate social circle, to a stage at which each individual thinks of him- or herself as unique. We are today much better placed to think of equality in terms of difference and not of identity.

The internalization of values is also linked to the 'inversion of social times', to borrow the expression of Herbert Marcuse. As early as 1967, Marcuse noted an inversion between work time and leisure time. It was excellent news, both for those who had yet to enter the world of work and for those preparing to leave it. We had thought that individuals affirmed themselves through work, but we were discovering that modernity made it possible for individuality to be asserted in one's own time, outside of work. This offers scope for redefining our values in such a way that they are not simply those of the hierarchy, authority and conformity with the world of work, which a large majority of the population find alienating.

The third development that has contributed to the internalization of values is undoubtedly the raising of the cultural level, which has enabled individuals to think for themselves. The appearance of so many examples of association and of associations, from community groups to NGOs, is incomprehensible if we do not bear in mind these foundations. Sociologists of the family go so far as to speak of association-type families and network societies. What is the network other than the technological metaphor of association? And as I do not believe in the chance development of technologies, I think that it is the strengthening of the associative social link that explains the development of these technologies, and not the opposite. These factors explain why eight out of ten French people are involved with associations.

We are seeing the development of a human capital economy in which the association plays a dynamic role. The closer we move towards a society in which knowledge and education are fundamental, the more individuals will be required to maintain associative relations. It will not be a case of setting individuals to work by saying: 'Sit down and be creative'; they will need to be associated with a process.

Associations are not created by chance. It so happens that the refocusing of the public debate on the topics of education and health serves to strengthen associations; for, by offering an alternative to the public service and the market, they develop human capital, which thereby becomes the source of 'growth within growth'.

Practical difficulties

The dynamic I have just described runs up, however, against certain limitations. The first has to do with the fact that we are still at stage two (the internalization of values) and not at stage three (the practical application of those values). This hiatus between the internalization and living out of values is moreover at the origin of the malaise of our societies. The state of men/women relations and work relations shows us just how long the practical realization of values takes. I note however that we would not be as sensitive as we are to certain subjects if the values of modernity had not progressed. We are much more inclined to denounce situations that strike us as all the more scandalous since our values are no longer those of yesterday but those of the modern world.

The second limitation of the current process is bound up with the fact that we are unable to translate the transformation of the bond between individuals into social, political and economic terms. It took several centuries for the emergence of the individual, around the fifteenth century, to bear its first fruits in the eighteenth century with the declarations of human rights. I therefore think that the spread of the associative link in civil society holds out the promise of major transformations, even if we do not yet know how to translate them into practice. In this context, one may wonder what political forms these new forms of association observed in civil society might take, the association being neither delegation nor representation.

How many people know that 2001 was the International Year of Voluntary Service, that is to say, a year that could have served for the constitution of a transnational civil society? The year 2001 also marked the centenary of France's law on associations. Why was it not reflected in the creation of a citizen's public forum? The road between stages two and three is long indeed, and the responsibility of those who exercise a measure of power is great in this regard.

Paul Ricoeur

Universal Project, Multiple Heritages

The first thing I would say about the 'future of values' is that it is not the task of intellectuals to anticipate developments that are totally opaque and subject to countless contingencies; they should stick to their role as public educators operating at a remove from politicians, economists and social scientists. I would add that, as we are no more than a minority, it is at the global level that we should seek to serve the cause of the majority—firstly by denouncing the prejudices that militate against the renewal of our inexhaustible heritages.

Cultural half-truths

I would begin by arguing the need to think of intercultural relations not in terms of frontiers but rather of cross-cutting influences emanating from sources whose radiance transcends frontiers. Admittedly, frontiers continue to exercise an intransgressible function since the nation-state remains the supreme political entity recognized by the United Nations. Frontiers mark the limits of the sovereignty of states, their jurisdiction and their military power. On the other hand, the cultural centres scattered throughout the world function rather in the manner of light sources that radiate outwards, their operative range depending as much on the capacity of other centres to receive them as on their own power of projection. I therefore see the cultural map of the world as a complex network of criss-crossing beams. To take an example: Russia today has a state frontier with all its neighbours, yet it does not form part of the political institutions of a united Europe, despite its many and varied military, commercial and political ties with this developing and expanding entity. However, the vagaries of politics have not prevented the influence of writers such as Pushkin, Tolstoy, Dostoyevsky and Solzhenitsyn, nor that of musicians and choreographers, from penetrating the barrier of political frontiers. It is in this way that I visualize the interplay of light sources extending all over the planet.

Another trap lurks in the idea of collective identity, whether at the national or community level. The human instinct for security tends to reduce this to the display of essential, substantial and unchanging characteristics. Identity is pre-eminently historical in nature, which is not to say that it is inconsistent, illusory and subject to the whims of time. To call it historical is to say that it is governed by a mode of change that gives it narrative consistency, density and intelligibility. A narrative plot turns a diversity of events, a plurality of protagonists and a jumble of chance events, discrete causalities, intentions and projects into a unity of meaning resting only on the intelligibility of the related action. I shall speak in that regard of a 'narrative identity'. But this is but one face of collective identity, the face turned towards a chronicled part. Its other face looks to the future: I shall liken it to a 'promise'. Making promises is easy; keeping them is to maintain one's identity—'I will maintain…' runs a national motto.[1] The identity deriving from the conjunction of narrative and promise avoids the trap of repetition, with its arrogance and humiliations alike. The profession of identity thus ceases to be subject to the interested parties' stratagems of forgetfulness or the artifices of repetition and its imposed commemorations. This applies particularly to the celebration of events that mark the foundation of a historical community, which is the occasion par excellence for professing an identity fixed for all time. One must learn to relate the same events differently, in terms of new projects that help to renew the way one interprets them. One must even learn to allow oneself to hear one's story related by others, particularly when the humiliation of one party is the victory of the other. We can in this case speak of a 'work of memory', equidistant between forgetfulness and repetition.

On the subject of ethical and spiritual values proclaimed as truth, we must reject a type of universality that has not been screened for both narrative identity and future promise. The only universality worthy of consideration is that predicated on interchanges between semantic inheritances shaped and transmitted through natural languages, themselves inescapably subject to human plurality. There is already much to be said about the variability of value horizons within a given culture, which do not all evolve at the same rate. I would compare them to the landscape profiles viewed from a moving train, which pass by at varying speeds as your gaze moves from the foreground, focuses on the middle distance or settles on the virtually motionless backdrop to the more rapidly moving outlines. It is a great mistake when evaluating the changes affecting moral values within a given community not to take account of the different rates at

---

1. National motto of the Netherlands.

which short-term, medium-term and long-term changes take place. For example, the upheavals in the marriage institution in the West should not blind us to the strength of the family bond, even its reconstructed form, and still less to the permanence of basic taboos such as the prohibition on incest, the condemnation of paedophilia, and the protection and love of children. The same is true of the demand for freedom and justice, which runs like an unbroken thread through the diversity of social and political conflicts down the centuries.

The miracle of translation

These remarks, limited so far to the development of cultural complexes of long duration, can be extended to comparisons between different cultural realms, with the addition of one factor anticipated in my earlier thoughts on the crossbeams emanating from cultural centres far removed from one another. This addition concerns the role of translation, which is the decisive rejoinder to the inescapable phenomenon of human plurality, with its implications of dispersion and confusion encapsulated in the Babel myth. We come 'after Babel', to quote a well-known title.[2] Translation cannot be reduced to a technique practised spontaneously by travellers, traders, ambassadors, smugglers and traitors, and elevated to a professional discipline by translators and interpreters. It constitutes a paradigm for all exchanges, not only between languages but also between cultures. The path is closed in the direction of abstract universals, detached from the cultural history of real communities. It is opening up again in the direction of concrete universals stemming from the work of translation. The primordial fact is that there is no universal language, only languages that are called natural to distinguish them from artificial languages. And even if, as Leibnitz tried to do, one could write an artificial language spoken by nobody, an unbridgeable gap would remain between it and the natural languages shaped by usage, with their complexities, their ambiguities and also their irrepressible inventiveness. In principle, we are all capable of learning another language apart from our mother tongue and thus of regarding our language as one among many and, by an effort of reflection on our native language, of imagining that what is said in our language is expressed otherwise in another language and that these other languages say something other than what we are used to saying in our own language. The miracle of translation is to create a presumed identity of meaning that, short of being identical for lack of a third term of comparison between the two languages, can claim to be the equivalent of the source meaning. It follows that the practice of translation, and above all of retranslation, can alone confirm this equivalence. Admittedly, no

---

2. George Steiner, *After Babel*, Oxford, Oxford University Press, 1998.

translation repeats the original, yet one can always translate or at least start to translate. The presupposition is that languages are not so alien to each other as to be radically untranslatable, even if one cannot reveal this common core other than by giving it shape in the work of translation, at the risk of betraying the two masters represented respectively by the foreign language and the host language. Not only has translation always taken place, but new cultures have arisen from the kind of hybridization resulting from the translation of vast corpora of texts: the translation of the Torah from Hebrew to Greek, from Greek to Latin and from Latin to the vernacular languages; and, at the other end of the world, from Sanskrit to Chinese in the case of the immense Buddhist corpus, and again from Korean to Japanese.

It is a phenomenon of this kind that I have in mind when I refer to the exchanges between cultural and spiritual heritages currently in search of a common language. This common language cannot be similar to those artificial languages invented in the eighteenth century. And while it does not often proceed by way of hybrids comparable to those mentioned above, it is invariably within each language, drawing in particular on the unexploited wealth of popular expressions in the host tongue, that what is said elsewhere directly starts to be said in our own language through a process of internal conversion. This patient labour of each language on itself is more fruitful than the official translations, which follow too literally the models of a dominant language, for which one is hard pressed to find equivalents in other cultures. And if the best thinkers within a certain culture seriously think that this culture is capable of transmitting universal values to others, they must admit that these are presumed universals, in search of ratification, appropriation, adoption and recognition. And once again it is the work of translation that underpins this quest for concrete universals, bearing the mark of history and of the critical scrutiny of history. One thing is certain: that there is no absolute untranslatability; that translation, though incomplete, creates resemblance where there only seemed to be plurality. It is in this resemblance created by the work of translation that the 'universal project' and 'multiple heritages' are reconciled.

The work of bereavement

Let me add a final touch to this picture of impasses and avenues of approach. It should not be thought that our cultural heritages consist simply of accumulated acquisitions; we must also think in terms of loss. The work of memory presupposes a work of bereavement. This necessarily impinges on our efforts to reshape our life stories, whether individual or collective, and particularly the events on which our traditions are founded. There is no country that has not suffered a loss of territory, population, influence, respectability or credibility in one age or another. The cruel history of twentieth-century Europe has made such a reckoning necessary. The ability to accept bereavement must be endlessly learned and relearned.

We must accept that there is something unintelligible in our life stories, irreconcilable in our differences, irreparable in the injuries suffered and inflicted.

Once we have recognized the place of bereavement in our existence, our memories are appeased and we can focus on the intersecting beams radiating out from our diverse cultures, on the mutual reinterpretation of our histories and on the forever renewed task of translation from one culture to another.

Towards the Century of the Spirit?

Thierry Gaudin highlights the emergence of a new model, that of cognitive analysis, which he sees as replacing the scientific model of the previous century and which raises the question of whether the century to come will be spiritual in character. Souleymane Bachir Diagne chooses to revisit the topic of religion, noting that it does not necessarily entail a petrifaction of identity so long as one chooses to develop its specifically spiritual dimension.

* * * *

President of Perspectives 2100 (an international association aimed at preparing global programmes for the twenty-first century), **Thierry Gaudin** directed the Centre de Prospective et d'Evaluation of the French Ministry for Research and Technology for ten years (1982–1992) as well as the publication of the work *2100, Récit d'un prochain siècle* (1993). He is the author of *2100, Odyssée de l'espèce* (1993), *Introduction à l'économie cognitive* (1997) and *Préliminaires à une prospective des religions* (1998).

Souleymane Bachir Diagne is professor of philosophy at Cheikh Anta Diop University in Dakar and Northwestern University in Chicago. A former pupil of the Ecole Normale Supérieure, agrégé of philosophy and former special adviser for education and culture to the president of the Republic of Senegal, he is also member of the Council for the Development of Social Science Research in Africa. His teaching is centred on epistemology, the history of philosophy in the Islamic world and cultural questions. He is the author of *Boole, l'oiseau de nuit en plein jour* (1989) and *Reconstruire le sens: textes et enjeux de prospectives africaines* (2001), *Islam et société ouverte: la fidélité et le mouvement dans la pensée de Muhammad Iqbal* (2001) and *100 mots pour dire l'Islam* (2002).

Thierry Gaudin

The Emergence of Cognitive Civilization

My close involvement from the early 1980s with technology monitoring enabled me to assemble a great deal of information about the way the world was moving, particularly in the technical field. The period was marked by that age-old phenomenon—a paradigm shift in the technology system. Technology interacts with society through a dual mechanism: society produces technology through innovation, while technology exerts a feedback effect on society by modifying social behaviour (the contraceptive pill being one of the most striking examples).

Technology and exclusion

In 2000, 1 billion people (out of 6 billion) were driven from their lands by the growth of industrialized agriculture and helped to swell the suburbs of cities the world over. By the year 2005, half the world's population will be urbanized, the proper balance between urban and rural populations in modern societies being 80 per cent urban and 20 per cent rural. The urban implosion is thus set to continue at the start of the century, along with exclusion and major social difficulties. It is time that science and technology served the needs of the poor and socially excluded…

When a change (such as the industrial revolution) occurs in the technological system, the new technology downgrades manual labour. In the nineteenth century, the drift from the countryside and the urban implosion led to the 1848 revolution. As a result, the ruling class resorted to a Saint-Simonian strategy of major international projects (the Panama Canal, the rail network, town planning on the Haussman model). Today, we are in a situation comparable to that in which Guizot found himself in 1830/35. 'Get rich' is the message constantly conveyed by the world about us. But that does not solve the problem posed by the socially excluded—quite the opposite.

Cognitive civilization

The industrial system, with its four poles (materials, energies, structuring of time and relationship with the living world), was based on a horizontal 'matter-energy' axis by producing a substantial number of tonnes of cement, steel and petrol per inhabitant. The new technological system known as the 'cognitive civilization' involves a vertical 'structuring of time/relationship with the living world' axis. Today it is possible to manipulate genes, i.e., the code of life, which gives human beings the powers of a demiurge (who nonetheless retains the instincts of a primate). Whereas in the industrial system the horizontal axis is characterized by materialism, scientism and rationalism in the manner of Auguste Comte, what is at stake in cognitive societies—even if life and time are linked by a relation as intimate as matter and energy ($E=mc^2$)—is no longer production, but recognition and awareness.

We live in an age of 'regulation', in which feminine values prevail. The centuries of assertion, conquest and authority are over. The human species is currently regulating its numbers and relationship with nature, as the demographic transition poses the question of decline with the increase in the number of elderly people and the new economic situation. Forecasts ten years ago predicted a stabilizing of the global population, which was supposed to reach 10 billion by 2100 (according to the United Nations). The same calculation today points to a peak of 8.5 billion inhabitants, along with the very unusual phenomenon of an inversion of the age pyramid. In 2030/40, the 60/65 age-group will be larger than the 0–50 age group. The children of the baby boom will have a less comfortable old age than their grandparents, even supposing that the financial problems of the pension funds are resolved.

All of this is having a fundamental impact on values. The scientistic paradigm that was valid in the era of all-conquering science and of nineteenth-century rationalism has made way for a cognitive paradigm. The impersonal 'it' that is the subject of science ('it is said that…', 'it is known that…', 'it will be seen that…', 'it is not possible to say anything about…') is a point at which scientific knowledge is being continuously accumulated and updated.

In a cognitive paradigm, there are a multitude of perceiving subjects, each having a different grid for interpreting the world—the problem being that of mutual recognition and intercommunication among those subjects. This raises the question of the constitution of collective conscious beings. Are companies or organizations such as UNESCO collective conscious beings? This line of thought moreover prompts the larger question concerning the human species and consciousness.

The paradigm shifts in the technosystem in the twelfth or the eighteenth century (the Industrial Revolution), or even in the sixth century BC (the Phoenician implosion) with the birth of Buddha in India and Lao-Tseu in China, were always accompanied by far-reaching changes in the spiritual domain, as if essential values were being revisited. May we conclude that the twenty-first century will be a 'century of the spirit'?

Souleymane Bachir Diagne

Religion and the Challenge of Spirituality in the Twenty-First Century

My argument hinges on the opposition between the *religious* and the *spiritual*. This is what separates insular, wholly self-centred groups from a pluralistic humanity whose unity encompasses a multiplicity of spiritual figures comparable (to borrow an image from Husserl) to the waves of a single ocean. The difference between religious and spiritual values lies in the fact that the latter—as I shall seek to demonstrate—are intimately bound up with the values of *decentring* and of *dialogue* with a panhuman focus. The spiritual thus understood can help to expand the narrowly commercial horizons of globalization in the direction of a 'civilization of the universal'—to employ an expression dear to the poet Léopold Sédar Senghor. I am talking here of a *civilization of the universal* and not of a *universal civilization*, to underline yet again the distinction between a civilization that produces or aspires to the universal and one deriving from the mere fact of being global.

Religion—the ultimate expression of identity?

The events of 11 September have singularly complicated our relationship with spirituality—as evidenced by the reaction of a section of public opinion in my own country. I was asked to take part in a broadcast on Senegalese radio to substantiate the idea that history was bearing out the views of Samuel Huntington,[1] who was in his own way endorsing André Malraux's claim that the twenty-first century would be spiritual in character. I was at pains

---

1. S.P. Huntington, *The Clash of Civilizations and the Remaking of the World Order*, New York, Simon & Schuster, 1996.

to deny what was taken to be the necessary premise of our discussion, emphasizing that Malraux's remark meant that religion (spirituality?) was what would save this century from the drabness and loss of meaning inherent in the cult of the material, whereas Huntington was arguing that the century that began with the fall of the Berlin Wall *is* religious and that we are therefore facing a threat of generalized conflict. In Huntington's view, it is the global impact of social, economic and cultural modernization in the second half of the twentieth century that has brought about, by way of a backlash, a re-enchantment of the world in the form of a return to, and hence revival of, religion. This has resulted in the fragmentation of the world, which has been reconfigured along the fault lines of 'civilizations'. The movements taking place in this world are movements of recentring calling themselves re-Islamization, re-Hinduization, re-Christianization, etc.

Huntington maintains that we are witnessing a pervasive process of 'indigenization', which in his view automatically entails a desecularization of the world since a return to origins will come up against religion at the core of our primordial identity. He argues that religion is the prime motivating and mobilizing force in the modern world, since religious affiliation captures within its orbit and assimilates all other forms of identification. Whereas Malraux's formula denoted an enrichment, an expansion of being, the reality is that we find ourselves faced with a simplification, a flattening and an impoverishment of existence.

Nothing is more illustrative of Huntington's simplistic vision of the world than what he says about 'Africanness'. Africa, loftily ignored in the first draft of his geopolitics of 'civilizations', makes a furtive appearance in the definitive 1995 version in the form of a large question mark. The reason for its inclusion is, in fact, to justify its earlier elimination from the map of the world. Most researchers on civilization, he writes, do not think that Africanness is a distinct civilization. He adds that the only exception is Braudel, but he does not dwell on that far from insignificant exception—and it is not clear what is meant by the phrase 'most researchers on civilization'.

The main thing to emerge, given the wealth of references in his book, is that he has no interest in what Africans say about themselves on the subject—their 'self-portrayal' to borrow Achille Mbembe's expression. The question mark that he deigns to add amounts to saying that it is possible that some sense of African identity centred on South Africa may emerge through a process of coalescence. The result of these assertions is the terrifying 1990 world map that Huntington draws, in which Africanness is virtually reduced to the Bantu world of southern Africa and a thin fringe north of the Equator—all the rest, in his view, being part of Islamic civilization.

That the country of Léopold Sédar Senghor has an Islamic identity is not in question; but its paradoxical exclusion from Africanness makes it fairly clear that Huntington's thinking is based on the negation of the pluralism inherent in identities. Identity, necessarily singular for him, is defined as that which can be petrified to form a 'bloc' within a simplistic geopolitics. Plurality is conceived in terms of blocs and signifies, in this 'ensemblist' conception of the state of nature, generalized conflict—open or latent and to varying degrees violent—pitting the various blocs against one another. It also means that values, to consider the question from this angle, no longer make sense out of their context or correspond to any transcultural reality. They belong to languages that are mutually untranslatable. Without exploring in detail the theses to which it gives rise, the vision I have just described thus poses the question of whether it is possible, that is to say *realistic*, in our turn-of-the century postcolonial world to continue thinking—outside of any imperial project—in terms of a civilization of the universal, to conceive of cultures as having a panhuman dimension rather than as a congeries of disparate human groups.

Panhumanism

In *Humanism of the Other*, Emmanuel Levinas similarly pondered the spectacle of the postcolonial era, with its 'saraband of myriad cultures', in a world as disoriented as it was 'de-Westernized'. The question of values thus comes down to that of a meeting of cultures that can occur only if it is informed by the idea of a society of human beings—something that globalization should make possible but which it currently impedes insofar as it signifies exclusion and poverty for the greater part of the peoples of the world. Such a society will be founded on the idea of *justice*, i.e., on the non-imperialist idea according to which other people do not have to be levelled down or assimilated to oneself, without their irreducible alterity thereby signifying conflict. Emmanuel Levinas formulates the requirement placed upon our age thus: 'Justice remains justice only in a society where there is no distinction between those close to and those remote from us, and equally where it is impossible to overlook those closest to us.'

There is a total contrast between the requirement of justice defined in this way and the realism based on the specious 'self-evident truth' that we prefer our daughters to our nieces, our nieces to our cousins and so on through the familiar process of reasoning by concentric circles until we arrive at the final circle in the form of the ultimate 'us', seen as synonymous with civilization. It is not therefore a matter of realism but rather of ethics and hence of moral requirement. To say that there is no difference between those close to and those remote from us is not realistic, and the lofty universalism characteristic of what is sometimes termed 'the Davos culture' effectively invites ridicule. But while it is not realistic, it *is* ethical. The relationship with the real is not so much *descriptive* as *prescriptive*. Are we not dealing here, then, with a mere formula that has no more impact than a sermon on the geopolitical logic of contending blocs as solid and sharply delineated as religions? This would be so if religions themselves offered little ethical leverage in support of a requirement of justice that does not distinguish between those 'close' to and those 'remote' from us. However, such a leverage exists at the heart of religion, that is to say, at the heart of the spirituality that it can embody. The importance of such leverage in cross-border transactions cannot moreover be overemphasized, since without it all we should have by way of dialogue between cultures would be juxtaposed monologues. It is indeed necessary that leverage for this ethical requirement should exist within every culture, always provided that the culture in question is tuned to an understanding of its own history, as Mohammed Arkoun has reminded us.

Spiritual openness

Huntington's paradigm posits that identity is, in the last analysis, essentially religious and that it is in the nature of religion to secrete this *petrifaction* that inescapably leads groups to oppose forms of identification conducive to a larger unity. A counter-paradigm might make the point that religion by its very nature enshrines this 'decentring' principle, this fluidity that constitutes its spiritual dimension. It may be argued that all the major world religions encompassed by Huntington's paradigm possess to the same degree this spiritual dimension, manifest in the literature that has developed at their heart alongside the scriptures and great foundational texts that this spirituality serves in a sense to subvert. This tradition often finds expression in lyric form, in the language of sensuality, through the medium of metaphor, allusion, anecdote, edifying tales or sometimes simply witty remarks and jokes. In short, this literature treats serious themes in a light-hearted way and sets out to be superficial with profundity. In this literature, the spiritual defines itself as an art of opposition, an art of decentring.

Spirituality is the art of distancing oneself from self, from the dogmatism, intolerance or violence that passionate conviction can engender. In this way, it is profoundly linked to the value of tolerance because it teaches us to be receptive to the varied ways in which truth is mirrored in all things. I should therefore like to propose this theme of truth being reflected in all things as a way of transcending the antithesis between relativism and universalism. To put it in the language of this same spirituality, the lover sees his beloved everywhere. If one does not see truth in what is different from oneself, it is because one does not love sufficiently and one does not see Layla through the eyes of Majnun.

To perceive spirituality in religion is to escape from the alternative within which the religious paradigm encloses us: a war *of* religions, or else a war *on* religions. It is the self-encounter implicit in the orientation described by Levinas, which is the precondition of true dialogue. An essential aspect of this orientation is the fundamental value of the critical mind, that is to say, self-criticism. In the new avatar of the comparative study of civilizations, one frequently comes across the idea that this spirit of self-scrutiny, of critical self-reflection is a value peculiar to a specifically 'Western' culture. Thus it is said that, while it is true that all cultures have the same intrinsic value and that each civilization is the equal of every other, the distinctive value of the West lies in its capacity for self-scrutiny, enabling it to understand and criticise itself and thereby foster not only innovation but also the ability to understand other people and different cultures. Marx moreover spoke of the possibility of understanding human communities that have never understood anything of themselves.

Thus recently,[2] by way of a critique of what Italy's leading political figure had chosen to term 'the superiority of the West', Umberto Eco rehearsed the lessons of cultural anthropology and explained how evaluation of the parameters of judgement *ipso facto* deprived them of any absolute status before proceeding to argue that the capacity to criticize those same parameters was a 'courage' specific to Western cultures! It follows, in this view, that the attributes essential to an open society and likewise to dialogue as a value have lodged themselves in a particular culture.

In such a case, there could be no escape from Huntington's vision of a specific identity characterized by a movement of continual decentring coming into contact not with other identities but rather with differences inherently manifesting themselves as hostility and petrifaction. As Amartya Sen, Nobel Prize winner in economics, recently wrote:[3] 'If the values fostering innovation, respect and the compassion necessary for a better understanding of other people and different societies are fundamentally Western, then there is every reason to worry'. This is a delicately euphemistic way of saying that the very idea of dialogue is then lost, since the *telos* that makes it possible is the prerogative of a single civilization.

Spirituality consists precisely in saying that there is no degree zero in the capacity for self-scrutiny, for critical self-reflection, which is a condition of the open society. While we must be realistic and recognize that authoritarian powers are engaged with the fundamentalist movements that oppose them in the same negation of pluralism, we must also hold firmly to the idea that, inasmuch as it constitutes a *spiritual* face of humanity, a culture always embodies—beneath the forces that can impede its expression—a rejection of self-confinement and the inertia implicit in the servile imitation of tradition (what Muslim spirituality condemns as *taqlid*) and an enduring capacity for decentring, which is the precondition of its encounter with others and thus with its own future.

---

2. In an article appearing in *Le Monde* on 10 October 2001.
3. In 'East and West: the Reach of Reason', *New York Review of Books*, July 2000.

PART II

Globalization, New Technologies and Culture

Globalization and the 'Third Industrial Revolution'

Does the third industrial revolution herald the emergence of a new set of unified social, cultural, economic and political ground rules valid worldwide? Expert opinion, it must be said, is divided.

Condemning the 'self-focused hype' concerning the arrival of a digital age, Paul Kennedy highlights the growing social divides that accompany this phenomenon.

Given the very real 'effects of globalization', whether with reference to the opportunities for an effective universality or to the strong risk of seeing hegemonies triumph, Jacques Derrida likewise advocates a posture of critical vigilance with regard to the glib rhetoric that speaks of the 'end of work' and the 'homogenizing impact of globalization'. By way of an analysis of the effects of globalization on work, forgiveness, peace and abolition of the death penalty, he formulates a series of hypotheses that underscore the importance of political decision-making and international law.

Noting the collapse of the Baconian ideology that hitherto guided scientific progress, Francisco Sagasti proposes an 'eccentric' vision of globalization, in the form of an attempt to base the necessary work of redefining the notions of 'development' and 'progress' on an intercultural North-South dialogue.

* * * *

Paul Kennedy is a historian, and professor and director of the International Security Studies programme at Yale University. A specialist in international politics, he is the author, among other publications, of *Strategy and Diplomacy 1870–1945* (1983), *The Rise and Fall of the Great Powers* (1987) and *Preparing for the 21st Century* (1993).

Algiers-born French philosopher **Jacques Derrida** is director of studies at the Ecole des Hautes Etudes en Sciences Sociales (EHESS) and conducts numerous seminars throughout the world, notably in the United States. His publications include *Of Grammatology* (1977), *Writing and Difference* (1978), *Dissemination* (1981), *Of Hospitality* (2000) and more recently *Who's Afraid of Philosophy? Right to Philosophy* (2002).

Peruvian economist **Francisco Sagasti** is a former adviser to the Prime Minister of Peru and president of the Agenda de Foro Nacional-Internacional. Previously director of Strategic Planning at the World Bank and chairman of the United Nations Committee of Advisers on Science and Technology for Development, he is the co-author of *The Uncertain Quest: Science, Technology and Development* (1994).

Paul Kennedy

Globalization and Its Discontents

My title is of course a play upon the title of Sigmund Freud's work, *Civilization and Its Discontents*. It has the same ironic double-meaning. Just as civilization, an eminently positive and agreeable principle, has produced challenges for those who live within it, our current trend toward globalization might bring us problems along with its undoubted benefits. It would not be useful in this context for me to define globalization or reflect on its origins and history. We are all struck by the increasing impact of science and technology upon the way we produce, trade and consume across borders. The hardware-cum-software revolution permits us to order clothes or books by computer, move money electronically over the world's currency markets at a colossal rate, etc.

Hundreds of millions of human beings are now engaged in production, not for the local market, but for the world market, whether in the fields of textiles, electronic goods, shoes or kitchenware. In Brazil, Mexico, Indonesia and China, instead of growing rice and logging trees, the young workers of today work on mergers and acquisitions of banks, automobile companies and chemical firms. Our university students report on their research progress from Beijing, Kiev, Madrid and New Delhi. Our children phone us from wherever they are. Although these possibilities came about only ten years ago, we already take them for granted.

This activity suggests that we are indeed becoming a single world market or community, an interconnected whole that is at last realizing the enlightened visions of people such as Adam Smith in his book *The Wealth of Nations*.

The excluded in a globalized world

In the United States, business journals, market gurus, economics professors and highly paid consultants talk incessantly about the coming global boom, the transformation of the workplace, the technology revolution and the knowledge explosion. It is implied that the world is slowly becoming a reproduction of Silicon Valley. It is asserted that this is the future.

Yet, instead of swallowing this self-focused hype (indeed, the proponents of globalization are almost always consultants, investors and business people who have a vested interest in encouraging such trends), perhaps we should pull back and look at the globe as a whole. The pessimist view would be to point out what is currently occurring in Kosovo, West Africa, Rwanda, Chechnya, Kashmir or elsewhere. These deeply troubled regions differ vastly from Silicon Valley or other advanced economic regions. We might also follow Robert Kaplan in the trips he describes in *To the Ends of the Earth*, only to discover that much of humanity is headed for disaster and self-destruction. I do not wish to follow that negativism. However, I would like to offer a caution to those who portray globalization in an uncritical and overly enthusiastic manner.

The Internet as a development tool

The technology revolution and the communications revolution still affects only a very small minority of the Earth's peoples, mainly those in the richer countries. It still bypasses billions of human beings elsewhere. From UNESCO's standpoint, the Internet may have the most influence of any single medium upon global educational and cultural developments in the coming century. Yet while over one North American in two uses the Internet, the worldwide proportion is no more than one in ten.[1]

I use the Internet every day of the year, sending and receiving up to forty messages per day. I can search the Web sites of the World Bank and the United Nations to find new data, read *The New York Times* and check the 9 million book titles in the Yale University Library from my home. The Internet gives me, my students and my children immediate access to knowledge. The knowledge explosion in which we are taking part is at the heart of the modernization and globalization of world society.

We speak of 'education for all' and of the 'knowledge society'. Yet we are in the midst of a technology revolution that seems less likely to close the gap between rich and poor countries than to widen the gap

---

1. The statistics presented herein have been updated on the basis of NUA statistics (http://www.nua.ie/surveys/) supplemented by UNFPA (United Nations Population Fund) demographic data.

even further. Thus far, the Internet has made the differences between the technologically advanced and the technologically weak even greater than before. Even within American society, the computer and e-mail have widened the gap between educated people (chiefly Whites and Asians) and the less-educated (chiefly Black Americans). This gap will be felt in every aspect of life, whether it is in opportunities, potential, education or job-hunting. The United States will be divided into two groups, one that is computer-literate and the other that is not.

This phenomenon has been replicated quite clearly at the international level. In the Arab states, only one person in 40 has Internet access while, in Africa, only one in 130 people are Internet users. This situation will not change as long as those lands lack electricity, telephone wires and infrastructure. They can afford neither computers nor the expensive software they require. If knowledge indeed equals power, the developing world may have less real power nowadays than it did thirty years ago, when the Internet was developed.

If we want to work toward a knowledge-based society in the coming century, we must bring countries together electronically rather than merely bringing together the discourses of European and American intellectuals. We need to make a concerted effort to bring poorer societies into the knowledge-rich system of electronic communications that has developed over the last twenty years. A world in which less than 10 percent of human beings have access to the new knowledge sources, and in which 90 percent are excluded, will be structurally unsound. This effort will need to be coordinated by the World Bank, UNDP, UNESCO, the NGO community and the global business community if it is to have any chance of success.

The alternative is simply to do nothing, to let the knowledge explosion deepen and intensify in technology-rich societies while poorer countries fall further and further behind. If this happens, the growing gap between haves and have-nots will lead to widespread discontents and threaten any prospect of global harmony and international understanding. This is the most significant challenge we face. We have no time to waste in responding.

Jacques Derrida

Globalization, Peace and Cosmopolitics

I am going to set out, bluntly, a series of propositions, submitting them for discussion not so much as theses and hypotheses but more as professions of faith. These quasi-professions of faith will be expressed by means of aporia, contradictory and seemingly incompatible injunctions, in other words the only situations where, having to obey two antinomic imperatives, I do not know what to do, which option to prefer or favour. In such a situation, I have to take what is called a decision and a responsibility—a responsible decision. I have to set myself or invent for myself a rule for accommodation, for compromise and negotiation, a rule that cannot be programmed in by reference to any kind of knowledge, science or awareness. Even if I possess, or seek to obtain, all possible knowledge, science or awareness of this subject, as indeed one should, I still have an infinite leap to make, since that responsible decision, that choice between two contradictory imperatives, is not something that any form of knowledge *per se* can dictate, programme in or prescribe. This is why I am tempted to refer to a 'profession of faith'.

The concept of globalization

Having laid down that basic principle, let us take the French word *mondialisation*, which in my opinion one should resist translating into, or replacing by, its supposed English or German equivalents 'globalization' and *Globalisierung*. That term, as statistics show, is being subjected to types of use and abuse highly symptomatic of our times, of this last decade in particular. The inflation, not to say rhetorical hypertrophy, from which it suffers not only in political discourse but also in the media, often masks one of its contradictions, the subject with which I would like to begin, a contradiction in respect of which a real critical culture, the contract for a new form of education, or indeed re-education, would no doubt be required, to counteract both the naive celebration and equally the demonization of the phenomenon of 'globalization'. Both celebration and demonization are often a cloak for interests and strategies that one must learn to detect.

There are indeed a number of unprecedented and irrefutable phenomena that justify this concept. Basically determined by technoscience (the products and benefits of which are, incidentally, unevenly and unfairly spread around the world), these effects of globalization relate to the speed and scope of transport and telecommunications in the electronic age (computerization, e-mail, the Internet), the movement of people, goods, modes of production and sociopolitical models in a market that is, with varying degrees of regulation, opening up. As regards the (very relative) opening up of frontiers (which at the same time have seldom given rise to so much inhospitable violence, so many prohibitions and exclusions), as regards legislative progress in, and the exercise of, international law, and as regards the concomitant limitations upon, and shifts in, sovereignty—these things depend less than ever before on technoscience and technoscientific know-how. Ethical-political decisions and political-economic-military strategies enter into play here. At this point, the ideal or euphoric image of globalization as a homogenizing and opening-up process needs to be seriously challenged with unfailing vigilance—not only because this homogenization, if and when it occurs, embodies both an opportunity and at the same time a terrifying risk, but also because behind apparent homogenization there often lurk disparities and hegemonies, 'homo-hegemonizations' as I call them, both new and old, which we must learn to detect and combat in their new guises.

The international institutions, whether governmental or non-governmental, are particularly well-placed to bring to light, analyse and experiment with these phenomena and to serve as a battleground and an arena for sensitive confrontation. They are also especially well-placed to organize resistance to those imbalances of which the most visible and most massive are the linguistic ones. Linguistic imbalance is all the more difficult to redress since—and this is another of the contradictions—the existing linguistic hegemony is also very useful for universal communication, and is hence ambiguous in its effects, and since a linguistic-cultural hegemony—I refer, of course, to the Anglo-American one—is being increasingly exerted or imposed across all the modes of technoscientific exchanges (the Web, the Internet, academic research, etc.), thus flying the flag either of sovereign, nation-state authorities or of supranational powers, in the sense of the corporations and the new forms of concentration of capital.

This is all familiar ground, and at this stage I shall only emphasize the aporetic contradiction within which responsible decisions have to be taken and contracts designed. If a linguistic-cultural hegemony, with the ethical, religious and legal models that it comprises, is both, as integrating homogenization, the positive precondition and the democratic pole of a desired form of globalization—seeing that it gives access to a common language, to interchange, to technoscience and to economic and social progress for communities, whether national or not, that would otherwise be without such access and would therefore be deprived, were it not for the Anglo-American language, of participation in the world forum—then how can one combat such a hegemony without jeopardizing the expansion of exchanges and of sharing? It is on this point that an accommodation must constantly be sought, in every specific circumstance. This is where it has to be invented, or reinvented, without pre-established criteria and without established norms. The very norm itself, i.e., the language of the norm, has to be reinvented for such an accommodation, such being the formidable responsibility of the norm. This reinvention of the norm—albeit that it needs each time to be a new beginning, different, without precedent and with no prior guarantees or ready-made criteria—should nevertheless not be left to relativism, empiricism, pragmatism or opportunism. It must justify itself by producing its principle of universalization in a universally convincing manner and by validating it in its very invention.

I am well aware that I am in this way formulating an apparently contradictory and *impossible* task, impossible, that is, as regards an instant, immediately coherent and self-identical response; but I maintain that only the impossible happens and that no event—and hence no groundbreaking and singular decision—can occur except when one does more than bring something possible, some possible knowledge, into play, except when an exception is made to what is possible.

The world: a concept born of Abraham's line

As my space is limited and instead of undertaking a direct analysis, I shall endeavour to illustrate this by an analogy, taking the example of the concept of 'world' [*monde* in French] and 'globalization' [*mondialisation*]. The reason why I make a point of distinguishing the concept of 'world' from that of 'globalization' or *Globalisierung* (and I note that use of the word 'globalization' [*globalisation*] is itself becoming globalized, to the point where it is coming to dominate more and more, even in France, in the rhetoric of party politics and the media) is that the concept of 'world' has a historical background. It retains a memory that distinguishes it from that of 'globe', 'universe', 'Earth' or even 'cosmos', at least cosmos in the pre-Christian sense, which Saint Paul later Christianized, giving it the meaning of the world as a *fraternal* community of humans, fellow men, brethren, sons of God and neighbours one unto another. 'World' firstly designates, in an Abrahamic (i.e., Judeo-Christian-Islamic but predominantly Christian) tradition, a certain space-time, a certain slant on the history of human brotherhood: what, in a Pauline language that still provides the framework and the precondition for the modern concepts of human rights or crime against humanity (domains within the purview of international law in its present form to which I would like to return and on which depends, in principle or in law, the further development of globalization), is referred to as 'citizens of the world'—*sympolitai*, fellow-citizens with the saints in God's house, brethren, fellow men, women, neighbours as creatures and children of God.

If you will concede, with me, that it is possible to trace back the concept of 'world' and all the ethical, political and legal concepts that tend to regulate the globalization process, the emergent future of the world, in particular by means of international law and even international criminal law, steering it through the difficulties encountered by the cosmopolitical international institutions and even the welcome crises of nation-states' sovereignty, then the most needful task and the most risky challenge would be to do two things at once, without renouncing either of them: firstly, to analyse, in rigorous and uncompromising fashion, all the genealogical features that lead the concept of 'world', the geopolitical axioms and prior assumptions of international law and everything that governs its interpretation, such as the process of globalization itself, back towards its European, Abrahamic and predominantly Christian or indeed Roman origins (with the hegemonic effects inherent therein); and secondly, never, through cultural relativism or facile criticism of Eurocentrism, to renounce the universal, universalizing, genuinely revolutionary demand that tends irresistibly to uproot that lineage, to remove it from its particular territorial and historical context, to challenge its limits and its hegemonic effects. It would be necessary also to extend this process to include that theologico-political concept of 'sovereignty', which is now experiencing the upheaval with which you are familiar, on the frontiers of war and peace and indeed on the frontiers between cosmopolitanism—which presupposes state sovereignty in the same way as citizenship of the world—and a different democratic International, transcending the nation-state and transcending citizenship. The point, therefore, is not to refrain from finding, from inventing—i.e., discovering what is already there *in posse*—within this very lineage the principle whereby it reaches beyond itself. Without ever yielding to empiricist relativism, the aim should be to give an account of that which, in this European genealogy, reaches beyond itself when it is exported, even if its exportation has been and may still be accompanied by unbounded violence, whether it is designated by relatively outdated terms such as imperialism, colonialism, neocolonialism or neo-imperialism, or whether it takes the form of more refined, more devious and more virtual modes of domination, now less easily identifiable and going by the names of 'nation-states' or 'groups of nation-states'.

The task of the philosopher in this connection, as I see it, a task both assigned and implied by the new world contract we are considering, would also be the task facing anyone undertaking political or legal responsibilities in this field: to render an account—while consciously accepting it by way of a profession of faith—of that which, within this heritage of the concept of 'world' and in the process of globalization, makes possible and necessary an effective universalization that frees itself from its own historical, geographical and nation-state roots or limitations, at the very time when out of loyalty—loyalty being an act of faith—it brings the best memory in that heritage into action and combats the effects of inequality, hegemony and homo-hegemonization which that same tradition may have produced and may still produce. For it is also from deep within that heritage that there arise the very motifs that today, by way of the profound change in international law and its new concepts, contain the potential for the universalization and hence the sharing or, if one prefers, expropriation of the Euro-Christian heritage.

Rather than remain on this plane of abstraction, I should like to give four interrelated examples in the direction of which, in putting forward these propositions, I should like to steer the discussion. These four interconnected instances are, respectively, work, forgiveness, peace and the death penalty.

The end of work—the ultimate shape of globalization?

The common premises I would choose in order to group these four themes together in the same set of problems would all come from a process of globalization that has been speeded up, pushed ahead to the level of a radical change or a break in continuity, and marked by a series of legal occurrences: firstly, the reaffirmation, renewed in the declarations thereon and constantly enriched, of 'human rights'; secondly, the performative production in 1945 of the concept of crime against humanity, which, together with the crimes of war, genocide and aggression, transforms the worldwide public space and opens the way for an international criminal justice system—which it is to be foreseen and hoped will be irreversibly developed, thus limiting correspondingly the sovereignty of nation-states (the four above-mentioned crimes indeed define the competence of the International Criminal Court); and thirdly, the challenging—albeit very uneven and in practice very problematical, but nevertheless quite decisive and irreversible—of the very incompletely secularized theological principle of the sovereignty of nation-states.

Let us imagine that the world begins where work ends, as if the globalization of the world were aimed towards, and at the same time originated from, the disappearance of what we call work, that old word painfully burdened with so much meaning and history—[in English in the text], *work*, *labour, travail*, etc.—which always signifies real, actual, non-virtual work. Using the expression 'as if' does not mean we are here in the fictitious realm of a possible future or engaged in resurrecting an historical or mythical past, or indeed a past of some revealed origin. This 'as if' trope belongs neither to the science fiction of some future Utopia (a world without work, 'at the end without end', *in fine sine fine*, of some eternal Sabbath rest, on some everlasting Sabbath, as in Saint Augustine's *City of God*), nor to the poetics of a nostalgia that harks back to a golden age or earthly paradise, at that point in Genesis when, before the Fall, the sweat of the labouring man or that of the woman in labour had not yet begun to flow.

In both of these interpretations of 'as if', science fiction or memory of time immemorial, it would indeed be as if the beginning of the world excluded work: work did not yet exist or else had ceased to exist. Work would have been brought into the world by the original sin, and the end of work would herald the terminal phase of an expiation. A choice would thus need to be made between the world and work, whereas common sense finds it hard to imagine a world without work, or work not of or in the world. In the Christian world, the Pauline conversion of the Greek *cosmos* introduces into the concept, among many other related meanings, that of assignment to expiatory work. The concept of work is loaded with meaning, history and ambiguity. It is difficult to conceive of it 'beyond good and evil', since although it is always associated, simultaneously, with dignity, life, production, history, good and freedom, it nevertheless often connotes evil, suffering, pain, sin, punishment and subjection.

No, this 'as if' takes into account, in the present, with a view to putting them to the test, two current commonplaces: there is on the one hand much talk of the end of work, and on the other of the globalization of the world, of the world becoming one, and the two are always linked to each other. I have borrowed the expression 'the end of work' from the title of Jeremy Rifkin's well-known book *The End of Work: The Decline of the Global Labour Force and the Dawn of the Post-market Era*.[1] This book brings together a kind of outpouring of *doxa* on what Rifkin calls a 'third industrial revolution', which he claims could serve the purposes of good as well as evil, when the new information and communication technologies are equally well able to liberate or to destabilize civilization. I do not know whether it is true, as Rifkin asserts, that we are entering a new phase in the history of the world. Fewer and fewer workers, he says, will be needed to produce goods and services for the population of the planet, adding that the end of work concerns technological innovations and the economism that is pushing us to the verge of a world without or almost without workers.

---

1. Jeremy Rifkin, *The End of Work: The Decline of the Global Labour Force and the Dawn of the Post-market Era*, New York, Tarcher/Putnam Books, 1995.

To test the truth of these propositions, we need to agree on the meaning of each of these words: end, history, world, work, production, goods. I have neither the time nor, accordingly, the intention of going into these vast and serious problems, in particular the concepts of world and work being employed therein. Something serious is indeed happening, or is about to happen, to what we call 'work', 'teleworking', virtual work, and to what we call the 'world', and hence to the being-in-the-world of what is still referred to as 'man'. It depends largely on a profound technological and scientific change that, in the cyberworld, the world of the Internet, e-mail and mobile phones, affects teleworking, time and the virtualization of work, at the same time as the communication of knowledge, any pooling of experience, any community; it affects the experience of place, of taking place, of the event and the completed task, in other words, of what *happens*.

This approach to the so-called 'end of work' was to be found in some of the writings of Marx or of Lenin, who linked the gradual reduction in the working day with the process leading to the withering away of the state.

Rifkin sees the third technological revolution as entailing an absolute transformation. The first two revolutions, of steam and coal, steel and textiles in the nineteenth century, then of electricity, oil and the motor car in the twentieth, did not radically affect the history of work, since they both left a sector where the machine had not penetrated and where non-mechanical human work, work that machines could not replace, was still available. It is claimed that after these two revolutions comes our own, the third, that of cyberspace, microcomputers and robotics: here, it seems, there is no fourth zone to provide work for the unemployed. Saturation mechanization would thus herald the end of the worker, or in a certain sense the end of work. Rifkin's book in fact allots a separate place in this ongoing transformation to the knowledge sector. Hitherto, when new technologies took the place of workers in a given sector, new openings occurred to absorb the workers who were losing their jobs. Now, however, as agriculture, industry and the service sector are laying off millions of people on grounds of technological progress, the only category of workers spared that fate are those in the 'knowledge' sector, an elite of industrial innovators, scientists, technicians, computer specialists, teachers and so forth. This remains, nonetheless, a narrow space, incapable of absorbing the mass of unemployed. Such, according to Rifkin, is the dangerous particularity of our times.

I do not intend to deal with the objections that could be raised to these propositions, either as regards the so-called 'end of work' or as regards so-called 'globalization'. In both cases, which are indeed closely linked, if I had to deal with them head-on, I would begin by trying to distinguish between the massive and more questionable phenomena recorded under the heading of these words, and the use made of these words without concepts. What is undeniable is that something is happening to work, to the reality and to the concept of work, in this century. What is happening is indeed an effect of technoscience, as a result of the virtualization and worldwide delocalization of teleworking, albeit that, as Le Goff has clearly shown, such contradictions on the subject of work time began very early on in the Christian Middle Ages. What is happening does indeed accentuate a certain trend towards the asymptotic reduction of work time in the sense of real-time work localized in the same place as the actual worker. All this, with our new experience of frontiers, of virtual communication and of the speed and volume of information, affects work as it has come down to us in its traditional forms. This evolution is moving in the direction of a certain form, incontestable and fairly well known, of globalization.

These signs on the level of phenomena remain, however, incomplete, heterogeneous and unevenly developed. They require painstaking analysis and, perhaps, new concepts. There is furthermore a gap between these obvious signs on the one hand and, on the other, the doxic use—or as some might say the ideological inflation—of these words 'the end of work' and 'globalization', or the glib and often woolly way in which they are employed. Those who overlook that gap should, in my opinion, be severely criticized, for they then try to hide, from others or from themselves, those parts of the world, those populations, nations, groups, classes and individuals who, in massive numbers, are the excluded victims of the movement known as 'the end of work' or 'globalization'. These victims suffer either because they are without the work they need or because they work too hard for the wages they receive, on a world market that is so violently inegalitarian. This capitalistic situation (where capital plays an essential role between the real and the virtual) is more tragic in absolute figures than ever before in all of history, which has never been farther from the globalizing and globalized homogeneity of 'work' and 'joblessness'. A large part of humanity is without work but would like work, more work. Another part has too much work and would like to have less, or even to have done with work that is so badly paid in that market.

Speech-making about human rights, if it fails to take account of this economic inequality, is in danger of descending into idle chatter, formalism or obscenity. We should be talking here about GATT, the IMF, foreign debt and so forth. This story has been going on for a long time. It is intertwined with the real and semantic history of the words job and profession. Rifkin shows awareness of the tragedy that could ensue from such an end of work, which would not have the meaning of Sabbath or Sunday rest it has in Augustine's *City of God*. In his moral and political conclusions, however, when he sets out to define the responsibilities to be shouldered in response to the technological storms building up on the horizon, and to a new age of globalization and automation, he falls back—in a way I think is neither accidental nor acceptable without scrutiny—on the Christian language of 'brotherhood', of virtues difficult to automate, of a 'new meaning to life', of the 'resurrection' of the third sector, of the rebirth of the human spirit. Rifkin even envisages new forms of charity, such as the payment of a virtual salary to volunteers, or VAT on the products and services of the hi-tech era, (ring-fenced to fund a social wage for poor people working in the third sector), etc. His remarks here have the rather incantatory ring of a discourse I referred to just now as requiring a complex but uncompromising genealogical analysis.

Had I had the space, I should probably have again stressed work time, often taking a lead from the work of my colleague Jacques Le Goff. In the chapter on time and work in his book *Time, Work and Culture in the Middle Ages*,[2] he demonstrates how, as long ago as the fourteenth century, parallel demands for both the extension and the reduction of work time were being made. What we have here are the premises for a right of work and a right to work, such as were later to be included among human rights. The figure of the humanist emerges as a response to the question of work. The humanist is someone who, within the theology of work that dominates the period—and no doubt still exists to this day—begins to secularize work time and the use of monastic time. Time, no longer simply a gift from God, can be measured out and sold. In fourteenth-century iconography, clocks often feature as the attribute of the humanist: the clock I am obliged to keep an eye on and which keeps a stern eye on the lay worker I now am. Le Goff shows that the unity of the world of work, as against the world of prayer and the world of war, if it ever existed at all, did not last long. Following on from the 'disdain for the crafts', a new 'frontier of disdain' is established, running through the middle of the new classes and through the very middle of the professions. Though he does not make a distinction, as I think one should, between 'craft' and 'profession', Le Goff also describes the process which, in the twelfth century, gave rise to a 'theology of work' and the transformation of the tripartite schema of *oratores, bellatores* and *laboratores* into more complex schemata, a process that may be explained by the differentiation of economic and social structures and a greater division of labour.

Forgiveness

The scene of repentance and forgiveness-seeking is today becoming globalized, presented on a worldwide stage. It stems both from the ground swell of the Abrahamic heritage and from the new situation in international law, and hence the new face of globalization that has, since the last war, been

---

2. Jacques Le Goff, *Time, Work and Culture in the Middle Ages*, trans. Arthur Goldhammer, Chicago, University of Chicago Press, 1982.

produced by the transformed concepts of human rights, the new concepts of crime against humanity, genocide, war and aggression, which are the charges to be answered in such self-indictments. It is difficult to measure up this issue, firstly because ambiguity is all too often kept up, especially in the course of the political debates which, the world over, are reactivating and shifting that concept. Forgiveness is often confused, sometimes deliberately, with a range of neighbouring themes—apologies, regrets, amnesty, statutes of limitations, etc.—some of which come under the heading of law, a criminal law in relation to which forgiveness should in principle remain heterogeneous and irreducible.

Enigmatic though the concept of forgiveness, in the strict sense, remains, the scene, the form and the language that people attempt to adjust to it belong within a religious heritage (which we may call Abrahamic in order to group together Judaism and the various forms of Christianity and Islam). Be that as it may, however complex, differentiated or even conflictual this tradition may be, it is both specific and at the same time in the process of becoming universal, precisely by way of that which the theatre of forgiveness brings into play or brings to light. That being the case, the very dimension of forgiveness—and with it all sense of proportion, all conceptual limit—tends to become obliterated in the course of this globalization. In all the scenes of repentance, confession, pardon or apologies, of which there have been more and more on the geopolitical stage since the last war and which have been enacted more and more often these last few years, we have witnessed not only individuals but entire communities, professional bodies, representatives of ecclesiastical hierarchies, sovereigns and heads of state asking for 'forgiveness'. In so doing they employ an Abrahamic language that is not (in the case of Japan or Korea, for instance) that of their society's dominant religion but which has already become, by that very fact, the common language of law, politics, economics or diplomacy: at once the agent and the symptom of that internationalization.

The proliferation of these scenes of repentance and of 'forgiveness' sought no doubt signifies, among other things, a *universal urgency* of memory: there *must* be a turning back towards the past; and this act of memory, of self-indictment, of 'repentance' and of being brought to justice *must* be carried beyond both the level of the courts and that of the nation-state. The question thus arises as to what happens on this level. There are many trails that might be followed. One of these regularly leads back to a series of extraordinary events which, before and during the Second World War, made possible or at least 'authorized', with the Nuremberg Tribunal, the international establishment of a legal concept such as that of 'crime against humanity'. This represented a 'performative' event of a scope that it is still hard to interpret, even though words such as 'crime against humanity' are now part of everyday language. That event was itself *produced* and authorized by an international community at a particular moment in its history and in a particular historically determined form, intermingled with but not merging with the history of a reaffirmation of human rights and of a new Declaration of Human Rights.

This sort of profound change has structured the theatre in which, sincerely or otherwise, the great forgiveness, the great scene of repentance with which we are concerned, is played out. It often takes on the characteristics, by virtue of its theatrical nature itself, of a great convulsion. Dare one say that this convulsion also sometimes resembles a frantic compulsion? No, fortunately it is also a response to a move in a 'good' direction; but the reason why one is at times tempted to detect therein, at least, a collective trance is that it often involves elements of sham, automatic ritual, hypocrisy, self-interest or tomfoolery, gate-crashers at this ceremony of guilt. Here we have the whole of humanity stirred by a purportedly unanimous impulse, a human race setting out all of a sudden to charge itself, in public and in spectacular fashion, with all the crimes it has indeed committed against itself, 'against humanity'. Indeed, if we start charging ourselves, while seeking forgiveness for them, with all of the past crimes against humanity, not a single innocent person would be left on earth, and hence there would be no-one left to sit in judgement or to arbitrate. We are all heirs, at least, of persons or events tainted in some basic, inward, ineradicable way by crimes against humanity. These events, these cruel, organized mass murders, which may have been revolutions, great canonical and supposedly 'legitimate' Revolutions, were sometimes those very same events that enabled concepts such as those of human rights or crime against humanity to emerge and make headway.

Such a convulsion would today, however, take the form or shape of a conversion, a de facto conversion tending towards the universal, on the way to becoming globalized. If, as I believe, the concept of crime against humanity is the count to be answered in this self-indictment, this repentance and this forgiveness-seeking; if, ultimately, the only justification for this concept lies in the sacral nature of the human (from this point of view, there is nothing worse than a crime against the humanity of the human being and against his or her rights); if the principal—if not indeed the only—resource of the meaning of that sacral nature is to be found in the Abrahamic memories of the faiths of the book and in a Jewish, but above all Christian, interpretation of the terms 'neighbour' and 'fellow man'; and if, accordingly, a crime against humanity is a crime against that which is most sacred in the living world and hence against the divine in humankind, in God-made-man or man-made-God-by-God (the death of man and the death of God would in that case result from the same crime), then the 'globalization' of forgiveness resembles an immense scene of ongoing confession, and hence of a virtually Christian convulsion-conversion-confession, a process of Christianization that no longer has need of the Christian Church. It may sometimes also (not that it makes any difference) take on the appearance of atheism, humanism or triumphant secularization: the whole of humanity would be prepared to charge itself with crime against humanity, to indict itself, to testify against itself, in other words to indict itself as if it were another: itself as the other.

Whether one regards this as a huge step forward, a historic change, and/or a concept still unclear in its limits and unsure in its foundations (one can take both positions at the same time, as I am inclined to do myself), the undeniable fact is that the concept of 'crime against humanity' remains on the horizon of any geopolitics of forgiveness, providing it with its discourse and its legitimation. To take the striking case of the South African Truth and Reconciliation Commission, which remains unique in spite of the analogies—analogies only—with certain South American precedents, in Chile in particular: what gave the Commission its ultimate justification, its declared legitimacy, is the definition, by the international community as represented by the United Nations, of apartheid as a 'crime against humanity'. We could take a hundred other examples; there are very many of them and they are *all* similarly underwritten.

Peace

As to peace, being unable to devote to it a more appropriate analysis and one more worthy of that great subject that concerns us, let me just make this remark, directly inspired by the title of these '21st-Century Talks'. If there is, as I believe, one lesson to be drawn from the most recent phenomena, phenomena that one no longer dares to call wars because of the semantic shifts involving, precisely, the ambiguous role of the state in such 'interventions' as the 'Gulf War', Rwanda, Kosovo, Timor, etc., all very different one from another as to the logic of the sovereignties at issue, that lesson is that, belated or not, well conducted or not, such interventions undertaken in the name of universal human rights, with the prospect in view of heads of State or military leaders being brought before international criminal tribunals, have, it is true, happily called into question the sacred sovereignty of the state, but have done so in conditions that often give cause for concern.

As Hannah Arendt observed, it is only the small states whose sovereignty is challenged and, albeit in the name of universal principles, called into question by powerful states who not only would not tolerate their own sovereignty being challenged but who influence or anticipate decisions, sometimes anticipating the deliberations of the competent international authorities, in the interests of their own politico-military-economic strategy and because they alone possess the necessary economic and technomilitary clout. Any future world contract would need to take account of this fact: until such time as the international authorities enjoy autonomy of deliberation, decision and, above all, of military implementation, until they have behind them the force of the law they are charged with representing, all infringements of sovereignty in the name of human rights, which should be just in the principle on which they are based, will be suspect and tainted by strategies in respect of which vigilance will always remain essential.

The death penalty

The serious worldwide issue of the death penalty is indissociable from what I have just been saying. Without going back over the long history of the abolitionist campaigns that have been going on for centuries, even in the United States, we should hold on at least to this obvious fact: since the last world war, there has been a long series of international conventions and declarations on human rights, on the right to life and on the banning of cruel treatment, hard to reconcile with the death penalty (declarations I do not have the time to quote but which almost all emanate from the United Nations), which have directly or indirectly created a pressure, at a level above that of the state, to which a great number of democratic countries have, let us say, been responsive at the time when they abolished the death penalty. It has always been an international authority, one transcending the sovereignty of the state, that has enjoined states (for whom the death penalty and the right to grant pardon had always been pre-eminent tokens of their sovereignty) to give up the death penalty—apparently of their own accord but in reality out of international obligation. This was obviously what happened in Europe—less than twenty years ago in the case of France—and in fifty or so countries in today's world. One could go along with certain legal experts in regarding this increasing trend towards abolition as becoming a 'customary norm of international law', to use the English term, or in Latin a norm of *jus cogens*;[3] but the fact is that, among the countries standing out against that trend, among the nation-states that present themselves as great Western democracies in the Christian, European tradition, the United States, after an eventful history in this respect (history old and recent that I do not have the time to retrace), is today, to my knowledge, the only country that not only has not abolished the death penalty but is applying it on a massive and increasing scale and in a cruel and, it must be said, discriminatory manner, when it is not indeed, as in many recent cases, applied blindly.

On behalf of other international associations and of the International Parliament of Writers, to which I have the honour to belong, and on my own behalf, I ask that the question of the death penalty be included in the form of a solemn appeal in any text concerning a new 'world contract'.

This brings me to the end of my professions of faith.

---

3. 'Constraining law.'

Francisco Sagasti

Science, Technology and Globalization

Perceptions of globalization North and South

Globalization looks very different when it is seen, not from the capitals of the West, but from the cities and villages of the South. I would like to begin by giving you four examples taken from my own country, Peru, to give you an understanding of how the paradoxical forces shaping globalization look when seen from the other side.

A few weeks ago, twenty-eight school children died in a remote village in the highlands of Peru after mixing water and powdered milk in a vat reserved for a powerful insecticide. Nobody could read the label and the children were simply poisoned. Incidentally, that insecticide has been banned in practically every industrialized nation; its sale continues only in places like my country.

Secondly, an important annual event recently took place in Cajamarca, in the north of Peru. Potato growers gather there to exchange the best seeds they have produced in the last year. It is an act of pride for communities to share with others the seeds that will help improve the production of potatoes. This year, transnational corporations attended the festival and are now working to patent the genes of these traditional foodstuffs in order to sell them at a profit.

Peru's macro-economic indicators are excellent. On Wall Street, or in the offices of investment bankers, people will advise you that Peru is a great investment opportunity with low inflation and punctual debt repayments. The situation is not so rosy, however, when considered from the perspective of Peruvians: 50 percent of the population have been living below the poverty line for the last ten years, 20 percent of the population are living below the critical poverty line, i.e., their income is insufficient to pay for even nourishment. Reference is often made to the end of work: perhaps it would be more appropriate to refer to the end of the workplace. In Peru, two-thirds of the work force is unemployed or under-employed, and between now and 2005, more people will enter the labour markets of Peru than in the whole of the European Union.

I recently attended an international conference with the distinguished political scientist, Dr Benjamin Barber. Summarizing his intervention, he pointed out that in the United States democracy had degenerated into bringing one group of rascals in for four years, only to throw them out and replace them with another group of rascals for four years. My reply was that, from the perspective of the South, that looks pretty good! In a context where the rascals manipulate elections and stay in power for fifteen or sixteen years, I would appreciate the chance to throw them out through peaceful elections every four years.

Thus, the complaints of the North are often the aspirations of the South. Progress in industrialized nations can be a threat to developing countries. Quite clearly, there now exist significant differences in these two viewpoints.

A fractured global order

In 1989, in the euphoria of globalization and the expansion of services and finance that followed the fall of the Berlin Wall, I advanced the idea that we were entering a fractured global order. I suggested that we were experiencing something extremely complicated, paradoxical and contradictory that had both good and bad sides. Globalization brings us into contact with one another, but it also maintains and strengthens profound divisions and fractures in terms of societies and income, and most importantly in our capacity to generate and utilize knowledge. These fractures are dividing the human race into two civilizations.

Today it has become clear that we have entered this fractured global order. The concentration of wealth and power has greatly increased both within and between societies. Even more striking is the growth in differences in ability to profit from knowledge. The current ratio in average income per capita between the twenty-four richest countries and the forty-two poorest is between 62 and 65 to one. However the ratio in annual expenditure per capita in research and development is over 250 to one. Extrapolate this figure over decades or even centuries and it is possible to see the enormous differences that have accumulated in the capacities to generate knowledge.

There is a real risk of two civilizations emerging with two ways of viewing and relating to the world: one based on the capacity to produce and utilize knowledge; the other passively receiving the knowledge that comes from abroad and deprived of the ability to modify it. To go even further, I was recently at a conference in Seattle where the spectre was raised of the emergence of two distinct subspecies of the human race brought about by the advances in human genomics and genetics.

What can be done? First of all, we need to find a sensible and balanced view away from the hype of those who portray globalization as the answer to every problem, and away from the pessimism of those who say that nothing can be done and that we are condemned to continue in the direction that current trends indicate. The second point on the agenda involves the revitalization of international cooperation in science and technology. This is not a new idea. In 1963, a United Nations conference was organized in Geneva to help the less developed countries progress in this domain. At the time, it was believed that advances in science and technology were like products in a huge supermarket. Developing countries could simply go along to buy and use what they needed. Twenty years ago a new program was issued with the objective of beginning to redress some of the imbalances. The industrialized countries had learned that science and technology possess the potential for creating harm as well as benefits, for creating enormous divisions and for being appropriated and used to increase profits or enrich a small part of humanity. In the twenty years since, we have seen a great number of declarations but nothing of substance has changed. Less than half a dozen countries from the developing world have been able to improve their own scientific and technical capabilities.

Redefining development and progress

We need the international community to return to the basic principles of international cooperation and introduce the idea that a minimum level of science and technological capability, including access to the Internet and sources of knowledge, is an absolute necessity for developing countries and should be the subject of international solidarity. This can be achieved. However, contrary to the situation twenty years ago, national governments are no longer the major players in the game of science and technology. Whether we desire it or not, the private sector and the international community of scholars have to be invited to the table with governments from the North and the South to begin discussing an agenda for the mobilization of science and technology for development objectives. One successful example of this approach is the WHO's new fund for vaccines. There is a particular role for UNESCO in this revitalization of international cooperation, since it is the only agency within the United Nations system with a mandate in scientific and technological affairs.

Over the next twenty or thirty years we need to embark on a joint effort to redefine what we mean by 'development' and 'progress'. It is clear that 'development" as we have understood it, that is, in terms of material consumption and standards of living in the highly industrialized nations, is not a viable interpretation for the whole world. This kind of development, measured through growth in the consumption of energy and materials is simply not going to happen in the developing countries. A different conception of 'development' and 'progress' will be required as we enter the twenty-first century.

We are witnessing the end of the Baconian programme, which had flourished for over 400 years. As articulated by Bacon at the beginning of the seventeenth century, this program consisted of three elements: using science as a new method for generating knowledge; generating knowledge not simply as a pastime for discovering the divine designs of God, but discovery for the benefit of humankind; taking advantage of institutions and state support in order to make knowledge even greater. Bacon believed in 'Man' and placed him at the centre of his thinking.

Science has undergone a transformation. Today, science is aware of its own limitations as a method for generating knowledge, and we are looking to ethics and aesthetics to supplement the discoveries we make through rationality and science. We are now aware of the ambiguous character of knowledge and its capacity for the betterment of humankind as well as for the creation of new dangers and problems. 'Progress' itself has been questioned and is in need of being redefined. Lastly, the Baconian conception of 'Man' has been modified by a more nuanced concept of the relation between men and women as well as between humanity and the biophysical environment. Today we are much clearer about the enormous and delicate balances we must strike.

Bacon's programme succeeded, but in doing so, undermined its own foundations. It is our task to redefine a new programme. We have that advantage of being able to learn from the mistakes of the last 400 years. We must enlarge our conception of knowledge generation to include considerations other than pure rationality: ethics and aesthetics are possible choices. Moreover, the Baconian programme was a creation of Western civilization. As it unfolded in unison with capitalist expansion throughout the world, the program obliterated or ignored other cultures. It is time to bring these cultures back into the picture. The third point on the agenda for change is a dialogue that involves all civilizations with the objective of redefining, over the next twenty or thirty years, what we mean by 'development' and 'progress'.

The New Technologies and Culture

Is the market economy, based on a set of transactions between buyers and sellers of goods, making way for a network economy bringing into play access providers and users of the flow of experience and involving no transfer of property? If the potential advantages of such a network economy are already foreseeable in terms of the internalization of certain costs, as in the case of environmental protection, the risks looming on the horizon are numerous: an increased concentration of power and the creation of patent ownership monopolies are often mentioned in this connection. In view of the danger of the wholesale commercialization of culture, Jeremy Rifkin stresses the need to establish checks and balances.

Redefining culture as an individual itinerary, based on local and personal appropriations and uses of technologies and content, Michel Serres argues that culture is not in danger. The transformations implicit in the new technologies, such as the emergence of a collective and objective memory at the expense of subjective memory, should not be a cause of alarm: they can, in the view of Michel Serres, be regarded as an integral part of the process of hominization.

* * * *

An economist and futurologist, founder president of the Foundation on Economic Trends based in Washington, **Jeremy Rifkin** is the author of two well-known works *The End of Work* (1995) and *The Biotech Century: Harnessing the Gene and Remaking the World* (1998), which sparked a great international debate. He has recently published *The Age of Access: The New Culture of Hypercapitalism Where All of Life Is a Paid-For Experience* (2000) and *The Hydrogen Economy: The Creation of the Worldwide Energy Web and the Redistribution of Power on Earth* (2002).

Philosopher and writer **Michel Serres** is a member of the Académie française and professor of French at Stanford University. His numerous publications include *Five Senses* (1985), *The Natural Contract* (1995), *Angels, A Modern Myth* (1995) and *Le retour au contrat naturel* (2000), *Hominescence* (2001), *L'Incandescent* (2003) and *Les Référents: éléments d'histoire des sciences* (2003). In 1994 he was awarded the Prix international de Prospective du Futuroscope.

Jeremy Rifkin

The Age of Access

There has been a great deal of discussion in recent times about the e-commerce revolution—the new software, telecommunications technologies, the Web, B2B (business-to-business), B2C (business-to-consumer), peer-to-peer and globalization.[1] What does this mean? At the Wharton School in the United States where I teach, the first question that visiting business leaders from all over the world ask me is: are we in a new economy? My answer is that it is not a new economy and that actually something far deeper is taking place.

An economic revolution

These technologies are giving birth to a new economic system that is as different from market capitalism as market capitalism was from the mercantilist economy that preceded it. We are beginning to see the outlines of a whole new economic era. Why has the NASDAQ suffered, why are high-tech stocks suffering? There are many reasons, but there is a fundamental one. We are trying to graft these new technologies on to an old market economy, and it does not work. We are now using technologies that will allow us to organize life at the speed of light. Markets were not designed for the speed of light. It is as simple and profound as that. By the mid-decade of the twenty-first century market capitalism will have become, I believe, a marginal part of the economics and commerce of this world. We are making a great historic shift from property exchange and markets to access relationships in networks.

---

1. This text, based on a presentation to the 17th session of the 'Twenty-First Century Talks' at UNESCO on 9 March 2001, was published in part in *Le Monde Diplomatique* of September 2001.

The last great change in economic systems occurred between the 1400s and the 1800s. A range of new technologies emerged in Europe that changed the possibilities for commerce. New agricultural technologies in the late medieval era increased food production. You had surpluses; you could begin trade for the first time since the fall of the Roman Empire. The compass allowed Europeans to circumnavigate the globe, explore new resources and create new markets for goods. The mechanical clock, that little invention by the Benedictine monks, was used by commerce to regulate time and commerce much more effectively. The print press, a new form of communication with great sweep and connectivity, served to speed up commercial life. Finally, there was steam power: we could now use stored sun and move at a pace way beyond solar flow. Together, these technologies were quick, fast and connective. What was the result? The feudal economy, based on barter, subsistence agriculture and proprietary obligations on the commons, proved too slow, too old-fashioned, too outdated. They could not accommodate the speed these technologies were making available for commercial life. The result was that proprietary obligations on the commons gave way to property exchange and markets.

Similarly today, we are at the midpoint of the electricity revolution. The technologies we are now introducing into our lives allow us to operate at the speed of light. Markets are going to prove too slow. This new economic system that is emerging, if it is a new economic system, changes everything: our notion of human nature, the social contract, and our relationship to our fellow human beings and the earth we live in. In the realm of primary commercial communications we are moving from geography to cyberspace. This is transparent, but it is worth dwelling on. We have been organizing economic life in geography for 10,000 years. What happens when primary communications and economics moves to the ether. It fundamentally changes the protocols: the result is a great shift from markets to networks. Now we are very familiar with markets: in markets you have a seller and a buyer; you come together to negotiate an exchange of goods and services. The seller makes money on the margins of the transaction and the volume of the units sold. At the Wharton School, this is what we teach as capitalism. In networks, the new model, there are no sellers and buyers: there are only suppliers and users, servers and clients. In networks, property still exists but it stays in the hands of the producer. It is accessed by clients in time segments through memberships, subscriptions, retainers, leases and licensing agreements. We do not pay for the transaction of the good in space; we pay for the flow of the experience in time.

From markets to networks

Markets are discrete; they are discontinuous and linear. You start, you stop, you start, you stop. The new technologies are cybernetic: they operate at the speed of light; they have continuous feedback 24/7. So discontinuous and discreet models are too slow.

Here is an example: Amazon.com is a market; Bertelsmann-Napster is attempting to be a network. Amazon uses the new technologies, but it is still a case of old-fashioned exchange. You have a CD, the seller sells it to the buyer using electronic commerce, and it is then transported to the buyer's house. At Bertelsmann-Napster you do not pay for the CD; you pay a thirty-day subscription if the new model works, which gives you unlimited access to the flow of the music for thirty days. In the time Amazon registers a single sale and transports that physical object to you, Bertelsmann-Napster can download to 1 million people. In markets we commodify goods; that is the scarce resource and valuable commodity. In networks we commodify human time; that is the scarce resource and valuable commodity. In marketing we call it LTV—lifetime value of the client. What are you worth if I can commodify every moment of your life? In markets you make money on the margins. The problem is that when you have technologies that operate at the speed of light your transaction costs start to approach zero. Every company that I work with in the world says to me that transaction costs are approaching zero, and when your transaction costs approach zero you cannot sustain markets because there are not enough margins to sustain profit. This is what is facing every industry.

Let me give you an example. I am an author; in a market I sell a book to a publisher. There is a mark-up at every stage, and the seller can take the cost and then charge more to the buyer. So you have the printer, the wholesaler, the distributor and the retailer—we are all making money here. Well, that was the case until Stephen King came along two years ago. He sold one book to Simon & Schuster for millions of dollars, and they can now put out one e-version. Not a million books, but one e-version. There are no transaction costs after the initial buy. How do you sustain markets with 1 million books that are physical when you can pay for the flow of the experience over time?

From ownership to access

There is a deeper change going on here: the shift from ownership to access. We grew up with the idea that to acquire physical goods in a market is valuable because then the property appreciates over time. But in a world that operates at the speed of light, when everything is immediately outdated, upgraded or evolving into something else, why would you want to hold onto anything? So we make a shift from markets to networks, from geography to cyberspace; we make a deep shift from ownership to access; we pay for the flow of experience over time, we do not pay for physical goods in space. The deepest change of all has to do with the nature of primary production. In the market capitalist era, primary production was physical goods and services. They are still essential, but there are no margins. In the new era, who are the big players in the twenty-first century? They are AOL, Time Warner and Disney, Vivendi, Sony and the News Corporation. So what is it that these new players sell? They call it 'content', which is a euphemism for taking thousands of years of cultural experience, the combined knowledge and metaphors upon which we live, and then deconstructing them into commercial fare that we pay for. We pay for the stories of our life. The new commerce is cultural, it is semiotic; we pay for the experiencing of life. It is called content.

So, how deep are these changes? When I was studying economics in the 1960s at the Wharton School, I was taught that your physical capital is your assets. This is ironic because today your physical capital is your liability—an operating expense at best. Nobody wants to be General Motors; everybody wants to be Nike. General Motors on paper—and this is the big difference between markets and networks—is the biggest, most powerful capitalist company in the world. It has capital—physical capital in the form of machines, equipment and inventory. Yet it is no longer in the top forty companies in the New York Stock Exchange. Now look at Nike. What is Nike? It has no equipment, it has no factories and it does not produce shoes. All its shoes are outsourced to anonymous subcontractors in Southeast Asia and Vietnam. It is a simple operating expense. I am glad to see that there are young people in Europe and the United States who protest against the exploitation of child labour in these subcontracting plants. The shoe in reality costs one dollar to produce. So why would the children and parents pay 100 dollars for a shoe that only costs one dollar? What are you paying for? You are paying to step into the Nike story. The shoe is a prop. It is both brilliant from a marketing perspective and pathological and sad from an experiential and cultural perspective. Nike purloins part of the cultural story; then we pay Nike so that we can experience it ourselves.

Nike is a design studio. It is a concept, an idea; it is intellectual capital, a marketing formula: cultural production. When they produced the idea of cultural commerce in the 1930s and 1940s, Jürgen Habermas and the Frankfurt school were a little naïve and premature, but I think they got a real prescient sense of what was coming. We still teach in accounting that your physical capital represents your assets, when every company that I work with thinks that physical capital is their liability. But if your real capital is intangible—intellectual capital, ideas, stories, experiences, brands, etc.—how do you measure it, how do you quantify it? If you overevaluate it, the government says you are not paying your taxes; and if you underevaluate it your shareholders say you are not giving us enough of the share. And the Nike story today could be worthless tomorrow morning. It is just a story. So we are going to have to rethink accounting, and we have no way of understanding how to do it yet. We are still living in the old market system.

To understand the shift from markets to networks, let us take the case of Lego toys. With the traditional Lego toy, you go to the store, you buy the toy and you take it home. If you want a new toy, you have to go to the store and bring it home. Remember I said markets are discreet, discontinuous and linear. They are too slow. In the future, the Lego toys—they are already beginning the transition—will be connected to the Internet, and you will pay for new things for the toy to do. The toy is just a platform. You will pay a membership or a subscription so that you can continually download new experiences with the toy. Your child will grow up to think of a toy not as a product they own, as a possession, but as a flow of experience they have over time. It is a great shift. Property is no longer the measure of a man or woman; access to the flow experience in time is the new status for the next generation. That is why this term 'access' has become such a powerful metaphor. It is as powerful as property was in my generation. It is not by chance that the word access entered the lexicon of the Oxford English Dictionary as a verb in 1991.

Let us look at the automobile. You could make the case that the twentieth century was about the automobile. It was the bedrock centre of market capitalism in the industrial way of life. The second most important piece of property we own is the automobile. I was with the CEO and staff of Ford Italy a few months ago in Rome. I began my talk to an audience of several hundred distributors and staff by saying: 'Get this straight! If it had its way, the Ford Motor Car Company would never sell another car again. They would much rather that you leased their car for two years and be connected to their network so that you would be paying for the experience of driving rather than the vehicle. The proof is in the pudding: the renewal rate for leasing is 54 percent, whereas the renewal rate if you buy a car from them is less than 25 percent. One out of every three cars and trucks on United States roads are now leased. People would much prefer paying for the flow of the experience of driving rather than having to pay for the vehicle itself. That is a sea change in how we perceive property. It is a network not a market.

Better environmental protection

People ask me the question: is this a good revolution or a bad revolution? Well, it is as if we were Franciscan monks sitting around here five centuries ago and one of the monks asked: this new thing called capitalism, do you think it is going to be a good thing or a bad thing? You know, the best we can say about great economic eras in history is that they are at once tumultuous, challenging, exciting, terrifying, destabilizing, disorienting, utopian and distopian. There are benefits for some, exploitation of others, a leap forward perhaps for humanity, a leap backwards for the environment. They are a mess. Economic systems are not neatly packaged. When we make the shift from property exchange in markets to access relationships in networks, it is going to be as tumultuous, challenging, exciting, terrifying and destabilizing as any economic era we have ever faced; and maybe more so. Let me give you an example of what I mean with reference to good and bad networks.

I have long been critical of corporations and their environmental policies. I have always believed that in a market economy companies always externalize their costs because they are exchanging the property or service so the bottom line always comes before sustainability. You cannot have sustainable development in a market economy because the producer is always externalizing the cost by transferring the property to the client, society and future generations. But in a network, property always stays with the producer; it is accessed by everyone else in time segments—through subscriptions, memberships, leases. We pay for the flow of the experience; we do not pay for the physical good. Will this change the way companies think about the environment?

Carrier, a big air-conditioning company in my country, is a good example. In a market economy they want to sell you the biggest air-conditioning unit you will buy. If it uses a lot of energy and creates global warming, that is money in the bank, they have externalized the cost. You pay for it, society pays for it, future generations pay for it. But now Carrier has a problem: I call it the Wang factor. Wang is the company that kept thinking it was going to make money by selling computer boxes in markets. But the transaction costs started to approach zero, the margins were not there, their product line was indistinguishable from that of their competitors, and in a global economy they went bankrupt. IBM just got out in time and went to service relationships in networks. Computers are now marginal to the way they make money.

So Carrier does not want to go the way of Wang. It cannot make any money on selling the air conditioners, so now it sets up something called cool services—a network. They put their air-conditioning unit into your business or residence, they keep the property and you pay a thirty-day subscription for cool air. They know you do not give a damn about an air conditioner, you just want comfort air. But now the property stays with them. Do they want to use as much energy as they can to give you that thirty-day subscription of cool air, or do they want to use as little energy as they can? Because the costs are internalized, they retrofit storm windows, special lighting—they are more pristine than Greenpeace. Is it because they care? It has nothing to do with that: it is all about the bottom line. But is it not interesting that we have a model here that may allow us to have a one-to-one relationship between the bottom line and the sustainability of the earth we live in? I said maybe.

Risk sharing

I will give you another example of a good network. In a market, the pharmaceutical companies want to sell you as many pharmaceutical drugs as they can. If you are sick the drug companies are doing well. But now, even in this high margin industry where there are terrific margins, they are facing generic drugs. We have seen recently the example of South Africa and the AIDS drugs. They are facing generic drugs, globalization and the new technologies that diminish the transaction costs towards zero. So now Glaxo Smith Klein sets up a little prototype programme in the U.K. called disease management. What do they do? They take five diseases—central nervous disorders, heart attacks, strokes, cancer and diabetes—and their new mission is to get you well and keep you well 24/7 for the rest of your life. Have they lost their mind in the corporate boardroom? Because if you are well, they are selling less drugs. How then do they make money? They set up a business-to-business economy-scale relationship with BUPA, the insurance company. If Glaxo Smith Klein can keep you well, it means less medical costs for the insurance company because you and I are on time segments; we are paying yearly subscriptions for membership. In this way, the two companies enter into a gain-saving arrangement. And now the two companies have put the employers into the mix: if you are sick we know that productivity goes down. The result is absenteeism, accidents on the job—you can measure it. But if you are well productivity goes up—you can measure that too. So now if Glaxo Smith Klein keeps the employee well, then the employer gain-saves back some of the savings and productivity with the other partners in the network. And these networks can continue to expand and expand all over the globe—with B2B, B2C, peer-to-peer.

Here is the distinction between a network and a market. In a market we make money by the margins of the transaction and the volume of the units we sell. In a network we make money in exactly the opposite way. We make money by minimizing production and by pooling the risk and sharing the savings. Because in networks there are no adversaries: think of it as one big economic family where everybody is pooling their interests as in a cooperative. The family can be the whole globe.

Increased concentration of power

In the future we may end up with just a handful of industries: the health industry, the leisure industry and the education industry—all operating as networks. But is there a problem here? Let us talk about bad networks. When Novartis and Monsanto sell a farmer a genetically engineered patented seed, we have an example of a bad network. When Monsanto and Novartis provide a seed to a farmer, there is no market, no sale, no seller and no buyer. We have not yet understood this; it is a new way of doing business. Novartis and Monsanto have the farmer enter into a licensing agreement. So the farmer gains access to the intellectual property in the DNA in the seed for one segment of time—a growing season. Remember that in networks property always stays with the producer—whether it is intellectual or physical property; you access it. Monsanto and Novartis would rather never sell another seed again. They would much rather every single farmer in France and in the world be totally dependent on them and have to access through time the use of that intellectual property in the seed. That is a tremendous concentration of power.

And here is the downside. The ability to use these new technologies, to create global B2B and B2C relationships means that the concentration of power in networks—in theory and practice—will dwarf the concentration of power in markets, even with vertical and horizontal organization. We are going to have to rethink anti-trust because all of our statutes are designed for markets; but networks inherently destroy markets. Moreover, they are global so we are going to have to have a global anti-trust regime. But there are good networks and bad networks. We are going to have to be sober and sophisticated so that we can surgically develop legislation on anti-trust to preserve the good networks and make sure the bad networks do not dominate. It is going to be one of the great political challenges of this new economic era in the twenty-first century.

Time is money

The real problem though with networks—and there are many benefits—is that we wake up one day and find that virtually every single activity we engage in with our fellow human beings is commercial. Remember that in networks you commodify and sell the flow of experience in time. We are embedded in network after network where we are paying for the flow of the experience through memberships, subscriptions, retainers, leases and licensing agreements. At least in markets there is off-time. Markets are discrete, discontinuous and linear, so after the exchange you have non-commercial time. But when you are commodifying time itself, 24/7, when you are connected to Ford for two years, you are connected day or night whether you are driving the car or not. You are paying for the flow of driving. Extend that toward Lego toys and every other single thing you can imagine and you begin to understand the problem. What happens when we find out one day that most of our relationships with each other are commercial and contractual rather than social and reciprocal—where time itself has become the ultimate commodity? Can civilization survive if most of our relationships with each other are commercial? Test it out, you older people: compared to ten or twenty years ago, are more and more of your family's relationships today commercial and contractual? And go to the United States, where it is much further advanced: life is more and more commercial and less civil and social. So Europeans come back from the United States and have two comments about America: firstly, that everyone is fat; and, secondly, that life—though exciting—is too commercial. I myself like the quality of life better in France. But I fear that the American way of life is coming to Europe.

I want to share with you a question I have been raising with CEOs in my private consultations in Silicon Valley and here in Europe. I ask them whether they believe that the quality of their own families' lives is increasing in direct proportion to all the technologies their companies are introducing. Is that not a fair question? Is there a payoff? We are on the cusp of the greatest technological and economic revolution in history. We are developing all these labour-saving, time-saving, convenience technologies; we are beginning to organize for the first time at the limit—the speed of light. Is it working? Do you know what every single CEO has told me in the last two years, to a person, although I have not checked with Bill Gates? They say no; their quality of life is deteriorating, they are stressed, they have less time. That is why we are selling time now, because we are so time-deprived that we now commodify time itself. And when I say to them, do you see any light at the end of the tunnel, they turn ashen because they see it is getting worse.

There is a cruelty in the way we are using the technology. You get the email to save time and for convenience. But then everyone else is playing the game. So the density of communication picks up. A few hours absence from the computer and we find a couple of hundred emails waiting for us when we get home. How are we ever going to catch up? We are just beginning to organize at the speed of light. Now the industry says we will have intelligent agents built into the software to help sort this out. Not when we move to picos and nanos, and DNA and quantum computing technology. You get the cell phone for convenience, and everyone else gets the cell phone; you are connected whether you want to be or not.

So, does the fault lie with the technology? Does the fault lie with this new economic system that is being born? Or does the fault lie with us, in our inability to ask the great question: how do we make this technology revolution an augment to our life but not a substitute for our existence? We are rushing to adapt ourselves to the technology; we have not yet stepped back and asked how we adapt the technology to the rest of our existence. And until we do that we will be further enslaved, further time-deprived, and the liberation we seek from the technology will be a distant memory.

The threat of culture as commodity

I should like now to talk about a deeper change; and if there was ever a place to discuss this it is here at UNESCO in Paris. The deeper shift involves a move from industrial to cultural commerce. The old economies do not disappear; they just become commodities and foundations for the new economies. Agriculture is still here; it is now a commodity—essential for the production economy. Production used to be where the margins are. Now it is a commodity; the Third World is going to do the production. But it is essential as a foundation for the service economy. The service economy was where the margins were in the last two decades of the twentieth century. Now it is a commodity, but essential for the experiential economy. The top 20 percent of the population no longer asks: what do we want to own? It already owns. It asks: what do we want to experience?

The top fifth of the world's population spends almost as much on experience now as on goods and services. We move to cultural commerce where the margins are: travel and tourism, theme parks, destination entertainment centres, film, television, video, computers, the Worldwide Web, sports, games, cuisine, even social causes become content. We pay for the stories that fill in our lives. But here is the message. If the new resource is cultural resources, what are the potential consequences if we use it up? Cultural diversity is as significant as biodiversity. In the nineteenth and twentieth century, we depleted species, habitats and physical resources. We end up with a tremendous narrowing of the gene pool and global warming. In the twenty-first century, the AOL-Time-Warners and the Vivendis move towards content; and that involves mining, exploiting, using and commercializing thousands of years of the human story. But cultural diversity can be depleted; and, when this occurs, it is as final as when we lose biodiversity.

Why am I saying this here? Well, France was the canary in the mine on this. It was UNESCO, if I recall correctly, that some years ago had a big battle with the United States, saying that culture counts. The French have always said that culture counts. The United States ridiculed, the United States threatened, other countries said you are wrong, and France was isolated from the world community on this question of culture and commerce. Well, let me tell you that France was right. It may have been premature in this debate, but it was right.

The big struggle in the twenty-first century is the struggle between culture and commerce. What happens if the commercial arena deconstructs our whole story into commercial fare? Can civilization survive when culture is completely put into the commercial arena? Now some people think the answer is yes. And this is where I want to part company with 'third-way politics'. Third-way politics is part of a noble tradition that began with the Enlightenment. If you go back and read the French and the English philosophers of the Enlightenment, if you go back and look at Locke and Newton and Condorcet and Descartes, they believed that material conditions were primary and set the foundations for the super-culture, the cultural milieu that was built from it. If you re-read Adam Smith, Ricardo, Karl Marx and Engels, they all agreed on this—the only thing they agreed upon: the material conditions are the primary foundation upon which human life is built; culture is secondary. But the French never bought the Enlightenment tradition, nor did most of continental Europe, even though the elite did.

President Clinton and Mr Blair believe that if you create a healthy global economy, through third-way politics, then you create healthy conditions for culture and society. If we can just have world trade and commercial relations, everything else will follow suit. They misunderstand the anthropology of history. They believe that commerce is a progenitor of culture when in fact it is a derivative and beneficiary. They believe commerce is the primary institution when in fact culture is the wellspring on which commerce and government rely. Do you know of an example in history where people first set up commercial relations and then create a culture later? Do you know of any examples in history where people first create a government and then set up a culture later? We have had it wrong from the Enlightenment through Adam Smith and Karl Marx and third-way politics, commerce is not the progenitor it is the beneficiary. But what happens when the beneficiary colonizes the benefactor? Can civilization survive the assault?

There are ways of resisting this pre-eminence of cyberspace and globalization: geography, locality, cultural diversity and all that culture brings. Now what is culture? Culture is all the affiliations, formal and informal, that we have in this room that are not commercial and not government. It is much bigger than the third sector: culture is church, secular, fraternal, sports, arts, civic, fun, games. Culture is where we have deep play; and the French have really talked more about deep play than anyone else. We create intrinsic value. The economy is where we have deep work; we create utility value. In the real world we live by both, by deep play and by deep work. We have got it all wrong in the modern era. Deep play is always more basic to people's lives, and work has always been something that enables us to have survival in order to play. We turned it all around in the nineteenth and twentieth centuries, saying that work is primary and play is what you do between work assignments.

So if culture precedes commerce, and the antidote to globalization, cyberspace and content is geography, locality and cultural diversity, where does the struggle head? Every young person I know on the streets of Seattle, Washington, Prague and Davos uses the new technologies. And I do not know one of them that is not in favour of trade. They just do not want their identity to be swept over in the process. How do we create an intelligent, Aristotelian balance between culture and commerce, between play and work, between intrinsic and utility value, so that we can have the best of this technology revolution, create a new economic system, not lose the wellspring—the culture that gave rise to it?

My hope lies here in Europe. More specifically, my hope lies in continental Europe—particularly here in France, in Italy and, hopefully, in Germany if it can get around its cultural past and see the light as well as the dark side. Here in continental Europe you still believe that culture precedes commerce. If you were to wake up one day in France and the entire culture was to disappear—all the institutions and affiliations—how long would France survive? But if you woke up tomorrow in France and your entire economy had collapsed, your whole government had collapsed but your cultural values, institutions and relationships remained, you could rebuild. That is how you know that culture precedes commerce.

By the way, you know how we figured it out in the business community? When the Soviet Union collapsed, the Berlin Wall came down, many of the businesses I work with rushed into Central Europe, Eastern Europe and Russia to set up shop. They failed. The Communists had eliminated even the thin remnants of the cultural sector, so there was not enough social capital in place to build predictable commercial relations—except in Hungary, Czechoslovakia and Poland because the cultural sector stayed alive in the dark days. It takes generations to build culture.

There has to be a countervailing power to globalization, so we can have both globalization and culture. The countervailing power is in the community. But what is the force that will give rise to that countervailing power? Governments are paring down, so they are less involved in local communities. Who fills the vacuum created by less government involvement? Corporations are less local, more global—operating in cyberspace, they are less involved in local communities. Who fills the vacuum? There are three contending forces vying for re-establishing locality, community and cultural conditioning. First, there is the fourth sector, that is the informal economy, the black market and organized crime. Because the third sector—culture—has been eliminated, the result is a rage of organized crime in Central and Eastern Europe and Russia. Secondly, there is a battle within each community to re-establish the community between the fundamentalist organizations and the civil society organizations. They both believe in locality, they both believe in culture; but the fundamentalist groups, the right-wing fascist groups, the ethnic cleansing groups, the religious fundamentalist groups believe that the only culture that counts is theirs and everyone else is the enemy outside the boundary. The civil society that you belong to in your families believes in local culture and geography, but also in respecting the diverse cultural traditions that make up the global experience. We see culture not as something to protect and defend as a possession; we see culture as a gift to share, to build and to create. Culture is a mosaic: it is something we fuse, we share, we create, or else it dies.

So, my hope lies here in Europe for this reason. I have never met a French man or woman who did not believe that your cultural identity precedes your commercial identity. You believe that commerce is essential to your life—and there are great business people in France—but you do not believe that it is sufficient to define who you are. That is your asset.

I have got news for you. In the next year or so, the European Union may take over the United States for the first time since the Second World War. We have not even thought about how we are going to respond to this. In our financial pages we are just beginning to say 'My God, the EU may be the number one economic power in the world in the next year'. This has not yet permeated into the general media. But does that mean that, with your new economic power, Europe will also be an intellectual and ideological power? It is my hope that here in Europe you can help lead a great debate, perhaps help steward America and other nations of the world into a debate on how we keep that delicate balance between culture and commerce, between deep play and deep work, between intrinsic and utility value. And if you can find the courage, the conviction, the will and the intellectual resolve to begin asking these tough questions on how to maintain this balance between globalization and the richness of cultural diversity, help us to find out how to re-empower community so that it is open and diverse and pluralistic and mosaic, then we may just have a shot at using this technology revolution, this new economic system, for a second renaissance, a leap forward in a legacy worthy of our children's generation.

Michel Serres

Is Culture Threatened?

The new technologies are older than we tend to think.[1] There are two kinds of technologies, as reflected in the French distinction between *techniques*—all of those devices employed by us as a species, from the nutcracker to the atom bomb—and *technologies*, by derivation from the English, referring to specifically informational techniques. The fact that the English word 'technology' covers both notions creates the false impression of a linear development from the 'hard' technologies (*techniques dures*) to the 'soft' technologies (*technologies douces*) that surround us today. This is simply not the case.

Soft technologies have evolved in step with human history and have even played a key role in the hominization process. Examples include the invention of writing, which is a technology involving informational or 'soft' energies, and the invention of printing, which is similarly a soft-energy technology. In the traditional economy, as Jeremy Rifkin has pointed out, hard technologies exploited hard energies.

But soft technologies already existed and had inaugurated the 'age of access'. Let us not forget that, while we ourselves have learned to write the languages familiar to us, over 950 in every 1,000 languages in the world still exist only as oral tradition. The peoples who speak them have not had access to writing. From the invention of printing onwards, access to reading, writing and libraries already involved soft energies. We should not therefore think in terms of a linear historical progression from hard to soft technologies. What we have is rather a dual history—that of soft energies, on the one hand, and hard energies, on the other.

---

1. This text, based on a presentation to the 17th session of the 'Twenty-First Century Talks' at UNESCO on 9 March 2001, was published in part in *Le Monde diplomatique* of September 2001.

The offence of simony

The soft technologies, which exploit soft energies and culture in particular, are expanding very rapidly. Now, within the European tradition, attitudes to the commercialization of culture were shaped by the canon-law concept of the *offence of simony*. This notion derives from the Acts of the Apostles and refers to Simon Magus, who sold consecrated objects or religious observances. Men of culture were thus in the habit of regarding someone who sold culture as 'simoniac'. This simoniac ideology has long protected us against the commercialization of culture. However, I was recently made brutally aware of the illusory nature of this sense of protection when I saw my image used against my will in a television advertisement. This act, which went against my convictions, could justifiably be described as 'simoniac'!

At this time of great change, we should try to weigh up our precise gains and losses. Are we putting culture at risk? Let us take two examples.

Our memory is becoming weaker from generation to generation. For by abandoning the oral tradition in favour of the written tradition, we are making less and less use of this mental capacity. In this way, contrary to what is thought, oral tradition is arguably more robust than written tradition. In our culture, memory is supposed to be subjective, a 'faculty of the soul' belonging to each individual. No one has identified the seat of memory in the human body. The vision I am proposing is different: with the invention of writing, memory was relieved of a certain burden, and writing became an object. Similarly, before the invention of the printing press, a cultivated man who wished to know Homer or Plutarch had to learn their texts by heart. Printing did away with that necessity and thereby freed up memory.

Montaigne's dictum 'a brain well formed rather than a brain well-filled' needs to be seen in this light. With the invention of writing, we have lost the power of memory. Memory has in this way become collective and objective, whereas we supposed it to be subjective and cognitive. This process is a constant feature of the process of hominization. We should not therefore fear this loss, since we gain by relieving ourselves of the crushing burden of remembering, enabling the 'well-formed brain' to devote itself to new activities, such as invention. The new technologies place at our disposal the memory of the world in its entirety.

The historian André Leroi-Gourhan described the process of hominization in this way: when man began to walk on two legs, he freed his forelimbs from the load-bearing function they had previously fulfilled. The hand was thus able to develop its prehensile capacity, and man became *homo faber*. However, at the same time as the hand acquired this prehensile faculty, the mouth ceased to fulfil that same function. The mouth was therefore able to speak... And if one were to set the acquisition of speech against the corresponding loss of the load-bearing function, there can be no doubt that the gain largely outweighs the loss. That is what is happening to us at present.

In this case, it is the human being, cognitively speaking, that is changing. But human beings have always changed in step with the development of soft technologies. This is particularly true in the scientific field. We certainly all have memories of lab work in secondary school involving experiments in which we had to make measurements, record them on a graph and derive a law from them. On the basis of a limited number of experiments and data, we were able in this way to arrive at major results. Newton's discovery of the law of universal gravity was likewise made on the basis of limited data and experimentation.

Today, technologies perform on our behalf, automatically and in real time, both the observations and the measurement of those observations, and then store the resulting data without any limit as to capacity. To such an extent that a current project is enlisting computer users the world over to link up nearly 2 million machines in order to process scientific data. We are therefore in the process of changing our scientific paradigm too: present-day science bears no resemblance to the science of only a few decades ago.

Three meanings of the word 'culture'

Culture is a word invented by Cicero, who declared that 'philosophy is the culture of the soul.' Culture as first defined thus formed part of a humanist vision, which the philosophers of the sixteenth century took up for their own purposes, initiating the tradition of the culture of the 'honnête homme'. The second sense of 'culture' is German. It was used for the first time by Kant, and then taken up by the Kulturkampf,[2] to designate all the acquired processes in a society. In this way, the breeding of pigs (*culture des cochons*) by the farmers of my childhood was part of the 'Gascon culture'. Yet this had very little in common with the dancers of the Opera, who rather come under the first definition of culture. I myself define culture as the path that leads from the pig to the Opéra, and back again. To my mind, then, a man who is refined in his artistic tastes but knows nothing about culture in the anthropological sense of the term is not cultivated, in the same way as the anthropologist who has no appreciation of artistic culture.

A third, more recent, definition is that of culture as a 'globalizable' commodity. Companies are already making huge profits by marketing cultural objets referring to human experience. The film *Titanic* is based on a universal maritime experience. *Vertical Limit* relates to a mountaineering

---

2. The 'struggle for culture' was the name given to the campaign conducted by Bismarck, from 1870 to 1885, against the Catholic Church.

experience that anyone could have had, even if we are in reality dealing with a dramatization or self-evident simulacrum of the experience in question.

One hears talk today of a battle between global culture, in the form of a globalized commodity, and local culture, in the anthropological sense of the term. Closing the frontiers in order to fend off the invasion of globalized culture would in my view be the most absurd way of dealing with the problem: this would be to condemn us to choose between Disneyland and the ayatollahs.

The cultural realm

How do we acquire a culture? Culture, in the anthropological sense, depends in the first instance on where we were born, on the language spoken by our parents and on a number of attitudes and customs handed down to us. But this is clearly not enough to make a cultivated person. Indeed, culture suffocates and dies when it is enclosed. It is the invention of a pathway that, from a given starting-point, takes us step by step from one neighbourhood to the next, on a journey that brings us into contact with cultures ever more distant from our own.

This pathway from one culture to another is strewn with obstacles, and it is difficult to meet with others, who are often different from what we thought. It does not always prove as easy as we imagine to familiarize ourselves with their language, customs and beliefs. We may nevertheless be charmed along the way and discover habits that are foreign to us. What is more beautiful than Brazilian craftwork or more extraordinary in some respects than the refinement of Japanese culture? Culture has no boundaries: it is porous. France was never so French as in the seventeenth century, despite the fact that Molière was strongly influenced by the Italians and Corneille by the Spanish.

The anticipated battle between the local and the global, that is to say, between culture designating the totality of acquired processes within a society and culture as commodity, reflects a profound misunderstanding of the nature of the cultural realm. Culture is not uniform but granular. It is complex, different for each person and composed of passages, obstacles, fords, passes and impenetrable mountain ranges... Above all, we all trace our own unique route within it and draw our own original map, which expresses the cultural singularity of each of us. Local cultures are in no way at risk—including from the Internet, which is also a granular and not a global domain.

Indeed, the use we make of these so-called global communication media, which are supposed to put us in touch immediately with any spot on the planet, is astonishingly local! Thus, contrary to received opinion, the mobile phone has strengthened family links. To be sure, they are also used for global communications. But it is precisely this combined local and global use of tools such as the mobile phone or the Internet that makes the domain in which they are used as crumpled, granular, obstacle-strewn and passage-riddled as the cultural realm. I have no fear on this score.

In some ways, 'true' culture is not in danger. There is, however, one point on which I would agree with Jeremy Rifkin: contrary to what Marx believed, culture is infrastructure. Europeans know that the Coal and Steel Community did not suffice to build Europe, for the economy is not the infrastructure. In truth, a European culture has existed since the Middle Ages. If it had been acknowledged at the time that culture was infrastructure, it would have been sufficient to set up the European University and to foster exchanges among young people and the shaping of a common culture through educational programmes. Europe would be speaking four languages, as is the case in Switzerland, and would be an accomplished fact!

But culture—if we really try to define it—designates in my view two things. In the first place, it is characterized by the process of acculturation, that is to say, the 'journey' from one neighbourhood to another that enables us to meet other people. Secondly, culture is based on a singular choice by the individual when he decides: no, I am not of that culture. We are living through a far-reaching transformation of our mental processes, of empirical science and of collective culture. It is this transformation that really makes me regret that I am no longer eighteen!

Cultural Globalization and the Preservation of Diversity

Does globalization necessarily lead to the imposition of a Western-oriented cultural model? Can this model be superimposed on plural identities? Is not the quest for meaning increasingly conducted at the individual level?

With reference to the example of Iran, Daryush Shayegan defines cultural modernity in terms of a cumulative and plural identity, at once reflexive and disenchanted, which far from being incompatible with other types of identity could play the role of a necessary universalist filter and pave the way for a 'tamed schizophrenia'. We are to this extent all Westerners.

Alain Touraine's point of departure is the observation of a growing split between an omnipresent instrumental world and an increasingly desocialized quest for self-consciousness, between a world devoid of content and a multitude of fragments of individual experience too readily termed 'culture'. Dissociating himself from the nostalgic advocates of totality and the apologists of pure movement who construct their discourse around postmodern disintegration, he defends the idea of a new individualism of rights in opposition to the social world of power.

* * * *

Daryush Shayegan is a philosopher, former director of the Iranian Centre for the Study of Civilizations and emeritus professor of Indian Studies and Comparative Philosophy at Teheran University. He is the author of *Qu'est-ce qu'une révolution religieuse?* (1991), *Le Regard mutilé* (1996) and *La Lumière vient de l'Occident* (2003).

Sociologist **Alain Touraine** is the founder of the Centre d'études des Mouvement Sociaux at the Paris Ecole des Hautes Etudes en Sciences Sociales (EHESS). A member of the Academy of Latinity and of the Academia Europea, he is the author of *Critique of Modernity* (1995), *Can We Live Together? Equality and Difference* (2000), *La recherche de soi* (2000) and *Beyond Neoliberalism* (2001).

Daryush Shayegan

A Tamed Schizophrenia?

Globalization and the new face of culture

It is hard to know what lies behind the term 'identity'. In the past, ethnic, national and religious identities were rooted in cultures that each possessed its own history. Today's world bears little relation to that discovered by Marco Polo in the thirteenth century when he travelled through Asia over the Silk Road. Worlds were worlds apart then: the Islamic, Indian and Chinese cultures were ethnocentric and self-contained entities. The coming of modernity shattered this cultural egocentricity. Today, these exclusive cultural identities are strung between the 'not yet' and the 'no longer', i.e., not yet modern and no longer traditional. The identities that inhabit this half-way house are totally fractured.

Samuel Huntington's 'war of cultures' is therefore paradoxical: for the paradigm, the dominant *episteme*, is that of a universal culture. All other cultures, or existential territories, create climates of being within the overall framework of modernity, remaining very rich in anthropological terms (sense of togetherness, close communication links, human warmth, etc.). The vestiges of these ancient cultures are a kind of opening onto 'the other side of the looking-glass'. Their survival is all the more interesting since all the great ontologies have today collapsed.

Globalization designates the omnipresent planetary culture. Whatever its basic premise, this new vision of the world always remains indifferent to ends. This global and somewhat anaemic culture functions on the basis of exclusively economic criteria. In so doing, it always remains operational, if only at the level of laws, institutions, *habeas corpus*, and so on. It serves as a vehicle for certain universal values, which we must accept irrespective of our individual culture. This disenchanted vision is a kind of universal cement or magnetic field within which all other modes of discourse (religious, communitarian, nationalist, etc.) can coexist without coming into direct conflict or degenerating into inter-ethnic disputes.

This globalized culture thus serves as a filter: it defuses the explosive charge of the most violent elements and 'de-ideologizes' them. Its rules of the game are very important: by rejecting them we should become embroiled in an endless inter-ethnic war, since all cultures are in essence ethnocentric. This is why the universalist discourse is necessary, particularly since we live in an ambivalent world. The proliferation of sects of all kinds is testimony to the frantic quest for a new form of transcendence. At the same time, the ties of gravity liberate unreason, consumerism and infantilism.

The empty wasteland of our existence is thus the setting for a desperate search for the absolute. Alongside the stupefying effects of the media, we witness the emergence of new modes of being attendant upon virtualization. Disenchantment is paralleled by the re-enchantment of the world through a kind of technological animism. We have entered what may be termed a 'post-era' (post-globalism, post-feminism, post-colonialism, etc.).

But here we come up against a paradox: any enrichment of the soul can only take place within a civil society conforming to the dictates of reason. To be spiritual, one has to live in a secularized environment. As Kant says in his *Critique of Pure Reason*, the two evils that threaten us are the 'sanctity of the sacred and the majesty of power'.

Interconnectivity

We live in a world of fragmented ontology, in which there is no longer any absolute truth, particularly a rational one. The critique of modernity by Nietzsche and Heidegger, which proclaims the end of metaphysics, leads to the 'weak ontology' of the Italian philosopher Gianni Vattimo, in which the main structures of the sacred have been dissolved. The consequence of this fragmentation is interconnectivity, in the broad sense of the term. Many authors have explored this notion, including Edouard Glissant through the concept of 'relational thought' and Gilles Deleuze with his 'rhizomatic relationships'. This interconnectivity is reflected at all levels of reality. In the cultural sphere, it manifests itself in a tangled web of relationships, in a configuration of mosaics in which all cultures interpenetrate and mingle at their borders. In the realm of knowledge, interconnectivity is apparent in the myriad ways whereby we interpret the world in keeping with our subjective values. This leads to a conflict of interpretations, which are all equally valid in their own domain. With the devaluation of the great metaphysical truths on which the old ontologies were based, every individual is now free to interpret the world as he or she wishes. In terms of identities, this interconnectivity is reflected in the Harlequin phenomenon: a single identity is no longer sufficient to meet all my needs; I move from one culture to another; I am a migrant at the interstices of cultures. In the media universe, it gives rise to networks and virtualization, which is weaving a worldwide web of interconnectivity. The instantaneity, immediacy and ubiquity characteristic of this interconnected world manifests itself cognitively not only in the contraction of time and space but also in synaesthesia of the senses. These all become interactive, as Marshall MacLuhan noted when he declared that the tyranny of the eye had given way to that of the other senses. Multisense perceptions today create a two-dimensional dynamic.

All of these developments correspond to a rejection of monolithic structures of belief, fundamental building blocks of matter and arborescent systems of thought. The stress is rather on nomadic thinking, empathetic modes of relation and cross-fertilization.

We are currently seeing a reaction to this 'Technicolor' globalization in the resurgence of extreme forms of nationalism, the old demons of the tribe and inflexible cultural allegiances. Yet, despite this resistance, the phenomenon of globalization is today irreversible and rearguard actions cannot block its progress. The fascination currently exerted by Buddhism is linked to this phenomenon: it is the only religion in the world that does not accept the idea of being or of divinity. Buddhism, a religion with a fragmented ontology, offers a cinematographic vision of the world, proposes an interdependent causality. These traits establish a link between this religion and the laws of the new science, notably quantum mechanics. This is no doubt why many scientists compare Buddhism and the new concepts in physics, which both embody the notions of dispersal of being and *quanta* of existence. There is no more being: it is the succession of instants that creates the appearance of duration.

It should be added that Buddhism today provides a coherent explanation of the absurdity of the world, while pointing the path to salvation divorced from any divinity, in particular the god of the tribe.

This interconnectivity creates an area of hybridization, as shown by the example of the United States examined from the standpoint of multiculturalism. In this country, people speak of *border identities* and *border passers* to designate those who cross the divides between these cultures, complete with hybrid consciousness. On a visit to Venice Beach in Los Angeles, in the space of a few kilometres I encountered a succession of shops encompassing a wide cultural spectrum: American Indian shamanistic rituals, the tarot, yoga positions, Chinese culture, Japanese massage, virtual reality technologies, etc. To walk along this beach is to see set out before you all states of consciousness from the Neolithic to the computer age, juxtaposed as though in a vast movement of recapitulation.

Thus the disappearance of the dominant mode of thought has engendered multiculturalism. Following the age of ideologies, everybody is free to have their say. Repressed levels of awareness resurface: the shaman next door lives alongside the technocrat. Of course, this proximity does not resolve the question of communication and understanding between minds that are not historically contemporaneous. How can these historical and epistemic divides be bridged?

In the end, we have all become 'bricoleurs'—do-it-yourself creators of composite cultures. Forty years ago one of Jung's disciples wrote: 'Modern art is situated between chaos and the archetype.'[1] Today, the Tibetan shaman has acquired the same dignity for us as Moses and the Buddha. An Aztec fresco has its place alongside a Chinese landscape or an Egyptian sculpture. Yet this do-it-yourself approach can also be dangerously ideological, as we can see in the Third World. In Iran, the most striking example is that of Chariati: this dabbler in ideas exploits the emotionally explosive potential of religion by casting it in a Marxist-Leninist mould. In so doing, he constructs explosive cocktails, ideological monstrosities.

The best known example is that of the Iranian Revolution, in which a religion seized power by overthrowing an imperial order that had lasted for 2,500 years. At the time, this revolution brought about a massive secularization of Islam, dragged religion into dangerous adventures, de-symbolized its spiritual content, and caused it to undergo, unopposed, a process of ideological radicalization. The entry of religion into the arena of history thereby led it to ideologization.

Apart from the revival of religion, the attraction of magic and the irrational are omnipresent phenomena. The modern individual seems haunted by the irrational in all its forms, which several centuries of secularization had confined to the oubliettes of history. He or she is interested in astrology and reincarnation and speaks of his or her former lives as if they were old acquaintances!

In recent decades, we have witnessed a dramatic rise of major sects: the Church of Scientology, the Moon Unification Church, Jehovah's Witnesses, New Acropolis, devotees of Krishna and New Age followers. Jacques Guyard's report on religious sects in France divides the movements concerned into thirteen groups: the healers, the orientalists, the apocalyptics, the psychoanalytic fraternity, the Satanists, etc. This unprecedented growth of sects in Western culture clearly reflects a malaise, which Christianity—too secularized for these spiritual castaways—cannot resolve.

Mention should also be made of the American religious challenge, referred to by Guy Sorman in *Le monde est ma tribu*[2] and by Harold Bloom in *The American Religion*.[3] It would seem that the United States is today entering a post-Christian era. This religion seems to focus on the forty days separating the resurrection of Christ from his ascension. It is thus markedly Gnostic in form. Combining the world of *high tech* with the

---

1. In Erich Neumann, 'Kunst und Zeit', in *Eranos Jahrbuch*, Zurich, Rhein-Verlag, 1951.
2. Guy Sorman, *Le monde est ma tribu*, Paris, Fayard, 1997.
3. Harold Bloom, *The American Religion: The Emergence of the Post-Christian Nation*, New York, Simon & Schuster, 1992.

star system and tele-evangelism, this religion manages to rally the masses worldwide, in Latin America as in Africa and Europe.

Cultural diversity

It is no longer possible to possess a single identity. A modern identity is today cumulative of many identities that we trail about with us; all beings, whatever their origins, possess a modern identity to the extent that they live in their time. This is the only identity capable of dividing, polarizing and scrutinizing itself from the outside, unlike those belonging to a closed world. This modern identity is capable of reflective awareness: it alone, being endowed with a critical faculty, is able to call everything into question. Paradoxically, it can activate the most archaic levels of consciousness, allow them scope for self-expression, further a multiplicity of interconnections and forge connections between worlds belonging to different ages. For example, every Iranian today possesses three identities: a pre-Islamic identity reaching back to the Iran of the King of Kings and crystallized in the Book of Kings; a relatively recent Islamic identity (1400 years old), which has integrated most of the myths of ancient Iran and shows how far Iranian Shiism has assimilated messianic ideas, such being the ease with which symbols move from one culture to another without passing through the realm of hybridization or the mediation of a meta-historical dialogue; and, finally, a modern identity.

Between these three identities, massive divides remain. However, by becoming aware of these divides and articulating these three levels of awareness, we become much richer than if we lived within the confines of a single culture. We become amphibious beings, living at once on land and in the water.

We currently find ourselves at the intersection of several epistemological fields. Doubly open-ended, we are at one and the same time a project directed towards the archaeological past of our knowledge (tradition) and the telos of our future. This combinatory art of reordering heterogeneous spaces and identities constitutes the 'third way'. It eschews likewise the reductionism of monolithic knowledge and the illusions of unattainable utopias.

It is perhaps the only viable option—that of a 'controlled schizophrenia' or, in Diderot's apt phrase, the option that enables you 'to speak with twenty mouths at the same time'.

Alain Touraine

Reconstructing Culture

My starting point in this purely problematic debate would be the profound conviction that there is no such thing as global society, culture or politics. We should therefore place the focus on the destruction of traditions, hegemonies and forms of social domination, taking as our point of departure the divorce between a modern tradition and certain civilizations, and between a form of rationalization and certain cultures. I should like to begin by applying this idea to the part of the world that invented modernity—the West. What is the explanation for the West's spectacular advance over a period of four to six centuries, enabling it to acquire overwhelming power?

The economic and cultural hegemony of the West

The West is the only part of the world whose history is predicated on discontinuities. Culturally speaking, the defining characteristic of the West is its acceptance of a total separation between the worlds of instrumentality and self-consciousness. More simply, the West is premised on the death of religion. In social terms too, the West has been a world of total discontinuity. The central principle that has shaped the social categories of thought and action is that of polarization—the opposition of positive and negative, of reason and unreason, of man and woman, of capitalist and worker, of colonizer and colonized, etc.

The West and modernity are defined in terms of this dual discontinuity: they do not have an ideal paradigm of the just society or of the end of history. On the way, some politicians and intellectuals have imagined a wholly modernized society, recovering its breath following a frantic chase. Today, the chase continues and the thinkers concerned are only names from the past.

Leaving aside nostalgic dreams of totality and apologies of pure movement, the problem common to Daryush Shayegan's vision of the world and my own definition of the West as discontinuity can be summed up in the following question. Can we imagine or achieve a certain recombination and integration of elements that have become dissociated, namely the inwardness of a civilization and the externality of an economy, the world of instrumental rationality and that of personal experience, whether individual or collective? In short, the main question is, can we point to any specific attempts to effect reconstructions of this kind? Have they come to anything? Will they do so? Can we conceive of a renaissance of the ideas of civilization, of society and *a fortiori* of religion? Or should we recognize that they will never return, that the direction in which the world is moving runs counter to any effort to revive what has been destroyed?

An irreversible break with the past

In the West, following the momentous break with the past represented by capitalism (i.e., the end of the 'political illusions' that Marx accused the French of harbouring), and following the end of the idea of the state when economics broke free of politics, the nineteenth century witnessed a tremendous effort of reconstruction. In England and Germany, and then half a century later in America and France, the highly novel notion of 'social rights' made its appearance, linking particular social situations with the concept of universal rights and citizenship. This idea was to come to the fore again in the concept of industrial democracy. And today we are similarly seeing the emergence of the notion of 'cultural rights'.

The same period was the setting for attempts at economic modernization on the part of non-Western countries. The first examples, Germany and Japan, departed from the main Dutch and English model, complemented by the French political model. Gradually, all countries attempted to build a modern economy, adopting different patterns (Soviet, Mexican, Egyptian, etc.) but invariably including substantial cultural components.

It is difficult to avoid the conclusion that these attempts, despite their positive outcomes in all parts of the world, have failed. Today, the overriding impression is one of a total separation between an omnipresent instrumental world and highly desocialized quests for self-awareness. In our world, there no longer exists anything that can be called 'society': what one finds are juxtapositions of endlessly fragmented experiences unreflectingly called 'cultures' and an juggernaut world embodying no particular content apart from commercially exploitable needs. In today's world, there are no grounds in my view for arguing that we are witnessing a recomposition of civilizations, their break-up being implicit in their modernity. The West's dual rupture with the past is irreversible. Nothing points to the formation of a new global system. At a time when the European countries such as Germany or France are typically falling behind while they debate their models and forms of organization, a country such as the United States is today the striking example of the juxtaposition of a globalized economy and fragmented identities. There is no common measure between this global economy, which has its own criteria of judgement and evaluation, and the definitions of self, or indeed of interactions with other people. A series of groups of individuals seek their identity or identities—that is to say, an inner definition—in a world defined solely in external terms. Everywhere, we encounter the search for purity and homogeneity, not to say the reduction of civilized conduct to the law of the market or of war.

We are thus living in a situation of desocialization, the abandonment even of any attempt to reintegrate social, economic, political and cultural activities. The crisis of the nation-state is part of a much more general phenomenon. The re-emergence of 'religions', for example, tends to take the most caricatural of forms: while religious awareness is more present than ever, churches (religious, political, or other varieties) are in irreversible decline.

Postmodernity or reconstruction?

The absolute, postmodern break-up of reality is not acceptable. Even if it is inevitable, to accept such an outcome would be to abandon the world to the violence of power, weapons and money. It is not possible to will the reconstruction of the world while affirming the total absence of a link between the different sectors of human experience.

Having effectively abandoned the search for social construction, progress and a universal civilization, we are all in different but complementary ways engaged in the same operation: the more modernity has detached us from systems, orders, societies and even universes, the more we acquire the ability to define ourselves in terms of that distance from ourselves produced by the artificiality and growing reflexivity of the world we live in. This is not a matter of 'modernity', which manifests itself in the break-up of the world and a rupture with the religious order. However, in 'modernity within modernity', in the heightened consciousness of modernity, in 'reflexivity in modernity', we feel the need to define ourselves non-socially. It is the nub of our experiences and aspirations: the main problem for all of us is the reorganization of religious inheritances, body management (life, death, sexuality, etc.) and our relationship with objects, in the form of an opposition to the worlds of instrumentality and new communitarianisms, which sacrifice the individual to a false collectivity. In other words, the question is whether it is possible to create an individualism that combats consumerist individualism, while spilling over into the political, social and economic spheres through the simultaneous agency of memory, reflection and sexuality.

The need, then, is to forge a grand alliance of all that is not social, given that the social has become the virtual preserve of power. This is why notions such as 'globalization', to the extent that they are powerful ideologies, point to the road not to take. We have a tendency to combat globalization in order to defend a local dimension; some optimists are already predicting the emergence of 'glocalization'. They are wrong: the global and the local are increasingly at odds. On the other hand, there is no reason to think that we cannot live, as in the last century, in a world in which the scope of human rights continues to expand at the expense of power. This construction of individualism can only take place if all are involved together: individualism, far from being a slave of economic success, must mobilize all memories and all forms of reflection and sexuality to oppose this multiform world of power.

The fundamental conflict on which everything turns has to do with the shaping of a vision—that of a cultural, social and political universe that is *feminine* in character, in opposition to the vacuous universe of power. The resexualization process is today being accomplished by women or with reference to women, but also with reference to a whole segment of cultural memory—that of continuity and the mother figure—as distinct from the search for the authority of the father. While the destruction process to which all societies, cultures and civilizations are subject is irreversible, this does not herald the triumph of a Western-type rationalism. We are moving rather towards a unification, integration and even 'recomposition' (to borrow the expression of Marcel Mauss) of all the experiences that go to make up an individual and develop the capacity to act autonomously and consequently to combat this impersonal, collective and calculating world representing the world of power in all its aspects.

As a Westerner, while I totally accept the West's discontinuities and its corresponding vocabulary (conflict, confrontation, investment, class struggle, etc.), I believe in the multiplicity of modes of *development*. Admittedly, we are today witnessing the establishment of a globalized capitalism and technologies. Yet, while nurturing no illusions about the 'dialogue of cultures', we can believe in the possibility of reshaping the conditions of individual existence, work, initiatives, suffering and happiness. In other words, the enemy is the social. From now on, we shall try to live outside this social realm, its rules of organization, its standards of judgement, and so on. In this way, we shall seek to develop the capacity to communicate with other parts of the world, other ways of thinking, other forms of reasoning and other kinds of experience, which no longer form civilizations but which provide us with the elements to reconstruct and manage the dimensions of the human individual, unified in the task of resisting a world without meaning, the world of instrumentality, profit, war and violence. Failing this flight from the social, the world of power threatens to dominate us.

The Future of Languages

It is in the nature of languages to be born, to live and to die. However, it would seem that at least half of the languages spoken throughout the world are fated to disappear in the course of the twenty-first century. Is humanity moving inescapably towards a form of linguistic hegemony? Despite this accelerated decline of languages, can we discern a process whereby new languages are being created?

We need to consider the context and the reasons that lead people to abandon their language. Salikoko Mufwene believes that globalization is not an adequate explanation. Adopting an ecological and a historical approach to the different types of colonization and their varied effects on languages, he highlights a complex situation in which prestige languages do not always impose themselves and sometimes allow scope for the development of lingua francas. Thus, the effects of linguistic hegemony, which are at the origin of the disappearance of a great many languages, are not always predictable.

Do languages behave like living species? Claude Hagège reveals the limits of the vitalist metaphor in linguistics: for languages are capable of being resurrected precisely because they are language as well as speech. Creolization is today proving the main factor in the (re)birth of languages.

* * * *

Born in Congo, **Salikoko S. Mufwene** is professor of linguistics at the University of Chicago, vice-president of the Society for Caribbean Linguistics and a member of the Conseil International Francophone des Langues. He is internationally renowned for his work, which is focused in particular on the phenomenon of creolization. His publications include *The Ecology of Language Evolution* (2001).

A doctor of linguistics, **Claude Hagège** is professor of linguistic theory at the Collège de France. Awarded the CNRS gold medal in 1995 for his scholarly achievements, he is also known to the general public for his essays restoring to linguistics its social and human dimension. His publications include *L'Homme de parole* (1985), *Le Français et les siècles* (1987), *Le Souffle de la langue* (1992) and *Halte à la mort des langues* (2000).

Salikoko S. Mufwene

Colonization, Globalization and the Future of Languages

I employ the term 'colonization' less with politics in mind than with reference to population genetics. In other words, colonization is here understood in terms of the displacement of part of a population from its country of origin to a new ecological setting. Analysis of the colonization process from this standpoint raises two particularly interesting questions: what effect does this change of ecology have on the immigrant population, and how is the 'host' ecology affected by the arrival of these new inhabitants?

The colonial phenomenon is often analysed in strictly political terms, as a process whereby one people exerts its domination over another. In my view, the political dimension is only an extension, a partial aspect, of the phenomenon of colonization as viewed from the standpoint of population genetics. Colonization, in the ecological sense, is clearly one of the factors responsible for the disappearance of certain languages and for the threats hanging over others. However, to say this is not to exhaust the subject, and we need to consider whether colonization operates in the same way worldwide.

Three types of colonization

I believe that a distinction needs to be made between three types of colonization inasmuch as they did not produce identical linguistic effects: settler colonization—like that of the New World by Europe; exploitative colonization—as experienced by Africa, particularly from the end of the nineteenth century and once again at the hands of Europe; and colonization linked to the slave trade—as manifest in the relations between

Europe and Africa from the sixteenth century onwards and characterized, politically speaking at least, by a relatively equal relationship, even if the balance subsequently swung in favour of Europe.

Colonization through the slave trade

Colonization linked to the slave trade did not have the effect of endangering languages, except insofar as it involved the deportation of those taken into slavery to other parts of the world. The African slave trade was not focused on a particular ethnic group and did not therefore lead to the extermination of entire peoples and, with them, the speakers of African languages on that continent. On the contrary, this type of colonization was accompanied by the emergence of new languages in Africa, in the form of pidgin tongues.

Settler colonization

In contrast, settler colonization of the kind that took place in the Americas and subsequently in Australia and New Zealand, which set out to reconstitute a new Europe and a new homeland for the settlers, saw the emergence of new varieties of European languages, such as the new forms of Portuguese and Spanish that developed in the Americas, Quebec French and American and Australian English.

The phenomenon of settler colonization also had the effect of placing the different European languages in competition. English, for example, was not the only language exported to the United States, having been confronted by French, Swedish and German. But these European languages gradually gave way to the new form of English that is spoken today in the United States

Similarly, the African languages that arrived in the Americas with the slaves have all disappeared. Currently we are witnessing the progressive disappearance of the Amerindian languages, in the same way as happened in the past with the African languages and the minority European languages. To understand why this phenomenon is occurring today, we need to set it in the context of the mechanics of settler colonization and to analyse it in the light of the socioeconomic evolution of American societies. Initially, the Amerindians were not integrated in the economic and political systems of the Americas and their marginalization favoured the survival of their languages. However, the more the process of integration progresses, the more minority languages are at risk. The link with the mother tongue is lost as speakers adopt colonial languages as new vernaculars. During periods of peace, minority languages are particularly threatened because of integration processes. Conversely, wars enable languages to maintain their autonomy and survive, provided that they do not result in the extermination of a whole people.

Thus the minority European languages have disappeared in United States territory because integration processes have functioned perfectly. As for the Africans, they lost their languages, despite racial segregation, because they were treated like cogs in the economic system. Apart from the integration of slaves into the economic system, the disappearance of their mother tongues was also a consequence of their multilingualism.

The linguistic process at work in the settler colonies can be analysed in the light of European history. A grasp of that history could possibly give us a better insight into the challenges and developments likely to arise in the future. Indeed, the history of the Old Continent is like a palimpsest of colonial phenomena and migrations. André Martinet's study *Des Steppes aux Océans*, published in 1986, retraces the history of the Indo-European languages, closely bound up with that of population movements and the domination of peoples over others. The imposition of the language of the dominant group is indeed a major vector of domination. In this way, the Celtic languages have disappeared from the territory that is today France, replaced by a Latin language, and survive only as traces, such as Breton, itself extremely threatened. It is generally overlooked that the Celtic languages once reigned supreme in the British Isles. In the fifth century, colonization by Germanic peoples resulted in the restructuring of their languages in the form of a new language, English, and in the progressive ascendancy of the latter over the Celtic languages.

Exploitative colonization

From a prospectivist standpoint, the problem of the future of languages in the Americas or Australia should not be taken as the model for analysing the problem in Africa. Since the nineteenth century, Africa, like much of Asia, has been subject to exploitative colonization. In this type of colony, the Europeans did not seek to constitute a new homeland but simply to establish economic bases and to develop new markets in the service of the metropolis. The social structure was in no way integrative, and the colonizers had no particular interest in imposing their language as the vernacular. However, they needed to enlist the help of African administrative assistants, who were taught European languages so that these gradually became the languages of the elite on the African continent and in certain parts of Asia.

As the privileged vehicles of the elite, European languages do not represent a real threat to African languages. The real danger comes rather from certain African languages themselves. Colonization was accompanied by the development of new languages such as *Lingala, Kikongo, Wolof* and *Swahili*; and these languages, initially lingua francas, progressively became vernacular in the great African cities. The prestige of the African metropolises has created a dynamic that is endangering ethnic languages and, in some cases even, the colonial languages such as English and French. It should however be specified that the threats to the colonial languages and the ethnic languages are not of the same nature, since in one case the language as such is not in jeopardy. The only threat is to its hegemonic and imperial claims over a territory that is not its own and over peoples whose mother tongue it is not.

The disappearance of languages

How may the present-day process of the disappearance of languages be understood? Too often, the scholarly literature treats languages as if they lead an existence independent of their speakers. I believe that we need to start thinking about the competition between languages and the dangers that arise not so much from direct conflicts between languages but from the behaviour of their speakers. We must ask ourselves why peoples attached to their languages and proud of their identity and their culture would risk giving up their mother tongue. We also need to reflect on the nature of languages and cultures: are they static notions or, on the contrary, dynamic processes? When a population abandons its language, does this automatically mean that it gives up its culture?

To explain the current loss of linguistic diversity, reference is frequently made to the globalization of the economy, which is said to lead some people to give up their language. This explanation seems to me rather simplistic, as a recent visit I made to Jamaica tended to bear out. English Creole has begun to flourish there with unprecedented vigour, whereas twenty years ago everyone was predicting its demise. In this Third World country where a large proportion of the population is facing unemployment, and in the ideological context of the promotion of a specific Jamaican identity, adherence to the ideology of the exploited class is accompanied by the rejection of the language considered prestigious and the adoption of the Creole language. The similarity of this phenomenon with other processes of this type in Africa is obvious: for example, the speakers of *Lingala* in Kinshasa frequently define their identity in opposition to the French speakers. As the gap grows between rich and poor countries, between the well-off and the exploited classes, the rejection of the prestige language by the 'oppressed' grows more marked and attests to a process of national- or social-identity building in opposition to the hegemonic model.

The choice by a population to abandon its language for another can thus be the result of very diverse and complex factors. In my view, the scholarly literature is mistaken when it claims that the prestige language will always prevail in the end. The fact is that its hegemony is likely to be challenged when it is perceived as an enemy. To grasp the linguistic processes under way, it is therefore necessary to abandon a specifically Western viewpoint and focus on the dynamics of the coexistence of languages in non-Western societies, analysing these issues in the light of the economic ecology specific to each country.

If globalization is a reality in France, Great Britain and the United States, it is not so in Jamaica, any more than in the Dominican Republic, Congo or Senegal. The following example seems to me particularly emblematic: the terrorist attacks that occurred in the United States on 11 September led to the suspension of aircraft flights in Europe and the United States, but they in no way affected African airports. It is worth noting, moreover, that the terms '*mondialisation*', adopted by the French, and 'globalization', favoured by the Anglo-Saxons, do not have the same meaning. The first applies to a process of universalization, whereas the second refers to a situation in which different elements in a very complex system are interconnected and interact. The world is not organized in a uniform way at the economic level. This divergence between the globalized and non-globalized world gives rise to a range of linguistic issues. In my view, the use of a language is always the result of a self-interested choice: people decide to speak a language because it is useful to them. The question we have to ask is the following: do speakers give up their mother tongue because it is less beautiful or less expressive or, on the contrary, because they are obliged to do so by economic circumstances that require them to adapt to the ecological changes taking place in the territory in which they live?

The problem of endangered languages thus shows itself to be more complex than at first sight, and it is impossible to comprehend it without taking account of the economic changes taking place within our societies and the way(s) in which they affect the speakers of the different languages.

Claude Hagège

The Life, Death and Resurrection of Languages

I should like to reflect on the comparison that is sometimes made between languages and living species. My position coincides to some extent with that of Salikoko Mufwene, since he is strongly in favour of an ecological view of languages that takes account of the social, cultural and political environment. However, I maintain that languages can be studied as biological entities only in metaphorical terms: it is true that languages are born, live and—unfortunately—die, but it is equally true that they can be revived.

The fact that languages regarded as dead can be resurrected points to a radical difference between languages and living species. While languages have many properties in common with living species, they are not fated to die, body and soul, in an irrevocable manner. Obviously, the circumstances required for a language to be resurrected are highly special and are very rarely met in full, but examples do exist.

The reason why the vitalist metaphors very much in vogue in the nineteenth century were so popular among the researchers of the period was precisely because languages were found to have properties that related them very closely to the living world as studied by biology, zoology, botany or, more broadly, the life sciences. What is involved in each case is the *struggle for life*. Darwin's concept needs to be set within and adapted to a linguistic context. The most resilient languages, those spoken by communities that are more powerful, more dominating and better able to fend for themselves, are the ones that sustain themselves at the expense of the more fragile languages. Languages are less prone to die when they have been successful in propagating themselves during their period of maximum vitality in relation to other more vulnerable or exposed languages.

Language ability as specific to the human species

While languages are similar to living species with regard to the struggle for life, they are very different in the way they evolve and in the way language families are constituted. They are as it were living species in the service of the societies that have 'created' them. The term may seem inappropriate since languages may be regarded as coeval with the human species, so that to speak in terms of the creation of languages is either purely metaphorical or wholly misleading. In reality, human societies have fashioned languages as means of communication but they have not created language, which is coeval with them and is written into the human genetic code. The distinction between 'language' (as a faculty) and 'languages' (as means of communication) is important and must be upheld. Together, they define us as a species. It is perhaps our sole defining characteristic, given that no animal species possesses language, as expressed in the historically and socially localized instruments called languages. Thus, neither languages nor language are written into the genetic code of any other species than our own.

In other words, I believe it is arguable—despite the increasing scientific uncertainty in this domain—that the human species, when it emerged some 2.2 million years ago (give or take some tens or hundreds of thousands of years), had language ability written into its genetic code. Of course, the volume of the cranium and brain were to increase considerably, further singularizing our species. However the transition between ourselves and our earliest human ancestors, themselves no longer ape-like anthropoids but tall and already human hominids, would appear from a distance to be sudden, even if it extended over a considerable period of time. The difference between the two species, which are very similar in terms of their morphology, has to do with the fact that only the second has language ability written into its genetic code, as well as with a series of mutations extending over very long periods. That does not however mean that the human species possessed languages immediately.

For reasons linked to the history of this first human species (which, until such time as we discover even older ancestors in Australia, New Guinea or elsewhere, may be said to have had its birthplace in Africa), we are African in origin. The Horn of Africa constituted, 2.2 million years ago, an ecological niche favourable to the emergence of a new species. This new species was born in a very special and very precarious environment—a tree-covered, game-rich savannah replete with water sources favourable to life, but subject to a series of dry and wet cycles. My hypothesis is that the recently emerged species was obliged to migrate tens of thousands of kilometres to avoid perishing for lack of food and water. This is no doubt why *homo pekinensis* developed a series of so-called 'flaked stone' cultures, displaying many similarities with those of the African birthplace.

Languages, as means of communication, are made possible by the inscription of language in the genetic code of humanity. However, they are not immediately indispensable and so did not necessarily come into being at the same time as humanity. In other words, the nomadic wanderings and great migrations dictated by the need to survive took place at a time when the species, although 'finished' since it possessed language ability, did not yet have languages as we define them today.

The proliferation of languages

The birth of languages extended over considerable periods of time. There followed a whole series of increasingly broad expansions. I believe that in an age relatively very close to us—the Neolithic (from 20,000 to 12,000 BC)—languages experienced an accelerated growth in the same way as societies, which themselves proliferated as human beings became sedentary, relinquishing a precarious and nomadic pastoral way of life entirely taken up with finding water for their herds. This period saw the appearance of the first embryonic towns: Jericho is described in the Bible as the first town in world history, but it was certainly preceded by others. With towns came the possibility of owning and cultivating fields. The humorist Alphonse Allais was right when he quipped: 'Towns should be built in the countryside.' Towns cannot be built anywhere but in the countryside, even if town life subsequently appears—largely artificially—radically different from rural life. While I cannot produce any real evidence for the hypothesis, I believe then that the Neolithic was a period strongly marked by the proliferation of languages.

The death of languages

Death by physical extinction

Let us now take a leap across the millennia and consider a period much closer to our own—the Renaissance, which marked the start of the colonial era. The wars of religion were transposed to the Americas and, in almost identical terms, to certain parts of South-East Asia with the arrival of mainly Spanish and Portuguese navigators, followed by the British, French and Dutch intent on setting up trading posts. The coming of the colonial era was accompanied by massacres carried out on such a scale and with such ruthless efficiency that the early decades of the sixteenth century—ironically called the Renaissance from the perspective of Western European cultures—may be seen as marking the start of a mass death for human languages.

Consider for example the case of Mexico, or New Spain as it was baptized by the Crown of Castile. In the space of a century, the thousands of languages existing in the Pre-Columbian era were reduced to just a few dozen by the 'epic' of the *conquistadores*. The problem in present-day Mexico of the survival of Nahuatl, of the Oto-Manguean languages of the central Mexican plateau or of the score or so Mayan languages bears no comparison with the loss of linguistic diversity in the sixteenth century as a result of the violent and massive incursions of the West in these 'new' countries.

In these circumstances, languages began to die in large numbers. Physical extinction through extermination was the result of other causes. Apart from the very heavy responsibility of the West, natural catastrophes wiped whole—or virtually whole—populations from the face of the globe, resulting in the extinction of languages through the extinction of its speakers. The Russians speak of the bearers, '*nositeli*', of a language; and one can indeed be said to 'bear' a language, like a treasure or an enigmatic beauty that enables you to communicate, to converse with your fellow beings and possibly to love them. So that when these people cease to live, they also cease to be the 'bearers' of their language. However, examples of the extinction of languages through natural catastrophes are ultimately restricted in number. The case of Salvador is often quoted. In the 1930s, a volcano eruption accompanied by an earthquake led to an Indian tribe in that country being almost totally wiped out. This said, other causes of language extinction are much more pernicious and formidable than the physical extinction of its speakers. What are these causes?

The imposition of a foreign model

One of the main threats to languages comes from acculturation, as the West conceives it, i.e., from contact between the intruding cultures and local cultures. I am not thinking only of the case of the Americas, but also of Australia and part at least of Africa. As pointed out by Salikoko Mufwene, African languages have resisted much better because that continent was lucky enough to escape the kind of colonization to which America, Australia and a part of South-East Asia were subject.

The intrusion of foreign models invites a comparison between old and new modes of life. The latter start out by being rejected, of course, but gradually come to be seen as worth imitating because they give the appearance of being more efficient and are felt to hold out the prospect of greater well-being. Imitation, here as elsewhere, is a key factor in the development of human societies. If he has the opportunity to observe sedentary communities, particularly foreign ones possessing military and economic power and the appearance of an efficient administrative and commercial system, a nomad living in poverty may be tempted to imitate this model, if not in his own generation at least through his children. It is precisely for this reason that traditional forms of education tend to be abandoned within human groups.

This phenomenon has been observed in Australia, Canada and the United States. In all these cases, the White population has gone much further than simply proposing or imposing a model: we are familiar with the story of those children snatched from their villages and forcibly enrolled in prison-type boarding establishments where they were strictly forbidden to use their native language. When the vernacular language has been demonized, the child who spoke it in his native village, and who has been made to feel ashamed of it in a thousand different ways, returns home as the vector of the new language, that of the foreigner, of the White Man, of the colonizer, of the one who came uninvited. This is the story of the extinction of many languages. In quoting the examples of Canada, Australia and the United States, I make no claim to be exhaustive.

At the Sydney 2000 Olympics, many Australian aborigines demonstrated in an effort to persuade the government to officially recognize the acts committed against their ancestors' children. Among the many demands made, I was particularly struck by their call for recognition of the fact that aborigine children, today English-speaking, had been snatched from their native environment. This had contributed to the extinction of linguistic diversity on this continent. Before the advent of Western culture, there were perhaps between 40,000 and 50,000 aborigine languages. Today, there remain no more than a few hundred, if not a few dozen. The most plausible estimate of the number of surviving languages is 200 or 300, all of them in a precarious situation and most of them on the way to extinction.

A failure of transmission

The mass death of languages has resulted not only from the imposition of foreign models but also from the imposition of domestic models. In a country such as Tanzania, the languages of the nomadic populations, the tribal languages, are seriously threatened by Swahili, which is promoted as the official national language and enjoys huge prestige. In these circumstances, regional languages are undoubtedly better equipped than tribal languages spoken by declining numbers of tribes pursuing a nomadic existence with their meagre herds. Some regional languages, it is true, have access to the press, education, even media such as radio and television. Yet it should not be forgotten that these regional languages can be counted on the fingers of one hand.

Account must also be taken in this context of personal phenomena such as marriage, which is a major factor in the life of languages because its effect can be either to ensure their survival or to seal their fate. Let us imagine that a man speaking the Kwego language marries a Masai woman speaking this major regional language of Tanzania and Kenya. While admittedly under threat from Swahili (although to a lesser extent than the tribal languages), Masai itself poses a threat to the tribal languages. Let us imagine, then, the case of a nomad cattle farmer possessing a wretched herd or, worse still, a hunter-gatherer whose survival depends on a subsistence economy. Let us suppose that he marries a Masai girl, who is given a few head of zebu as a dowry by her father. For this reason alone, he is liable to be tempted by the prestige of his wife's culture and by the desire to marry into the status of cattle-breeder. His life comes to be ruled by imitation of the Masai. What, then, will he pass on to his children? It will certainly not be Kwego but rather his wife's language, Masai, which he will himself have learnt. As for his wife, she will naturally not teach her children Kwego, but rather Masai, the language of her father, her family and her region. In this process of transmission, we see extremely clearly and sharply the different stages in the extinction of languages, which first become precarious, are then marginalized and finally become extinct for lack of transmission.

The attraction of prestige languages

Another cause of the death of languages is the attraction of prestige languages, as popularized by the media. Let us stay with Africa, which provides excellent examples of the process whereby languages disappear, independently of the machinations of the colonizers who have uprooted and been responsible for the extinction of some of the languages of the people that they have colonized.

Many African languages are indeed threatened by the languages of peoples that were themselves subject to colonial rule. Let us then imagine an Egyptian who is a speaker of Nubian, a major African language belonging to the family of Nilotic languages. Our Nubian Egyptian, a frequent visitor to the large towns of the north, perhaps even to Cairo or Khartoum, is a Muslim. Although a follower of Islam, he does not read the Koran in the original Arabic, or if he does he recites it without really understanding it; he listens however to the Cairo radio and the religious broadcasts. He listens to everything that is said in Arabic. When he returns to his village, this Nubian speaker has become a transmitter of the Arabic language, the language of the Koran, of the holy book of his faith, of the capital cities. This language has great prestige because it embodies a strong national—not to say, nationalist—assertion of identity in opposition to the former colonial system and to different kinds of present-day economic pressures. In these circumstances, the demise of Nubian is a foregone conclusion since the villager returning from a stay in Cairo, or who simply remains in touch with the newspapers and particularly radio and television, which are all in Arabic in both Egypt and Sudan, will become a vehicle of total Arabization. Islamization has been in progress for centuries but it tends to be linked to a process of Arabization. In this way, local tribal languages lacking the means to defend themselves are made extinct—often with the consent, sometimes enthusiastic, of the populations that were their depositories. In such cases, the language is the victim of a failure of transmission, the children being sent to schools that teach the prestige language, rather than to local teachers. The contact with prestige language thus constitutes an additional factor making for the extinction of languages.

One could cite very many other causes. The question has to be asked in particular whether the users of languages in the process of disappearing really wish to defend them. Like ethnologists, linguists generally wish to do their utmost to ensure their survival because of their love for languages. Paradoxically and tragically, the main adversaries they encounter in this enterprise are often the users of these languages themselves, who do not wish to revive their languages and do not regard them as particularly useful tools in gaining access to modernity. *Modernity*—this is the word that embodies a serious threat to languages.

Fashion and snobbery

Another factor in the extinction of languages should be mentioned. It is neither economic nor social in character and could even be seen as marginal to the weighty 'scientific' arguments generally adduced, involving as it does a purely psychological factor, not to say a question of mood. Fashion and snobbery nevertheless constitute an extremely serious threat. In many cases, where there are no solid grounds for thinking that efficiency will lead to well-being, when there is no professional need, when there is no economic or social justification, when there is no real pressure, political or otherwise, to give up one's vernacular language in favour of a dominant language, there is one other reason at least that prompts people to flock to the latter. I refer to snobbery and the fact that the language in question is perceived as being chic to know, even if it is murdered with each syllable uttered.

The resurrection of languages

Languages are born, live and die, but they can also be revived. There is a fundamental reason why this is so: languages are not merely languages. I have spoken of language ability as a defining characteristic of the species and of languages as the historical and social materialization of that ability. Another distinction needs however to be borne in mind—that made by Ferdinand de Saussure, the great linguist of the beginning of the last century, between 'language' and 'speech'. Language is also *speech*.

Language, indeed, is the conjunction of a phonological system (the consonants and vowels are arranged in syllables, and the syllables ordered in words), a morphosyntactical system (the syntactic structure orders the words) and a semantic and lexical system (words are conveyors of meaning). Even where a language is not spoken, where these various systems are not orally performative in everyday exchanges, the language remains a language. It lacks the speech necessary for performance, but it is not necessarily threatened with extinction. It is precisely because languages are language as well as speech that they can be reborn. When one of them 'dies', what is lost is merely speech and not existence. It is not lost as a language. Speech has been lost because, in the aetiology of extinction I developed earlier, its speakers have ceased to utter it. Yet its phonology, its morphosyntax, its lexicon and its semantics will not necessarily disappear. They are in no way fated to die, always provided they have been set down somewhere.

In Africa, the subject of my thesis, I observed at first hand the extraordinary phenomenon of collective memory, when I was told by my elderly informers that they had acquired their language from their ancestors, who had themselves learned it from their forebears. I believe in the reality of an oral tradition, but it seems to me less easily grasped, even if it is perfectly tangible, than a written tradition that has left a document as a material trace. All these written media, including their current virtual form, are certainly threatened with deterioration as physical objects, but they are nonetheless conduits for the conservation of language. Some are even able to preserve speech. In the case of many dead languages where speech has been extinguished, written testimonies are all we have left.

A resurrection: Hebrew

Where there exists a powerful human will to breathe life into a language, then its revival is possible. The example generally cited is that of Hebrew, revived following the progressive arrival of Jewish communities in Palestine after the Dreyfus Affair, in the wake of the pogroms of the Tsarist era and subsequently during the early decades of the twentieth century. After the Second World War, when the State of Israel was created, the Jews arrived in a country that had since the 1920s equipped itself with a language: Hebrew.

How had the Jewish communities been able, from the early years of the twentieth century, to revive this language? They had simply reconstructed it on the basis of written documents, starting with the Bible but also texts from the Rabbinical, Talmudic and Midrashic tradition and all the learned correspondence exchanged down the centuries in Hebrew. Yet Hebrew had been a dead language since 600 BC, as in 594, following the victory of Babylon over the Jewish communities, the Judean aristocracy had been deported en masse to Babylon, where it had discovered Aramaic, a language spoken by nomadic traders operating over vast stretches of territory and whose descendants are the inhabitants of modern-day Syria, Lebanon, Jordan and part of Iraq. The Aramaic language, moreover, survives to this day: there are still some Aramaean communities in Lebanon who speak a form of Aramaic called Syriac or eastern neo-Syriac. In 530 or 525 BC, when the Jewish communities were repatriated by Cyrus, the victorious emperor of the Babylonians, these communities of elite Jews brought with them Aramaic. Thus Joshua of Nazareth, a young Jew brought up in the language of his community, spoke Aramaic and not Hebrew, which was already a learned language.

The resurrection of Hebrew, following a long endeavour going back to the last decades of the nineteenth century, is a quite extraordinary phenomenon, but not without equal nor exemplary value. All that was required was human will. The communities concerned considered that, given the ideal that brought them to the country at that time, the only language that would enable Jews going to Palestine to communicate was Hebrew and not Yiddish or Judeo-Arabic, any more than Yemenite or Iraqi Arabic, Serbo-Croat, Russian, Polish, Hungarian or Romanian, or any of the languages of the Jewish communities established for centuries in Central and Eastern Europe and subject to the authority of first the Ottoman, then the Russian and finally the Hapsburg Empire. All these communities spoke very many languages, all of them Indo-European. For them, Hebrew was an alien and liturgical language, but it seemed to them the only conceivable language of communication. Accordingly, as that language had been dead for 2,600 years without being extinct, since many written testimonies remained, it was 'sufficient' to decide that it would be the language of the new communities. And this is what happened, albeit not without difficulty, protest and problems both within and between communities.

Creolization—the future of languages

The example of Hebrew shows that a language can be revived, just as it can be promoted, if the human will exists. Having reached the optimistic panel of the life-death-resurrection triptych, I shall conclude by citing other cases of the revival of languages regarded as dead.

The Cornish language, which had been dead since the end of the sixteenth century, has been revived and seems in the process of spreading in the south-west tip of Great Britain, among a Celtic population that has shown a very strong wish to bring it back into being in the face of the pressure exerted by British English.

Nynorsk, or neo-Norsk, in Norway has not been revived but rather constituted, virtually created, on the basis of the country dialects of the southwest of the country to counter the Dano-Norwegian of the bourgeoisie of Oslo and other large cities, which is the language of the communities of Danish origin, imposed over centuries of Danish colonization of Norway.

Another example is the Nagamais language of Nagaland. Nagaland is situated on the Himalayan uplands in the most eastern state of India. It is inhabited by tribal communities speaking Assamese, Tibetan or a language that, through pidginization followed by creolization, is on the way to becoming a national language, created virtually on the basis of trading relations. Markets are indeed an ideal location for the creation of pidgins and creoles.

Timorese is spoken as the lingua franca more or less throughout Timor, via Tetun, one of the main languages of the country. It has been creolized and pidginized with very limited structural support.

Whereas the renaissance of Hebrew was based on an ancient written tradition of Biblical and Talmudic texts, the case of the above-mentioned languages is radically different. With the exception of Cornish, which is another instance of 'resurrection', they are all examples of creolization.

The number of languages that die is considerable. At the rate of twenty-five languages disappearing every year, it could be that only 2,500 of the 5,000 languages existing today will remain at the start of the twenty-second century. However, it must not be forgotten that new languages are being born. Unfortunately, many fewer are born than die. The main process whereby languages are born is creolization, that is to say, the emergence of a language that initially did not belong as a mother tongue and ancestral heritage to any of the individuals or the communities that come to employ it as a means of plying their trade in the towns and marketplaces. A means of communication arising from a process of mixing, of distillation of all the languages present, these creoles represent in large measure the future of languages. One language of worldwide scope can moreover look forward to a bright future as a result of the creolization process it is currently undergoing: I am talking of course of Anglo-American!

PART III

Towards New Social Contracts?

The New Social Contract and Lifelong Education for All

The educational legacy of the twentieth century is by no means slight: illiteracy has declined significantly, particularly in relative terms, and enrolments in secondary and higher education have increased. But the persistence of disparities both internationally and even within societies would seem to call for the framing of new social contracts. Furthermore, the increasingly close links between the economic sector and knowledge production, and the rapid changes in the labour market, prescribe the need for a new definition of education. This can no longer be linked to a limited period of life and must now rest on the four pillars of learning to know, learning to do, learning to be and learning to live together. The new technologies also open up new approaches to teaching and learning. Through the opportunities for access that they offer, they can contribute to the goal of universal education, provided the possibilities that they embody are matched by the necessary political will.

Jacques Delors analyses the forms that lifelong education might take in our evolving societies, and the dialectic that needs to be established between democracy and education. Jeliou Jelev stresses the role that education should play in developing a sense of individual citizenship and responsibility. Fay Chung, finally, underlines the social, political and economic importance of women's access to education, particularly in the developing countries.

* * * *

French Finance Minister from 1981 to 1984 and president of the European Commission from 1985 to 1994, **Jacques Delors** was also at the origin of French legislation on continuing education (1969). Previously president of the International Commission on Education for the 21st Century set up by UNESCO, he coordinated the international report entitled *Learning, the Treasure Within* (1996).

Philosopher, initiator and coordinator of the democratic movement in Bulgaria, **Jeliou Jelev** in 1992 became the first Bulgarian president to be democratically elected (1992–1997), after being one of the leading dissidents under the Communist regime. His critique of Communism is set out in *Bulgarie, Terre d'Europe* (1998). He currently directs a foundation for cooperation in the Balkans.

A former Minister of Education and Culture and former State Minister for the Creation of Employment and Cooperatives of Zimbabwe, **Fay Chung** was a member of the International Commission on Education for the 21st Century. She was also chief of the Education Sector of UNICEF and special adviser for education to the Africa Union. She served as founding director of the UNESCO International Institute for Capacity Building in Africa until her retirement at the end of 2003.

Jacques Delors

Towards Lifelong Education for All

My topic—the role of education in our societies—confronts me with a choice between two key issues. On the one hand, there is the problem of the persistent, indeed growing, inequalities in education worldwide; on the other, there is the impact on all societies of radical technological, economic and geopolitical change. After touching briefly on the first, I shall direct my attention to the second issue, focusing on the definition of a new social contract at the national level.

Educational inequalities

Let us remember that, at the end of the 1990s, there were 900 million illiterates in the world and 100 million children having no access to education. It should also be borne in mind that progress towards education for all is at a standstill in some countries and that 70 percent of the world's 57 million teachers live in difficult circumstances incompatible with their calling and with the role they should be playing in society. I naturally acknowledge the efforts of UNESCO, the World Bank and other agencies in this regard, but more needs to be done. Perhaps the global contract could include a new clause providing for the creation of a worldwide fund for education. The Member States of the United Nations would need to contribute only 1 percent of their current military expenditure to the fund for it to have the necessary scope and capacity.

This being said, I should like to revert to the challenge posed by the radical changes affecting our societies, while underlining that education is founded on universal principles inspired by thinkers going back, in some cases, 3,000 years.

Radical change and unchanging principles

Whenever a technological revolution occurs, the question arises as to what exactly is going to change and whether everything is going to change. Experience shows that there is always an unchanging element in society. Knowing what that element will be in the context of the technological changes we are experiencing is a difficult question that seems to me beyond the scope of this contribution.

I shall confine myself to outlining the parameters of the radical changes taking place. They are the technological revolution (the new information technologies and biotechnology), the globalization of markets and the economy, the expansion of trade, the emergence of new stakeholders, the transformation of capitalism and a certain decline of the nation-state. This list might suggest that economics is in the process of ousting the other human sciences. If this were so, it would be a serious error. My list could also suggest, not without reason, that economics has hijacked the role of politics. This is regrettable from the standpoint of nurturing healthy democracies and wise governance. It has a direct bearing on education, highlighted only in the English language. Most people when they talk of lifelong education are speaking of *training*; I myself prefer to speak of *learning*, which is not the same thing.

Some other factors affecting this transformation should be mentioned. They include: the media revolution; the emergence of a global public opinion; changes in values linked to such major trends in the second half of the twentieth century as the advancement of women, evolving lifestyles, the break-up of the family and growing aspirations to self-realization; the rise of identity-based groups and communities; and finally the formidable tension between global and local dimensions. Our leaders increasingly think globally, whereas the citizens they are addressing think in local terms. For many of our contemporaries confronted by globalization, this tension is disorienting.

I should like, in all modesty, to underscore the importance of the unchanging element in human affairs. Emmanuel Mounier said that 'man is perpetually renewing the appearance of his indignations.' The battle for human progress continues. It is never finally won, but it is worth resuming. We should always remember that the economy exists to serve man and society and that education should promote the values of freedom and solidarity, while not overlooking the dimension of competition—with its element of aggression—that has always existed among human beings.

Such an approach—which is hardly out of the ordinary—should make us wary of the cult of novelty, the exclusive media focus on the immediate and instantaneous, without regard for past and future (what a responsibility for the education system!), and the emotion-ruled society and its corollaries—the dictatorship of opinion polls and the loss of authority. At the basis of education is a relationship between pupil and teacher resting on an authority recognized by the one and wisely exercised by the other.

This said, we must confront novelty, not least the process of globalization, which should result in the near future in new global rules of the game and a reshaping of international organizations. The role and content of work in society is also an inescapable novelty. We must likewise take account of the upheavals in the job market, arising from technological changes and globalization. Taking a lead from Robert Reich, former United States Minister of Labour, I would distinguish between: the manipulators of symbols, who are perfectly at ease in the information society; the organizers and managers, who will always be necessary; the professionals, working inside or outside companies; the companies themselves; and all the others, workers and service providers, who are subject to the constraints of the market and the requirement of flexibility.

Education should play a central role in re-establishing a degree of equality of opportunity. Those falling within the forty-to-fifty years age group are often at a loss to cope with the changes in the job market.

The role of work

Contrary to what Jeremy Rifkin thinks, I continue to uphold the essential role of work in society. My position is anti-Malthusian, based on the experience of history and on our discussions following the publication of the Club of Rome's 'zero growth' report thirty years ago. My position is essentially normative. The fact of affirming the importance of work in society does not imply a passive or professorial attitude. We must act, taking into account the time freed up by technological progress and social organization. In earlier times, men and women in industrial societies spent on average 100,000 hours of their life at work. The present-day figure is 70,000 to 75,000 hours. In fifty years time, it may have fallen to 45,000. This is a considerable change, and it has consequences for the organization of society.

We therefore need to redefine the bases of the social contract. Do we accept a democracy ruled by the media and opinion polls or do we want to return to a mediated democracy, reasserting the role of civil society? Are we then to adopt a new model of development, more respectful of human time and of the needs of nature? This would imply the creation, between the market and the public sector, of a third sector of activity in which initiative, spontaneity, imagination and community life could play their full role.

The four pillars of education

What is the potential contribution of education in this domain? The four pillars of education as defined in the report of the International Commission on Education for the 21st Century[1] are: learning to know, learning to do, learning to be and learning to live together.

Whether in developed or developing countries, the basics of education are reading, writing, arithmetic and self-expression, without which there would be no equality of opportunity or future prospects. Studies conducted in Great Britain by Tony Blair's Government revealed that 18–20 percent of the twelve-to-thirteen age group did not possess these rudiments of knowledge. There is no need, then, to mention the developing countries, where children quickly lapse into illiteracy after a period of schooling. Learning to know means imparting a desire to learn. Education must have its place in society like a fish in water. Work-study training, for so long criticized in France, is not dead simply because we have moved from an industrial to a postindustrial society. The principle remains the same: to enable young people to measure up to the demands of economic and social reality while pursuing their studies.

Learning to do is clearly related to specific trades, but it is essential today to be familiar with the new information technologies. Given the uncertainties of working life and the growing autonomy of many workers, who must not only produce but also control their production, it is necessary to master the new professional skills and sift through the available knowledge and information. Technically speaking, we can today talk of the need to acquire skills and not simply a trade or profession.

The Edgar Faure report, which preceded ours, focused mainly on the third pillar of education: learning to be. This report was written in the enthusiastic spirit of post-1968. Learning to be means not overlooking any of the potentialities of every child. It is incompatible therefore with selecting children at the primary school stage for their literary, conceptual or mathematical skills. It is necessary to establish varied patterns of provision, taking account of the rate at which different pupils mature, the possibility of their wanting to return to education and the chances of bringing out their potential. Finally, education should help individuals to become aware of their strengths and weaknesses, so as to enable them to exercise personal responsibility.

If we wish to avoid the market society, if we wish to avoid the disappearance of the European model of society, we have to accept a reconciliation between collective and individual responsibility.

Learning to live together means working to ensure that mutual understanding is already a reality in our classrooms, which are so diverse in

---

1. *Learning: The Treasure Within,* Report of the International Commission on Education for the 21st Century, chaired by Jacques Delors, Paris, UNESCO Publications, 1996.

terms of pupils' ethnic and religious affiliations. Learning to live together from the classroom onwards is a guarantee for the future. It means understanding other people, being encouraged to play an active part in society. In this connection, I would underline the importance of civic education, which sparks a great deal of controversy. The teaching of history and the history of religions is essential. The experience of a united Europe is instructive in this regard: we have genuinely learned to live together over the last fifty years.

The terms *lifelong training* and *lifelong education* (I prefer the latter) are often employed, but unfortunately the practical construction work has not yet begun. The time has come to devise and put into practice the basic principles of lifelong education. Political leaders and teachers must be urged to reflect on the question, be made to face up to their responsibilities. In arguing the case for lifelong education for all, our report starts from the premise that every individual should be given the means to exist as a person, to renew him- or herself at any time and thereby to cope with the problems, both personal and professional, that life throws up. In the words of the report, the mission of education 'is to enable each of us, without exception, to develop all our talents to the full and to realize our creative potential, including responsibility for our own lives and achievement of our personal aims.'

With this end in mind, some principles could serve as guidelines in devising and undertaking the necessary reforms. Firstly, lifelong education is not merely the sum of initial and continuing education. It is a new system that must be conceived as such. The authorities responsible for education must establish the framework, architecture and principles of this lifelong education.

Secondly, basic education—a close concern of UNESCO—is a prerequisite for all countries and all pupils.

Thirdly, the diversity of educational provision from the secondary level onwards should enable all pupils to test their abilities, choose a career path and thus use their potential to the full.

Fourthly, equality of opportunity means that those leaving school between sixteen and eighteen should be given a study-time entitlement voucher. The aim is not to prevent people from pursuing higher education but rather to ensure that those preferring to start work between sixteen and eighteen should be given priority if they wish to resume their education at a later date. With the education voucher, they will enjoy a second or third chance.

Fifthly, higher education should regain its status in society and should organize itself. It should recover its authoritative voice as a producer and dispenser of knowledge and research, while fulfilling its role in lifelong education. Universities must respond to the radical changes taking place by adapting knowledge structures and reshaping academic disciplines accordingly.

These reforms will only be possible if they form part of a new social contract, involving government, the education authorities, employers' organizations, trade unions and local communities. For this to occur, there first needs to be an awareness that the traditional way of dividing life into cycles is inadequate and outdated. There used to be an age for getting educated, an age for working and an age for enjoying one's retirement. This arrangement no longer holds good. We should understand that education is possible throughout life, and that those wanting to work beyond seventy may continue to do so if they wish.

Moreover, we should be conscious of the consequences of these changes for the welfare state by making the link between individual and collective responsibilities. When contemplating with alarm the spiralling costs of lifelong education, we should ask ourselves whether citizens, in an act of individual responsibility and forethought, should not participate in the cost of lifelong education by saving up for study-time entitlements or educational credits for their children or themselves.

Finally, we must turn equality of opportunity into a reality and abandon the dangerous myth of a form of equality based on results. I am certain in my own mind that the future will belong to those who are best able to create, transmit, absorb and apply knowledge. This is what is meant by a 'knowledge society'. A knowledge society can only contribute to the enhancement of democracy, and vice versa, if it is in constant dialectic with an ever-changing society organized on a participative basis. From this standpoint education and democracy are intimately linked.

Jeliou Jelev

Education and Citizenship in the Twenty-First Century

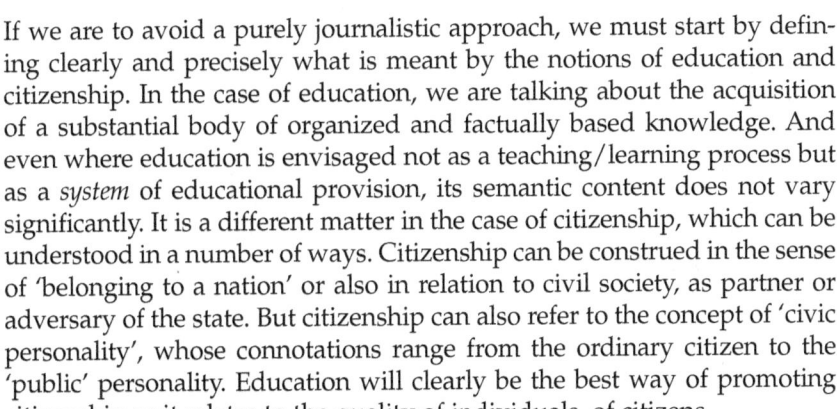

If we are to avoid a purely journalistic approach, we must start by defining clearly and precisely what is meant by the notions of education and citizenship. In the case of education, we are talking about the acquisition of a substantial body of organized and factually based knowledge. And even where education is envisaged not as a teaching/learning process but as a *system* of educational provision, its semantic content does not vary significantly. It is a different matter in the case of citizenship, which can be understood in a number of ways. Citizenship can be construed in the sense of 'belonging to a nation' or also in relation to civil society, as partner or adversary of the state. But citizenship can also refer to the concept of 'civic personality', whose connotations range from the ordinary citizen to the 'public' personality. Education will clearly be the best way of promoting citizenship as it relates to the quality of individuals, of citizens.

Becoming a citizen

At what point do individuals become citizens? They become citizens when they acquire a 'civic personality', which they do less through their relationship with the state than through the relations they establish between themselves and civil society, of which they will be an active member. The individual becomes a 'civic personality' when he progressively takes his place and successfully integrates himself in the mainstream of social life by defending the fundamental values of democracy. In this context, he stands as the representative of civil society and, as such, becomes both a partner and adversary of the state.

Obviously, the relationship between 'civic personalities' and the state will depend in the last analysis on the degree of democracy in the state concerned. The more democratic a state, the more it will seek to pursue the path of dialogue and compromise whenever it finds itself in disagreement with its citizens. That is why, in a democracy, divergences and contradictions between citizens and the state can serve to enlarge the scope of freedom, which is a prerequisite for the renewal of science, the arts and culture. For only free citizens can realize their full creative potential.

Democracy, totalitarianism and education

History and the contemporary world clearly demonstrate that democracy and civil society are essential to the full development of science, culture and the education system. Indeed, it is not by chance that Athenian democracy left such a vital imprint on educational principle. Even if its concept of education was different, it is an undeniable fact that it gave rise to multidirectional research, which is only conceivable in a democratic society. Our age offers equally striking examples of the links that exist between democracy and civil society and between the teaching and education system. We naturally think in this connection of the rivalry between the two superpowers, the totalitarian Soviet Union and the democratic United States. Everyone knows the sad finale to this adventure. The Soviet Union not only lost the contest, but it collapsed as a political system and as an education system. How and why did this happen, given the extent of the Soviet Union's natural, human and intellectual resources, which were in no way inferior to those of the United States?

The answer is simple: the Soviet Union lacked two key resources, namely a free civil society and a democratic state system. A state in which an independent citizen automatically becomes a dissident or is treated as an 'enemy of the people' cannot create the conditions for the flourishing of creative human energies and the spirit of initiative, which are the fount of all social prosperity and progress. The main principle that informs education systems in totalitarian states is collectivism, which enables the state to produce subjects but not citizens. Education thus conceived is based on the following premises: that the collectivity or community shall be placed above the individual; that the individual, *qua* individual, must subordinate himself to the will of the community, without discussion as to the rights and wrongs of the question; and that the individual must rely above all on the 'collective' and not on his own resources.

It is important to analyse very carefully the practice of totalitarian regimes with respect to their education systems. For the key educational issue in the years to come will concern the integration of the notion of the civic spirit in education.

Education in the Internet age

The wide-scale introduction of computers and the rise of the Internet have made access to information virtually unlimited. We can now receive all the information we need and communicate whatever we consider important or useful for others. In practice, the key question in this context is whether those possessing this information will be capable of using it wisely and rationally.

What is the quality of the information to which the public has and will have access? Does it provide the basis for acquiring a sound and systematic education or scientific grounding? If the answer is no, what will be the nature of the interaction between the unlimited information on the Internet and the education system proper? What will be the role of the school and of the teacher in this process? There is no easy answer to all these questions. It is clear, however, that it is the education system that must tailor and continuously adapt itself to the new situations created by information technology and the Internet, and not the opposite. As past examples show, radical changes in the means of communication and information systems invariably have the effect of modifying the existing education system.

In Antiquity, children did their calculations in the sand or on clay tablets. But the system evolved, notably following Gutenberg's revolutionary invention or again when, in the twentieth century, audiovisual media became the major source of information. In the years to come, the education system will undergo even more significant changes arising from the Internet. It naturally follows that the role of the school and the teacher will also change. At a time when information was limited, the teacher represented for children and parents alike a messianic figure opening up the portals of knowledge, since it was from the teacher that they first learned about the origins of the Earth and the significance of the sun and moon, the planets and stars, and the continents and oceans. The teacher's role is no longer the same. Teachers have lost their Promethean aura and can no longer be regarded as the fount of all knowledge. From the radio, television, newspapers and magazines received in the home, children learn all sorts of things at a very early age. These early inputs may not be logically structured but the fact remains that they are assimilated along with the multiple facets of reality. In this context, it is clear that the teacher's function is progressively shifting and is becoming focused on the organization and presentation of knowledge in a logical and coherent manner.

In the age of the Internet and globalization, the moral problems that arise call for the exercise of citizenship, responsibility and civic control over the dissemination and use of information. I emphasize that this is a civic and moral responsibility. Governments must not introduce censorship or limit access to information. The young can have access on the Internet to potentially dangerous information and may be tempted to use it. In this case, the danger comes from the flagrant discrepancy that can exist between the free access to information and the absence of any sense of civic responsibility concerning its use. It would perhaps be desirable, despite their limited scope for action, if schools could be responsible not only for the task of dispensing knowledge but also that of educating young people in the sense of awakening their sense of moral responsibility. This task is moreover incumbent not only on the school and the education system: it should mobilize all the institutions of the state, public organizations and above all the family.

The legacy of the twentieth century

As we enter the twenty-first century, we have a duty to state openly and clearly what we accept and what we reject in the educational legacy of the twentieth century. What are the lessons we must learn for the century to come? I think they can be formulated as follows.

We should say no to centralized and standardized education systems controlled by the state. The state should not disengage from the education of young people, but its involvement should never jeopardize the basic values of democracy—including human rights, civil and political liberties, the rule of law, a market economy, free enterprise and the rights of minorities.

Nor can we accept collectivist doctrines and systems of educating young people and adults. They produce individuals who rely entirely on the state, rather than citizens who rely on their own strength, their intellectual abilities and individual talents, their willpower and their creative energy.

Conversely, we should further the development of a civil society that not only fosters citizenship but also serves as a firm foundation for the construction of a democratic state; and we should likewise promote the development of a rule-governed state whose democratic institutions and laws ensure that all its citizens may enjoy respect for human rights, political and civil liberties, minority rights and equality in all things.

Fay Chung

Women and the Future of Education

Statistics indicate that the gender gap remains a very serious problem in nearly all developing countries at all levels of education. This gap becomes larger at secondary and tertiary education levels. However, some 40 percent of girls in the Least Developed Countries (LDCs) are not able to access even primary education.

There have been a number of studies indicating that having better educated girls and women, particularly at secondary education level and above, results in a number of social benefits such as lower infant mortality rates, lower birth rates, greater productivity, etc. It is incontrovertible that increasing the number of better educated women brings about measurable social benefits.

The situation of women today and the potential for change

In examining our subject, it is important to consider the situation of the world today, the situation of women within that context, and the potential for women to change that situation for the better over the next few decades. I shall concentrate on the situation of women in developing countries, and the possibilities offered by education for improvement of the situation of women in particular and of society in general.

Physical and economic needs

It is not uncommon to find that about half the population in developing countries, particularly in the LDCs, are living below the poverty datum line. This high degree of poverty affects women and children adversely, as measured by high infant and maternal mortality rates. There is clearly a relationship between high levels of human development, higher levels of income and a higher standard of living. However while greater access to quality education is of critical importance in the reduction of poverty, it would be too simplistic to assume that education alone can serve as a panacea for all problems. Basic education for all needs to be combined with a number of other improvements, many of which are physical in nature. Better understanding and control of nature for example, such as better access to clean water supply, better sanitation and low-cost and readily available sources of energy, would bring about benefits to impoverished women. Good quality and relevant basic education are of critical importance in enabling women to better utilize facilities.

The need to make some physical changes that would enable people in poverty-stricken situations to have greater control over nature is an important one. This is particularly so in the many drought-prone areas in Africa. Inability to control the forces of nature is one of the most serious obstacles to overcoming poverty. This has implications for education: countries need to produce sufficient middle- and high-level engineers to make this conquest of nature possible. It is a well-known phenomenon that there are few if any women in engineering courses.

However, in addition to making physical changes to have better control over the vagaries of nature and providing access to knowledge and skills to boost agricultural productivity, there is an equally critical area in terms of women's right to own property. In many developing countries, particularly in many Sub-Saharan African countries, women have very limited rights to own property. Without access to land rights for example, women agriculturalists who produce the bulk of the food in developing countries, may find it difficult to increase their productivity. Land rights require legal reform as well as the education of women regarding their legal rights. Even when legislation exists in favour of women, the majority of women may be too ignorant of the legal niceties to enable them to claim this basic human right.

Political power

The leadership available to women is highly influenced by the educational facilities available to women. Where large numbers of women are illiterate or poorly educated, it is unlikely that they can produce a leadership that can raise the majority of them to higher levels of empowerment, whether this be economic, political or social empowerment. Women are often politically weak and are not well represented in decision-making bodies. It is important to provide women with education linked to understanding of their basic human rights and how these can be translated into reality.

Social situation

Education can help to improve the social situation of women in many societies. This touches on the issue of social values within a society, and how this reflects on social organization within the society. The need to ensure gender equality and gender equity within the society, in particular by respecting the role and contribution of women to their societies, raises the whole question of how gender is treated within the education system. Curricular, teaching and administrative processes within societies, and in particular within educational institutions, need to be examined to ensure that gender bias and gender stereotyping are not insidiously integrated into the processes.

One important change that is seriously affected by the type and quality of education is that of job opportunities for women, including their promotion prospects. All too often women have limited job and promotion prospects. If women are to hold posts in all areas and at all levels, then educational programmes need to be geared towards providing girls and women with equal access to employment and promotion.

Specific educational interventions to bring about change

Primary and basic education for girls and women

Despite numerous international as well as national plans to provide education for all, the fact remains that in the LDCs almost 40 percent of girls do not attend primary school. Almost half the world's adults are still illiterate, and most of the illiterates are women.[1] One of the most pressing requirements is therefore establishing primary education for all girls and providing basic education opportunities for women.

While the world trend is towards co-educational institutions where girls and boys, and men and women, can study together as equals, the predominance of co-educational institutions may have had a negative effect to some extent on the number as well as the quality of education available to girls and women. In some societies, single-sex schools, particularly at secondary and tertiary levels, may play a very important role in ensuring that women are prepared for leadership roles outside of their family roles and in providing women with the necessary tools to control their own destinies.

It is also important to examine the content and quality of the education that will be offered to girls and women, and how this content and quality will link up with the needs of the societies in which the women will operate. It is not unusual to find that the educational opportunities

---

1. UNESCO, 'World Education Report', 2000, pp. 114–15.

offered to girls and women in some societies are geared to strengthening their traditional subjugation. In brief, a modern curriculum that would include mathematics and natural sciences, technology, an international language, health education, and a knowledge of their legal rights should be fundamental.

The use of distance education to increase and improve educational access

Distance education is particularly important for groups that are handicapped by geographical as well as cultural constraints. Girls and women are particularly affected, as concern for their safety may make parents hesitate to allow girls to travel long distances on their own. Even in industrialized countries, women may find opportunities for further education severely limited because of their responsibilities as wives and mothers. Educational opportunities targeted at young women, including young married women, can do much to strengthen the economic and professional potential of these young women.

Of particular importance is the possibility of distance education programmes specifically designed to improve and strengthen leadership qualities in women. In most countries women are poorly represented in leadership positions.

Technology offers many new opportunities for women. For example, the problem of distances between home and work can now be minimized, possibly making it easier for women to join the work force while at the same time fulfilling their roles as mothers. Job locations are now not as problematic as before, as it is possible for work required in one locality to be carried out in another locality, and indeed in another country. Examples are multiplying of cross-country transfer of work through electronic mail, such as the growth of India as a centre for computer technology for the United States. It is therefore important to have educational programmes to enable women to enjoy the flexibility and broadening of range that access to technology offers.

Conclusion

The position of women in a society is a key indicator of the level of development of that society. Where the majority of women in a society are underprivileged and poverty-stricken, it is unlikely that the society can free itself from the constraints of poverty and underdevelopment. These constraints are physical, political, legal, and technological. In each of these domains, education can play an important part in overcoming problems and in transforming systems. Democratic political systems cannot function well when a large proportion of the population is impoverished and illiterate: democracy requires the existence of a well-educated society and strong civil society institutions covering legal rights, banking, industry, business, religion and other areas of social interaction. The institution of multi-party democracies in the absence of strong civil society institutions is a contradiction in terms, and can lead to the type of chaos that we have witnessed in recent times in Rwanda and Yugoslavia.

A Natural Contract and the Future of Development

———⚬⚬⚬———

The unbridled exploitation of natural resources, the alarming impoverishment of biodiversity, pollution of all kinds, the scornful dismissal or plundering of indigenous environmental knowledge—the human race is exploiting the earth in an increasingly parasitical manner. How can we meet today's needs without jeopardizing the ability of future generations to meet their own needs? How can we best turn to account the reservoir of scientific knowledge embodied in the natural heritage, and how can we share the benefits of this knowledge more fairly? 'Mastering our mastery', this must be the watchword in drawing up a natural contract that will promote development without enslaving nature.

Jérôme Bindé opens the discussion by re-examining the idea of a natural contract as put forward by the philosopher Michel Serres. Thomas Odhiambo highlights the challenges posed by the preservation of biodiversity. Mostafa Tolba sets the environmental question in a broader context by discussing the prospects for development in the approaches to the year 2020.

* * * *

Jérôme Bindé is deputy assistant director-general of the Social and Human Sciences Sector and director of the Division of Foresight, Philosophy and Human Sciences at UNESCO. He is also secretary-general of the Conseil du Futur, as well as founding member of the Academy of Latinity. A graduate of the Ecole Normale Supérieure and agrégé, he has contributed to numerous works and published many articles on cultural, social and future studies issues, including *L'éthique du futur: pourquoi faut-il retrouver le temps perdu?* (1997) and *Prêts pour le XXIe siècle?* (1998). He was editor of *Keys to the 21st Century* (2001), the first anthology of '21st-Century

Talks', and is the coordinator and primary co-author of the future-oriented world report *The World Ahead: Our Future in the Making* (2001).

An entomologist by training, **Thomas Odhiambo** was the founder-director of the International Centre of Insect Physiology and Ecology (ICIPE). He was also the founder of the Nairobi-based RANDFORUM (Research and Development Forum for Science-Led Development in Africa). A former president of the University of Tropical Medicine of Kenya and of the African Academy of Science, he was the author of numerous scientific publications, for which he was awarded the UNESCO Albert Einstein gold medal in 1991. Thomas Odhiambo died in 2003.

Mostafa Tolba is a microbiology professor and was secretary of state for education, then youth minister, of Egypt from 1971 to 1973 and executive director of the United Nations Environmental Programme from 1976 to 1992. Since 1994, he has been founder president of the International Centre for Environment and Development.

Jérôme Bindé

The Natural Contract and Development in the Twenty-First Century

At the time when the first social contract was beginning to take shape, in the seventeenth century, the philosopher Hobbes set out the following equation: the state of nature equals the state of war. For the author of *Leviathan*, the state of nature was one of total insecurity, that of the 'war of all against all', in which 'homo homini lupus.' For Hobbes, a social contract was the only possible safeguard against the risk of such a struggle to the death. This idea, as transmitted through the very complex reformulations of the proponents of 'natural law' theory, was the source of modern political constructs and of the democratic tradition stemming from the Enlightenment.

The limitations of the social contract

As we enter the twenty-first century, we find ourselves confronted by a new challenge: the war against nature, against the environment. The notions of security and insecurity have expanded to include all the conditions of human existence. Security therefore encompasses the ecological, health, social, cultural and human dimensions no less than that of politics.

We are today obliged to acknowledge an omission, an increasingly glaring shortcoming, in the social contract: in the same way as declarations of human rights, it excludes nature and everything defined as non-human. Hobbes, for example, excluded stones, animals, children and God from the social contract as formulated in *Leviathan*. Women are likewise excluded. Certainly, the social contract is essentially oriented towards the future, but this future orientation is strictly limited by the instantaneity also characteristic of the contract, which is always concluded between parties present in the here and now. While bearing in principle upon the future, the social contract *de facto* excludes future generations. This instantaneity is becoming increasingly marked in the age of globalization, which by making the short term and the market the measure of all things subjects the social contract to the tyranny of urgency.

The limitations of the social contract, which had already been noted by philosophers of history (one thinks of Hegel's striking retort to Hobbes in the *Phenomenology of Mind* when he declared that 'none are innocent, not even the stones, not even the child'), are becoming ever more apparent. The social contract is no longer a sufficient foundation for peace since war has now been declared on the environment. It no longer suffices to guarantee the kind of development promised by the Enlightenment since a contract focused on the here and now cannot underwrite a sustainable form of development, one that meets the needs of present generations without compromising those of future generations. Hence our present need for a natural contract. The philosopher Michel Serres was the first to put forward this idea in a work entitled *The Natural Contract*,[1] which develops a thesis that I now propose to summarize and discuss.

The foundations of the natural contract

The first key idea advanced by Michel Serres is that there is a strict equivalence between the mainspring of the social and natural contracts. Just as in Hobbes' view it was fear that precipitated the social contract (he indeed thought that he himself was born of the extraordinary fear experienced by his mother when she saw the Invincible Armada sailing off the coasts of England), so the basis of the natural contract is what the philosopher Hans Jonas called the 'heuristics of fear'. As Michel Serres says, 'We must decide on peace among ourselves to protect the world, and peace with the world to protect ourselves.'

Michel Serres's second key idea is that the natural contract is made necessary by a change in scale in the psycho-political history of the human species. The 'I' has now become impossible and the 'we' outmoded. Action on Planet Earth today comes 'not so much from man as individual and subject (...), not so much from the groups analysed by the old social sciences—assemblies, parties, nations, armies, tiny villages—no, the decisive actions are now, massively, those of enormous and dense tectonic plates of humanity.' 'A major contractual actor of the human community', Michel Serres writes, '[today] weighs at least a quarter-billion souls'. The human being now exists only in the aggregate. 'Yes, the megalopolises are becoming physical variables; they neither think nor graze, they weigh.'[2]

---

1. Michel Serres, *The Natural Contract*, trans. Elizabeth MacArthur and William Paulson, Ann Arbor, University of Michigan Press, 1995.

The third key idea of Michel Serres is that there is an equivalence between human beings in the aggregate and nature in its totality. 'The new counterpart of these new plates of humanity is global nature, Planet Earth in its totality, the seat of reciprocal and crossed interrelations among its local elements and its giant components—oceans, deserts, atmospheres, or stocks of ice. The new plates themselves are the seat of reciprocal and crossed interrelations among individuals and subgroups, their tools, their world-objects, and their knowledge, assemblages that are little by little losing their relations with place, locality, neighbourhood, proximity.' In other words, 'being-there' is becoming rarer.

The fourth key idea of Michel Serres is that the hypothetical natural contract cannot ignore the growing role of science in human history. Science's role in this respect is very ambiguous. It reinforces the social contract through a knowledge pact. Indeed, the origin of science 'resembles the origin of human societies as if they were sisters: the pact of knowing, a type of social contract, controls the expressions of knowledge. But this pact does not make peace with the world, even though it is closer to it.'

The fifth key idea is that we are going to have to master our mastery. This programme is inevitable: according to a Canadian study, three Planet Earths would be necessary if the development models and consumption patterns of North America were to be extended to all human societies. If North American prosperity were to spread to the planet as a whole, which would be a positive scenario, the situation would be literally unmanageable given the current state of development models. These approaches therefore need to be completely changed. Many experts have welcomed the fact that the developed democracies are no longer fighting among themselves. However, they should have added that they have ganged up against the world, which has become a kind of scapegoat of development. This war is 'literally a world war, and doubly so, since the whole world, meaning all men, imposes losses on the world, meaning things. [...] Why must we now seek to master our mastery? Because, unregulated, exceeding its purpose, counterproductive, pure mastery is turning against itself. [...] We must then change direction and abandon the heading imposed by Descartes's philosophy. Because of these crossed interactions, mastery only lasts for the short term before turning into servitude; property, similarly, has a rapid ascendancy or else ends in destruction'.

The sixth key idea is that we find ourselves, as we enter the twenty-first century, at a bifurcation in history—encapsulated by Michel Serres in the phrase 'either death or symbiosis'. This means that we must break with a parasitic vision—still widespread—of our place in the world. I have underlined that the social contract, as exemplified in the Universal Declaration of

---

2. 'Elles ne pensent, ni ne paissent. Elles pèsent.' The alliterative assonance of the original French is necessarily 'lost in translation'.—Translator's note.

Human Rights, overlooked nature and the world. We continue to conceive rights on the basis of a progressively expanding conception of the entity invested with rights. Michel Serres notes that in the past 'not just anyone could attain this status'. The Declaration of the Rights of Man and of the Citizen enabled every man, but not every woman, to obtain the status of subject invested with rights. The social contract was completed with the integration of women. But it closed upon itself, 'leaving the world on the sidelines, an enormous collection of things reduced to the status of passive objects to be appropriated. [...] Exclusively social, our contract is becoming poisonous for the perpetuation of the species, its global and objective immortality'.

What, though, is nature? It is firstly, we are told, 'all the conditions of human nature itself, its global constraints of birth and extinction, the hostelry that gives us lodging, heat and food. But nature also takes them away from us as soon as we abuse them. It influences human nature, which, in turn, influences nature'. Nature behaves as if it were a subject.

Michel Serres's seventh key idea is that the time has come to give an essential new dimension to the exclusively social contract through the addition of a natural contract of symbiosis and reciprocity, whereby we would set aside mastery and possession in our relationship with things in favour of reciprocity and respect and whereby knowledge would no longer imply property, nor action mastery. This contract would be, literally, a peace and armistice contract, which would put an end to the war on nature. It would thus be a contract of symbiosis. Michel Serres explains that the 'symbiont recognizes the hosts rights, whereas a parasite—which is what we are now—condemns to death the one he pillages and inhabits, not realizing that in the long run he is condemning himself to death too.' Today, rights to mastery and property are increasingly tantamount to parasitism. Conversely, rights of symbiosis 'are defined by reciprocity: however much nature gives to man, man must give that much back to nature, now a legal entity'. The most ancient civilizations, as studied by anthropologists, were the first to cultivate this wisdom.

Is nature a legal entity?

The eighth key idea of Michel Serres takes the form of a question. Is the conclusion of a natural contract dependent on the recognition of nature as a subject invested with rights? I do not think so. I said that nature acted 'as if it were a subject' and not 'as a subject'. It would always be easy for a critic of the natural contract to object that the promotion of nature to the rank of a legal person is no more than a philosophical metaphor. In recent years, a polemic has blown up, particularly in the Anglo-Saxon world, between those who are mooting or advocating the extension of rights to the non-human world, to non-human entities in the sense not only of animals and plants but even the inanimate world, and those who reject such an extension, while recognizing that we have duties and responsibilities to species or to the planet. The dispute in question divides those who think, unlike Hobbes, that animals and stones are legal entities and those who hold to the traditional view that, since they lack language, reasoning and the ability to validate the contract by signs or marks, animals and stones have no legal personality.

However, the metaphorical hypothesis that recognizes nature as a legal subject seems to me largely superfluous for the purpose of concluding a natural contract—on two grounds. The first is that, as Gregory Bateson argued with visionary insight several decades ago in a work entitled *Steps to an Ecology of Mind*,[3] the unit of survival is not, contrary to Darwin's belief, the reproductive individual, nor the lineage, nor the species or subspecies, but rather that subtle entity constituted by the organism in its environment. If we grasp this notion of ecological security, we also understand that the party to the social contract can without discontinuity be party to the natural contract, and that an ecology of nature must be matched by an ecology of the human mind. Human rights must be proclaimed in the human being's natural setting, as was done two centuries ago for the human being divorced from the environment.

Secondly, the natural contract is not concluded simply between persons and living organisms in their environment in the present, but also with the virtual legal persons constituted by the members of future generations. I know that many legal experts still have a problem with this notion. But this is to overlook that the Roman law of succession recognizes the right of children to be born and thus makes them virtual legal persons. From this standpoint, the natural contract thus gives the social contract a future dimension.

The keywords of the natural contract

The ninth key idea of Michel Serres is that the natural contract would remain a dead letter if we did not devise a new conception of politics and of political leadership. Our current bureaucracy is underpinned by a form of 'bureaulogy', in other words, a world that exists only when seen from a bureau, or a laboratory. Those who govern must now go outside of the human sciences, outside the streets and walls of the city, become physicists, emerge from the social contract, invent a new contract by giving back to the word *nature* its original meaning of our natal and native conditions, the conditions in which we are born—or ought to be reborn tomorrow. We must therefore give the name 'cybernetic' to this art of steering, literally 'symbiotic, to this art of governing (as in the art of

---

3. Gregory Bateson, *Steps to an Ecology of Mind*, San Francisco, Chandler Publishing, 1972.

navigation) by loops engendered by angles that engender in turn other directional angles, a 'technique [...] specific to helmsmen's work'. This new cartography of power is seen as the potential source of a form of geopolitics, in the full etymological sense of the term, meaning a real Earth policy rather than the erstwhile games of international relations.

The tenth key idea is that the natural contract is both virtual and unsigned, in the same way as the social contract and the scientific contract, since it seems to be the case that the great fundamental contracts remain tacit. Yet if the natural contract remains virtual, it is nevertheless a contract that is binding and that binds people together. For any contract 'creates a collection of bonds, whose network canonizes relations; today nature is defined by a set of relations whose network unifies the whole Earth'. In this sense, the natural contract can be said to connect in a single network the social and the scientific contracts. Connect and love, these are the keywords of the natural contract, which relate it closer to the spiritual realm than to modernity, which has progressively imposed in the sphere of nature the opposite of religion, which is not atheism but negligence.

The last key idea, finally, is that the natural contract is inseparable from the ethic of the future, whose outlines I have attempted to define in a number of texts that conclude the report *The World Ahead*[4] and which is the cornerstone of a forward-looking conception of democracy. For it will be necessary in the twenty-first century to extend the reach of democracy, not only in space—through a form of international governance capable of dealing with problems that have become crossborder and transnational in character—but also in time, for the problems are transtemporal. Reintroducing transmission into the contract will be one of the main thrusts of the natural contract. To be sure, as the poet René Char said, 'our heritage is preceded by no testament', but the natural contract should constitute a kind of blank legacy that safeguards the options of future generations.

Such a contract will be all the more crucial since we are currently faced by a major danger: the appropriation of the living via the patenting of the discoveries of genetic engineering. The natural contract should set limits to such procedures and should forestall abuses. It is worth pointing out in this connection that Locke's social contract prohibited the appropriation of the human body, unlike that of Hobbes, who sanctioned slavery and the appropriation of another's body. Freedom of industry cannot prevail over the fundamental rights of the individual. The natural contract will therefore, in my view, be a key element in the future global contract.

---

4. *The World Ahead: Our Future in the Making*, London, UNESCO Publishing/Zed Books, 2001.

Thomas Odhiambo

The Future of Biodiversity

Biodiversity is an amazing consequence of the creative fecundity of nature. It is demonstrated in that genetic diversity which, in the terrestrial landscape, is closely associated with the diversity of ecosystems. Over a quarter of a million species of vascular plants are already known to science. They are found all over the world, but the majority are native to the tropics and subtropics. It is believed that another 25,000 species await discovery.

However, it is also estimated that some 20 to 24 million hectares of tropical forest, which contain the vast majority of the world's vascular plants, are cleared or degraded each year. Since the beginning of the millennium, approximately 60 percent of the world's forests have been permanently cleared. Such horrendous statistics evoke doomsday images for many people, including Peter Raven of the Missouri Institute. He stated that 'not since the end of the Cretaceous period, 65 million years ago, when about two-thirds of the organisms on land disappeared along with dinosaurs, have extinction rates approached those of the present.' Scientists estimate that as many as 40,000 of our approximately 170,000 species of tropical plants may soon become extinct. These biologically diverse ecosystems are being destroyed at a rate far greater than that at which biologists can learn about them. Simply cataloguing these species before they disappear is not enough. If they are to provide us with new products, it is important that we learn about their biology, the role they play in the ecosystem and their relationship to nature.

The necessary partnership between biodiversity and biotechnologies

Twenty-nine nations have recently set up the Global Diversity Information Facility. Using a fund of $39 million, it will attempt to catalogue all of the world's biological species. This is a mammoth task that, in reality, requires the billion dollar funding that was provided to the Human Genome Project. Cataloguing plant species is probably the simplest assignment this facility has. Given that herbaria and botanical gardens throughout the world have already developed their own compendiums, the essential task of the facility will be to cross-reference these databases. The cataloguing of other organisms, particularly micro-organisms and invertebrates, is a far more arduous task. For example, there exist an estimated 3 million insect species, the majority of which are to be found in the tropics and most of which are still unknown to science.

The great scientific expeditions that took place from the eighteenth century to the beginning of the twentieth century are the zeniths of history's survey of flora and fauna. These expeditions created the solid foundation on which much of bioscience was based. The theory of evolution, the basics of economics in botany and the understanding of functional morphology are examples of this.

For all this vast progress in taxonomic and bio-geographic knowledge, built up over the last 250 years, we still have only a modicum of knowledge on the enormous array of living organisms. If we were to spend the next few decades building up a body of physiological, ecological and genetic knowledge of a representative group of species living in a representative ecosystem, and further, if this profound understanding were to be interactively linked to a body of knowledge of the microworld of genomes of these organisms, the scientific world would possess an explosive new clarity in its comprehension of the biosphere. It is probable that the technological advances engendered by this more holistic approach will lead to the creation of exciting new products and services derived from our biological knowledge.

This approach gives biodiversity a future far beyond a quantitative interest in survival and conservation. The Crucible Group, which did so much between 1988 and 1993 to sensitize the world to the looming crisis in biodiversity, puts it well: 'Although there is no doubt that today's conservation of biological diversity will yield considerable economic and social benefits in the years ahead, we recognize that economic gains will grow slowly, that there will be few economic windfalls, and that only those countries that have both conservation and development strategies for diversity are likely to reap significant rewards.'[1] The world at large and the trustees of biodiversity must take this into account.

---

1. The Crucible Group, *People, Plants and Patents: The Impact of Intellectual Property on Trade, Plant Biodiversity and Rural Society*, Ottawa, IDRC, 1994.

This conservation-cum-development strategy would constitute the first real quantum leap in biological knowledge and its application since biotechnology exploded in 1973. Nations that show rich biological diversity, most of which are developing countries located in the tropics, must finally undertake what should have been started twenty years ago: acquiring and enhancing their knowledge of molecular biology; developing the capacity to begin biotechnological research and technological development for a new scientific understanding; and innovating the new products and services that will ensure food security in the developing countries and human health everywhere. I include in this category protection from AIDS, cancer, degenerative diseases and the major tropical diseases. This partnership between biodiversity and biotechnology, which must be designed for the benefit of humanity in developing countries and around the globe, is a challenge that every scientist in the developing world should adopt.

New systems

Early in the twenty-first century, we must set out to effect an intimate marriage between the vast body of knowledge that has been developed over millennia in the agrarian culture of the tropics, and the modern scientific knowledge that has accumulated through experimentation and testable observation in modern industrial culture. The world is beginning to recognize that the community-innovation system is vibrant in the tropical developing countries. Particularly in respect of medicinal plants and in seed selection for domestic food reserves. This knowledge occurs within the context of the ethical-religious-cultural heritage that indigenous peoples have always sustained. The Crucible Group concludes succinctly: 'Although [we] fully recognize that the protection of species and ecosystems is a powerful moral obligation, we also know that any sound conservation strategy must correspond with the interests of the people who depend upon diversity most closely. Conservation programs that meet the needs of these people—that is, the indigenous peoples—have a good chance of working, and we ignore this fact at our peril.' Artificial barriers between conservation and sustainable use must be broken down. Rural communities use diversity because they need to. To them, diversity means choices and opportunities. Acknowledged and empowered, rural communities are arguably the most effective, efficient and economical servers of biological diversity.

As they are currently formulated, intellectual property rights are an immovable roadblock to this intimate marriage. They prevent the international community from recognizing and acknowledging indigenous peoples' full ownership of the innovations and knowledge they have developed. During discussions that were stimulated by the Rio Earth

Summit in June 1992, and the subsequent negotiations that were engendered by Agenda 21, intellectual property rights over living resources became the most contentious political and commercial issue ever considered. The issue is not likely to go away. Even as the rules are being ratified by the WTO, critical elements of intellectual property rights relating to this area are still under debate.

Patentability

Signatory states can exclude plants and animals from patentability as long as they provide for the protection of plant varieties by way of patents or an effective *sui generis* system. In addition, they must allow for the patenting of micro-organisms.

A community research program to rationalize opposition

A proposal has been made to establish a community research program on traditional values and forest-related knowledge, integrating the traditional and academic methodologies of community innovation systems and hypothesis-based innovation systems. Such a program involves a variety of stakeholders, encompassing elders of traditional communities, community-based organizations, indigenous peoples' organizations, local communities, non-governmental organizations, governmental establishments, academic research institutions, and even agency institutions such as FAO and UNESCO. This program is intended to forge a rational alignment from the widely opposing positions now taken by the two different sources of knowledge and innovation.

Farmers' rights

Using the mechanisms established by the FAO Commission on Plant Genetic Resources and the Convention on Biological Diversity signed at the Rio Summit, several groups intend to establish a convention on Farmers' Rights. The Indigenous Peoples' Biodiversity Network is among these.

Balancing demands over patents

At the heart of the raging controversy concerning patents on life lie questions about both genetic resources and the sharing of benefits. It is important that we strike a balance between the demands of the North and those of the South. Industrialized countries seek to embrace the entire intellectual property rights regime, while rural communities and indigenous societies reject the monopolistic system that threatens biodiversity and food security and shows disrespect for their unique community-innovation systems.

The language of Agenda 21, which repeatedly refers to a fair and equitable sharing of benefits, remains purely rhetorical as not a single country has met this international commitment to protect and strengthen the rights of community-innovation systems and the benefits arising from them. Indeed, the intellectual property rights regimes are increasingly being characterized as predators of indigenous knowledge.

Patenting genes

Natural genes cannot be patented since they already exist and are merely 'discovered' by geneticists. Engineered genes, however, can be patented as they have been invented by the linking or splicing together of segments of natural genes. That which is patented is the newly existing gene and the product it produces. A bitter brawl is in the making, however, as Europeans in general, and Britons in particular, vehemently reject genetically modified foods imported from the United States. Consequently, even though scientists pronounce genetically modified foods as safe, consumers consider scientific judgment to be inadequate. They demand absolute assurance against risk.

Co-equals in innovation

Efforts in bio-prospecting, which are intended to find new chemicals or compounds for pharmaceutical use, have become highly controversial, especially since multinational pharmaceutical firms have concluded apparently unfair contracts with indigenous peoples. For example, the contracts recently signed by Merck Pharmaceuticals do not include provisions for the sharing of scientific knowledge and techniques with community innovators. Similarly, no R&D programs providing for joint registration of accruing patents have been established. Clearly, the two innovation groups have not been treated as equals in terms of work, results or benefits. If we are to protect the present and future of biodiversity, we must ensure that partners are treated as equals.

The world heritage model

Thirty thousand protected areas, located in some 150 countries worldwide, have been designated. They cover a total area of 13.2 million square kilometres or approximately 9 percent of the world's land surface. There are several types of protected areas: habitat and species management areas, national parks, nature reserves and managed resource protected areas. The latter are managed for the sustainable use of natural ecosystems. Perhaps the protected areas that possess the most potential for biodiversity in the future are the biosphere reserves and the wild heritage areas. These are managed in cooperation with host nations. UNESCO has been very closely associated with this quantum leap.

The World Heritage Sites operate under the World Heritage Convention, which was adopted by UNESCO's General Assembly in 1972. It is the most widely recognized conservation agreement in the world, with 153 countries currently adhering to it. The World Conservation Union coordinates the natural heritage programme, which has led to the inscription of 142 natural heritage sites on the World Heritage list. These sites were established in order to fulfil the following objectives: to identify, protect and reserve areas of outstanding universal value; to encourage countries to nominate sites for inclusion in the World Heritage list (New Zealand is currently considering the prospect of including some of its sub-Antarctic islands); to assist countries in the protection of these areas through professional training, technical assistance and financial support; to create a duty for the international community to cooperate in the conservation of natural heritage.

These objectives are important in that they put into practice cooperation, solidarity and universal values, all of which will be the hallmark of the twenty-first century. Accommodating traditions of tenure within new arrangements can be a powerful means of promoting forest conservation and centres of biodiversity.

One of the most attractive features of the World Heritage sites lies in the fact that they are intended to form a comprehensive network and embrace a full range of forest ecosystems. This network will allow us to maintain ecological viability and integrity and to preserve the biotic diversity within these ecosystems. The sites are also large enough to be viable and are contiguous or are connected by ecological corridors. This ecological innovation should ultimately accomplish the conservation of biodiversity.

In conclusion, humanity as a whole can only use its natural heritage to the fullest if it does not lose sight of the library of knowledge that has been left to it by generations past. That library has been accumulated and tested through the community innovation system as well by the hypothesis-based R&D innovation system. Like the human brain, it is only useful if it is integral and accessible exactly when it is needed.

Mostafa Tolba

Environment and Development in the Approaches to 2020

The 1992 United Nations Conference on Environment and Development, at which the famous Agenda 21 was negotiated, required three years of preparation. Both before and after this event, a huge number of legally binding treaties were signed. These established rules about the environment at the global, regional and inter-regional levels. I mention these events to lay down the background against which the drafting of any future environmental contracts will take place as well as to show the difficulty in sifting through this material to reach a meaningful strategy that can take us into the next century.

Sustainable development

As we approach the twenty-first century, our concept of environmental responsibility is based on tenets first expressed nearly 200 years ago. George Perkins Marsh, in his 1864 classic *Man and Nature*, tells us that '[m]an can control the environment for good, as well as ill'. He also states that '[w]isdom lies in seeking to preserve the balance of Nature' and that '[t]he present generation has an obligation, above all, to secure the welfare of future generations'. The discussion we are having today is nothing more than a rehearsal of ideas which were summed up more than 200 years ago. It is time to stop re-inventing the wheel and to move onto action.

At the turn of the century, Mahatma Ghandi was asked if he would like a free India to become like Great Britain. He replied, 'Certainly not! If it took Great Britain half the resources of the globe to become what it is today, how many globes would India need?'

The concerns voiced at the 1972 Stockholm United Nations Conference on the Human Environment and subsequent international conferences leading up to the 1992 Earth Summit in Rio de Janeiro and the Commission on Sustainable Development have led to the present theory and practice of sustainable development. Central to this conception are the following tenets: current practices must not undermine future standards of living; economic systems must maintain or improve their resource and environmental base for future generations. To ensure that future generations have the same, or better, opportunities than the present generation, there is full accord that sustainable development should cover economic growth, social development and environmental protection.

Challenges in the twenty-first century

I would like to describe some of the challenges that I believe we will face in the next century.

Socio-economic and political challenges

Poverty levels continue to be high in the three regions where developing countries exist, but most particularly in Africa. This poverty exists in contrast to the continuing wasteful pattern of consumption by rich countries in the North and the rich segments of societies in the South. The world's population continues to grow, all the while migrating to different regions of the planet and changing in age structure. This is coupled with a continuing high percentage of illiteracy in developing countries.

We have been witness to changes in the status and role of women in the labour force. Economic business markets have been changed by globalization while trade regimes and information systems continue to evolve. The regionalization of economies is another noticeable trend. Still in the labour market, our concepts of the labour force, work, leisure, and underemployment are changing due in large part to automation. Finally, companies are shifting toward a focus on low labour costs, improved productivity and the drive for improved corporate efficiency.

Other major trends include: a proliferation of terrorism, which is becoming increasingly destructive and difficult to prevent; the growing sophistication of organized crime, which has now created links with terrorism; the increasing severity of religious, ethnic and racial conflicts; the introduction of trading in pollution, tradable permits, carbon dioxide credits, and joint implementation programs; the increasing importance of foreign direct investment, coupled with a continuing decline in social-development assistance; the issue of the interrelationship between trade and the environment. The gap between the living standards of the rich and the poor promises to become more extreme and divisive. World Bank figures show that average per capita income in low-income countries grew by 3.4 percent form 1986 to 1994. This compares with 1.9 percent for high-income countries. It is tempting to conclude that wealth is increasing for both the rich and the poor. In reality, if we exclude India and China from the figures, income in the low-income countries fell by 1.1 percent. According to the *1996 Human Development Report*,[1] nearly ninety countries are in poorer economic condition than they were ten years earlier. The gap in per capita income between the industrial countries and the developing world tripled between 1960 and 1993.

Today, the net worth of the world's 358 richest billionaires is equal to the combined income of the poorest 45 percent of the world's population, or 2.3 billion people. Leaving aside the moral implications of this figure, this issue could lead to increased instability and social migrations that could economically and politically swamp richer nations. The income gap is widening, not only between the countries of the first and third worlds, but also within countries. In the United States, the richest 1 percent of society have more wealth that the poorest 90 percent. Finally, I think we are moving dangerously towards the twenty-first century without a framework for democracy and justice. This will probably be the most difficult issue we will come to face.

Environmental, scientific and technological challenges

Turning to the domains of the environment, science and technology, the challenges we will face at the beginning of the next millennium can be summarized as follows:

- The increasing industrialization of developing countries, implying significant pressure on environmental and natural resources.

- The rapid change in all forms of technology, including biotechnology (especially genetic engineering), micro-electronics and information technology.

- Persistent and growing shortages in natural resources—water shortages being of particular concern.

- Continuing serious global environmental problems. We are concerned with problems such as climatic change, global warming, the depletion of the ozone layer, and the loss of biodiversity. Problems arising from the production and transportation of toxic waste and hazardous chemicals, air and water pollution, pollution of the marine environment etc. will also be among the challenges that we carry with us into the next century.

---

1. *1996 Human Development Report*, UNDP, 1996.

- The threat of new and re-emerging diseases and micro-organisms that have developed immunity. Recent outbreaks of bubonic plague in India, the Ebola virus in Africa, and drug-resistant tuberculosis in the United States are causing the world to rethink its public health policies. The continuing spread of the AIDS epidemic is obviously another major concern.

- The aging of nuclear power plants around the world. Plants that are currently in existence are designed to operate for a period of between thirty and fifty years. At the end of this period, the plants have to be dismantled, and the sites made safe for other uses. As a consequence, more than three hundred facilities around the world will have to be decommissioned by the year 2010. Only about seventy commercial reactors have been removed from operation to date, and it is my strong belief that the scientific techniques for the decommissioning of reactors are not satisfactory.

- The unexpected and the unknown. Thirty years ago, climate change, ozone depletion and the loss of biodiversity were unspoken of. Today, they are major issues on our agenda.

Areas for action

Without wishing to be presumptuous, I can imagine a number of areas which could be considered for action in the next twenty or thirty years.

Firstly, we must aim to devise appropriate means for empowering women, youth, and the poor in the design and implementation of development policies and programs using new information technologies. This subject has aroused much discussion, but thus far no practical answer has been forthcoming. We lack methodologies for empowerment.

The promotion of democracy is, naturally, an important area for action, but we should ask if this can really be achieved. Can we impose democracy by force? Are the democracies of the developing world really democratic or do we most often see lip-service being paid to democratic ideals? We are in sore need of a frank and honest discussion. This remains a basic requirement for further development.

International water authorities must provide as much help as possible in establishing policies and strategies to efficiently manage diminishing freshwater resources. The availability of freshwater, and particularly shared resources, is going to be *the* issue of the twenty-first century, whether we like it or not. It is pointless to hide our heads in the sand. We need to prepare the mechanisms for the resolution of the conflicts that are going to occur between countries sharing water resources.

Careful use of genetic engineering in food and pharmaceutical production should become an overall strategy for the development of technology.

There is also much progress to be made in furthering our understanding of climate change, ozone depletion, and the loss of biodiversity.

A major role has to be given to the issues arising from the use of economic instruments for the implementation of relevant global treaties and to the setting of price tags for the services of the environment and its natural resources. Without resolving the questions that these issues raise, there can be no rational use of the environment, its components, or its natural resources.

A strategic focus must be maintained on the issues of ensuring global food security, conserving natural resources, and bringing about an urgent shift in power generation to new and renewable sources of energy, within the context of a change from the irrational non-sustainable patterns of consumption that undermine the environment and natural resources.

We should strive towards achieving an improved understanding of the content and impact of the market-driven globalization that is taking place.

Conclusion

Certainly the road ahead will not be smooth. It will demand a series of reforms to confront failed economic policies and to instigate new structural adjustment programs. Above all, it will require money. These reforms offer the opportunity, in the long term, to alleviate poverty and to meet basic human needs as well as to bring about the end of economic conditions that promote environmental degradation. Imagination, determination and courage will be required if we are to oust the rigidly unfair and protectionist international economic order, eliminate commodity price volatility and overcome the crippling debt and chronic poverty that presently strangle society.

The road is a long and hard one. Five years after the 1992 Earth Summit in Rio, a United Nations General Assembly Special Session was organized in order to evaluate progress in the implementation of Agenda 21. At that time, the heads of state in attendance declared that, although some progress had been made, the overall situation was worse in June 1997 than it had been five years before. A commitment was then made to move from words to deeds. Today, that action has still to materialize.

Framing a Cultural Contract for the Twenty-First Century

Since 11 September 2001, Samuel Huntington's concept of a 'clash of civilizations' has returned to the headlines with a vengeance. In the view of many specialists, this over-simplistic notion—which has something of the self-fulfilling prophesy about it—masks the profound complexity of the cultural question viewed from a global perspective. Others, rather than thinking in terms of a clash of civilizations or cultures, prefer to argue the need for a 'cultural contract'. At a time when culture is no longer regarded as a fixed entity and when globalization seems paradoxically to be giving rise to a dual movement of standardization and fragmentation in the cultural domain, the framing of a cultural contract would seem both necessary and problematic. How can one reaffirm certain universalist principles without running the risk of establishing a new order dominated by a single culture? Is it even possible to conceive of a cultural project, to the extent that culture always presupposes scope for transgression?

Reflecting on the conditions under which such a contract might be possible, Alain Touraine places the issue of cultural rights in a historical perspective and proposes an approach centred on the theme of recognition. Hélé Béji argues that the preservation of cultural diversity should not serve to advance the claim that culture is all that there is to be said about the human being. Finally, Eduardo Portella contrasts the technological model of reproduction, or cultural cloning, with an approach to culture viewed in terms of hybridization.

* * * *

Sociologist **Alain Touraine** is the founder of the Centre d'Etudes des Mouvements Sociaux at the Paris Ecole des Hautes Etudes en Sciences Sociales (EHESS). A member of the Academy of Latinity and of the Academia Europea, he is the author of *Critique of Modernity* (1995), *Can We*

Live Together? Equality and Difference (2000), *La recherche de soi* (2000) and *Beyond Neoliberalism* (2001).

Essayist, writer and former professor at the Faculty of Tunis, **Hélé Béji** was the founder in 1998 of the International College of Tunis, of which she is president. Her research is centred on the anthropology of decolonization. The author of numerous articles in *Le Débat* and *Esprit*, her published works include *Désenchantement national, essai sur la décolonisation* (1982), *Itinéraire de Paris à Tunis* (1992) and *L'Imposture culturelle* (1997).

Philosopher, writer, literary critic, **Eduardo Portella** is emeritus professor of the Federal University of Rio de Janeiro, founder president of the Organization for the Development of Science and Culture and director of research at the Colegio do Brasil, ex-president of the Brasilian National Library Foundation, and president of the International Fund for the Development of Culture. He is also a member of the Brazilian Academy of Letters. A former minister of culture of Brazil, he has also been deputy director-general of UNESCO and president of the UNESCO General Conference.

Alain Touraine

The Case for a Cultural Contract

I take it that my task is not to spell out what a cultural contract might look like but rather to justify an expression that is by no means self-evident. 'Culture' and 'contract' are words that seem diametrically opposed. Whereas we can grasp the idea of a natural contract or a social contract, the concept of a cultural contract is difficult, impossible even, to comprehend. Culture always has a simultaneously universal and particular dimension. If we place exclusive stress on the differences, we are pitched into a world of incommunicability, which is sometimes one of indifference or pure tolerance, but more usually one of warring deities and violence.

From political rights to cultural rights

How might this universal be defined in specific terms? Religions regularly try to frame ecumenical projects. But attempts of this kind invariably founder, either because the proposed ecumenism amounts to no more than pious sentiment, or because it cannot withstand the tensions between the different religions. We are thus in a situation where we cannot see how it is possible to treat separately or, conversely, to combine the universalistic and particular character of each culture. Devising a contract between cultures is such a contradictory undertaking that we traditionally maintain that the only way of establishing rules of communication and respect among cultures is to accord autonomy to the political order.

Cultures have always seemed either head-in-the-clouds or too earthbound, that is to say, midway between the divine and the social. Politics was invented with the specific task of coming up with the definition of a society reconciling different and competing cultures. Yet if politics were the right answer, the debate would be over. It would have ended with the Declaration of the Rights of Man and of the Citizen in 1789, and there would be no obvious reason to re-open it today. Why, then, is it being so reopened?

The main problem confronting us today is the weakening of political institutions. So long as non-citizens existed alongside citizens, what mattered was to ensure that all people had access to citizenship. For some 150 years now, we have started to assert ourselves as more than just citizens, to consider that our rights do not end with citizenship. Being a citizen is of little consequence to us if we are ground down by our working conditions, by discrimination or by segregation. In 1848, we began to ask ourselves a critical question: how can we maintain a universality of rights while applying those rights not to the political structures overlaying the social realm but rather to the social and cultural world as a whole?

We started, with great difficulty, by thinking about social rights, that is, about work. The industrialized countries proceeded to proclaim the intention to defend workers' rights and the dictatorship of the proletariat. Taking a lead from the British, we gradually invented the idea of an industrial democracy or social democracy. For a period of fifty to a hundred years, this remained our basic response. Citizenship is a universal attribute. The worker is defined by social relationships.

Today we find ourselves facing a similar problem. We want a democracy that is both political and social, but we also want a cultural democracy. Cultural rights are not the right to be different, just as workers' rights are not the rights of a particular social category. What is at issue today is the right of each and everyone to combine participation in the modern world—we all want to enjoy the technical and economic benefits of modernity, whose communication and production technology are globally present—with the possibility of preserving, reinterpreting and even inventing one or more identities. At a time when political universalism threatens to disintegrate and dissolve in social conflicts and cultural incomprehension, we wish to affirm that the universal is not a content but rather a right. The universal is the right that we all have to be both equal and different. It is the right that we possess, not to construct a modern and rational society but rather to fashion an individual response. What is important is to recognize that we are all, each in our own way, in search of individual solutions to the same problem. We can only look for our own solution if we recognize the right of others to seek their own solution. We communicate not because we discover that the possibilities for universal communication exist but because we recognize that we are all in the process of fashioning responses, all of them individual yet all communicable.

Contracts of communication

What is the condition that makes it possible for each of us to forge an individual connection between the technological and economic globalization of the world and our particular inheritances, creations and cultural transformations? I believe that the essential condition is rejection of the idea that everything is all of a piece. Communication between cultural elements and individual experience is only possible if beliefs, law and customs are dissociated. Communication between beliefs is always possible. Communication between institutionalized beliefs is difficult. Communication between customs is totally impossible. To take the view that the economy should be free of any social bond and should even exercise a kind of hegemony over the other dimensions of the social system is to envisage society as 'all of a piece'. It is not possible to achieve the kind of social construction I have described, one allowing people to express individual responses, within a strictly capitalist conception of the world. Such a conception is totalizing in the same way as a theocratic outlook.

We cannot communicate and we cannot establish contracts of mutual communication, cultural contracts of form and content, unless we recognize that culture is not an essence or an identity but an evolving construction. This presupposes separating out the different economic, political, social and cultural dimensions. It accordingly supposes that we accord a measure of autonomy to the political realm, to the public domain and even to civil society. The point is to accommodate the multiplicity of cultural commitments and affiliations within the overall political order.

I began by expressing a doubt about the word 'contract'. I now accept the idea of a contract. I would even go so far as to say that there is no system of communication and integration between what is similar and what is different without an institutionalized recognition of the relationship between the general and the particular, based on every individual's right to combine the two. The idea of a cultural contract is one that should not be divorced from the idea of cultural rights. I repeat, cultural rights do not signify the right to be different, but the right to participate in a global world and at the same time to be culturally specific, particular and singular. In this sense, it is fitting that this issue of the cultural contract should concern us in this new century, just as the short century from 1848 to 1914 was dominated by the issue of the recognition of social rights within the framework of political democracy. Today, it is within this same framework of political democracy, extended to include social rights, that we need to secure democratic recognition of the cultural rights of all.

Hélé Béji

What Future for Cultural Pluralism?

I should like to begin by highlighting a fundamental characteristic of modern evolution—the equality of cultures, which has become a principle inseparable from our democratic awareness. One can no longer point to a hierarchy of cultures, to superior or inferior cultures. They all possess human dignity, an equivalent spiritual value and an equal right to recognition. This is the historical principle that decolonization has made irreversible. However, this positive trend whereby all cultures are becoming emancipated as part of the egalitarian design for a single global civilization conceals another tendency in the form of an intractable and divisive concern with origins, the resurgence of a cultural outlook shaped by a highly subjective vision of the past. Modernity exists in the tension between these two poles.

Civilization is raising us all aloft, like the interrelated parts of some vast construction. But so that we shall not become mere machine-like shadows of ourselves and so that our humanity shall not be lost, it is offering us an alternative in humanitarian self-gratification, in the expression of all our cultural particularities, in a passionate sense of belonging.

This inner schism is at the heart of modern awareness. Technology, in ironing out human differences, provokes an inevitable resistance, rather as if a too impersonal and abstract future itinerary were being absorbed into that of our origins, or as if becoming could today only be experienced in terms of a return.

Cultural passions

Has this multiform renaissance of cultural traditions, which was supposed to result in a significant expansion of the symbolic potential of future societies, lived up to its promise? Following the loss of prestige of European civilization (in the wake of the colonial debacle), has the rise of other cultural *imaginaires* generated new insights? Have we seen the emergence of more viable and humane societies in response to the disarray of a world that is threatening to become 'insane by virtue of being rational', in Eric Weil's admirable phrase? Has the search for cultural origins been successful in forging a more amicable, sociable and humane compact between human beings to offset the loss of social bonds in the modern world?

It would seem not. The diversity of the cultural dream has not resulted in more humane political imaginings. For example, the rehabilitation of indigenous cultural values in the decolonized states has not proved a fruitful source of political freedoms. It has thrown up a few ministries of culture, but the cultural resistance that had constituted a decisive critique of colonial domination has not itself been transformed into a higher political vision. There has been no convincing alternative to the established European model of society. Non-Europe has not yet established itself as a new utopia.

What is the reason for this discrepancy between the ambitious cultural message and its meagre translation into politics? It may firstly be linked to the fact that cultural idealism can be a cloak for dubious ideological stances. We should not think that belonging to a particular culture is a guarantee of sound political administration. A shared tradition is no protection against the negligence, wickedness or injustice of our compatriots. Cultural fraternity is not a sufficient assurance of the humane governance of one's fellow citizens. Our cultural sympathies do not wholly coincide with our political virtues. The political link is not cultural in nature, but rather *civil*. Civic values, not cultural values, are the basis for humanity in politics.

Above all, the exalting of cultural origins may harbour a fantasy of purity close to the delusions of racism. One discerns in the subjective apology of one's own culture (the extreme metaphor for which would be religious ideology) a psychological or moral constraint whose roots are not far removed from obscurantist systems of thought. The original cultural criterion is always obscure. Culture is not always elegance of mind and tolerance of heart. It may be informed by hatred and brutality, conceived as a refinement of culture itself. It follows that cultural discourse may also have the effect of feeding all kinds of despotic longings and oaths of allegiance.

We were under the impression that this tyrannical potential, lurking in the exclusive vision that individuals can have of their own culture, could be checked by cultural pluralism. Indeed, what better apprenticeship of mutual understanding could there be than for cultures to live out their differences, to experience the sustained promiscuity that obliges them to tolerate one another, even where their aspirations are in conflict, and to accept the need for give-and-take when exercising the right to be heard and to express themselves?

Yet a difficulty arises. How can one establish a common principle governing the recognition of cultural rights, inherent to every culture, when each culture is known to be a law unto itself, its own yardstick, and will not readily relinquish its own criteria of the lawful and unlawful, justice and injustice, good and evil, obedience and transgression, and innocence and force? There is a specific hermeticism built into every cultural conviction, which renders ontological discord between cultures intractable. The notion of cultural rights, implying the specific legitimacy of each culture, presupposes the non-recognition of a universally valid moral code. It follows that no act can any longer be reprehensible from a universal moral standpoint, not because it is not blameworthy in itself but because there is no longer any universal conscience in a position to affirm it.

To overcome this dilemma, one would have to think in terms of a higher authority whose comparative genius has managed to derive a new supra-cultural syncretism that could be prescribed for all cultures. But who could occupy this position of indisputable sovereignty? What form of higher *reason* could quell all cultural *passions*, always supposing that the word 'reason' has a similar meaning in all cultures and that the multiplicity of criteria of cultural judgement is not a challenge to reason itself? Pluralism is bound up with the question of the intellectual and emotional misunderstanding between cultures.

The inescapable issue of human rights

When one thinks about it, has not this ideal contract based on sovereign reason and capable of reconciling the irreconcilable already found historical expression in the 1789 Declaration of the Rights of Man and of the Citizen? Do human rights hold the key to the higher formula that would resolve the mutual incompatibility of cultures? The answer turns out to be no, for the simple reason that human rights and cultural rights are diametrically opposed. Human rights are defined as natural rights, in contradistinction to cultural rights. The principle on which human rights are based is precisely that of wrenching the human being from his cultural determinations, also known as his 'prejudices'. Human rights presuppose an end to cultural distinctions and to the pre-eminence of culture. The cultural argument itself is denied any claim to legitimacy. We are all free and equal in rights, whatever our origin, language and beliefs. In contrast, cultural rights give key importance to cultural origin as the principle of recognition between people. They make cultural origin a prior postulate and a decisive argument in human relationships, whereas human rights suspend the cultural criterion in consideration of the individual.

But human rights differ from cultural rights in another equally crucial respect: human rights are subject to a civil law that defines them in terms that are valid for all, whereas the scope of cultural rights is a matter for their defenders to determine. Let me quote Article 4 of the 1789 Declaration of Human Rights: 'Liberty consists in being able to do anything that does not harm other people. Thus, the exercise of the natural rights of each man has only those limits that ensure to the other members of society the enjoyment of these same rights. These limits may be determined only by the law.' The law thus makes rights subject to the authority of the police. A right is never left unconstrained; it is not a right to undefined enjoyment or to unlimited satisfaction. It must always answer to the law for its misuse.

What law is in a position to regulate the enjoyment of cultural rights? As matters stand, no adequate legal code exists. How, then, may we prevent cultural rights being used to justify the unjustifiable? It is one thing to say that every culture embodies some inalienable part of what it means to be human, but it is quite another to make it a ground for impunity, irresponsibility or the exercise of cruelty. Rights without obligations are only appetites, expressing or masking the desire for arbitrary power.

Cultural rights can therefore very easily lead to undertakings rooted in force. From its own standpoint, colonization was a cultural right—the right to civilize the uncivilized. Today, who can prevent some cultures from claiming to have a global mission, precisely because of the right of every culture to heed the promptings of its own genius? After all, Western society may very well be viewed as a vast and highly complex tribe, which derives its energy and its *raison d'être* from the values implicit in exploration, discovery and curiosity and from its Promethean proclivities, even if this is to the detriment of those who are happy to savour their existence without bothering about anything beyond their immediate horizon.

Cultural doctrines, while they may have elevated the weak, have conferred formidable advantages on the strong, those for whom the challenge is to exercise cultural control over their age so as not to let it enslave them.

Here another difficulty looms. Modern cultures, even with the best intentions in the world, can scarcely avoid trampling on older cultures, not because they are superior in intelligence or humanity—they are sometimes more stupid and more inhuman—but because they are the culture of the present. The present is not qualitatively better than the past, but it exists, whereas the past is no longer and will always seem weak and unreal alongside the ability of the present to give shape to its age. We see here the extent to which the question of the equivalence of cultures comes up against the effective inequality of the cultural forces at work.

Is communication a tool of cultural harmonization?

The phenomenon of modernity, in other respects so unremitting, may also conceal its own antidotes. It has given every culture not wishing to be fated to disappear the possibility of linking up with the very essence of modern culture—namely communication. Communication presents every culture with the challenge of devising for itself a persona that is perceptible and identifiable by humanity as a whole. It arguably offers us a unique instrument of cultural orchestration capable of encompassing plurality without sacrificing diversity, in such a way that all cultures may acknowledge each other without crushing one other, confront each other without destroying one other, and express themselves without oppressing each other? Communication sets itself up as that great regulating and ordering authority, that elusive reason arbitrating between cultures, which could convert them to a common method of transmission. The necessity of communicating is to the modern mind what prayer was to the religious mind—the act by which we shall be saved and failing which we shall be damned.

Let us examine the changes that communication brings about to see whether the principle of a cultural compact thereby becomes possible. The first point to make is that the act of communicating has less to do with the content or truth of the message than with the scope and scale of its impact. In this process, understanding is secondary to the perception of images or signals, whose low degree of intellection fosters, through its reductive simplifications, the illusion of a kind of equivalence between falsehood and truth. It follows that communication, while it is our principal channel of information, may not necessarily serve to promote intelligibility. Through communication, every culture perhaps becomes less intelligible than we imagine.

My second observation is that this relative loss of discernment increases in proportion to the inordinate nature of the appeal. It is perhaps in the glorification of difference by competing cultural claims that *indifference* most easily triumphs. Conversely, this growing lack of cultural difference fuels the desire to be different. The more cultures mingle, the more they display a need for purity. There is no certainty that pressure from other cultures will cause us to stop regarding our own values as central. When multiplicity leads us astray, we are brought back to reality by what is central to us. Assertion of one's difference may here be no more than the veiled assertion of one's superiority. The age of communication is no doubt making cultures more accessible to each other, but it may also be making them more narcissistic. Their ceaseless visibility places them in perpetual rivalry.

Thirdly, by sacrificing the complexity of signs to the ubiquity of signs in the interest of propagating them, and by sacrificing depth to display, communication is tending to foster a form of mental domestication and hence the rise of a hegemonic control, not as a result of a conspiracy but through a gradual levelling of opinions and beliefs. It is in this way that communication is tending to become 'global', along the lines of a cultural search for supremacy, whereas the 'universal' presupposes a search for the unity (*unus + versus*: directed towards the one) of the human race, the protection of a shared world by free consent of all its constituents.

My final observation concerns the constraint exercised on every culture by the cult of the topical in the world of communication. The topical must be distinguished from the present. The present is a category of the intemporal, whereas the topical is the world in which signs expire in the very act of appearing and being immediately forgotten. We may thus be witnessing the possible emergence for the first time in history of a *culture without memory*.

There is thus no real certainty that communication can satisfy all the strict requirements of justice and truth implied by a cultural contract. It is a platform that offers all cultures the illusion of self-expression but not the possibility of knowing one another.

The ethical requirement

The difficulties associated with cultural pluralism, some of whose characteristics I have outlined, show that an exclusively cultural contract would be liable to be flawed in principle and inconsistent in content since it would lack a vital ingredient—namely, ethical concern. In other words, culture must no longer be made the pretext for evading the moral issue. If the eulogy of difference heralds a new sophism that can sanction a silent conscience, then I must declare myself in favour of the *disrespect of difference*. It may even be the case that this cultural bias, this frenzied flagging of identity, betrays a lack of moral feeling, a void in the representation of the human, a loss of the sense of the human, in which the search for identity becomes a sort of hypertrophied or hyperbolic compensation for loss of humanity.

But it must be acknowledged that all this is not devoid of meaning. It is not without reason that cultural grievances are being voiced in reaction to the implacable character of modernity, since they coincide with the modern individual's tragic premonition of the absence of a homeland. These cultural grievances tell us that we cannot resist adversity in the abstract. We can only manage to do so with the support of beliefs, reflexes and familiar balances that give us a feeling of invulnerability against the insensitivity of the world. It is simply that there is a danger that these grievances may pit the absence of homeland against another kind of inhumanity in the form of an *excess of homeland*.

Fanaticism on the one hand and rootlessness on the other—these, in a way, are the two immoral dispositions that a human contract between cultures must avoid if it is not to elude the ethical question, situated between the muddle of cultural passions and the generalized torture of their disincarnation.

Despite the profusion of cultures, there is at least one moral question on which a common focus is possible. Can the cultural prerogative provide a foundation for a morality of mutual recognition, a genuine method whereby human beings will recognize each other? Is it not a diminishment of our humanity to reduce human dignity to cultural origin? Can the cultural credo claim to say *everything* about the human? Has not the cultural credo become a pretext for evading the human, for forgetting that the cultural mask may assume not only the features of fraternity but also those of oppression?

Is one a human being simply because one has a culture? The answer is quite clearly no. One is also human 'by nature', as Rousseau[1] would say. Human beings are possessed of a 'natural reason' that prevents them from taking cultural identifications for moral considerations. This natural humanity, which precedes reason and any culture, is what Rousseau defined as sensitivity, 'the natural repugnance at seeing any sentient being, and chiefly our own kind, perish or suffer'. It is that pure impulse of nature, independent of any cultural precept, which Rousseau calls *commiseration*, the basis of morality. 'If I am obliged to do no ill to my fellow men, it is not so much because I am a reasonable being but more because I am a sentient being'. We know that it is because they appeared not to be endowed with reason, i.e., because their culture was not the same as ours, that the natives in the colonies were treated with such cruelty. It was simply forgotten that, even if they were not reasonable beings, they were nonetheless sentient.

Yet, in the last analysis, could this nature of which we are speaking have any meaning without a culture to apprehend it? If we had not read Rousseau, would we even have fashioned an ideal of nature? Is it not the beauty of Rousseau's language that restores to us the strength of our natural feelings? Without culture, would we see nature as a picture? Without culture, would nature speak to us? Would it have a language? The answer is clearly no. And this is why it is for culture to answer for its own aberrations.

A cultural contract must therefore, as a prerequisite, stop believing in the innocence of every culture, state the moral ambiguity of each of them, acknowledge its share of violent or peaceful impulses and of human or inhuman proclivities, recognize its acts of liberty or tyranny, and sooner or later agree to revisit the standpoint of conscience, stop

---

1. Jean-Jacques Rousseau, *Discours sur l'origine et les fondements de l'inégalité parmi les hommes*, Paris, Flammarion, [1754] 1952.

making its origins into a superior reason, its convictions into rights, its differences into a religion, its allegiances into a source of vanity and its identity into a virtue. In a word, it must be able to construe the 'non-me' as a being no less sensitive than the 'me' through a resurgence of the natural and original instinct of compassion. Rousseau said of compassion that 'having lost, from one society to the next (the word "society" could here be replaced by "culture"), all the strength that it commanded between one man and another, lives on only in a few great cosmopolitan souls, who cross the imaginary barriers that separate peoples and who, like the sovereign being who created them, embrace the whole human race in their benevolence.'[2]

---

2. Ibid.

Eduardo Portella

Culture in the Twenty-First Century: Cloning or Hybridization?

What is the state of play concerning the cultural contract today? I think it is fair to say that it is in total disarray. I approach the question from a Latin American perspective, remote from the dominant currents of thought in the West. The issues confronting us stem largely from the problem of intercultural relations. There is every reason to think that the intangible, the subjective and the cultural will play an increasingly important role in the transformation of our societies. In this connection, cultural perception could well turn out to be as important for the new information societies as scientific knowledge has been for industrial societies.

The cultural question is coming to the fore at a time when the advance of globalization is bringing it into conflict with tenacious national identities. While cultures remain rooted in national contexts, it is proving increasingly difficult and untenable to treat as sacrosanct canonical concepts such as 'identity', 'people' and 'nation', predicated on more or less stable patterns. Our societies have never known such a radical break with age-old tradition, even if we cannot live without traditions, albeit reinvented ones. We are indeed entitled to wonder whether those developments usually seen as potential threats to the nation-state might not provide fertile terrain for culture, that is to say, favour the coexistence of diversity as distinct from domesticated cohesion and artificial uniformity.

Culture today

Whatever the case, culture can today no longer be conceived in the absence of an intrinsic, existential and vital tension between the universal, regional, national and local dimensions. The theme of cultural identity, which has been with us since the earliest manifestations of globalization, has run its course. The hegemonic model of identity had its roots in an exclusive, monolithic, autocratic and highly incarcerating concept of culture. Identity was conceived as something fixed and pre-determined that could also be removed, destroyed, dispensed and disseminated. It was brandished like a weapon. We have been slow to realize that racism thrives when cultural identity is elevated into an absolute, including where the concept of race has replaced that of culture. In the twentieth century, we have seen the supposedly most 'sophisticated' cultures succumb to barbarism. The culture of exclusion leads inevitably to the exclusion of culture.

Today, the concept of cultural identity is influenced by the prospect of a planetary culture and is set to modify the profile of universalism, which has shaped and sometimes distorted our outlook. But postnational identities have yet to demonstrate their ability to oppose inequality, injustice, exclusion and violence. To say that culture eludes nationalization is not to sacrifice it on the altar of globalization and privatization. To subordinate culture to the synthetic criteria of the dominant ideology, which is only interested in the ups and downs of the stock market and the fluctuations of supply and demand, and to the siren calls of functionality and urgency is to deprive it of essential social oxygenization and substitute the stress of the market for creative tension.

This form of culturally deprived development is not entirely foreign to the intellectual, moral, subjective and social deficit at the core of the impasses with which we are today confronted. It is too often forgotten that overcoming the social divide implies making good the cultural deficit. Cultural investment is also social investment. The standard approach to culture today, however out of touch with reality and behind the times it may be, is to range it among the superfluous products. There is no escaping the fact that culture, one of the defining traits of modernity, is under strain as we enter the new millennium. That is one of the reasons why I tend to describe the present juncture in the modern age as a period of 'low modernity'. It is not difficult to see why some like to bury modernity behind the prefix 'post'. We live in an age that is too beset by anxiety to carry this project through to its conclusion. The promise of emancipation implicit in modernity still lives on in our hopes; but, engulfed by the one-way metaphysical tide, it looks on puzzled, powerless and paralyzed by the endless procession of inequalities, exclusions and power struggles. Meanwhile, in parts of the world that have still not recovered from colonial domination, wars continue to be waged with total disregard for the most elementary principles of human dignity. There is no shortage of deconstructive energies certainly, but the will to reconstruct is regrettably in short supply.

In the hubbub of the global information society, which lowers communication costs in spectacular fashion and from which zapping provides the only form of escape, the authoritarian face of so-called democratic regimes shows itself. We glimpse the antidemocratic forces concealed within a democracy immersed in video-politics. A kind of electronic fundamentalism lies in wait for us. Under the apathetic gaze of an indolent public, the famous opinion polls—as improvised as they are volatile—reflect little more than the sedentary aspirations of captive consumers. Medical utopias, stupefying audiovisual processes and the spin-offs from scientific progress provide the setting for proclamations concerning the end of history, not to say of humankind. If contemporary art and culture still have anything to say, it is to reject such subservience, this 'chronicle of a cloning foretold'. From prenatal selection to cultural biotechnologization and from serial reproduction to the recycling of modern icons, we hear the ironic message of a revolt of the pre-clones against a profit-motivated eugenicist culture. Technologized culture proclaims itself voided of the natural. Cloning is nothing more than technologizing taken to its limit.

The creative potential of cultural hybridization

How can one technologize culture, reduce it to a series of uniformities and claim that it is still culture? A cloned culture is an abortive culture. When culture ceases to be relationship it ceases to be culture. Relationships are the main identifying mark of culture. Culture is hybrid; and the hybrid is the opposite of the clone. Whereas the clone is the replication of itself, the hybrid is a creation that transcends yet comprehends its progenitors. A distinction should be drawn here between hybrids and GMOs (Genetically Modified Organisms). Often perceived in centralized, or 'pure', civilizations as an unusual, eccentric or even exotic phenomenon, hybridization has nonetheless evinced a wholly spontaneous naturalness wherever it has occurred. Transcending the notion of belonging, it is predicated upon the creation of a new solidarity. It can be an antidote to exclusion. If I may be allowed to parody André Malraux, I would say that the third millennium will be hybrid or nothing.

To argue the case for cultural intermixing is not to deny the universality of science and technology, the fact of modernization and the impact of the network society on our everyday lives. We have to rethink cultural media in terms distinct from the patrimonialist concepts of the fundamentalists and the intellectualist prejudices of hidebound academies. We cannot prejudge the quality of the message according to whether its vehicle is a show, stadium, circle, web, screen or network, any more than a book, library or theatre. We can no longer conceive of culture without taking into account the complexity of the images and languages with which the nervous systems of individuals and society are confronted. In the past, education was the irreplaceable link of cultural transmission, its main aim being the instruction of men and women. With the explosion of the mass media in modern societies, the school has lost or has had to share what used to be seen as its exclusive task. Alongside it, beyond the limits of time and space, *de facto* learning facilities have sprung up, often in haphazard fashion, so as to constitute a new form of 'peripatetic' pedagogy, at once anxious and voracious. The auditoria of modernity, from factories to cultural supermarkets, from kiosques to cinema screens, provide the setting for a process of education and re-education in one's own image.

Traditional cultural mechanisms are no longer sufficient to emancipate culture from the massification that merges human faces and individualities in the crowd. In this connection, it has to be recognized without nostalgia that we live in a mass society. But we must also realize that one of the functions of education today is to 'demassify' the masses. This presupposes that we relinquish our elitist cultural prejudices and open ourselves up to the possibility of new approaches to cultural construction and action.

The challenge, then, is to give an expanded ethical dimension to the cybercommunity. Rather than allowing audience ratings to dictate our choices, we must cultivate excellence of understanding and perception. The political self-consciousness of the citizenry is always shaped in the realm of public communication. There is an urgent need to draw a critical distinction between essentially passive spectators who are mere consumers of images and citizens, whose social individuality has been purged of its individualism and who are in a position to make responsible choices. An active civic community is incompatible with disinformation, lack of information, false information and misinformation, as well as with the multiform traps of videomania and videophobia. I am arguing here for a reshaping of the hegemonic model of the media and thus for a salutary reassertion of cultural differences, pluralistic rationality and the creation of a world assembly of spectators that would counter the apocalyptic drift of the historical process. Globalization will only be conducive to a global democracy if it is underpinned by nations founded on the notion of citizenship.

In mass society, the debate on culture and democracy is bound up not only with the legitimation of plausible authorities but also with a rejection of tradition as the inert depository of identity. In escaping the confines of an identity shaped by a universalistic tradition, we must avoid being drawn to particularisms with their religious and ethnic distortions as well as to mere capricious or revanchist differentialism. National identity cannot be reduced to some untouchable essence, as patriots and ideologues preoccupied with national security imagine. To my knowledge, no genuine culture has never sprung from state-owned factories, even if the state has up to now been well placed to democratize and promote culture or, conversely, to stifle it. The relationship between the state and culture must be radically revamped. There can no longer be any question of inventing culture according to fixed state benchmarks. What is required is to reconstruct the state with open cultural identities. This calls for a change in political culture rather than cultural policy. Emancipating ourselves from identity in its self-centred form leads us to reconstruct a potential cultural identity as an intersubjective experience: a freedom of identity situated at the confluence of adulterated logics, hitherto unpredictable perceptions and currently imperceptible predictions. Identity must be understood as non-autistic. That is why the emancipation of identity is a permanent undertaking.

Towards a cultural contract?

Can we and should we frame a cultural contract? This question gives rise to many paradoxes. Firstly, contracts are drawn up on the basis of standards, whereas culture is sustained by cultural transgressions. The cultural contract would therefore have to include some open clauses, some scope for transcendence of the norm, if it was to have any legal legitimacy. Secondly, such a contract would be situated somewhere between a social contract and a natural contract. Over the course of its development, modern rationality in its hegemonic form has increasingly separated the social from the natural, culminating in the division of the individual into two dissociated halves. From this standpoint, the framing of a cultural contract could be seen as something of an intellectual obstacle race, inasmuch as the culture of discussion is predicated on the discussion of culture. The aim should be to take up the discussion from a post-metaphysical perspective capable of transcending without abolishing the limits of practical reason. We need to preserve the right to be different while avoiding impulses of purification, which in their various manifestations—including the most recent—have shown themselves to harbour much violence.

The hybrid is the open contract, and the clone the closed contract. New values, based on vigorous discussion and dialogue within the civic community, can only be forged through the vital, natural and hence hazardous process of cultural hybridization.

Towards an Ethical Contract?

---ꝏ---

The question of the relationship between ethics and politics is not new: divided as they often are between moral rigour and cynical realism, the two have been seen as irreconcilable. Similarly, doubts about the moral implications of science did not arise with the new century. Today, the biotechnology revolution places us in an unprecedented situation in relation to the living world. At the same time, a world that is tending to become more interdependent as a consequence of globalization encourages us to envisage the ethical question from a new planetary perspective, which makes it impossible to ignore our common destiny. However, we have yet to conceive of a genuine ethical project for humanity that would give renewed meaning to the quest of individuals and societies: this would be the challenge of an ethical contract.

Ryuichi Ida sets out the theoretical, legal and practical difficulties associated with the adoption of a bioethical code at the international level. Edgar Morin, recalling the conflictual relationship between ethics and politics, expresses the aspiration towards a democratic political framework that would enable an ethic of humankind to flourish within the setting of a 'Homeland Earth'. Lord Desai considers the requirements for a more equitable form of development on a global scale; while Luc Montagnier invites us to expand our horizons even more by cultivating a keener awareness of the relationship of humanity to time and space.

* * * *

Ryuichi Ida is professor of international law at the University of Kyoto. He is president of UNESCO's International Bioethics Committee, of which he was chairman from 1998 to 2002 and a member of UNESCO's World Commission on the Ethics of Scientific Knowledge and Technology (COMEST).

A sociologist and emeritus director of research at the CNRS, **Edgar Morin** is also president of the European Cultural Agency (UNESCO) and president of the Association pour la Pensée Complexe. His many publications include *Method* (1992), *Introduction à une politique de l'Homme* (1999), *L'Humanité de l'humanité: l'identité humaine* (2001) and, with Jean Baudrillard, *La violence du monde* (2003).

Lord Meghnad Desai is professor of economics and founder director of the Centre for Global Governance at the London School of Economics and a consultant with numerous organizations such as FAO and the World Bank. He is currently editor-in-chief of the *Journal of Applied Economics* and a member of the editorial board of the *International Review of Applied Econometrics* and several other specialized reviews.

French scientific researcher, joint discoverer of the AIDS virus, a member of the National Academy of Medicine and the National Academy of Sciences (France), **Luc Montagnier** is emeritus director of research at the CNRS and emeritus professor at the Pasteur Institute. From 1997 to 2001, he was also professor and director of the Center for Molecular and Cellular Biology at Queen's College, New York University. In 1993, he created with Federico Mayor the World Foundation for AIDS Research and Prevention, of which he is president. He is the author of a work that has become a classic, *Des Virus et des hommes* (1994), and has recently written an article entitled 'Où va la recherche biomédicale en France?', published in the collective work *Quel avenir pour la recherche? Cinquante savants s'engagent* (2003).

Ryuichi Ida

Bioethics and the Future of Living Things

Scientific progress, particularly in the life sciences, is one of the key phenomena of the twentieth century. It represents both a triumph of the human mind and a momentous challenge to human existence. Human life, the very concept of living matter even, is thrown into question by advances in the biosciences and the development of biomedical and genetic technologies. A couple previously diagnosed as sterile has a chance today of fertilization through techniques of assisted reproduction. Whereas genetic abnormalities could previously not be detected until after birth, it is today possible to test an embryo and if necessary perform an abortion. Huntington's disease[1] can be diagnosed in a young person seemingly in perfect health by means of genetic testing. A child lacking an element of DNA[2] crucial to his or her survival can be helped through gene therapy. These examples give some idea of the applications of present-day biomedical research. They show how blurred the distinction has become between life and death, between normal and abnormal, between justice and injustice. The progress of the life sciences raises a whole series of social, ethical, legal and cultural questions.

Defining the living

What is a living thing? The frontier between the life and death of humankind is hard to define. In what does the life of a living thing consist? When does it start to live? What does living signify? When does a living thing die? All these questions lead us to ponder the value

---

1. A neuro-degenerative disease.
2. DNA deficit is a serious and very rare immune disease (affecting one newborn child in every 100,000). It is often mentioned in connection with 'bubble babies'.

of living entities. Underlying them is the question of the distinction between living and non-living matter, as well as that of the potential use of non-living bodies, organs and tissues for the purposes of scientific research or medical treatment. We are talking here of the possibility of using a living being before its birth and after its cerebral or cardiac death.

Let us take embryo research as an example. There is a fundamental issue as to whether embryos can be used as objects of research. The legal responses to this question vary according to national laws, but they fall roughly into two categories. One holds that use of the embryo for scientific research should be banned because human life is involved. The other maintains that the embryo cannot be equated with a living human being and that embryo research is therefore permissible. These two opposing responses pose the question of the nature of the embryo. For the embryo is not just another cell; it is the cell that will become a human being. Because of these two stances, we do not have a definitive, universal answer. Thus, in many countries embryo research is not prohibited for a specified period after fertilization, whereas other countries ban it outright.

Another question concerns genetic testing. Should it be allowed or not? Such testing makes it possible to determine whether any genetic abnormalities are present in the foetus. If the result is positive, an abortion can be performed or genetic modifications carried out. The risk here is that of moving towards a new form of eugenics. However, so long as the purpose of the research remains purely biological, aimed at understanding the mechanisms of human life, it is not easy to find grounds for any outright ban on embryo research. Yet here again another problem arises: what is the origin of the embryo used for research purposes? It is often the case that embryos used in scientific research come from abortions or multiple pregnancies; and it can be argued that these embryos, which would otherwise be discarded, will serve the cause of scientific progress. But this line of argument, with its *a posteriori* justification of abortion and embryo reduction treatment, can of itself lead to abuses.

I should like to give another example relating to the human genome. Research on the human genome lifts the veil surrounding the mystery of human life. It reveals the genetic particularities of every living being and the differences between individuals; it identifies diseases of genetic origin and genetic anomalies. The results of this research can be usefully employed for disease prevention and genetic therapy. This is what is known as 'customized treatment'. The complete analysis of the human genome will serve to highlight the differences between the genomes of various individuals since genetic specificities are the scientific foundation of an individual's identity. Knowledge of those genomes could give rise to various forms of discrimination relating to race, ethnic origin, employment, insurance, marriage and education. It is essential to recognize that human beings are genetically equal. Yet the interpretation of genetic tests could be biased by the search for elements corresponding to social values considered inferior, thereby opening the way to discrimination against a given community. What is at stake here is the value of a living being. The dignity of life should underpin every ethical consideration in this realm. Human dignity is always the fundamental framework of bioethics, which involves three principles: the sanctity of human life, the equality of human existence, and the prohibition on manipulating human life.

True, we have already suggested how difficult it would seem to be to uphold respect for these three bioethical principles given the development of the life sciences and of medical and genetic technology. But the question arises as to what is human dignity. While it remains at the core of bioethics, we have to ask whether we should also think in terms of the dignity of animals and plants. Does the concept of human dignity entail a distinction between human and other forms of life? Does it entail a distinction between the human personality and other living entities? It seems to me that the concept of human dignity is self-evident in the Christian world where, from its origins, the human being has been viewed as different from other living entities. On the other hand, Buddhism is based on a cyclical conception of the life of living beings. A man may have been a dog in a previous life, and a woman may become a bird in a future existence. The life of every being is cyclical, so all lives have the same value. Human dignity, then, cannot be conceived solely in contradistinction to animals and plants. We have to find a concept of dignity applicable to living things as such.

Another conception of life is possible according to which a living entity is not a thing. Here again we may appeal to dignity so as not to treat a person as a thing. It could be said that what is important is the mind and not the body of a human being. But mind and body are inseparable according to one conception. In short, the concept of human dignity is far from being self-evident.

This concept was recently discussed in Japan in the course of a debate on the banning of reproductive cloning. A large majority of the Japanese population puts human dignity foremost, but the point was to specify the essence of that dignity. We finally concluded that the exploitation of the human person, the predetermination of the human genome and the potential risks that a cloned individual would run were all matters that affected human dignity. Discussions also took place regarding legislation on human organ transplants. The key question was whether brain death could be considered a death worthy of the human person. The upholders of cardiac death are strongly opposed to the recognition of brain death. According to them, so long as the heart is beating, a person is not dead. In the end, the law strikes a compromise between these two positions: it authorizes the transplantation of organs from a body in a state of brain death provided the person has given his or her written consent and the family is in agreement. If transplantation is authorized, the person is considered dead. Otherwise, death is pronounced only after cardiac death. In this way, Japanese law avoids taking a clear-cut stance and bioethics does not seem in the end to have influenced the outcome of the discussions.

The universality of bioethics

Is bioethics universal? Is it possible to conceive of a new bioethics applicable to all conceptions and all living forms in all the countries of the globe? How could it be established? To answer these questions, a number of factors have to be taken into account. Firstly, it must be recognized that we live in a diverse world: diverse in terms of race, levels of development, environment, religion, thought, etc. It is by taking this fact into account that we shall be able to construct a new bioethics. It is true that ethics is strongly dependent on the habits, customs, religion and social values of a given society. It is often said that each human community has its own ethical system. The question, however, is whether there is not a single ethic, and thus a single bioethics, applicable to the world.

Diversity does not mean fragmentation, and the world itself, though uniquely diverse, is not fragmented. Another characteristic of the human community should therefore be recognized: its interdependence. No one can live alone. No state can any longer live in isolation. If these two characteristics of diversity and interdependence are recognized, we can hope to construct a bioethics for the world of the twenty-first century. Even if the concept of human dignity is not clearly defined, we should recognize it as a fundamental principle of bioethics. Irrespective of nationality, race or religion, no one would deny the fundamental value of the dignity of living beings. Each human person has his or her own dignity and the differences of bioethical principles from one society to another derive from conceptions and applications of the notion of human dignity in each society. In the West, individualism is a primordial value, whereas in the Asian countries collectivism is a prime concern. But Asian collectivism is not incompatible with Western individualism. Each individual lives in a human community. He or she cannot enjoy respect if that community is not able to guarantee human dignity. What is at issue, rather than the superiority of this or that value, is the way in which effect is given to human dignity.

We also need to take account of the concept of human rights, which is the legal expression of human dignity. Article 1 of the Universal Declaration of Human Rights stipulates that all human beings are born free and equal in dignity and rights. Thus the concept of human rights forms a link between bioethics and law. Moreover, the Universal Declaration on the Human Genome and Human Rights, adopted by the UNESCO General Conference in 1997 and ratified by the United

Nations General Assembly, is both a bioethical declaration and an instrument with which the international community has equipped itself in the field of human rights. The dignity of life is inscribed and protected therein as a human right. Since the protection of human rights is recognized as a universal precept, this means that respect for human dignity is also recognized as universal.

Diversity, interdependence and human rights are the tripod on which universal bioethics rests. It is the framework within which each society establishes its own bioethics. That is why the Universal Declaration on the Human Genome underlines the important role of national bioethics committees as independent, multidisciplinary and pluralistic bodies. Bioethics is becoming established at all levels, from the national through the regional to the universal. The UNESCO International Bioethics Committee, which I have chaired since last year, has the important role of coordinating the efforts of national, regional and international groups with a view to constructing a common bioethical framework in the twenty-first century.

Two further elements should be taken into account in our thinking about the framing of a new bioethical contract. These are the freedom of scientific research and the economy. There can be no doubt that scientific progress is dependent on freedom of research. If I have underlined the difficulty of adapting bioethics to the rapid pace of scientific advance, I do not mean to say that scientific research should slow down. Some maintain that scientists have let loose devils upon the Earth: the atomic bomb, environmental pollution, etc. It has to be recognized that there is no good or bad research in science. What is good or bad is the application of the findings of research, and this is where bioethics enters the picture. Research remains an intrinsic value.

The market economy has a tremendous influence on scientific research. Advanced scientific research on the human genome is dependent on financial resources and on economically significant results. The application of research findings also depends on their economic viability in the realm of the life sciences. If the cost of applying and disseminating them is too high, it is to be feared that the corresponding treatments will not be made available, given the general state of public health funding. For example, sufferers from hepatitis C had to wait a long time for the marketing of low-cost Interferon. Again, public health systems started reimbursing kidney transplants only when the cost fell below that of other treatments. Patentability is also an important issue for genomics. Patents are in principle granted to inventions, and it is a moot point whether the results of human genome research are patentable. In my view, economic interests place bioethical principles in jeopardy.

Many questions remain open. Bioethics cannot be imposed from above, but must be established through public debate. I have stressed the importance of national bioethics committees that do not dictate bioethical principles but propose possible approaches to solutions. It is through a combination of discussion within national committees and public debate that bioethical principles are crystallized. UNESCO's International Bioethics Committee is likewise a forum for discussion and has the aim of identifying universal bioethical principles. How can we reach an agreement on universal ethical principles when, as I have described, positions on the subject are often contradictory? Our committee fosters a spirit of harmony and symbiosis as the basis for a worldwide human community. It is in this way that bioethics will achieve universality. All of our discussions on bioethics converge on those two key concepts of harmony and symbiosis.

Edgar Morin

Future Ethics and Politics

The relationship between ethics and politics, which should be a complementary one, is often antagonistic. The policy-making of states and governments tends at best to subordinate ethical considerations to practical concerns of *Realpolitik* and power politics, and at worst to stifle them altogether. However, it is not just a matter of politics tending to exclude ethical concerns. Ethics can also oppose political realism in a variety of ways.

Ethics against politics

In the first place, this may take the form of dissidence. Ancient mythology provides us with an example in the person of Antigone. We have also seen acts of dissidence closer to our own time. Dissidence corresponds to a demand for justice, for truth or for truth and justice simultaneously, which would seem like pure folly. It is not by chance that mental homes were considered suitable places for accommodating dissidents in the former USSR. There was something apparently insane in the act of dissidence of the young Siniavski when he wrote a letter to *Komsomolskaya Pravda* voicing his criticism of the Soviet system. By giving his address, he was virtually asking to be arrested. Such dissidence may be deemed madness or, even worse, an absolute crime. In Nazi Germany, a brother and sister—the Scholls—were put to death in Munich for taking part in student dissidence. From Antigone to Solzhenitsyn, dissidence seems absurd, unrealistic. Yet I am one of those who think that there is something necessary and far-sighted in this madness, because it testifies to an ethical imperative irreducible to reason.

As well as dissidence, there is also resistance. Resistance involves the use of political means to pursue a rebellion that is ethical in character. Of course, such means can go astray and become unethical, as in the case of terrorism. But it is interesting to note that resistance always seems unrealistic at the outset. Think of the French Resistance fighters in the summer of 1940, when France was totally defeated, conquered by the Nazi armies. That year Europe was entirely under the heel of Hitler's Germany. Resistance seemed completely unrealistic. Yet, in the two or three years that followed, it became more and more realistic as hopes of a German defeat were transformed into a likelihood.

There is also the approach based on the refusal to lie. Something that greatly impressed me in Solzhenitsyn's letter to the leaders of the USSR was the fact that he simply called on them not to lie. There are some people who refuse to cooperate with oppression or hypocritical propaganda by keeping silent.

Political realism

The notion of political realism should itself be called into question. It is a goal-oriented realism, and it ends up as a realism that opts for the lesser of two evils. If one thinks that the domination of Nazi Germany is an accomplished fact that will prove irreversible for several decades and if one chooses to accept it and salvage what one can from the wreckage, one is working for the lesser of two evils—in other words, collaborating. This kind of realism always remains at the surface of reality, which is provisional. History is uncertain and changing. In 1943, there was a turnaround in the situation regarding Hitler's domination, and realism became lack of realism as the impossible became possible.

In a standardized world, underground forces are at work, what Hegel called the 'old mole', undermining little by little the bases and foundations of the status quo. The USSR was not defeated in battle. Its foundations were eroded from the inside.

So ethics are not necessarily unrealistic. Likewise, utopia does not only signify the impossible. There exists, it is true, a bad utopia, that of a perfect society, totally harmonious, without conflicts and contradictions. Good utopias are based on possibilities that are not yet realizable. It would seem impossible today, for political reasons, to feed all the people on the planet. But it is technically and materially possible. Peace on earth is also a possibility—one that we may hope to see realized in the next millennium.

In politics, a logic of dialogue is necessary, that is to say, a complementary and antagonistic relationship between ethics and politics. The ethical pole must be maintained in politics. I wish to stress the need for future policy-making to develop the role of ethics in this dialogue between ethics and politics. There has been much discussion, wholly ambiguous, on the right of humanitarian intervention. The idea that, for humanitarian reasons, it is right to transgress some of the ground rules of the current political setup is a forward-looking notion.

The philosopher Jonas has also outlined an ethics oriented specifically towards the future, based on the idea that we are not only responsible to each other for the state of the planet but are also responsible to our children and our children's children for the future of the planet. Today, because of the ecological threat to the biosphere, the nuclear threat and all the other threats deriving from the latest outbreak of human folly, we must assume our responsibilities towards the future. We cannot predict the shape of the future; but we can try to avoid disasters of all kinds so as to improve the lot of humanity.

Towards an ethics of humankind

I should like to make a link here between future ethics and 'anthropo-ethics', or the ethics of humankind. What is the human being? The human being is at once an individual and part of society and of the human species. However, this does not mean that the human being is 33 percent individual, 33 percent social and 33 percent biological. The relationship is much more complex. The species is present in the individual. We know that the species can only maintain itself if two individuals mate. The species is thus genetically present within the individual. But just as we are in society, so society can be said to be within us. From our birth, society inculcates in us its language and its culture. The individual and society are therefore inseparable; they interpenetrate one another. The relationship is rotational or recursive: individuals are needed to reproduce the species and produce society, but society is also needed to produce individuals by endowing them with culture and language.

We may draw from this analysis a number of conclusions for the ethics of the future, as regards the relationship between society and the individual and that between the individual and the human species. What is the society that allows for reciprocal control as between individuals and society? This answer is obviously a democratic society. Democratic society is today experiencing problems, and is regressing in some cases. However, any attempt in the future to establish an ethical system for society and individuals alike must have democratic society as its basis. The democratic relationship is the one that offers the individual possibilities of self-realization. It also accommodates social complexity. Democratic society embodies the plurality of ideas and opinions, including tolerance of deviance. Working for democracy means working at one and the same time for individuals and society.

As concerns the relationship between individuals and humankind, it is important to remember that humanity, understood as the totality of human beings, is today a multidimensional and not simply a biological notion. Humankind recognizes itself as such in all parts of the planet, with legitimate cultural and individual differences. The relationship between humankind and the individual can only flourish in a context of earth citizenship. Techno-economic globalization is dangerous if checks and balances are lacking. The explosive growth of communications, the reciprocal influence of cultures on each another, the opening up of cultures to the world at large and the desire to know one another will ensure the preservation of differences jeopardized by techno-economic globalization.

Today, the notion of Homeland Earth must encompass that of particular homelands, not undermine it. The relationship between humankind and the individual requires the development of an earth citizenship. The citizen is someone with a sense of responsibility and social solidarity. Médecins Sans Frontières, Amnesty International, Greenpeace and many other intergovernmental organizations are movements inspired by earth citizenship.

The future is not scripted. However, we can already discern the outlines of a new logic of dialogue between ethics and politics, underpinned by democracy and a sense of earth citizenship.

Lord Meghnad Desai

Development in the Twenty-First Century?

Since I am an economist and not a specialist in ethics, I will try to use an economic starting point to reach an ethical conclusion. At the end of the twentieth century, 6 billion people are alive and are living longer than their parents or grandparents could have hoped to live. The ability to extend human life is among the superb achievements of the century, most of which have occurred over the last thirty years. The world's population has tripled while income has increased even more. We are rightly and thankfully troubled today by inequity, poverty, the environment, globalization, human rights, etc. Indeed, it is wrong to be smug as we were in the 1950s and 1960s, when we thought the world to be a well-ordered place, or in the 1970s and 1980s, when we chose to overlook suffering all over the globe.

India and China have achieved something great by eliminating hunger and starvation despite having to manage gigantic populations of 1 billion people. In the 1960s, it was not clear that this would be possible. At the same period, no one imagined that a South Korean entity could run a company in Scotland or that the Scottish would worry about the Asian crisis one day. These are all positive developments. While it is tragic that Africa has not taken part in this global progress, we can only hope that Africa will achieve what Asia has done. Kenya, Ghana, Mauritius and Botswana all show signs of moving toward such advances.

We have learned about the meaning of development over the last twenty years. We know that it is no longer a matter of income per capita alone, but also includes health, education, gender, equity and human rights. We have moved away from the conception of the 1960s, during which development was measured in terms of steel production or weapon production. Instead, we ask how many women are among the poor, how many people are illiterate and how many people can sustain their livelihood on their own. We have realized that development is found in individual behaviours and not in governmental decisions. As long as discrimination persists, development cannot take place. In summary, development is a matter of human dignity, human rights and human opportunity.

Globalization is a positive development in that, for the first time, the First World feels as vulnerable as the Third World. It is paradoxical that the 15 percent of the world's population that lives in the First World and controls 85 percent of the world's resources is complaining as much about the adverse effects of globalization as the remainder of the planet. When unemployment rates rise by 3 percent in the First World, countries panic, thinking that work has come to an end. In reality, it is only a minor inconvenience when compared to the Third World. The twenty-five years known as the Golden Age of Keynesianism or capitalism after the Second World War were not necessarily golden for the Third World. The First World gave very little foreign aid and was careful to control its contributions politically. Today, some $300 billion flows to the Third World through the market. Despite the Asian crisis and other problems, capital still flows. The difference is striking. In 1980, when Mexico experienced a debt crisis, it took eight years to recover. In 1994, the peso crisis required only eighteen months to recover. Indeed, private capital is far more forgiving than public capital.

Of course, globalization threatens many interests, including those of the powerful labour aristocracy in the First World. Since it finances political parties in the Third World, it wants to slow industrialization there. That is why the NGOs in the First World complain about wages in the Third World. Yet if wages were not low, the countries would never move toward industrialization. If one gave the Third World wages similar to those of the First World, the system would come to a standstill. East Germany is proof of this.

The twenty-first century could be much better than the twentieth century; it would be difficult not to do better. However, in order to achieve this, we must provide equity and rule of law. The First World must obey the rules it establishes for the Third World. The United Nations must do away with the asymmetry that currently prevails in the Security Council, where the five veto-holding countries make all of the decisions. Bretton Woods institutions must be run by countries other than the rich, and preventing genocide in Rwanda must be as important as preventing genocide in Kosovo. The rule of law will only exist if the First World stops feeling sorry for itself and stops bullying other nations.

The arms spending in rich countries has fallen significantly, while that of poor countries has risen. The rich countries use their peace dividend to finance unemployment, tax cuts or the welfare state rather than spending it on the Third World. I am inclined to trust foreign capital that flows through equity markets far more than that which comes with strings attached. Indeed, governments can blackmail recipient countries to whom they give foreign aid. I would rather avoid this if possible.

I do not know what the role of the mass media will be. In the past, we thought that if citizens saw violence on television, they would never be able to tolerate it. Rwanda proved this false, indicting both the mass media and the United Nations. At the same time, new media such as the Internet have allowed NGO groups to mount global resistance to certain projects. For example, in India, a democratically elected government is building a dam that has generated significant discontent. Two hundred people are being displaced. The NGO movement made use of 'the imperialist link', appealing to the World Bank and Western states. Similarly, Greenpeace used its transnational grassroots system to stop the construction of an oil rig. The media will not play a unique, one-dimensional role. Sometimes it will be harmful while at other times it will be helpful. The world is complex and sometimes contradictory.

Luc Montagnier

Shaping a Universal Consciousness

Prediction is an impossible undertaking. All we can do is to exercise forethought and write our own history. In this respect, we are no different from other living systems, which are similarly capable, by different genetic mechanisms, of anticipating the events that occur over the course of their evolution. The notion that the twenty-first century will be 'spiritual' in character seems to me somewhat optimistic. Personally, I think we find ourselves at the apex of an extremely fragile pyramid.

The abyss of time and space

Scientific knowledge over the last fifty years has opened up an abyss in time. We have evolved for over three and a half billion years on the basis of a genetic language shared by the other species. Indeed, it is perfectly possible to produce human proteins (insulin, for example) from bacteria.

This unique history of life on earth, from which humanity stemmed, was necessarily preceded by lengthy competition between different genetic codes. But we have managed to detach ourselves from this selection process, our code having come to dominate. We consequently have a responsibility to nature. As dominant species, we must maintain the genetic diversity that has led to our emergence.

Advances in physics have shattered our vision of the dimensions of the universe. We now know that we are not at the centre of the universe; we are a minuscule point, surrounded by stars, nebulae and galaxies. This vision of the world gives us a certain consciousness of infinity and dictates the need for modesty on our part.

But, as a highly organized system, we are also prone to pride. If we were to replace the photons by a degree of negative entropy, the earth would become a very brilliant point and the sun a black dot. It seems to me that this should prompt the emergence of a new awareness. Yet this is unfortunately not the case.

The dangers ahead

Without mechanically projecting onto it the processes that govern living organisms, there are grounds for thinking that our society lacks a regulatory system (such as a brain), particularly in the current context of very powerful communication systems and information exchanges (comparable to nerves). It is true that some systems are self-regulating, such as population growth. But the lack of regulation may become alarming for the future of humanity, as in the case of the environment.

The twentieth century experienced Spanish influenza and AIDS, and the latter continues to ravage the countries of the South. But other more terrible epidemics may arise. While it is true that genetic diversity will always enable a few individuals to survive, there is a danger of devastation that could place our civilization at risk.

The extension of human life span also raises new questions relating to the growing incidence of chronic diseases. It is not certain that biology and medicine can come up with answers. If we were to overcome neurodegenerative diseases and cancers, the working life of human societies could be prolonged by twenty years, which would transform the socio-economic structures of our planet.

Finally, the greatest danger is doubtless the growth in inequalities, which is tending to accelerate with the development of the new technologies. True, the impact of these is such that more and more 'emerging' countries are deriving benefit from them. But it is not tolerable that twenty-first century society should exclude 1 billion human beings.

Globalization can help us to acquire this universal and anticipatory awareness. It may enable us to avoid chaos and evolve towards societies freed from the anachronistic blights that we half-see at the present time.

PART IV

Science, Knowledge and Foresight

The Human Impact of the Genetic Revolution

Genetic engineering technologies are now sufficiently operational to open up the possibility that human beings will be able to choose their own hereditary characteristics. As Edward Wilson points out, natural selection is no longer the sole driving force of evolution. It remains to be seen whether it will be replaced by genetic selection: such a development will stem not from technical and scientific necessity but rather from human choice.

A certain amount of media mystification has moreover surrounded the supposed powers of genetics, both in relation to GMOs, often presented as the miracle solution to the problem of hunger, and to 'genomics' with its attendant uncertainties. According to Jacques Testart, the real danger of genetics lies in its routine use and the possibilities that this opens up for restrictive monitoring and competitive eugenism.

In the view of Gianni Vattimo, the problems relating to the application of genetics need to be addressed first and foremost politically, if we wish to guard against their appropriation by absolute powers or economic interests.

* * * *

A biologist and entomologist, **Edward Wilson** is professor of zoology at Harvard University. A distinguished advocate of the preservation of biodiversity, the inventor of sociobiology and recipient of numerous prizes and awards, he is the author of *Sociobiology: The New Synthesis* (1975), *On Human Nature* (1978), *Consilience: the Unity of Knowledge* (1998) and *The Future of Life* (2002).

Jacques Testart is a biologist and research director at the Institut National de Santé et de Recherche Médicale (INSERM). The scientific father of the first French test-tube baby, he is also the author of numerous essays highlighting his commitment to a science that respects human dignity: *Le Désir du Gène* (1994), *Pour une éthique planétaire* (1997), *Des Hommes probables: de la procréation aléatoire à la reproduction normative* (1999) and *Le Vivant manipulé* (2003).

Gianni Vattimo, professor of philosophy at the University of Turin and a member of the European Parliament, is considered one of the leading figures of philosophical postmodernism. He has taught at various American universities, including Yale, UCLA and New York University. His published works include *The End of Modernity* (1988), *Belief* (2000), *Dialogo con Nietzsche* (2002) and *Nichilismo ed emancipazione* (2003).

Edward Wilson

Does Natural Selection Still Drive Evolution?

The question of the future of natural selection does not arise solely in the context of the new possibilities opened up by human genetic engineering. It first came to the fore as a key issue in the 1970s as a result of significant advances in the genetic engineering of crops. Before discussing the problems posed by the genetic engineering of our own species, I wish to touch upon the topic of what are known as genetically modified organisms (GMOs) and the questions they raise.

Genetically modified organisms

The world's food supply hangs by a slender thread of biodiversity. Ninety percent of it is provided by slightly more than 100 plant species, out of 250,000 currently known to man. Twenty species carry most of the load. Only three of these—wheat, maize and rice—stand between humanity and starvation.

All of the plant species and organisms known on the planet are potential donors of genes that can be transferred, through genetic engineering, into crop species in order to improve their performance. With the insertion of the right pieces of DNA, new strains—whether cold-hardy, pest-proof, perennial, fast-growing or highly nutritious—can be created.

The spin-off from the revolution in molecular genetics was first developed in the 1970s. In the 1980s and 1990s, before the world could realize what was happening, it came of age. A gene from the bacterium *bacillus thurengiensis* was inserted into the chromosomes of corn, cotton and potato plants, allowing them to manufacture a toxin that kills insect pests. There was no need to spray insecticides; the engineered plants now performed this task on their own. Other examples of this kind could be quoted, showing that agricultural fields can now be treated against diseases, with no harm to crops growing there.

The enormous potential of genetic engineering made it possible to take this process much further: a bacterial gene was implanted into a monkey, and a jellyfish's bioluminescence gene was implanted into a plant. It was overlooked that these breakthroughs would be less than universally acceptable and could stir opposition. For many, human existence was being transformed in a fundamental and insidious way. With little warning, GMOs had entered our lives, possibly changing the order of nature. Protest movements against the new industry began in the 1990s and exploded in 1999, just in time to rank as a millennial event with apocalyptic overtones. The European Union banned transgenic crops, and radical activists called for a global embargo on all GMOs.

Today, public opinion and official policy have come to vary greatly from one country to the next. France and Britain are strongly opposed to GMOs, while China is strongly favourable to them. Brazil, India, Japan and the United States are favourable, with varying degrees of caution. In the United States, particularly, the public awoke to this issue only after the 'trans-genie' escaped from the bottle. From 1996 to 1999, the amount of United States farmland devoted to genetically modified crops had exploded, from 3.8 million to 70.9 million acres. As the century ended, more than half of soya bean and cotton grown was engineered, as well as 28 percent of corn.

The risks of genetic engineering

There are several sound reasons for anxiety over genetic engineering.

Many people—not only philosophers and theologians—are troubled by the ethics of the transgenic evolution. While it is true that human beings have been creating new strains of organisms since agriculture began, this has never been done at the pace inaugurated by genetic engineering. During the past era of traditional plant breeding, hybridization was used to mix genes almost always among varieties of the same species or, at most, highly similar species. Now, genetic engineering takes place across entire kingdoms. The extent to which this process should be allowed to continue remains an open ethical issue.

The effects of new transgenic food on human health are difficult to predict and never free of risk. However, the product can be tested like any other new food product on the market. There is no reason to assume that their effects differ in any fundamental way. Yet scientists generally agree that a high degree of alertness is essential.

Transgenes can escape from modified crops into wild relatives of the crops, where the two forms live closely together. Yet hybridization has always occurred in nature, even before the advent of genetic engineering. However, the traditionally derived hybrids have not modified their wild parents. Domesticated species and strains are usually less competitive than their wild counterparts in both natural and modified environments. Of course, transgenes could change that picture in the future. It is too early to tell at present. Again, we will have to maintain a high level of surveillance.

Genetically modified crops can diminish biodiversity in other ways, as a result of unintended consequences. This is known as collateral damage. These elementary effects on the environment have not been studied on the field. How severe they will become remains to be seen, and will require a high level of surveillance.

Many people having become aware of the potential threats of genetic engineering to their food supply understandably believe that yet another bit of their freedom to choose has been taken from them by corporations, using technology beyond their control or understanding. They also fear that an industrialized agriculture, dependent on high technology can, by one unanticipated mistake, go terribly wrong. In the realm of public opinion, genetic engineering is to agriculture as nuclear engineering is to energy.

Yet how will we manage to feed billions of people over the next decades, and save the natural environment and the diversity of life living in it, without being trapped in a Faustian bargain that threatens freedom and security? No one knows the solution to this dilemma. Most scientists and economists who have studied both sides of it agree that the benefits outweigh the risks. Some have even spoken of an 'evergreen revolution'—one that is sustainable.

Over 130 countries have tentatively agreed to the Cartagena Protocol on Bio-Safety, which provides the right to block import of transgenic products. The Protocol also establishes a Joint Bio-Safety Clearinghouse, which is in charge of publishing information on national policy. At approximately the same time, the United States National Academy of Sciences, joined by those of Brazil, China, India, Mexico, endorsed the development of transgenic crops. They made recommendations for risk assessment and licensing agreements, and stressed the needs of developing countries in future research programmes and capital investment.

Along with improving science and technology, this is the path to progress for humanity as a whole in the realm of transgenic crops.

The genetic engineering of humans

Is genetic change still occurring in human beings, as in past millennia, or has civilization brought directional evolution in our genes to a halt? Is natural selection still operating to drive evolution? The answer, basically, is 'no'.

The only undoubted global change is a change in frequency—occurring throughout the world—of racial traits such as skin colour and hair type due to more rapid population growth in developing countries. In 1950, 68 percent of the world's population lived in developing countries. In 2001, the figure will rise to 80 percent. That amount of change is having an effect on the amount of previously existing genes. However, none of the traits involved affect intellectual capacity or the fundamentals of human nature.

The major event in the human revolution is not the directional change of the species, but homogenization through immigration and inter-breeding. Homogenization is not dynamic on a global or evolutionary scale. It changes local populations, often swiftly, but cannot drive the evolution of the human species in one direction or another on its own. Many more combinations of skin colour, facial features, talents and other traits influenced by genes are now arising than ever previously existed. Yet the average differences between people in different localities around the world are narrowing. If continued over tens or thousands of generations, the present rates of immigration and inter-marriage could eliminate all population differences around the world.

Medical researchers, motivated by the need to understand the genetic bases of disease, have begun to map the 50,000 components of genes. Reproductive biologists have cloned sheep and, presumably, could do the same for human genes, if the procedure were allowed. Thanks to the Human Genome Project, geneticists will be able to read off the complete sequences within several years. Scientists are also experimenting with a limited form of molecular engineering in which genes are altered in the desired direction by substituting the appropriate snippets of DNA.

If these advances in knowledge are just partially attained, and if they can be made generally available (something problematic), humanity will be positioned to take control of its own ultimate fate. It can, if it chooses, alter not just the anatomy and intelligence of the species, but also the emotions and creative drive that compose the very core of human nature. If it occurs, the engineering of the human genome will be the final of three distinguishable periods in the history of human evolution.

Throughout almost all of the 2-million-year history of the genus *homo*, culminating in the species *homo sapiens*, people were unaware of the ultra-microscopic hereditary code that shapes it. At historical times during the past 10,000 years, populations still experienced racial differentiation, largely in response to local climatic conditions, just as they had in the distant past. During this passage through evolutionary time, shared with other species, the human population was also subject to stabilizing selection. Gene mutants that cause disease or infertility were weeded out. However, with the advent of modern medicine, human evolution entered its second period. Increasingly now, hereditary defects could be deliberately modified or averted. Physicians are now able to prevent symptoms entirely through this kind of treatment. We should not worry, however, that such destabilizing of selection will go too far, because the second period of human selection is ephemeral. It will not last long enough to have an impact on the heredity of the species as a whole, because the knowledge that made it possible has brought us swiftly to the third period—that of volitional evolution.

Progress in gene therapy has been slow in the early period, but it will accelerate. Too much hope and venture capital is at stake to permit failure. Yet I predict that future generations will be genetically conservative. Aside from repairing disabling defects, they will resist hereditary change. They will do so in order to save the emotions and rules of mental development that define us as a species, because these elements compose the human soul.

Jacques Testart

From Genetic Mystification to Molecular Policing

A review of the state of technoscience at any given point in time will yield at least two diametrically opposed ways of predicting and arguing the case for the future shape of the world.[1] The first seizes on the most optimistic promises of science to conjure up visions of a happier, healthier and freer society. The second focuses on the uncertainties and shortcomings of our technologies, their adverse effects on health and their economic and social drawbacks in order to paint a gloomy picture of the misfortunes that await us in tomorrow's world. Between these opposing outlooks, any number of compromises with the inevitable—invariably deemed sagacious—jostle for position in the centre ground.

Yet to anticipate that the truth lies somewhere in the middle of this range of possibilities rather than at one of its extremes is merely to apply a statistical rule. Such a prediction is reassuring but it is also immobilizing since we are only roused to sustained action by causes of maximum gravity. This weak attitude, passing for moderate, would only be justified if the varied threads of technoscience were incapable of combining to form a technological weft running through every practice and linking up with all modes of life. Moreover, the moderate stance presumes to pass itself off as reasonable while ignoring the fact that the same degree of probability does not attach to all the hypotheses concerned. Feasibility apart, each technology stands or falls by its ability to meet a social demand or to create such a demand. We should therefore regard as most realistic the forecast that takes fullest account

---

1. This contribution, read on 15 May 2001 at the 18th session of the '21st-Century Talks', had previously been published in the review *Futuribles*, July–August 2001.

of those objectively verified forces capable of stimulating or arresting an evolving situation.

This is as relevant to the application of genetics as it is to climate change, and a scientific approach of this kind is very different from the wishful thinking based on an irrational confidence in humanity or its collective destiny. This relies on the sledgehammer argument that the worst has never happened despite the forecasts of doom that have accompanied each major innovation, on appeals to unimagined and quasi-magical resources, on the postulation of a mysterious and benevolent force guiding human destiny, and on the belief in a neutral and beneficent science. In this way, experts and politicians deliver pious and comforting messages to society at large, while simultaneously denouncing a 'return to the irrational' because a few individuals reject the catechism of technoscience.

What is the real nature and scope of the genetic revolution? Let us briefly see where matters stand at present.

Control over genetic processes—fact and fiction

Under the heading of the 'genetic revolution', the media lump together the mapping of the genome and methods of identifying DNA[2] with voluntary modifications to the genome of living beings (gene transplants and genetically modified organisms) and deficient tissues (gene therapies) as well as with techniques that owe absolutely nothing to the progress of genetics, such as *in vitro* fertilization or cloning.

The *mapping of the genome* consists in describing in detail the structure of the DNA molecule. Geneticists claim to have completed this recently but remain incapable of separating out the genes, those portions of DNA responsible for specific activities. It is worth noting that geneticists credited us with 100,000 genes in 1999, reduced this to 30,000 in 2000 and subsequently revised their estimates upwards (to some 60,000) in 2001. The fact is that the mapping of the genome is limited to molecular anatomy and, despite the mystification accompanying genetic research, we are a long way from recognizing the function(s) of DNA constituents.

Thus for the most part genes are still only virtual entities. However, the mystification begins with the much-trumpeted 'human genome' projects since the structural conformation of a protein, or 'gene product', is not inscribed in the gene sequence, as demonstrated by the prion protein. It is thus clear that the genome does not embody a programme but only information and that most physical or pathological characteristics are the

---

2. DNA (deoxyribonucleic acid) is the essential substance of chromosomes; the part organized as genes contains information differing from one individual to another, which as a whole constitutes the genome.

result of interactions between this complex information and a large number of elements foreign to the genome.

The procedures for identifying each segment of the genome are remarkably effective. This is why the law increasingly has recourse to 'genetic fingerprinting' and why medicine can make predictions about pathologies on the basis of a sample of a person's DNA. Whether in the form of legal evidence or medical diagnosis, identification of the peculiarities of DNA is the logical application of molecular anatomy.

However, the diagnostic test result is based on interpretation whenever the target gene is not part of a system involving the expression of a single gene; and this system, which postulates that a single gene is responsible for a single characteristic, is rarely attested in practice. It follows that diagnosis is almost always based on probabilities since the co-factors of the genome and the environment are not all known, and their complex interactions increase still further the indeterminacy of their ultimate effect. That is why predictive medicine is observational: it is based on findings rather than physiological understanding: the finding that a given genetic marker[3] is present in the genome of an individual, and the finding that this genetic characteristic leads to this or that characteristic in a certain proportion of the population. Predictive medicine is the management of ignorance, working on the basis of sophisticated statistics. It shades into duplicity when it preaches individual diagnosis since its practical effectiveness is exclusively collective. It will increasingly turn us all into timid survivors, imposing on us forms of behaviour for which there will never be any certain need given the key role of chance in human existence.

We know that in the United States people thus identified as being 'at risk' from pathologies agree to preventive mutilation of the organs concerned, such as the breast or prostate, and that everywhere insurance companies and the pharmaceutical industry are gearing up for the new markets linked to probability-based health care. But what is overlooked is the setback suffered by a certain vision of progress when curative medicine, concerned with treating illness, evolves into predictive or preventive medicine, which prophesies and pigeonholes each individual in his or her patient slot. Science was invented in a quest for knowledge, for certainty, and all that has been achieved through science is to give uncertainty a learned gloss. Perhaps we have allowed ourselves to be misled from the start about the true powers of science? Perhaps we have overlooked the fact that knowledge consists in pinpointing probabilities more and more accurately, without ever eliminating probabilism? Whatever the case, the result falls far short of the triumphant claims of the specialists, who pride themselves on having achieved 'mastery over living matter' or having

---

3. This may involve a normal gene, a missing gene or one structurally modified relative to the so-called 'normal' structure, i.e., that most frequently encountered.

discovered 'the secrets of life' and are then surprised that the public, its appetite whetted, should demand more certain and conclusive results.

Genetically modified organisms (GMOs) represent yet another step in the quest for mastery: the aim is no longer simply to identify the genome but to modify it deliberately by adding a gene of particular interest. What is standing in the way of the creation of a human GMO is perhaps the difficulty of defining the genes that would constitute a 'superior individual'. Such a genetic designation of a 'superman' would constitute a challenge to ethics as well as reason. So GMOs are only to be found at the present time among plants, animals and micro-organisms, all of them forms of life that we have taken it upon ourselves to manage in a controlled form for our exclusive benefit with the aim of deriving maximum profit from them.

The point of the GMO is to raise animal and plant productivity or to stimulate resistance to natural or industrial enemies, or again to manufacture substances useful to human beings. The mere announcement of a project to produce this or that GMO is immediately presented to the public as a new success. We are swamped with announcements of plants resistant to frost or parasites, rich in vitamins and even productive of petrol, as well as of animals serving as organ donors or secreting human proteins in their milk. The picture is unfortunately less rosy in reality since, setting aside the socioeconomic and public-health debates sparked by GMOs, it has to be said that the proclaimed advantages have yet to be demonstrated in practice: no plant or animal modified in this way has proved capable of significantly improving, in a regular and reproducible fashion, the services rendered to humankind.

It is thus mere mystification to suggest that we exercise genetic control over nature, and such suggestions by industrialists and their experts, taken up by politicians, bankers and the media, provoke indignation and disquiet. People are indignant that GMOs, whatever their future effectiveness, have been imposed without prior demonstration not simply of their risks but also of their advantages; and they are uneasy because the attitude of scientific and political leaders reveals an ideological concern, bordering on deceit and irresponsibility, to convince themselves and others of the reality of genetic control. How can we look to the future with serenity when the technological drive is not subject to scientific validation, despite the fact that science is made to serve as its justification? Coinciding with the interests of powerful lobbies, the institutional mystique surrounding genetics is preparing the way for a twenty-first century in which 'progress' is imposed through a combination of lies and *faits accomplis*.

It is interesting to note that, unlike animals and plants, micro-organisms and culture cells lend themselves to genetic engineering. It is as though the complexity of multicell living matter was at odds with the simplistic mechanistic view that one can control an organism by modifying its cells. Yet it was through a gene transplant *ex vivo* (outside the body) on stem cells extracted from the bone marrow of sick children prior to reinjection, that 'gene therapy' finally notched up a minor success recently. What the subsequent media hype failed to bring out was that the cell therapy in question involved an *in vitro* GMO technique difficult to apply to other pathologies, which underlines the fact that we know how to obtain the desired effect by introducing a gene into an isolated cell but not into a complex organism.

We may provisionally conclude that genetics does not yet have any direct means of acting upon human beings but that it is rapidly developing a diagnostic function on the basis of DNA identifiers.

The potential use of genetics

It would be unreasonable to claim that progress in genetic techniques is impossible. Compliant GMOs and effective gene therapies may one day become a reality. Our concern so far has been to show that the mystification that has taken hold of genetics will have a major impact in the years to come. It remains for us to consider what may seriously be expected of the technologies under development and to return to the question of prediction, which is the true paradigm of the medicine of the future. For common sense dictates that, in keeping with medical logic, health economics and the concern with well-being and quality of life, everyone should have a sound organism rather than relying on medical help (even if effective) and on replacement organs. It is moreover established that the biological quality of each organism depends primarily on its genetic constitution, even if the hazards of development play many tricks on the genome. Thus it is logical to predict that the essential focus of health action will be to bring into the world children whose genome is potentially 'normal', i.e., with the least number of pathologies. This is in the interest of the medical world (geneticists, biologists and doctors), the biotechnology industry and medical-insurance industries, and also of the future parents.

It is thus very likely that medicine will increasingly be directed towards the twin task of disease prevention through the genetic selection of individuals and the subsequent definition of the optimum conditions for their survival. For even if all children were in the future to be conceived and selected in the laboratory, it would still be necessary to manage the lack of perfection characteristic of living beings. Already pharmaceutical groups are investing in the production of health-management software, capable of proposing the natural and artificial environment best adapted to each genome. The discovery of genetic susceptibilities for all illnesses, including infectious ones, is transformed into a proclamation of generalized genetic causalities, as if the pathological state depended more on fate, as inscribed in the genome, than on living conditions. In this way, governments dispense with welfare policies while industry imposes superfluous prescriptions and insurance companies profit from the right to statistical security.

Thanks to the study of the genome, all human beings become potential patients previously unaware of the seriousness of their condition. They accordingly become a permanent target of the health industry. Already in the United States, each newborn child is subjected to five genetic tests on average, and up to twenty tests in some states. The cost of a standard combination of three genetic tests is $25, ten times less than two years ago. But it would obviously be more effective to apply batteries of tests at a stage when it was still possible to choose 'acceptable' genomes and reject others, that is to say, shortly after fertilization.

The normative power of embryo selection has to do with the variety of embryonic genomes deriving from a single couple, which is capable of engendering billions of offspring that would all be different at some point of their DNA, with the rare exception of true twins. This random nature of procreation points up the absurdity of early-twentieth-century eugenic enterprises that sought to improve humankind by selecting progenitors, whereas it is only at fertilization that the genome of a new being is formed.

My opinion is that genetic medicine will increasingly be directed towards the selection of children in the egg, a strategy that requires an increased production of gametes[4] in the reproductive process. The reason why the fertility of human couples, and of mammals in general, is relatively low compared with other animal groups (e.g. fish or insects) has to do with several characteristics of gametogenesis (production of gametes by both sexes), fertilization and development.

Obviously, the development of the embryo within the female body drastically limits the number of offspring in simultaneous gestation (from one to fifteen depending on the species). As we know, the development of twins in the human species is possible and free of risk, given a proper medical environment. Thus half the children born by assisted procreation techniques are false twins. It seems that the mechanisms selected by evolution, operating at different levels, limit the procreative yield of mammals and, strangely enough, of the human species in particular. The limits in question, well in advance of gestation, concern the number of embryos resulting from fertilization, that is to say, the rate of production and the quantity of the available gametes. The male is characterized rather by an excess of gametes: man produces 100 million spermatozoids daily, a naturally useless surfeit drastically reduced by assisted procreation, which requires only one spermatozoid to fertilize an ovule. It is on the female side that the many barriers limiting child birth are found. These include:

---

4. Gamete: a mature haploid germ cell (male or female) that unites with another of the opposite sex in sexual reproduction to form a zygote (*Shorter Oxford English Dictionary*, 5th edition, Oxford, Oxford University Press, 2002).

- the number of oocytes[5] moving around in fertilizable ovules: the ovaries of the feminine foetus contain 6 to 7 million oocytes, of which only 3 or 4 hundred escape degeneration before being exposed to the risk of fertilization;
- the fertile period, which runs from puberty to menopause and thus occupies less than half of a woman's lifetime;
- the cyclical phases of fertility, which restrict the time when fertilization can take place between menstrual episodes to some 20 percent of the fertile period, i.e., about 5 percent of a woman's lifetime;
- the number of foetuses tolerable in a single gestation, already mentioned, and the number of offspring that a mother is capable of feeding and raising.

Wastage and restrictions are thus constants of procreation, particularly in the human species, and these diverse processes are so convergent that they prompt the question of whether they are not an evolutionary necessity. It may be noted that if woman could produce children in their millions, a few couples blessed by fate could prevent other couples from reproducing by restricting their access to the available resources. The limits imposed upon all establish a kind of gene democracy whose advantage is to maintain and increase biodiversity, giving the species the ability to survive in uncertain conditions. It should be said that so-called 'artificial' procreation supports this process of genetic diversification by enabling sterile couples to contribute to the next generation. On the other hand, embryo selection by geneticists would quickly become a way of promoting arbitrary limitations on human diversity. Is it credible that embryo selection, which is currently the target of substantial medical investment, will remain limited to 'particularly serious pathologies', which affect no more than one child in a thousand?

Imagine that it becomes possible to create a multitude of embryos for each couple with the aim of selecting a single child. The prospect of extracting the 'best' genomic pairing would undoubtedly be appealing since it would offer parents the opportunity to select their offspring from more potential children than if they had been fertile for millennia. We may compare such a prospect with that of cloning, which is infinitely conservative, and wonder which would prove the greater temptation—the identical or the ideal. There can be no doubt that society would spurn the egocentrism underlying indiscriminate cloning in favour of the purification of the genome.

---

5. Oocyte: an egg mother cell, which gives rise to a mature ovum by meiosis (*Shorter Oxford English Dictionary*, 5th edition, Oxford, Oxford University Press, 2002).

Yet the artifice of embryo selection would, among other things, be in conflict with biodiversity through the application of arbitrary criteria of choice based on aesthetic taste, social competitiveness and inadequate knowledge, which would establish adventitious norms that would progressively take the place of structural genetic resources.

We shall not detail here the technical processes that will open the way to the near-generalization of embryo screening. We shall simply enumerate the stages in a pre-implementation genetic diagnosis (PGD) strategy of this kind.

- *Reducing the constraints on the couple*: we are already able to carry out a biopsy on the ovarian cortex, which is very rich in small follicles, particularly in young women, and freeze the resulting sample with a view to subsequent *in vitro* fertilization. In this way, stocks of female gametes can be built up alongside those of male gametes, limiting the interventions upon the woman to the taking of a single ovarian sample, without any monitoring or hormonal stimulation.

- *Producing numerous embryos:* provided we were able to make the oocytes contained in the primordial follicles thus preserved evolve into ovules, embryos could be conceived by the dozen. Research carried out on a number of animal species show the feasibility of this approach, which makes it possible to limit the degeneration of oocytes observed under natural conditions. It is possible to cultivate oocyte-follicular complexes *in vivo*, possibly in a female belonging to another species, but we shall soon be able to cultivate these complexes *in vitro* to the point of obtaining ovules competent for fertilization.

- *Selecting the 'best quality' embryo:* the large number of embryos available will justify a wide range of genetic tests to identify—'particularly serious illnesses' apart—predispositions to various ailments, and even probabilities of physical or mental characteristics. The limited number of blastomeres[6] in these young embryos will not reduce the number of tests, these cells being capable of being multiplied intentionally or scrutinized by 'biochips' capable of recognizing a very large number of DNA configurations within a single cell.

- *Transforming the chosen embryo into a child*: even if the chances of birth by way of *in utero* embryo transplant are not increasing (about 10 percent today), embryonic cloning—medically justified in this way—should ensure that every PGD results in the birth of a child, provided the clones of the chosen embryo are preserved by freezing with a view to successive transfers. Giving birth to a single child starting from an embryo is a procedure that should bring about a reconciliation between bioethics and reproductive cloning.

---

6. Cell deriving from the initial divisions of the fertilized egg.

Some serious side-issues

Does such a scenario, juggling existing or emerging techniques to cater to collective fantasies nourished by commercial interests, belong to the realm of science fiction? Does the selection of human beings on the basis of the 'best offer' in molecular terms still qualify as preventive medicine? Is there any real difference between individual parent selection of children against a background of convergent expert opinion and what a welfare state might propose in the name of the map of the 'normal genome'?

The age of soft, consensual and benign eugenics is upon us. Under the new breeding paradigm, any parent will be able to opt for the best-looking of his or her virtual children from among the hundreds of embryos assessed for their merits. We may well continue to be ignorant even of the number of our genes, but this will not prevent us from correlating given DNA structures with given individual characteristics and deriving statistical laws on this basis. The situation recalls that of traditional knowledge, which establishes a causal relationship between visible characters and certain risks. But the reference to those intimate and highly individualized characters contained in the genome prepares the way for a disturbing instrumentation of the status of every individual.

According to the American scientist Jacques Cohen, who has been a pioneer in this kind of genetic policing, we shall soon be 'fortunate' enough to be able to choose our children's height, weight, hair and skin colour and even their IQ. The protean nature of living matter, which will undoubtedly prevent human beings from living up to their genomic horoscope, may well become the only area of freedom remaining. It is for the very reason that perfection does not exist that industrialists tolerate PGD projects, a market that appeals to them only insofar as it does not restrict that of preventive medicine.

Many important questions arise relating to the subjectivity of the manufactured child, the outlook for scientific failures and the right to a distinct status of those children who continue to be conceived in bed. A major risk is the substitution of a genetic racism for the old forms of racism based on skin colour or origin, and the claim that it has the imprimatur of science. The genetic mysticism that has taken hold not only of science and medicine but also of culture, the collective imagination and politics has been matched by the imposition in law of a certain conception of the norms to which human beings should correspond and the purposes they should serve: embryos can be manufactured for research purposes, i.e., human life can be created for the purpose of destroying human life (this was the aim of a ministerial project for revising the bioethics laws in France, which was finally rejected); and a child handicapped from birth can obtain damages by virtue of a right not to be born or to be born 'normal' (the Perruche ruling of November 2000).

It would be pointless to correct embryos deficient in a given gene since the possibility always exists of preserving a 'normal' twin embryo. Thus genetic purification will operate according to the laws of the free-market society as regards the acceptance or rejection of the human embryo, that is to say, in terms of its competitive status. The time will come when the concern is to improve the species by grafting on new characteristics. The question is with what qualities in view?

The most worrying aspect of this Promethean posturing is our inability to exercise effectively the control that we constantly claim to possess. What remains is the adventure, which may also be labelled experimenting with human life and which could well prove irreversible. It is not in the laboratories that this tendency will be halted. The stakes are political and ideological rather than scientific.

The fear of giving birth to a handicapped child is immemorial and reasonable, and there is no restrictive definition of handicap when everyone's place in society depends on their conformity to an abstract and 'competitive' model. Thus the search for the 'ideal' child is only new because it is claimed to be possible. A certain cultural standardization of human beings is already a reality in the industrialized countries. If it is true that personality is the result of both genetic inheritance and the physical and social environment (nature and nurture), then the convergent choice of certain genomes made possible by PGD will combine with cultural globalization to create a trend towards out-and-out social cloning. In future, human evolution will take place through culture, through psychic development. Research in biology progresses by moving from the study of the organism (physiology) to the study of molecules, that is to say, it becomes localized whereas culture becomes globalized. In fact, biology also tends towards globalization once the molecules are classified, ranked and selected in terms of the interest accorded to them, as in the case of genes.

Genetics may have a less grandiose future than its scientific dominance and its mystical aura currently suggest. What if genetic medicine was in the end no more than a simple but formidable form of molecular policing? As Hans Jonas forecast: 'the real threat embodied in science-based technology lies not in its destructive possibilities but in its peaceful everyday use.'[7]

If humanity were today to decide to choose its own future, it should focus its efforts on the shaping of a civilization in which recognition of others occupies a key place, for in the absence of others I lose my freedom. It should also debunk the spurious promises of genetics so as to bring technoscience within the confines of democracy. This is no easy task for an often fascinated public and for politicians anxious to appear modern....

---

7. Hans Jonas, *The Imperative of Responsibility. In Search of an Ethics for the Technological Age*, Chicago, University of Chicago Press, 1984.

Gianni Vattimo

The Political Challenge of Genetic Engineering

I am one of those who does not feel the need to demystify biogenetics since I believe its influence to be less crucial than we imagine. Many of our worries concerning the use of genetic engineering techniques have to do with the somewhat deterministic way in which we view the question, which ought to be approached in political terms.

Nature and ethics

Nietzsche was the first philosopher to speak of genetics. He looked forward to a society based on genetic selection, doubtless exaggerating the power of science in so doing. In particular, he believed that the time had come to do what nature had always done serendipitously—i.e., give birth to supermen. Nietzsche was also the theoretician of the death of God. Believing that the bounds of nature could be transcended thus amounted to thinking in terms of the death of God.

Nowadays, to speak of the need for an argumentative ethic is equivalent to announcing—in less scandalous terms perhaps—the death of God. It would seem that we need an argumentative ethic since we no longer have any obvious and absolute foundation for our values.

Technological and scientific progress in the field of human engineering, combined with the dissolution of the conceptual foundations of values, confronts us with the question of the rules that should govern our research and practice in the field of genetics. These rules can no longer derive from the natural order. It is true that some authorities continue to preach a morality founded on respect for nature; but if we examine their arguments it is clear that they are not speaking of nature but of an ideology that fixes nature in a particular historical form deemed preferable. For example, the church does not allow women to be ordained priests on the grounds that the nature of women precludes it. This conception is based on the perception of the nature of women in the time of Jesus, that is to say, at a time when women could not occupy positions of authority and power. However, we do not need to think that a principle is natural to comply with an ethical command.

Nature becomes important when authorities are in conflict. What can we substitute for the rule of nature? In the current situation, we should not forget that we pose questions not in an abstract manner but in determinate contexts pertaining to the natural sciences, philosophy, the social sciences or ethical thought. In our societies, the debates on genetics take place between authorities regarded as absolute. An authority proclaiming itself natural would be the invisible hand of natural selection.

I fear that the revolt against sociobiology is a revolt against the idea that ethics affirms principles that seem superior to us because they are more useful. As a philosopher, I should like to recall Baudelaire's remark to the effect that 'where I have encountered virtue, I have always encountered anti-nature.'[1] I am not persuaded that the nature of human evolution is such as to favour the principles of altruism or collaboration. The question posed by ethics is probably that of non-theoretical reciprocal recognition. Take the example of freedom: freedom is not something we can demonstrate, but something we conquer. It is true that where freedom is asserted, it has to be respected on theoretical grounds. However, no one has ever changed a political order by demonstrating that freedom was a natural right.

The enemies of genetics are neither natural principle nor some intransgressible limit. One such enemy, on the other hand, could be political power insofar as it might wish to gain control of this mechanism either to oppress or dominate. The principle of consent is the only principle that we can oppose to all forms of authoritarianism. What we must ask ourselves is whether we can apply the principle of informed consent to all the problems of genetics. Let us draw a parallel: the Church, when it bans abortion, speaks in the name of those who do not yet have a voice; I would prefer that the mother be named the natural guardian of the newborn child. Indeed, we cannot impose a totally alien will on the woman who carries the foetus. We cannot prescribe something in the name of a conception of nature that the free being does not recognize.

Christianity has taught me that the human being is a free individual and that violence is to be defined as violence against our own freedom.

---

1. Cf. Charles Baudelaire in *The Painter of Modern Life* ('Praise of Cosmetics'): 'Crime, the taste for which the human animal draws from the womb of his mother, is natural in its origins. Virtue, on the contrary, is artificial and supernatural...'.

We must therefore work, either in the political sphere to make sure that absolute powers do not predominate, or else in the economic sphere to ensure that the potential of genetics is not monopolized by private interests.

We should also reflect on how to resolve the problems of genetics in a human and non-naturalistic fashion. These are long-term projects. It is because we cannot answer these questions that we turn to the absolute authority, mystery, or once again nature. Personally speaking, I prefer to recognize the authority of my fellow human beings.

We should not refer to an authority chosen simply because it resembles us, because it is of our species, or because it belongs to our party. These are problems central to contemporary democracies: how may we broaden the process of consultation? I do not wish the majority to block research. However, as an individual wishing to live in a free society, I can accept that the democratic decision should slow down excessively rapid or very rapid scientific development. Is such development immoral from a natural standpoint? Is it technically feasible? These questions remain to be answered.

The New Faces of Racism

The scientific deconstruction of the foundations of racism has not sufficed to eliminate this scourge. It is today assuming new social and cultural forms, reflecting new urban realities and the paradoxical reinforcement of immigration control policies alongside the liberalization of markets. At the same time, the genetic revolution is highlighting the risk of a new type of discrimination: genism, whereby the distinctive characteristics and qualities of individuals would be determined mainly by their genes.

The critical project deriving from the Enlightenment having proved inadequate to the task of eradicating racism, the contributors to this section propose forward-looking diagnoses and a range of preventive measures that seek to address previous shortcomings. Jérôme Bindé, Nadine Gordimer and Pierre Sané deal with new aspects of racism in the age of globalization and the genetic revolution. Warning against the dangers of 'genism', the new forms of racism it implies and 'genetic genocide', George J. Annas proposes the drafting of an international treaty on the preservation of the human species. Axel Kahn challenges the ideologies of genetic determinism and shows that modern biology offers no support for racist prejudice. Achille Mbembe reflects on the imaginative roots of racism, and Elikia M'bokolo analyses the changing faces of racism, underlining that the notion of culture has today sadly replaced that of race in the ideological discussion of 'difference'.

* * * *

Pierre Sané is assistant director-general for the Social and Human Sciences Sector at UNESCO. Born in Senegal, he is a graduate of the London School of Economics and was Africa director of the Canadian International Development Research Center (IDRC). In 1992, he became secretary-general of Amnesty International, where for ten years he presided over the expansion of the organization's mandate to take account of the post–Cold War context.

Jérôme Bindé is deputy assistant director-general of the Social and Human Sciences Sector and director of the Division of Foresight, Philosophy and Human Sciences at UNESCO. He is also secretary-general of the Council of the Future, as well as founding member of the Academy of Latinity. A graduate of the Ecole Normale Supérieure and agrégé, he has contributed to numerous works and published many articles on cultural, social and future studies issues, including *L'éthique du futur: pourquoi faut-il retrouver le temps perdu?* (1997) and *Prêts pour le XXIe siècle?* (1998). He was editor of *Keys to the 21st Century* (2001), the first anthology of '21st-Century Talks', and is the coordinator and primary co-author of the future-oriented world report *The World Ahead: Our Future in the Making* (2001).

Novelist, screenwriter and essayist, **Nadime Gordimer** was awarded the Nobel Prize for Literature in 1991, in recognition of a creative achievement strongly marked by the struggle against the apartheid regime in Africa. Her work includes: *A World of Strangers* (1958), *A Guest of Honour* (1970), *Sport of Nature* (1987), *My Son's Story* (1990), *The House Gun* (1998), *The Pickup* (2001). Vice-president of PEN International, she is also a Goodwill Ambassador for UNDP.

George J. Annas is professor in the Department of Health, Law, Bioethics & Human Rights at Boston University. His publications include *The Rights of Patients* (1975), *Some Choice: Law, Medicine, and The Market* (1998) and *Health and Human Rights* (1999).

Geneticist and doctor, **Axel Kahn** is director of the Cochin Institute of Molecular Genetics in Paris, a member of France's National Ethics Consultative Committee and president of the European Commission's Life Sciences High-Level Group. His published works include: *La Médecine du XXIème siècle: des gènes et des hommes* (1996), *Copies conformes: le clonage en question* (1998), *Et l'homme dans tout ça?* (2000). He is also the co-author of *L'Avenir n'est pas écrit* (2001).

Born in Cameroon, **Achille Mbembe** is a research associate at the Institute for Economic and Social Research of Witwatersrand University in Johannesburg. From 1996 to 2000, he was executive secretary of the Council for the Development of Social Science Research in Africa (CODESRIA) and in 2001 he taught at the University of California (Berkeley) as visiting professor. His publications include *Afriques indociles* (1988) and *De la postcolonie. Essai sur l'imagination politique dans l'Afrique contemporaine* (2000).

Born in Congo (RDC), the historian **Elikia M'Bokolo** was for ten years director of the African Studies Centre at the Paris Ecole des Hautes Etudes en Sciences Sociales (EHESS), where he is currently director of studies. He is the author of many books on Africa, including: *Noirs et Blancs en Afrique équatoriale* (1981), *L'Afrique noire. Histoire et civilisations* (1992) and *L'Afrique entre l'Europe et l'Amérique* (volume editor, 1997). He recently received, with Philippe Sainteny, the Audiovisual Research Prize for the documentary *Afrique, une histoire sonore*.

Pierre Sané and Jérôme Bindé

Racism, Globalization and the Genetic Revolution

―∞―

Over the last two centuries, pseudo-biological theories of 'racial' inequality have often been enlisted in an attempt to bolster ideologies of racism, racial discrimination, xenophobia and intolerance. In recent decades, however, the inanity of these theories and the vacuity of the very notion of race have been amply demonstrated. Science, and modern genetics in particular, has constantly affirmed the unity of the human species and the lack of any foundation for the notion of 'race'. In the words of Article 1 of the Universal Declaration on the Human Genome and Human Rights, adopted by UNESCO's General Conference on 11 November 1997, and endorsed by the United Nations General Assembly on 9 December 1998, 'the human genome underlies the fundamental unity of all members of the human family, as well as the recognition of their inherent dignity and diversity'.

Yet racism and racial discrimination, far from vanishing, have survived the scientific deconstruction of the concept of 'race' and seem to be gaining ground in most parts of the world. Significantly, racism, racial discrimination and xenophobia are currently attempting to establish their legitimacy by means of arguments that seek to assert the inequality of cultures. The far-reaching technological, economic, political, social and cultural changes associated with the third industrial revolution—the revolution of the new technologies—and often subsumed in the word 'globalization' seem to favour the spread of new forms of racism and discrimination. For globalization is accompanied by a growth of social inequality and uncertainty and by a corresponding explosion of communitarian reactions and the flaring up of passions regarding ethnic, national, 'racial' and religious identities. This is apparent in the worldwide proliferation of ethnic, 'racial' and religious violence, which often assumes the fanatical form of massacres among neighbouring populations, 'ethnic cleansing' and renewed genocide.

Thus, even as we celebrate the dismantling of institutional apartheid in South Africa, we witness the rise in most regions of the world of diverse forms of social and urban apartheid based on a structural discrimination that is 'racial' in character; whether explicitly or implicitly, while no longer having consciously to draw on 'racial' representations. In this universe of walled-up housing projects and no-go neighbourhoods, the very concept of public space—which is inseparable from the concept of democracy—is on the wane, and sometimes even disappearing. This growing separatism of urban space is reinforced by the emergence of various forms of academic and educational apartheid. These proliferating forms of social, urban and educational apartheid constitute a system of 'invisible racism' and veiled racial discrimination, which is no less formidable than the overt varieties.

There would seem to be a need, then, to rethink these questions in a forward-looking way. If it were only a matter of being 'enlightened', the progress achieved in mass education and the 'deconstruction' of pseudo-racial ideologies would long ago have led to the eradication of these scourges. Unfortunately this has not happened. Indeed, racism and racial discrimination have often been carried to their farthest extremes in countries with the highest levels of education. To understand the persistence of racist prejudice, should we not therefore undertake new kinds of exploration into these dark reaches, this time making better use of the tools provided by disciplines such as psychology and psychoanalysis?

In addition, the revolution in contemporary genetics, while opening up great prospects for humanity, also poses disturbing questions. In the temptation to perfect our species, are we not witnessing the revival of eugenics, more specifically a commercial form of eugenics that threatens to create a 'two-track humanity' and with it the eventuality of a 'post-humanity' that could lead to a form of dehumanization or self-domestication of humanity? Have we properly understood the risks attached to humanity's dream of taking control of itself—or should we say, of being controlled by those who master the new procedures? Does the progress in modern genetics not threaten to lead one day to that 'brave new world' prophesied by Aldous Huxley, with a new species of genetically engineered 'supermen' dominating the masses of 'subhumans', who will either be excluded from the new 'genetic paradise' or themselves be genetically manipulated for the purposes of social control or more complete exploitation?

Clearly, ethics needs to remain in step with scientific progress and technological developments so that they do not lead to new forms of discrimination. First of all, we must ponder the risk that the identification of characteristic gene sequences in populations living in a given geographic area could lead to the instrumentalization of this data for purposes of racial or ethnic discrimination.

Secondly, we must ask ourselves whether the new techniques of human reproduction are not liable to lead to the selection of embryos—and thereby to discrimination. Selection may be employed to favour certain phenotypes so that fewer people will be born with a genetic profile that is deemed undesirable or, conversely, to favour the birth of individuals with desirable characteristics—for example, the physical qualities needed to perform a certain kind of work. It is therefore important to define an ethical framework to guide states in the use of such techniques and in preventing their being used for discriminatory purposes.

Thirdly, research on the human genetic heritage could increase the temptation to deny the very existence of human liberty. Many geneticists today are working on human genome sequences that may have a role in predisposing individuals to certain kinds of behaviour (depression, rage, memory capacity, etc.). Furthermore, new theories are emerging, such as sociobiology, that attempt to make biology the foundation for individual and group behaviour and which could lead to our being dispossessed of the concept of human liberty. Bioethics must confront these questions so as to ensure that the dignity, rights and fundamental liberties of the human being are respected and that some individuals are not stigmatized in relation to others.

In conclusion, there is a risk that new forms of racism and discrimination will emerge in the twenty-first century, based on the idea of inequality among cultures and furthered by globalization and the uncertainties that it has engendered, as well as by the growth of material inequality and the dissociation of social and educational systems. Furthermore, this new social and cultural racism may also converge with another threat: the possible emergence of a new kind of eugenics, based primarily on consumerism and commerce, and new forms of discrimination fostered by the progress of modern genetics and the new, almost demiurgic powers of technoscience.

All of these threats call for searching, forward-looking reflection and for preventive measures at the international and national levels, especially in the following three domains.

- *Education*: there can be no question of assigning schools and other educational institutions the impossible task of curing the ills that society itself cannot or will not tackle. Nevertheless, education could be a valuable tool in combating racism and racial discrimination, so long as we reject the various forms of 'educational apartheid' that are currently taking shape and so long as efforts are focused both on formal education at all levels and also on non-formal education. Educational programmes, textbooks and pedagogical methods should be radically rethought in order to meet these new challenges, and help should likewise be sought from the new technologies and 'networked' education.

- *Bioethics:* safeguards must be introduced to prevent misapplications of the new genetics and to protect humanity from the spread of new techniques informed by genetic racism and discrimination. There is a danger that humanity's old demons will return if groups are allowed to be stigmatized as somehow genetically 'less capable'. Above all, there is a greater risk than ever of eugenics or the manipulation of the human species in the name of the 'transcendence of humanism' or a dream of 'post-humanity'. A bioethical framework should be established at the national and international level in order to deal with this gravest of dangers for human rights, and provision should be made for a worldwide monitoring and debate function to alert the human species to the possible misuses of technological and scientific applications, and their economic and commercial exploitation.

- *Urban policies and human rights:* manifestations of 'urban apartheid' have become increasingly extreme, thereby challenging the fight against poverty and threatening democracy. Is it now time to reconsider urban policies so that, along with the security of citizens, public space can also be renewed politically, culturally and ecologically. If we wish to change our lives in the twenty-first century and carry on an effective fight against racism, racial discrimination, xenophobia and intolerance, it will be necessary to change our cities as well.

It is important to emphasize that the developments anticipated here are in no way inevitable. Governments must demonstrate civic will by adopting policies commensurate with the challenges facing us. Leading figures in civil society must also mobilize their efforts to ensure that the rights of every human being are fully recognized, and that their societies do not become essentially uncivil.

Nadine Gordimer

New Aspects of Racism in the Age of Globalization and the Gene Revolution

Is globalization a new face of racism?

Many communities in the world, and many individuals outside but humanly concerned about such communities, believe globalization to be a new form of discrimination by a world group of economically privileged people expanding and protecting their own powerful interests. Globalization is seen as a phenomenon that started in the twentieth century. But it may be useful to look at its historical precedents, examining its pitfalls and success potential from all aspects including those of scientific research now that it has become the prevalent motive for human good in the twenty-first century. Its inception goes back centuries.

Exploration was the first idealist form of globalization, distinct from ancient wars that succeeded in conquering and homogenizing territories under dominant powers, and from the ancient trade routes of the Chinese and Arabs. The premise of explorers was to expand the concept of 'The World' through knowledge: that was its intellectual, scientific ethic, and its philanthropic one, following close, was to bring what was regarded as the only unifying spiritual enlightenment possible for humankind, the Christian faith, to peoples who had faiths of their own, discounted within the ethnic boundaries of the countries from which the explorers came. Along with the globalizing mission of Christianity came that of Western-world trade—in goods other than slaves, in which they were already involved, that unspeakable form of globalizing, the purchase of people in one country and homogenizing of them as slaves within the social hierarchy of another.

The Dutch East India Company, founded 1602, is one of the best examples of multinational corporate trade as an early form of globalization. Its outpost at the Cape in South Africa was not supposed to be a settlement, but a supply station for its ships on the route to India. A purely business enterprise. The fact that its supply station led to the Dutch Empire's occupation of the Cape takes us to the next stage of globalization: colonialism. If I cite the example of my own country's history, the same thing had happened, was happening in the Americas and other territories, 'undiscovered' until Europe penetrated them.

One world, a just world under the new name of globalization, that is the ideal we have before us, as politicians, scientists, artists, and other intellectuals, after the disparate national and international institutional combinations of modern times.

The boldest attempt to realize globalization in contemporary history has been politically ideological: Communism, in particular Soviet Communism. As we all know, the ethic of Communism calls for, counted on, human self-seeking to be transformed by revolutionary control of the means of production for the general good, an economic praxis. It was without question a noble ideal and many of us believed that it had a better chance of success than the religious ideal, which believed this end would be achieved above and beyond politics. Soviet Communism failed to globalize firstly because one cannot count on the transformation of human self-seeking; secondly because its means grew instead to a form of unbridled power that could not in turn match that of capitalism.

Neither East nor West has succeeded in getting the people and powers of the world to unite for the good of all.

What chance of success has the one-world concept in its less grandiloquently termed equivalent: globalization?

If we look at the past we cannot ignore that previous attempts have always turned out, of necessity, to be forced partnerships. Globalization has always needed both to contest on moral grounds, and also to work with the forces of other forms of power. The transformation of human self-seeking into human justice has to have agents. Politics and high finance have always taken a hand to the reins, whatever the noble declared direction of the charge into the future. So has scientific experiment. But it would be simplistic not to admit, along with the widespread movement of protest against globalization, that globalization as the function of the world's economy has been managed so far by agents of the rich countries, in their own interest and without recognition of the other aspects of just dispersion of the world's resources, which a reality of globalization demands.

We surely do not need reminding that the global scene, these days, is the image of a world made up of multinational corporations—that is globalization. One of its greatest beneficiaries, Bill Gates, has come to the conclusion that '[c]omputers are amazing in what they can do, but they have to be put into the perspective of human values. And certainly as the father of two children, thinking about the medicines I take for granted that are not available elsewhere, that rises to the top of this list.'[1] The responsibilities of science and medicine towards the world's poor are implied here, along with high finance.

The facts of contemporary reality have come not only to Bill Gates. Klaus Schwab, founder of the World Economic Forum, has recently declared 'that the systematic failure of world financial control makes it hard to escape a dismaying conclusion. The global institutions that we have so painstakingly built—the United Nations, IMF and World Bank and WTO—are inadequate to deal with the many problems we face. [...] Systemic failure threatens us all. [...] I am deeply sceptical [...] that the institutions responsible for promoting world peace, financial stability, socioeconomic development and the free flow of goods and services will ever again be able to address these challenges on their own.'[2]

A first move towards creating a new and effective collaboration is his suggestion that the G8 should become the Group of 20, a move already envisaged by President Thabo Mbeki. What I would hope to see is recognition of this as a correction of the part racism, unacknowledged, has played against the concept of bringing about globalization. It would not be an exaggeration to see this as having been the last international expression of colonialism, coming from its old home in the Western world. It implies that globalization, in all its implications, has the final obligation as the means to put an end to colonialism forever.

Is genetic engineering a new face of racism appearing in globalization?

I do not feel qualified to speak on the subject of the gene revolution announced for the millennium of globalization. As a concerned, activist individual I can only express disquiet and alarm based on nefarious genetic theories and subsequent practice on human beings in the century just left behind us. I refer, of course, to the Nazi regime.

It is difficult for us to judge at present—when not enough knowledge of the theories of cell reproduction, creation of embryos and the human genome project[3] that holds hereditary information has become available in

---

1. Quoted by Mark Malloch Brown, UNDP Administrator, in *Choice Magazine*, June 2001.
2. Quoted by Klaus Schwab, 'The World Needs A Bigger Stage', *Newsweek International*, 25 July 2001.
3. The human genome sequence—the ordered structure of 3 million DNA units comprising genetic information—was obtained (by the National Human Genome Research Institute) in a provisional form in June 2000. See Nicholas Wade, 'Tapping The Human Root', *Sunday Independent*, Johannesburg, 22 July 2001.

terms fully to be understood by lay persons like myself—whether the medicinal benefits of these discoveries will be the ethical limit of such research, or whether the end result will be that form of discrimination produced by the breeding of a world class of genetically privileged people, a scientific way to new overlordship, with strong possibilities of practice of racism, even unintentional. For within even approved fields of medicine, while vast economic differences continue to prevail between the haves and the have-nots, it will be the haves, mainly Western and white-skinned, and not the have-nots, mainly dark-skinned, who will afford to counter physical affliction and live longer and better.

This is the aspect of racism, the question to be asked of and answered by scientists.

George J. Annas

Genism, Racism and the Prospect of Genetic Genocide

I think there is little doubt that the twenty-first century will be the century of human genetics. New genetic technologies have the potential not only to change what we can do to ourselves and each other but, more importantly, to change the very way we see ourselves and each other.

Our superficial perceptions of each other have often fostered racism in the past. Simply defined, racism is 'the theory that distinctive human characteristics and abilities are determined by race'.[1] The hunt for genes, especially in groups identified by racial classifications, could lead to 'genism' (a term not yet officially recognized, but one I would define as the theory that distinctive human characteristics and abilities are determined by genes) based on DNA sequence characteristics with resulting discrimination as pernicious as racism.

A second consequence of the new genetics will be a temptation to use our new powers to transform ourselves by attempting to create a 'better baby' or even whole new categories of post-humans, eventualities warned of in Huxley's *Brave New World*. Huxley's world relied on conditioning to enable the enslavement of categorically 'inferior' humans by their genetic 'superiors'. A more likely outcome is genetic genocide: the elimination of the new human by the old, or vice-versa. Let me briefly explain each of these dangers and suggest ways that we might avoid them.

Genetic universality or genism?

The great hope of genomics is that it will scientifically demonstrate that humans are all essentially the same, and that this demonstration will lead

---

1. *Oxford English Dictionary*, 2nd ed., Oxford, Oxford University Press, 1989.

us to exchange our penchant for making distinctions among humans for a view that all humans are essentially the same. And genomics has already accomplished the science part. After the draft of the human genome was announced last summer, for example, Chris Stringer of London's Natural History Museum observed: 'We are all Africans under the skin.' The same point was made by other geneticists in different words, one noting that 'race is only skin deep', and another that 'there is nothing scientific about race: no genes of any sort pattern along racial lines'. Craig Venter, the leader of the private genome mapping effort, concluded: 'Race is a social concept, not a scientific one. We all evolved in the last 100,000 years from the same small number of tribes that migrated out of Africa and colonized the world.'[2]

This is all to the good, and geneticists deserve praise for getting this antiracism message out to the public. Unfortunately, the message of genetics, while undercutting racism, can simultaneously invigorate its evil brother, genism. This is how it works. Eric Lander, the genomics leader from the Massachusetts Institute of Technology has noted that, although we are all 99.9 percent genetically identical, 0.1 percent of difference is made up of 3 million spelling variations in our genomes. Each of these genetic variations could be used as a pseudoscientific basis for discrimination based on genetic endowment. Genome leaders have recognized this, and have called for legislation to prohibit genetic discrimination in employment, health insurance, life insurance and disability insurance. These are not the only arenas of discrimination that should concern us. Most important are the ways in which knowledge of our genomes will affect how we view our own life's possibilities, and even how our friends and families view us. The geneticists have said that understanding the genomic code will enable us to understand life at the molecular level. But we do not live life on the molecular (or atomic or subatomic) level, but as full-bodied human beings. It is this reductionistic view of humans as a collection of genes that is at the core of genism.

An example is provided by the now defunct 'Human Genome Diversity Project,' which sought to collect DNA samples from some 700 of the world's isolated ethnic groups, sometimes referred to as the world's 'vanishing tribes'. In the project's view, it was more important that science seize the opportunity to collect DNA from these peoples than that any action be taken to actually help the peoples themselves. The indigenous peoples around the world properly and forcefully rejected this project, and insisted that their human rights be placed above this dubious and reductionistic project.

It is true that 'we are all Africans under the skin'. It is also true, however, that if we decide to search for genetic differences in the 0.1 percent

---

2. Announcement of 26 June 2000, Washington.

of our DNA that is different, we will find them and use them against each other. Philosopher Eric Juengst put it well: 'No matter how great the potential of population genomics to show our interconnections, if it begins by describing our differences it will inevitably produce scientific wedges to hammer into the social cracks that already divide us.'

Preventing genism from taking over where racism left off by substituting molecular differences for skin colour differences will not be easy. Two actions, however, seem necessary. First, genetic privacy must be protected. No one's genes should be analyzed without express authorization; and, of course, no 'genetic identity cards' should be permitted. Second, pseudoscientific projects that purport to identify genetic differences between 'races' should be rejected.

The prospect of genetic genocide

Screening genomes to detect differences creates more opportunities for discrimination. Using the new genetics to try to make a 'better human' by genetic engineering goes beyond discrimination to elimination by raising the prospect of genetic genocide. Is this inflammatory language justified?

The project of genetic engineering will begin with the genetic replication of humans by somatic cell nuclear transfer, known simply as cloning. Cloning to create a child who is a genetic replica of an existing human makes a mockery of human dignity, both by undermining the individuality and liberty of the clone child, and by turning the child into a product of our own will and technique. The immediate danger, of course, is that, as products, the clone children will have their human rights called into question and, as copies of originals, they will inevitably be treated (and treat themselves) as second-class citizens.

Cloning, however, is only the beginning of the genetic engineering project. The next steps involve attempts to 'cure' or 'prevent' genetic diseases, and then to 'improve' or 'enhance' genetic characteristics to create the superhuman or post-human.

It is this project that creates the prospect of genetic genocide as its most likely conclusion. This is because, given the history of humankind, it is extremely unlikely that we will see the post-humans as equal in rights and dignity to us, or that they will see us as equals. Instead, it is most likely that we will see them as a threat to us, and thus seek to imprison or simply kill them before they kill us. Alternatively, the post-human will come to see us (the garden-variety human) as an inferior subspecies without human rights to be enslaved or slaughtered pre-emptively.

It is this potential for genocide based on genetic difference, which I have termed 'genetic genocide', that makes species-altering genetic engineering a potential weapon of mass destruction, and makes the unaccountable genetic engineer a potential bioterrorist. This may seem overblown; but, as an analysis of the failure of the United States to take action to prevent the genocide in Rwanda concludes, failure to act need not be based on failure to understand the facts: 'Any failure to fully appreciate the genocide stemmed from political, moral, and imaginative weaknesses, not information ones.' The hopeful aspect of the new genetics is that it can lead us to see our species in new and deeper ways, and help us to form what Vaclav Havel has termed our 'species consciousness'. A species-level consciousness will help us to imagine the likely consequences of our genetic science and to take effective steps to try to prevent predictable disasters.

What should be done?

Bioethics has been called upon to save us from the potential harms of the new genetics; but, with its focus on individual decisions made in the context of the doctor-patient relationship, it cannot help us confront species-wide issues. Although bioethics can help, a much more potentially effective framework is the language and practice of international human rights. My own view is that the threat by cults and others operating on the margins of human society to clone a human being creates an opportunity for the world to act preventively in ways that have been either extremely difficult or impossible.

Specifically, I believe it is now reasonable and responsible to suggest that UNESCO's Universal Declaration on the Human Genome and Human Rights, and the overwhelming repulsion of peoples and governments around the world to the plan to clone humans, can be followed by a formal treaty on The Preservation of the Human Species. This treaty should ban both species-altering techniques and species-endangering experiments. Specifically, techniques that propose to alter a fundamental beneficial characteristic of being human should be banned. (The alteration could be accomplished either by making the characteristic optional, such as by making sexual reproduction optional by adding cloning—asexual replication—to the ways humans could have children, or by altering the genetic code of an embryo in a way that the resulting child would be seen as a member of a human subspecies or of a new species.) Species-endangering experiments are those that would put the entire species at risk, such as current proposals to use pig organs for xenografts, which risk the creation of a new lethal human virus that could be similar to HIV.

This treaty should also contain a democratic and accountable enforcement mechanism through a monitoring and review body. No experiments in the species-altering or species-endangering categories would be legal without this body's prior review and approval. By shifting the burden of proof to scientists and corporations to demonstrate that their interventions would more likely be beneficial than harmful to the species, the treaty would adopt the environmental movement's precautionary principle to species-altering and species-endangering interventions.

We have a tendency simply to let science take us wherever it will. But science has become so powerful, both in terms of making our lives better and raising the risk of species suicide, that we can no longer abdicate our mutual responsibility to each other as members of the human species.

Conclusion

In her disturbing and evocative novel of post-apartheid South Africa, *The House Gun*, Nadine Gordimer writes of Harold and Claudia Lindgard (the parents of a young man who has killed his friend):

> The Lindgards were not racist, if racist means having revulsion against skin of a different colour, believing or wanting to believe that anyone who is not your own colour or religion or nationality is intellectually and morally inferior. Claudia [a physician] surely had her proof that flesh, blood and suffering are the same, under the skin. Harold surely had his proof in his faith that all humans are God's creatures in Christ's image, none above the other. Yet neither had joined movements, protested, marched in open display, spoken out in defence of these convictions. They thought of themselves as simply not that kind of person; as if it were a matter of immutable determination, such as one's blood group, and not failed courage.[3]

It took direct action to overcome apartheid. Although the Lindgards seemed to believe in behavioural genetic determinism, there is no gene (or blood characteristic) that codes for or excuses inaction in the face of actual or threatening human rights abuses. Inaction in the face of genism is not an option. We must work together to promote genetic privacy, prevent the cloning and genetic engineering of humans, and promote and protect universal human rights based on dignity and equality.

Without action on the species level, genism will eclipse racism as the most destructive disease on the planet. We are all Africans. We are all humans.

---

3. Nadine Gordimer, *The House Gun*, Rockland, Compass Press, 1998.

Axel Kahn

The Genome, Biology and Racism

On 12 February 2001, *Nature* and *Science*, two of the world's leading scientific reviews, published simultaneously two versions of the human genome sequence, one of them the result of cooperation between a number of university laboratories in different countries and the other stemming from the efforts of a private American company, Celera Genomics.[1] We learned in this way that human beings possess some 35,000 genes, differing only slightly from one person to another. The genetic alphabet is composed of four letters, A, C, G and T, forming a chain of 3.2 billion signs inherited from each of our parents. This chain of letters moreover shows a variation of only one in 10,000 as between men and women originating from Africa, Asia or Europe. Throughout the world, commentators have marvelled that such a prodigious creature as *homo sapiens* could spring from so few genes—no more than in other mammals, only two times more than in an insect such as a vinegar fly, a third more than in a worm, and less than in the batrachians and certain plants, such as wheat and tulips. Yet the very close resemblance between people of different ethnic backgrounds, coming from regions several thousand kilometres apart, seemed reassuring. This was proof, it was claimed, that races did not exist and that there was no longer any possible justification for racism, which would hopefully soon be on its way out.

Alas, I fear that this was to leap to a premature conclusion, out of ignorance or ideological presupposition. We must first look again at the role of the genes. Obviously, a single gene does not exist for each physical or psychic characteristic, for each attribute, for each specific behavioural trait, otherwise it would be inevitable that a creature with

---

1. This paper, delivered on 3 September in Durban (South Africa) at the 19th session of the '21st-Century Talks', was published in *Le Monde* on 4 September 2001.

cognitive capacities as developed as those of *homo sapiens* would possess far more genes than a mere animal. In fact, the mode of action of genes, i.e., the mechanism whereby they influence the properties of living beings, is combinatory, in the same way as the combination of words gives meaning to the phrase or text. Indeed, it is not the number of words used that determines the literary quality of a text, just as it is not the number of genes that explains the scope of human potentialities. I use the term potentiality advisedly, for the combination of genes does no more than govern the possibility of a human individual being educated within a community of like beings. When isolated and raised by animals, a young human being will evolve in the manner of those child savages, well documented in history, who are incapable of attaining the mental capacities characteristic of the human species. The combinatory effect of genes explains why small genetic differences can have considerable consequences for the beings concerned, as evidenced by the difference in appearance and ability between the human and the chimpanzee, whose genes are nonetheless 98.4 percent identical.

The reductionist ideology according to which genes directly determine the qualities and behaviour of individuals and human societies remains widespread. It explains the puzzlement of many when confronted by the news that human beings have no more genes than an ass or ox, and far less even than a toad. The same kind of prejudice lurks behind the sensational, unscientific announcements claiming that science has identified the genes controlling intelligence, aggression and many other mental characteristics. The connection between such persistent ideologies and racism is obvious: it is easy to imagine the devastating effect on populations often predisposed to believe in the omnipotence of the gene by the simultaneous announcement that scientists have located a region on the chromosome linked to intelligence and that this region varies in form according to the different ethnic groups. The fact that people the world over are to a large extent genetically homogeneous, as confirmed by study of the genome, is unfortunately not sufficient to avert the threat of biology taking a racist turn. There are two kinds of reasons why this is so.

Firstly, the combinatory nature of the effect of genes means that very slight differences can have far-reaching consequences for living beings. Secondly, the assertion that racism is illegitimate since races do not exist at the biological and particularly genetic level is tantamount to acknowledging that, if they were to exist, racism would be tolerable. However, this is in no way the origin of racism nor the justification for anti-racism. It is true that human races do not exist in the sense in which we talk of different races of animals. Think of German shepherd dogs and poodles, heavy carthorses and racing thoroughbreds. Homogeneity is in this case artificially maintained by breeders. In the human species, the variability of types is also significant but it is continuous because of the incessant crossbreeding between peoples. All human beings are in fact highly homogenous genetically since our common ancestor—who lived 200,000 years ago at the most in Africa—is young in terms of the evolution of life. All the continents seem to have been populated by groups of peoples who left Africa some 70,000 years ago. Skin colour, which plays such an important role in racial prejudice, reflects not so much a genetic divergence as a phenomenon of progressive darkening of the skin as one moves from the North towards the equator. There is greater genetic diversity, on average, among the individuals in a particular ethnic group than between two different ethnic groups, even where they are as apparently dissimilar as the Scandinavian and Melanesian populations.

This scientific demonstration, while essential, is likely to be inadequate. First, because such a demonstration has little impact on the lived experience of ordinary people, who have no difficulty in picking out in the street Asians, Whites, Blacks, dark-haired Mediterraneans and fair-haired Scandinavians. Second, it does not take into account the very frequent socioeconomic roots of racism, which is often the reflection of social malaise and discontent, for example among the deprived communities of large cities. Third and most important, there is paradoxically little relationship between the reality of race and racism. Indeed, it is a commonly observed fact that the worst racist excesses are in no way impeded by the non-existence of races. In ex-Yugoslavia, the worst kinds of racist behaviour set the Southern Slavs at each other's throats, one side being converted to Catholicism (the Croats), another to Islam (the Bosnians) and the third to Orthodoxy (the Serbs). I think one could readily cite many examples of the same phenomenon in Asia and Africa. In the speeches of latter-day racists, it is often no longer races that are declared incompatible or unequal but rather customs, beliefs and civilizations. The talk is of the clash of cultures. What is rejected is not so much the black-, white- or yellow-skinned person but the eating habits, the smells, the style of worship, the noise levels and the customs of the other groups.

Often, the increasing pressure of cultural uniformity and the imposition of Western standards in step with economic globalization provoke a reaction in the form of community isolationalism. This is a protective reflex against a wealthy and dominant civilization posing the twin threat of exclusion and loss of cultural roots. Sometimes this can even lead to something like cultural apartheid, resulting from the combined effect of the assertion of identity by minority groups and the intolerance or—what is sometimes worse—the disdain and indifference of the majority. There is in this exclusive form of communitarianism a tendency that seems to me inhuman. For cultural exchanges are what characterize civilizations and their development. Thus the Phoenicians were influenced by the Hittites, the Sumerians, the Assyrians and the Babylonians, who themselves traded with Egypt and Greece. The Etruscans, whose civilization was rooted in Greek and Phoenician arts and techniques, were at the origin of Roman culture. The same Roman culture was later remodelled in Constantinople by Greek civilization and subsequently incorporated many Eastern elements.

The dynamism of human cultures has always involved cultural exchanges and borrowings, which—contrary to the uniformity imposed by a dominant culture—creates diversity and with it new scope for the development of the human mind. The role played by African music, dance and sculpture in the emergence of modern art is an eloquent illustration of this process. Conversely, the animal races rarely exchange habits; they retain their ethological particularities, which essentially evolve only in response to genetic and ecological variations.

Thus human diversity is a source of mutual enrichment only if it is associated with exchanges. Uniformity has the same effect as isolationism: in both cases, dialogue is sterilized and civilization declines.

To sum up, biology and modern genetics offer no support to racial prejudice, and it is undoubtedly the responsibility of scientists to refute the pseudo-biological theses that too often continue to be enlisted in its support. This is a relatively easy task, but it is certainly not sufficient; for it is clear that racism has no need of the biological facts concerning race in order to proliferate. Conversely, it would be misguided to try to base an anti-racist commitment on science. There is no scientific definition of human dignity, which is a philosophical concept. Thus the struggle against racism and for recognition of the equal dignity of all human beings is above all a moral one—the reflection of a profound conviction that is obviously in no way the prerogative of the scientist.

Achille Mbembe

The Imaginative Roots of Racism

Despite the advances in various fields of knowledge, the case for the fundamental unity of the human species continues, in practice and above all in the realm of the imagination, to be disputed. In the case of racism, what is challenged is the very distinction between practice and imagination: the racist imagination is in itself no less than a social and cultural practice. This explains the persistence of racial prejudice, the emergence indeed of new forms of racism in virtually all parts of the world, including societies characterized at first sight by cultural homogeneity and subject to very limited migratory pressures.

A baseless prejudice?

There can be no other explanation for the persistence of racism inasmuch as race, strictly speaking, does not exist. For if race does not exist, what are the grounds for racism? What is the nature and driving force of this vacuous prejudice?

It could be that racists are simply ignorant of their own ignorance, believing as they do in something that has no existence. Racism would in this case derive from a belief characterized by a lack of knowledge of its absence of rational foundation. If this is indeed the case, knowledge cannot of itself eradicate racism. Belief and knowledge correspond to two distinct modes of judgement and valuation, and it is not certain that reason is the best critic of faith; they rest on two antagonistic definitions of truth. The truth of science is not sufficient to undermine the truth of belief. Knowledge is not therefore a certain cure for racism.

It is thus important to move from a perception of racism as a purely sociological concept (i.e., a mere prejudice that knowledge and reason could cure) to a realization that racial prejudice is rooted in mental structures whose determinants and main indicators lie beyond the dividing line established by the Enlightenment—that separating reason from the irrational and the imaginative. It will then be apparent that the force of racism lies in the unique link it establishes between reason, the irrational and the imaginative realm.

This unique connection is centred on the accident—the basically arbitrary fact—of the human body, as mediated through the equally arbitrary attribute of skin colour. Racism transforms this arbitrary attribute into a receptacle of our most secret and sometimes shameful fears, desires and impulses, and even into subjective and self-sustaining psychological structures that open the door to a multitude of conscious and unconscious meanings that are uncontrollable from start to finish because they belong, properly speaking, to the realm of the imagination and its functioning.

Awareness of this psychological dimension of racism should not blind us to the specifically sociological factors conducive to the spread of racism in the modern world. A number of trends in recent decades have paradoxically had the effect of reopening, on a global scale, the floodgates of the racist imagination.

The most important of these is doubtless the paradox arising from the worldwide movement of people, goods and signs (the phenomenon known as globalization, whose cultural dimensions have been so well analysed by the Indian anthropologist Arjun Appadurai). The obverse of this movement is not only the increasing number of quests for cultural and political identity based on the reinvention of difference but also the proliferation of micro-practices and policies aimed at controlling, regulating, immobilizing and, in some cases even, eliminating populations regarded as superfluous.

Globalization is reflected worldwide in the accelerated movement of people and commodities, the rapid circulation of images and the emergence of a world in flux, which, while originating from a particular location, is almost always domesticated and taken back into local ownership. Globalization has initiated a new phase in what may be termed the history of mobility.

This new phase is taking place in a context marked by a dual process of de-territorialization/re-territorialization, leading to new structural relationships between the poles of production and consumption, between city-worlds with increasingly complex functions and their regional environments. A key aspect of the dynamics of de-territorialization is the emergence of megacities, cosmopolitan meeting places for cultural diasporas, whose very existence often contradicts the traditional concept of the nation-state.

The new forms of racism linked to this dual process are related to three phenomena. The first concerns the growing discrepancy between the rights of people and that of objects and commodities. As a result of deregulation, financial movements go virtually unchecked, even if capital invariably flows in the same direction and bypasses in the process whole regions of the globe. The movement of people, on the other hand, remains strictly regulated.

The second phenomenon is that of migration. This assumes a variety of forms. Given the strict regulation of international migration and the introduction of increasingly draconian policies to limit and curb it, illegal and clandestine migration is today an integral part of globalization. Trafficking in human beings (whether children, women or illegal workers) is today part of a global economy whose underside remains increasingly hidden. The presence of immigrants in a foreign land moreover poses in acute form the problem of the relationship between citizens and foreigners, native and non-native populations.

One of the issues in conflicts between natives and non-natives often concerns access to resources. These conflicts are exacerbated by the fact that such access is dependent on belonging to a clearly defined group, whether it be the nation or a more restricted community. The close interrelationship between access, property and belonging has the effect of denying individuals the possibility of living on the basis of their work capability alone, irrespective of their origins. It places the emphasis on belonging and exclusion, thereby obliging individuals within society to fashion the tokens of belonging and invent those of exclusion, even where such tokens are not self-evident.

At the political level, we have witnessed from the early 1980s onwards the introduction of legislation aimed not only at discouraging immigration as such but also blocking the movement of people to parts of the globe that have become out-and-out fortresses. The best illustration of these developments is the visa policy. By targeting certain countries and establishing various forms of categorization, this policy has redrawn—in all legality—a map of authorized movements coinciding in large measure with the racial map of the world.

What is termed globalization thus goes hand in hand with the closure of frontiers at their entry points, by means of the deployment of externally directed surveillance technologies, the construction of new walls and the establishment of holding and no-go areas, often located at the very heart of airports, those symbols of mobility par excellence. Within the same frontiers, one has only to note the complexity of the definitions of 'clandestine', 'illegal' or 'person without identity or working papers'. The administrative labyrinth facilitates the practice of mass expulsions and makes the existence of foreigners more precarious. Thus the promise of universality inherent in the democratic ideal is frustrated by the form of regulation known as the nation-state. Globalization does not necessarily lead to universal citizenship. The right of free movement remains, from this standpoint, the precondition of a truly cosmopolitan world.

The third phenomenon is war—in theory an exceptional situation but one that is unfortunately tending to become the norm and even routine in some parts of the world. Increasingly, war and poverty are interlinked and constitute two forms of extreme violence. A useful distinction can be made here between the two faces of contemporary war, both related to the problem of 'race' (in the broadest sense of the term) or, more generally, of difference.

Firstly, there is war as a general phenomenon, which is aimed at destroying the enemy. The primary reflex is the physical destruction of the enemy's body, property and infrastructures, the point being to capture his wealth or simply incapacitate him without necessarily occupying his territory. In Africa in particular—but it is also the case in other, non-Western regions of the world—new configurations of war have emerged.

Except in rare cases, most wars are no longer aimed at liberating people from oppression (which was the case, for example, with the wars of decolonization). Nor are they any longer waged uniquely between standing armies. Very often, they set armed individuals against unarmed ones. In these circumstances, the distinction between a state of civil peace and a state of war has become tenuous.

The equation at the heart of present-day wars concerns the relationship between resources and life. They are wars of predation involving two distinctive kinds of material stakes: that of wealth—particularly in the form of minerals—and that of bodies. If one excludes wars aimed at the physical annihilation of the enemy (genocides), most of these wars are targeted at the bodies of the adversary in an attempt to maim or incapacitate. Thus war is no longer geared to obtaining reparation for a supposed injury. It no longer takes place between 'political entities'. The occasion for wars and genocide is now the relationship of man to man, insofar as this is equivalent to the relationship between human beings and things (this being the very definition of racism).

We see then how the new forms of racism continue, like the earlier ones, to have the human body as language and target. Why does the body of the other person play such a key role?

The essential reason is that the body—particularly its colour—is the most immediate, visual and physical aspect of the other person. It is the reality that is patently not fiction because it is there, present before us and occupying the same space as our own body. This immediacy and contiguity are irrefragable. The body has an anatomy. You can see it, touch it, smell it and wound it physically. In this sense, it is the enigma or the wall with which racism in all its forms maintains a conflictual relationship.

The more the human organism gains in transparency through the new genetic revolution, the more one may expect imaginative representations of the body of the Other to plunge deeper into opacity. This body thus becomes, more than ever perhaps, the receptacle of those primordial fears and superstitions that the progress of science paradoxically serves only to crystalize.

In the last analysis, the focus and target of what is termed racism is in very large measure human life. Racism can be defined as an active, practical and imaginative doubt concerning the proposition that every human life, in and of itself, is of equal worth and has the same price, density and value—a proposition whose corollary is that we are equally accountable for each life. Racists deny the principle of equal accountability for every life and, out of imaginative habit, experience the presence of others as an obstacle prefiguring their own demise.

It is this principle—that we are equally accountable for all human life—that ideologies of difference seek to abolish. And it is this same principle that any new humanism must affirm. Science can perhaps contribute to this new humanism. Yet since racism is by definition a practice rooted in the imagination, we should not overestimate the help that science can bring.

Elikia M'Bokolo

The Changing Face of Racism

To grasp the complex problem of racism, we have appealed variously to the social and other sciences; we have focused alternatively on the past and the future. We have likewise oscillated between the collective imagination and the material aspects of everyday life, between psychology and moral issues. The ensuing pessimism regarding new forms of racism would seem to have three main sources.

A pessimistic outlook

Firstly, we have recognized the existence of a number of paradoxes in the process of progressive 'enlightenment' through the sciences and social sciences. Although all of the research findings tend to invalidate the notions of racism and race, prejudice born of racism and racist practice seems to persist. We have the feeling that this phenomenon will persist, and experience over recent centuries suggests that this will indeed be the case.

Secondly, there is a paradoxical discrepancy between the potential that exists in our world for harmonious understanding between ethnic groups and the difficulties that remain in the form of exclusion, domination by majority cultures and oppression of minority and ethnic groups, which are deprived of all their rights.

The third paradox concerns the process of globalization and all that it entails. The free circulation of goods, capitals and ideas is at odds with the tightening up of passport requirements and frontier restrictions. These three elements fuel our pessimism.

It is moreover discouraging to note that we do not seem to have learnt the lessons of the past. Over the past two centuries, we have witnessed an explosion of racist practices. In spite of the intellectual, legal and cultural lessons we have learnt, we are still confronted by racism, in old or new guises. Racism in its old form focuses on people in faraway places and takes as its 'justification' the individual's skin colour or economic situation. The new racism targets people geographically closer—our neighbours, those alongside whom we live, as we have seen in the Balkans and some parts of Africa. Why are we unable to profit from the lessons of the past? Or, to put the question another way: have societies, states, intellectuals and activists derived all that they should from the historical facts available to them?

Another factor conducive to pessimism concerns the close relationship that exists between the imaginative universe, ideologies and language of racism and the everyday practice of violence, on the one hand, and the major economic and political issues and interests that preoccupy our governments, on the other.

I should like to return to the new and old forms of racism—the racism that focuses on distant populations and that which targets neighbours. To borrow an expression from Achille Mbembe, how is it that racism is still spreading despite all that has been discovered through research and science? I would say that we have exchanged one state of affairs for another. This is apparent in the development of the social sciences and the line taken by the media or by individuals who consider themselves experts and take it upon themselves to make judgements about faraway peoples (the media, development experts, NGOs).

Having invalidated the biological foundations of the notion of race, we have gone on to invalidate civilizations. When one sees the trickery used by certain groups to serve their interests or that of their heritage, one realizes that the notion of race has become a cultural concept. This shift points in a new and disquieting direction. According to the social sciences, cultures are processes rooted in history. Yet according to everyday speech, which is backed by strong convictions, cultures are constituted by states and governments. They today represent a set of preconceived notions linked to an individual or a community. Consequently, asylum seekers or clandestine immigrants no longer have an individual identity but the identity of a government, a state or a nation.

In the view of the social sciences, culture has always been an open and participative process. It is an invitation to exchange. But in the contemporary popular view culture has become something closed, originating from elsewhere, an enclosed place in space. In the social sciences we have tried to demonstrate that culture embodies many points of convergence, in different temporal universes, which can come together, even show themselves to be complementary. There is an internal and an external time, a time for proximity and a time for distance, a prolonged and an abbreviated time. But according to the other line of reasoning, culture is one-dimensional, repetitive and circular.

We have also affirmed that culture is an ensemble of spaces, places and products born of a multiplicity of struggles. Yet in the present-day view, rather than being an element of the heritage or an opening towards others, it has become a constraint. Just as races served in the past to generate difference, so culture is now used to demonstrate that others—the Asians and Africans, for example—are different. There is now a historical exception for these minority populations. This use of culture serves today as the basis for a strong ideological discourse, in the same way as did race previously. The entry of this new concept into discussions on development, good governance and modernization worries and disturbs me. Too often, culture is reduced to difference, inequalities and closed access. We have entered a world from which history has been expelled—not only history as it is written today, but history as it has unfolded down the centuries. Let it be said, however, that the current debate on the 'duty of memory' and the calls currently being made for the payment of reparations seem to signal a new approach, contrasting with the negative effects of the evolution of the concept of culture, which has regretfully taken the place of that of race.

Self-Knowledge: Anticipating and Preventing Sickness of the Soul

Has the soul become an outdated concept for modern societies, strongly marked in many parts of the world by the continuing advance of secularization? Does the soul still exist and has it a future? Does a future-oriented enquiry into analysis of the soul have any meaning outside the realm of theological questionings. For some, the soul remains the spiritual core of every human being. For others, the soul is simply another way of designating our psychic apparatus, which is as vital to human beings as their bodies. Very often, indeed, a psychological malaise manifests itself in bodily pain. At a time when the North is characterized by the cult of performance, by the growth of stress as a way of life and by the emergence of new inequalities, and when the South is suffering from poverty and exclusion, we are rediscovering a suffering soul, manifesting itself in the new forms of depression, addiction, compulsion, violence directed against the self or others, etc. How can we prevent and cure these new maladies of the soul?

Julia Kristeva examines the psychic deficiencies of the contemporary soul and describes the psychoanalytic experience in terms of a rebellious creativity. Denise Bombardier stresses the deleterious effect of the devaluation of time in modern societies. Adalberto Barreto reports on his experience as a therapist in a context of social exclusion, underlining the need to break out of the habitual university or medical settings to create new kinds of community therapy.

* * * *

Linguist, semiologist and psychoanalyst, **Julia Kristeva** is a professor at the Institut Universitaire de France, at the Université Paris VII Denis-Diderot and teaches regularly at Columbia University in New York and at the University of Toronto. As a writer, she has published *New Maladies of the Soul* (1995), *The Feminine and the Sacred*, with Catherine Clément

(2001), and *Female Genius: Hannah Arendt* (2001), *Melanie Klein* (2001) and *Colette* (2002).

Denise Bombardier, who holds a doctorate in the sociology of communication, is an essayist and a novelist. As a journalist with Radio-Canada, she is the author of internationally acclaimed television broadcasts. Her numerous publications include the very successful *Une enfance à l'eau bénite* (1985), *La Déroute des sexes* (1983) and *Ouf* (2002), as well as a volume written in collaboration with the psychiatrist and psychoanalyst Claude Saint-Laurent and entitled *Le Mal de l'âme. Essais sur le mal de vivre au temps present.*

A psychiatrist and ethnologist, **Adalberto Barreto** holds a professorship at the Faculty of Medicine of the Federal University of Ceará, and is Brazilian coordinator of the Integrated Community Mental Health Movement. He works in the *favelas* of the Nordeste, particularly Fortaleza. He has published a number of works, including, *L'Indien qui est en moi* (1996) et *Du Sertão à la favela: de l'errance à l'insertion*. His experience is described in a work by Éliane Contini, *Un psychiatre dans la favela* (1995).

Julia Kristeva

The New Maladies of the Soul

My topic places us at a hazardous but vital crossroads, where biology and meaning, body and mind, and psychiatry, psychoanalysis and psychology intersect with metaphysics. I shall try to focus my presentation on this junction of the material and the spiritual. I shall not refer to the examples of clinical cases related in my book *The New Maladies of the Soul*[1] but simply to the substantive questions they raise, as they relate to the question at issue and at the risk of being somewhat abstract.

I should like, in fact, to demonstrate the relevance of psychoanalysis to the contemporary crises of society and the modern discontents of civilization by responding to three questions. The first is whether you, whether we, have a soul? The second is whether this soul is still capable of rebelling? Thirdly, why is psychoanalysis, or why could it be, a new avatar of atheism and hope?

Do we have a soul?

The question as it stands might seem obsolete. But I shall attempt to show, as I do in my book, that psychoanalysis proposes a vision of the human being according to which being alive is predicated on the human being's possessing a soul, on having what Freud called—in the tradition of Greek philosophy, the Jewish experience and the Christian heritage—a 'psychic apparatus'.

Psychoanalysis is based on the principle that you are alive if, and only if, you have a psychic life. It accordingly tries to reconstitute that life and alleviate its traumas so as to make possible the psychic life that enables your body to live. From this perspective, psychoanalysis can

---

1. Julia Kristeva, *New Maladies of the Soul*, New York, Columbia University Press, 1995.

be seen as heir to the personal ethics developed within the Western philosophical, religious and scientific tradition. According to Freud, the psychic apparatus represents a kind of transition between the body and meaning. Psychoanalysis can thus be seen as a theory and practice of the 'co-presence' of sexuality and thought: it is because our sexuality is rooted in the biology of the body and additionally bound up with the sense of communication that psychoanalysis, by intervening upon the meaning of the sexual discourse, can intervene upon the meaning/direction of your life and your body. Freud thus offered us, with his model of the psychic apparatus, a complex and psychosomatic conception of the soul organized around three topics: the conscious, subconscious and preconscious; the ego, superego and id.

Has this conception of the soul, novel in the history of thought, which effects a transition between substance and mind and revisits the classic dichotomies of metaphysics, survived the test of time? Is Freud's conception of psychic life still relevant at the opening of the twenty-first century? Has the soul disappeared? Or, on the contrary, can this Freudian vision of the soul help us to reconstruct our inner lives and, in so doing, revitalize our bodies?

It might be thought that advances in biology and the neurosciences have replaced the soul with chemical substances and molecules. Yet nothing is less certain. In this connection, I have assembled some particularly interesting quotations from biologists and neuroscientists: 'The image is present before the object in the brain'; 'It is the neural network that is penetrated by the cognitive activity that takes place within it and not the cognitive architecture that obeys the constraints of the nervous system'; 'One cannot do without the goal and the subject. I do not see how we might conceive of mental functioning that did not include a representation of the goal, that is, that did not imply a subject that attempts to represent both itself and the expected goal'. In other words, even the most technical and biological models need to integrate the notions of subject and goal. Far from eliminating meaning, we are obliged to reintroduce it; and far from seeing the birth of a new form of spiritualism, we find ourselves witnessing the reintegration predicted by Freud between body and spirit, sexuality and thought.

Given the scientific pointers in this direction, are there not grounds for thinking that some aspects of modern life are leading us to eliminate and disturb the soul? One has only to look at American soap operas, assailing us with their self-indulgent psychological dramas, to realize that the characters in these series are incapable of coming to terms with their conflicts, that they suffer as a consequence, and that their hysterical self-indulgence is a confession of unhappiness and of an inability to give meaning to their psychic life.

As for the renewed interest in religions, does it stem from a quest for the spiritual life or is it a confession of psychic impoverishment that demands an artificial soul to replace an amputated subjectivity? 'I don't know who I am'. Hamlet's 'To be or not to be' is rephrased in terms of the dilemma 'Take a pill or not take a pill?' The subjects thus call on religion to make good a deficit of soul! They seek in an ancient and archaic code that which they are unable shape in the form of a singular soul or subjective singularity.

This whole question ties in closely for me with the experience of the psychoanalyst's couch. For several years now, we have observed that seemingly classic cases (neurotics, obsessives, hysterics, etc.) mask far more serious maladies of the soul, even if obsessional neurosis and hysteria remain present. These maladies of the soul are bound up with wounded narcissism, false personalities, borderline conditions and psychosomatic illnesses. For all their differences, these illnesses share a common denominator with each other and with other sicknesses of the soul such as drug addiction, crime and vandalism: the difficulty of psychic representation.

This deficit of psychic representation can take the form of mutism or can express itself in a variety of signals experienced as empty or artificial (patients, even when socialized and surrounded by others, admit to the impression of speaking only false and artificial words, as if they were puppets). Such a deficiency hampers sensory, sexual and intellectual life and can undermine biological functioning itself, i.e., can become a physiological ailment, ranging from headaches or stomach aches to cancer. Patients then appeal, in disguised form, to the psychoanalyst to restore their psychic life and, thereby, the life of the body.

Are these new patients the product of modern life, which aggravates the situation of families and young children? We all know that mothers are less present in the home, that fathers no longer have any authority and that, consequently, the traditional structures that enabled the subjectivity to develop have disappeared. Is the inability of these patients to represent conflicts subjectively and personally tied up with medical dependency, with the idea that everything is rooted in biology and material factors, entailing massive recourse to medication and turning the image into a drug and a tranquillizer?

Or is it simply a matter of analysts listening more? Are analysts themselves not more alert to deep personality conflicts? Rather than seeing everything in terms of hysteria and obsessions linked to inhibition or suppression of the libido, do they not observe more serious deficiencies relating to pre-Oedipal situations and to more archaic structures of the personality, involving the relationship with the mother and extensively explored by Melanie Klein[2] as the entry point to symbolization?

Patients who suffer from this inability to represent and symbolize conflicts can be divided into two categories: on the one hand, those who

---

2. Melanie Klein, *The Psycho-Analysis of Children*, London, Hogarth, 1932.

have difficulty in living out their desires and who are confronted by various forms of perversion, driving subjectivity into its innermost recesses and going so far as to destroy the relationship with others and their own body; on the other, those who have not discovered their desires and who turn against themselves in acts of self-destruction, which frequently take the form of anorexia or bulimia.

Can the soul rebel?

Modern culture can no longer be a culture of interdiction. We have referred to the various constraints weighing on the family, which can give rise to problems of representation. But we have yet to speak of the loosening, not to say lack, of moral, religious and political prohibitions, which goes hand in hand with the weakening of authority and the crisis of values. Of course, some interdictions will always remain, and their forms are far from being fully explored, not least the economic constraint. But contemporary societies are characterized by the fact that interdiction is so to speak negotiated, since it is confronted by rebellion. This is commonly observable in everyday life in the unease, discontent and dissent aroused by plans to reform education and retirement benefits, for example.

The problem, in fact, goes much deeper and concerns mental and psychic life. In the Judeo-Christian tradition, the soul is characterized precisely in terms of its capacity for revolt. I shall return later to Freud, whom I consider to be one of the great rebels of our time, and to psychoanalysis, which is a form of revolt. But, before that, I should like to dwell for a moment on Saint Augustine, for one cannot talk about the soul without mentioning him. In the mystical and Christian theological tradition, Saint Augustine considered that the soul is soul insofar as it is capable of interrogating itself and calling itself into question. Now, etymologically speaking, the word 'revolt' means 'return and renewal', which is precisely what is involved in calling oneself into question. Moreover, Saint Augustine thought that prayer was a form of questioning: the ego is founded on questioning. But when the believer called himself into question in this way under God's authority, he was protected by an absolute: the promise of eternity, an untroubled life, reconciliation and immortality. The self-questioning proposed by psychoanalysis is much more demanding. By entering into analytical therapy and exploring our traumas and despairs, we confront our capacities for pleasure and suffering. These are so deep-rooted and powerful that we quickly perceive their reconciliation and stability to be provisional. Only their intensity seems eternal to us. The soul is in a way sadomasochistic! And our absolute is not a divine authority to be turned to account by this or that institution, but rather the indistinct voice that speaks to another. In other words, what psychoanalysis offers us, by 'articulating the conflict', by learning to represent it in an indefinite way in the course of self-questioning, is to reconstitute our soul, not as an inner fortress but as a constant interrogation.

That is why, confronted by these new maladies of the soul (vandalism, drugs, psychosomatic troubles) masking profound inadequacies of psychic life, analytical listening (and interpretation) is a form of forgiveness. To forgive, in my view, does not come down to removing the malaise, suffering or exultation that the pervert finds in acts that are in reality destroying him, but rather to giving a meaning, above and beyond the unrepresentable, to the suffering and ecstatic body.

Now this experience of forgiveness does not exist in the social realm, which is rather that of judgement. A society is there to judge when it is confronted with the crimes of the pedophile or sadist, or those of the politician. Yet there is a place where pedophiles, sadists, drug addicts or those suffering from psychosomatic disorders can question themselves with the help of a benevolent listener enabling them to arrive at an indefinite and optimally far-reaching representation of suffering, pleasure and the impossibility of being. This act of listening, which serves to bestow meaning, has a function of forgiveness, not in the sense of erasing but of beginning anew. The patient, then, searches with the psychoanalyst for other, shareable ways of experiencing pleasure and suffering.

Initially, the patient shares his suffering with his analyst and joins or rejoins the human community in the singular form of a dialogue. Only later will the patient perhaps be able to 're-establish the link' with others. It is a minimal form of socialization, but one that is firmly grounded and reliable and which enables those unaware of the meaning of their suffering to discover, define and share it.

Psychoanalysis, a rebellious creativity

Analysis discloses the irreconcilable conflictuality and dramatic splits that constitute every human being, which dictate that no unity and no absolute are possible. We are all beings 'thrown'—as Heidegger put it, or rebels in the Freudian view—into a unity that cannot be stable and where self-questioning in the sense of calling oneself into question is the only solution. At the same time, this capacity for revolt made possible by analysis leads us to create links. Once the analysis is over, I shall be able to separate myself from the absolute that the analyst has represented for me so as to recreate new links on each occasion and to enter into a phase of creativity that will enable me to face new situations and lead a life in society.

Sartre said that 'atheism is a cruel and lengthy undertaking'. In the same way, the analytical experience, understood as the uncovering of suffering and the unrepresentable and as a permanent search for the meaning of the unrepresentable, may be seen as a form of atheism that is indeed cruel and long drawn out. While it does not afford us any hope of stability, it does on the other hand offer us the hope of rebellious creativity.

Denise Bombardier

The Compression of Time and Sickness of the Soul

Who today still believes in the respect due to time? I myself am closely concerned by the modern problem of time. As a television journalist, I belong to a profession that has fragmented time, that mocks it and is constantly frustrating it. Yet as a writer I must submit myself to time, the more or less inescapable time involved in writing. Time, I confess, haunts and preoccupies me. I leave it to psychiatrists and psychoanalysts to analyse the harm done to the soul by this disrespect for time. I shall simply set down a few ideas suggested to me by this constant race against it.

Time in today's world

Today, people own more than one watch, some of them waterproof so that they can check the time not only on land but also under water, where time in fact stands still. Clocks are now to be found in every part of the house and in all public places—apart from casinos, since gamblers are told they have their whole life in which to win (or lose!).

We are also witnessing the development of a new kind of mental illness: the cell-phone craze. And, as we know, the mobile telephone does away with the notion of waiting, not to mention privacy.

Everyone says: 'I have no time to lose'. We need, then, to think about the way in which society is abbreviating all human activities. In medicine, for example, doctors are not only attempting to replace natural organs subject to wear and tear with more robust artificial organs (about which we have absolutely no complaint) but are also studying ways of lessening the time that wounds take to heal. In our too costly health systems, time is money! In the much-vaunted day surgeries, they remove your cancerous growth in the morning and send you home in the afternoon. The time that patients spend in hospital is being systematically reduced.

Similarly, the traditional period for viewing a dead person in a funeral parlour has been reduced from three days to one. One also hears of deceased people who have stipulated in their will that they should be buried or cremated immediately. The rite of passage that enabled those close to the deceased to come to terms with the parting of a loved one is no longer observed.

Conventional clock time is valued at a premium or a discount depending on whether it is that of an affluent or a Third-World society. In Western societies, time is perhaps the most valuable economic resource. Share prices rocket on the back of instantaneous technological communications. A fraction of a second is transformed into gains or losses of millions of dollars. In the calculation of economic returns, the 'time' factor is of prime importance. Every element in the life of a commodity—its production, consumption, degradation and, in the near future, elimination—has its time coefficient. The person who stipulates in his will how long his friends and relatives will be able to mourn him after death thus finds justification in this mercantile approach to the time of the living. What is most shocking is that we are denied the privilege of excluding certain aspects of our life—events, states of mind, moments of happiness and misfortune—from this odious calculation.

Living in the fast lane

Nowadays, the organization of leisure activities no longer leaves any time for solitude. In North America, everything is organized down to the last second. Yet, by definition, leisure surely means not consulting one's watch and not being pressed for time.

I have worked in television for over twenty-five years. Television is the enemy of time. What is zapping if not a state of irritation linked to a sense of time as being inadequately filled or boring? One day we should question—as certain philosophers have already begun to do—the impact of zapping on the transmission of knowledge, on children's capacity to concentrate and on the building of relationships with other people. Zapping certainly has something to do with the difficulty that young people have in concentrating in class. It is understandable that children who spend their time zapping in front of the television soon become aggressive when they realize that they cannot 'zap' their teachers!

Is there not an essential relationship between time spent in creative solitude, spare time and freedom? Could it not be said that the only free being is the person who, through a singular deployment of spiritual energy, is able to break away from this mercantile model of time in order to devote him- or herself to 'the contemplation of the beautiful and the good', as was said in the time of the Saints?

Should we not sound the alarm at our collective capitulation before this insidious appropriation of something essential to ourselves? The love relationship induces a kind of return to perfect harmony. When you are invaded by happiness, you feel a compelling need for time to stand still. Does it not follow that love, like other feelings, will in future be a privilege reserved for the happy few who have given everything to attain it, in the manner of saintliness in former times? We know that the love relationship is tending to become progressively shorter in duration—one couple in two divorces in North America. These emotional fractures, in the circumscribed lifetime of an individual, tend to involve the loss of fragments of the self-belief inherent in all of us.

'Oh time, suspend your flight, and you, propitious hours, suspend your course', wrote the poet. Has Lamartine, a poet of the past, been overtaken by the present? What if, on the contrary, we were to heed him more so as to avoid replacing the greeting 'How are you?' with that terrible and all-too-frequent question 'Do you have time...?'.

Adalberto Barreto

Exclusion and Sickness of the Soul

For over twelve years I have been working in a *favela* of 281,000 inhabitants, situated near Fortaleza, a city of 2 million people. To escape from the drought, the inhabitants of the *favela* migrate from the countryside to the city, participants in a silent and invisible war resulting from an unfair economic policy that generates exclusion. Although seemingly weapon-free, this battle inflicts deep wounds that penetrate to the very soul of these individuals. This drift from the countryside sets the individuals concerned on a downward path, leading from economic hardship to cultural deprivation and a loss of know-how, social bonds and self-respect.

The experience of arriving in large cities is one of profound desolation. The city does not welcome them or open its doors to receive them. The migrants remain on the poverty-stricken fringes of the city, and very soon realize that their dream of a better future is nothing short of a nightmare. Another set of problems then confronts them. Where are they to live? How can they build a house without the means to do so? How are they to feed their children? How can they find a job without work training? The life of a *favelado* is as harrowing and frustrating as that of a lost soul, searching to make contact without ever managing to make itself heard or seen in the world of the living. The prevalence of this theme among the socially excluded may mirror their own sense of living a faceless existence, deprived of the right to living space. Could it be that the 'lost soul' is the prototype of twenty-first-century maladies of the soul in Brazil?

Devising a community therapy

We first became involved in this context through the *favela*'s human rights centre, which asked us to provide psychiatric support for people in psychological distress. In the course of our very sporadic interventions, we were regularly confronted by the question of how to treat an individual in such a setting—for example, how to treat a woman whose husband is unemployed and who has no roof over her head and no food. As academics, we had to extend our treatment beyond the individual and the biomedical realm to encompass the family and community as a whole. In the university, one learns to train people so that they can go on to treat others. But that method is not valid for the *favela*, where hundreds of people require immediate treatment. We therefore had to change our working methods in order to get closer to a wider public. We also had to break away from the model of the saviour figure, the technician who arrives with solution in hand, and to look beyond the failings to the human and cultural potential. In the first instance, one is so moved by the failings that one invariably tends to want to lecture, medicate and offer advice; but this is not what these communities are looking for.

To address this challenge, we organized weekly meetings with people in crisis and developed what we have called 'community therapy'. This provides a forum for reflection, awareness-raising and collective thinking, where everyone listens to everyone else and tries to express him- or herself. In this *favela*, where raised voices quickly escalate into violence and the law of the strong prevails, we dared create a place where people could express themselves and find words to 'articulate these ills'. The project was ambitious but it bore fruit.

These meetings enabled us to awaken the group's therapeutic capacity. For it is within the group, through the reciprocal expression of suffering and the exchange of individual experience, mutual support and the strengthening of affective links and cultural values, that the social fabric is consolidated and a sense of social belonging awakened. Individuals discover how to transcend their problems and eventually integrate themselves more successfully in society.

Our approach is closely aligned on that of the Participatory Action Research (PAR) network, whose method we have been following for a number of years. This is based on a rejection of the academic monopoly of knowledge production and seeks to generate knowledge at the local level, from and for the local community. Our experience has convinced us that maladies of the soul can be treated by the group itself. Those who suffer contain solutions within themselves, even if they need help in finding them.

This model is today widely applied throughout the country since we have already trained 600 mental-health workers, whom we call community therapists, with the help of the Pastoral da Criança, an agency of the Brazilian Catholic Church active among 130,000 of the country's impoverished communities. These therapists do not practise psychiatric interpretation or analysis but mobilize the group to find a solution to a particular problem. For example, if one of the group members suffers from insomnia, the therapist calls on the other members to reveal whether they have experienced something similar in the past and how they have overcome it.

The principal pathogenic axes

The inhabitants of the *favelas* are social outcasts, consumed by a sense of neglect and bereavement. Nobody supports them. Neglect is manifest at the individual level in their physical appearance: the relatively young are prematurely wrinkled, gap-toothed and dishevelled. It is also apparent at the family level, where women abandoned by their husband must shoulder the responsibility of raising several children. Families are found living in the streets. The effects of neglect are also apparent at the social level: the geographical layout of the *favelas*, with their ramshackle constructions of wood and cardboard, reflects the life stories of their inhabitants, the fragmented existence of families and the private wounds of individual existences.

A whole range of methods exist to overcome these situations of neglect. In some cases, neighbourhood groups and trade unions combine to meet basic food and housing needs and form networks. In other cases, the young people get together and sometimes lapse into delinquency, with the most sensitive of them developing neurotic compensations (depression, alcoholism, drug addiction).

Appeal is also made to religious cults. Increasingly, they are becoming places of collective catharsis. The suffering of the body touches the soul within. There is a tendency for all religious assemblies—whether Catholic, Afro-Brazilian or Protestant—to become the providers of intensive existential care, where people come to revitalize souls devitalized by the harshness of existence. Some forms of worship are tremendously aggressive, particularly the new Pentecostal churches and the Universal Church of the Kingdom of God. These require their followers to reject any cultural belief and to break with models of conduct internalized for generations, giving rise to a veritable loss of identity, the creation of a false ego modelled on the values of a religion from which everything is to be expected and which affirms itself through the negation of others. On the pretext of exorcizing evil, such cults exorcize the core of people's own being and beliefs, of the critical foundation of their values, and of their innermost soul. However, other religions such as the Afro-Brazilian cult Umbanda hold out the possibility of integration into a neo-family reconciling multiple images of identity that, by respecting the grassroots culture, can forge a more tolerant kind of community.

Insecurity

The climate of insecurity is a ferment of violence and division in society, stimulated and sustained by fear of the irrational actions it generates. In the *favela*, violence—theft, crime, aggression—has grown more acute with unemployment. While the rich access the Web through their keyboards, the poor generate their own asocial Internet in the form of networks organized as a source of livelihood in delinquency. These groups impose their rule and create a climate of insecurity and fear that extends to all social groups. I do not wish to speak of the culture of violence, which is the paradigm of every developed society, maintained through a technological counter-culture expressed in films. In Brazil, the television even broadcasts programmes featuring live violence, particularly in the *favelas*.

Just as security is a necessary social factor for the development of mutual trust, so living in security is essential for the possession of self-confidence and the capacity to master one's instincts in order to transform them into existential strengths.

The loss of self-esteem

The most tragic form of destitution is not the visible one but that which people internalize, namely a profound sense of inadequacy. They no longer believe in themselves, are excluded and lose all ability to love and be loved. One way in which this loss of self-esteem manifests itself in the individual is the withdrawal into silence. In Brazil, we say that when the mouth is silent the body speaks. It goes without saying that it takes a great deal of work to help these people express themselves within the group so as not to deprive them of the possibility of learning from contact with others.

Within the family, the result of a repressive and disparaging upbringing is to destroy the child's self-confidence. Socially, this lack of self-confidence produces professional failures. Many find a job but do not remain in it more than a month: the distress is so great that they eventually give up trying.

Along with the sessions of community therapy, we have implemented a group programme for the fostering of self-esteem, to enable individuals to rediscover their personal and cultural potential and harness it to an individual and collective dynamic so as to become the subject of their own history and responsible for their own existence.

The case for a policy of prevention

The troubles associated with neglect, insecurity and loss of self-esteem constitute a disturbing situation nationwide. They sustain the ferment of violence and division at the core of society. The irrational fears and actions they engender worsen the climate of tension, despair and anguish, which can only be dispelled by the presence of committed institutions, working alongside the community. When these institutions are absent or inoperative, individuals create their own rules and institutions. This devil-take-the-hindmost mentality ratchets up the fratricidal violence.

Devising tools capable of stimulating creative action among individuals in distress must be based on specifically individual values and on previously rejected cultural values. These new tools can only be conceived within a participatory and community framework. The group is the source of the most relevant solutions, ones fashioned by itself and reflecting the diversity and lived experience of all concerned, avoiding the imposition of any *a priori* scale of values. This approach demands that the health professionals distance themselves critically from explicative models of distress and the involvement they imply, since they are too often linear and reductive: one thinks of the biomedical model, for example, which advocates drug treatment; or the social model, which imposes from the outside actions that are alternately educational or repressive.

Self-realization by the individual as a factor in the transformation of the social fabric should make it possible to get away from paternalistic models such as the all-powerful welfare state, which reinforces dependence and stifles creativity. The aim, rather than waiting for budget investments, is to turn to account the sociocultural capital of excluded individuals so as to enable them to move from the status of passive victims to that of actors in the shaping of their destiny and thereby become jointly responsible for reconstructing society and capable of making critical choices as autonomous beings.

The creation of locations that foster affective and social links and promote a sense of cultural belonging within a community context is vital. The point is to move from location to link, transcending the individual model whereby the solution for all ills is expected to derive from an outside individual or from the political sphere. We maintain that the solution is collective: it is necessary to set in train participatory movements in which each person makes his or her contribution, thereby enabling the group to develop as a whole and enrich itself in the process.

The loss of self-esteem is a state of deprivation with respect to one's own knowledge. It is important to establish and develop places where identity can be restored, where speech can liberate itself. Scientific knowledge should finally recognize and incorporate so-called 'popular' knowledge. The restoration of self-esteem by victims of social exclusion constitutes the cornerstone of the struggle against the maladies of the twenty-first-century soul.

I shall close with an anecdote that was reported to me from a therapy session. A father, wishing to pacify his son in revolt against the chaos and confusion of the world, tore a map of the planet into tiny pieces and asked the son to put it back together in his own way, thinking he would be unable to do so. Yet thirty minutes later the map had been pieced together again. The father was amazed until his son explained that, before his father had torn it up, he had noticed that the map bore the portrait of a man on the back. So all he had to do was to 'repair' the man, and in repairing the man he had repaired the world.

Human Beings and the Future of the Universe

Questioning as to the origin and structure of the universe is central to all the world's mythologies, which are almost always cosmologies. The question is indeed fundamental, for in raising it we are pondering no less than the origin of our being-in-the-world, our place in the cosmos and the meaning of our existence. Astronomy, which has gradually emerged from the religious and mystical domain, can today pose these questions in scientific form. Will the expansion of the universe continue indefinitely? Will the Big Bang be matched by the Big Crunch? How can we conceive of what will happen after the extinction of the stars, in conditions wholly inexplicable in terms of the laws of traditional physics? Up to what point will human beings and human intelligence adapt to the future evolution of the universe? Such questions involve a time scale incommensurate with that of human existence or even of history; but the death of the universe, however remote, remains a vertiginous prospect for the human mind.

Trinh Xuan Thuan points to the reasoning whereby we can predict the future of the universe in the short and long term, and the limits of such prediction. Nicolas Prantzos traces the path that leads from a cosmology conceived on the model of cyclical time to the idea of the probable death of the universe, with its possible implications for our conception of our place in the cosmos. Finally, André Brahic offers a defense and illustration of scientific reasoning, with particular reference to astronomy.

* * * *

Born in Vietnam, **Trinh Xuan Thuan** studied astrophysics at the California Institute of Technology (CALTECH), then at Princeton University. Professor of astrophysics at the University of Virginia, he is a specialist in extra-galactic astronomy and has written numerous scientific articles on the formation and evolution of galaxies. He is the author of a number of very successful works: *Secret Melody* (1988), *The Birth of the Universe: The Big Bang and After* (1993) and *Chaos and Harmony* (2000), *The Quantum and the Lotus: A Journey to the Frontiers Where Science and Buddhism Meet* (2001). He has recently published *Origines* (2003).

Nicolas Prantzos is a Greek-born astrophysicist. A researcher with CNRS, he studies the evolution of galaxies and high-energy astronomy at the Paris Institute of Astrophysics. He has received a number of awards, including the Académie Française Astronomy Prize in 1994, the Henri de Parville Prize from the Académie des Sciences and the Golden Pen award from the Association des Ecrivains Scientifiques de France for his work *Soleils éclatés* (1988), written in collaboration with T. Montmerle, and the 1999 Jean Rostand Prize from the Mouvement Universel de la Responsabilité Scientifique for *Naissance, vie et mort des étoiles* (1998) published in the 'Que sais-je' series. Finally, he is one of the four authors (including Hubert Reeves) of the best-seller *Sommes-nous seuls dans l'univers?* (2000).

André Brahic is also an astrophysicist. A professor at the University Paris-VII Denis-Diderot and director of the Atomic Energy Commission Gamma Gravitation Laboratory at Saclay, he is famous for having discovered, with William Hubbard, the rings of Neptune. His research is mainly focused on the origins of the solar system, on which he is a leading world expert. He has participated in the exploration of the solar system as a member of imaging teams for the *Voyager* and *Cassini* probes. He is the author, among other works, of the best-seller *Enfants du soleil* (1999).

Trinh Xuan Thuan

The Future of the Universe: Big Bang or Big Crunch?

The universe was born 15 billion years ago from an extremely small, hot and dense point. An immense explosion occurred, the energy of which engendered the matter contained within the universe, in accordance with Einstein's formula $E = mc^2$ (energy = mass × speed of light squared), creating space and time.

In the three minutes immediately following this explosion, a multitude of quarks—particles that, according to physicists, form the basis of matter—assembled in threes to form protons and neutrons. The universe then cooled as it became diluted, enabling matter to be formed. Matter as it is today corresponds to this dilution. I must make it clear that this theory of the Big Bang was worked out on the basis of observations of matter that is very distant in time and space.

Cooling to 1 million degrees prevented matter from 'breaking up' (temperature being equivalent to the movements of the particles) and enabled atomic nuclei to form, particularly hydrogen and helium that account for 98 percent of the visible mass of the universe. Under the influence of gravity, this matter coalesced to create stars; the hundreds of billions of which clustered together to form galaxies.

There exist today 100 billion milky ways, each of which contains 100 billion stars. This mass of galaxies forms an immense cosmic 'tapestry', some parts of which are hundreds of millions of light years away. It is possible to study this interesting topography by means of telescopes.

Finite expansion or limitless expansion?

Is the expansion of the universe eternal? Is the universe going to attain a maximum radius? Are the galaxies going to come closer together?

Will there be a kind of Big Bang in reverse (Big Crunch), leading to a crushing or collapse in which everything will become energy and light once more?

There is in fact a continual struggle between the original explosive force of the Big Bang and the force of gravity, the force that pulls us earthwards. It is gravity that makes planets orbit around stars, which holds stars within the milky ways and makes the galaxies interact with each other. This struggle will decide the fate of the universe. If the force of gravity is powerful enough, it may be able to stop the expansion of the universe and take us towards the Big Crunch.

The original force of expansion is known through the movement of the galaxies. On the other hand, to measure the force of gravity we have to measure the total mass of the universe and use the idea of critical density (mass per unit of volume) beyond which the force of gravity is greater than the original explosive force.

This density corresponds in fact to three hydrogen atoms per cubic metre. This is the most complete vacuum that humankind can create on Earth, remembering that one gramme of water contains 1 million billion billion atoms. The universe is so vast that this density of three hydrogen atoms per cubic metre is enough to stop the universe expanding. The question is whether the density of the universe is greater than the critical density. If it is, the universe will experience the Big Crunch (closed universe). If it is not, the universe will expand forever (open universe). If the density of the universe is equal to the critical density—an extreme case in which time is infinite—expansion will also be eternal.

It may seem easy to solve this problem by counting the stars, remembering that each of the 100 billion galaxies contains 100 billion stars. This multiplication makes it possible only to calculate the density of shining matter, however. The density obtained is equal to 1 or 2 percent of the critical density. A factor of fifty to one hundred is thus missing in order to stop the expansion of the universe. Astronomers have nevertheless discovered the existence of matter that gives out no radiation of any kind, including X-rays, gamma rays or radio waves. Without light, the astronomers are literally in the dark. How can this dark mass be calculated?

Astronomers detect the presence of this invisible 'dark' mass because it exerts a gravitational pull and hence modifies the orbits of planets or the movements of galaxies. Thus, taking account of data on the invisible mass, the density of the universe represents 30 percent of the critical density. In other words, it would require a factor of three to stop the expansion of the universe. We are thus living in an iceberg universe, 90 to 98 percent of whose mass is inaccessible to our measuring instruments.

Astronomers have no idea of the nature of this invisible mass. It may be everything that is not light, i.e., planets, comets or corridors. Speculation is rife as no theory has elicited any enthusiasm in this field. In recent years we have also seen the appearance of studies on the existence of an anti-gravitational force that it is claimed would speed up the expansion of the universe. Some clues based on observation of the heat of the Big Bang seem to indicate that the geometry of the universe is without any curve, i.e., the universe is 'flat'. It is half-way between an open universe with the topology of a horse saddle, and a universe closed like a sphere.

Evidence indicates that expansion will be forever. Nobody is certain of this, however, chiefly because of the existence of particles born in the first seconds after the Big Bang that have a mass not attached to the galaxies and hence impossible to measure through the movement of the galaxies.

The near future: the Milky Way and the solar system

In 3 billion years, our galaxy will absorb the Magellan cloud—two 'dwarf' satellite galaxies with just 1 billion stars circling round our galaxy, the principle of 'cannibalism' being very much alive in the universe, which is rather Darwinian. I should explain that it is called the Magellan cloud because it is only visible in the sky above the equator and Magellan was the first to have seen it.

In 7 billion years, Andromeda—a galaxy of the same size as ours and also the closest—will collide with our Milky Way. I should make it clear that this galaxy is 2 million light years from Earth. In other words, the light reaching us today from Andromeda set out when the first human appeared on Earth. However, this galaxy, which is approaching us at 90 kilometres per second, will not cause great catastrophes as there are big spaces between the stars (between three and four light years). At the very most one might fear a small deviation in the orbit of the sun or the Earth, with a few earthquakes.

From our human point of view, however, what is of more importance is the evolution of the sun. Without the sun's energy, we would not be here talking about it and life on Earth would not exist. In 5 billion years, when the sun has finished converting its reserve of hydrogen into helium, it will swell one hundred times and become redder, engulfing Mercury and Venus and taking up 10 percent of the sky as seen from Earth. The temperature at the surface of the Earth will be 1,000°C, causing the seas to evaporate and the forests to burn. Our descendants will thus preferably have to live on Pluto, as the most distant planet of the solar system would escape the clutches of the red giant. Their respite would nevertheless not last long. In fact, 2 billion years later, the sun will have used up its reserve of helium and will collapse in on itself, becoming a white dwarf.

Indeed, once the nuclear reactions stop, the force of gravity will gain the upper hand. The sun will then be unimaginably dense (one tonne per cubic centimetre and it will measure about 10,000 kilometres across, like the Earth. In other words, our descendants will have to look for another sun in their search for energy. The colonization of space so popular with science fiction writers can then begin.

The extinguishing of the stars

In the long run, the stars will use up their fuel and the universe will become dark for us, who are unable to see X-rays and other invisible sources of radiation. In any event, in a thousand billion years the stars will be extinguished. In 10^{18} years, the galaxies will become galactic black holes, given the disappearance of radiation. In 10^{27} years, the masses of galaxies will become intergalactic black holes. Then these black holes, despite being 'black', will evaporate and change into light, in conformity with the principles of quantum mechanics.

In any event, at a very distant time (all the books in the world would not be enough to write down the zeroes for this number of years), the universe will end in an extremely glacial cold. The temperature between galaxies is even now at -270°C. As the universe becomes diluted, we shall tend towards absolute zero. If we work things out in terms of the galaxies drawing closer to each other, the masses of galaxies will end up by joining together 100 million years before the Big Crunch. The stars will evaporate through the heat 100,000 years before the Big Crunch. Matter will become increasingly hot until it becomes an infernal brazier, and the stars will explode 1,000 years before the Big Crunch. In the end, the universe will be filled with sulphur, electrons, neutrons, anti-particles and anti-matter, which will be collapsing.

It is hard to know what will happen next. In such extreme densities, traditional physics can no longer offer any explanations. This is called 'Planck's Wall', or the wall of knowledge. Will the universe rise again from its ashes, like the Phoenix? Will another universe with different physical laws come into being? No one knows, but it is possible today to measure very accurately the density of matter in the universe and to determine the future of the universe using Einstein's equations.

Nicolas Prantzos

Cosmologies of the Future

Our view of the future has for long been dominated by the idea of the Eternal Recurrence. All the great civilizations of the past (Hindu, Mayan, Babylonian) developed a cosmology based on the notion of cyclical time. In other words, after a certain time, the universe was regenerated and set itself in motion again. Periodic natural phenomena, such as the phases of the moon or the cycle of the seasons, which were of great importance to the agrarian civilizations of the past, doubtless lay behind this notion of cyclical time.

However, the advent of Christianity brought with it the notion of linear time, based on the unique event of the death and resurrection of Christ. In the words of Saint Augustine in the *City of God*: 'Christ died once for our sins and, once resurrected, will never die again'. These concepts of cyclical and linear time are found again in modern cosmology, although in slightly different forms.

According to current theories, the uniform, hot and dense state of the universe following the Big Bang is gradually transformed as structures appear within it under the combined effect of expansion and gravitation (stars, galaxies, clusters of galaxies, etc.). Its future is determined by its density. Below a critical threshold, expansion will continue indefinitely (the open universe) and the universe will evolve towards a state that is always different from the previous one, within the framework of a linear conception of time. Beyond that density (the closed universe), expansion would be halted and become contraction so that the universe would return to something like its initial state (Big Crunch). But no one knows whether a new cycle would follow, as the concept of cyclical time would have it. Indeed, according to the latest ideas, the expansion of the universe is actually accelerating and will continue forever.

The heat death of the stars and galaxies

In the nineteenth century, scientists suspected for the first time that the marvellous complexity that surrounds us may be no more than a temporary state fated to disappear. At the origin of this suspicion was the development of thermodynamics, which made a notable contribution to the industrial revolution. This brought with it the understanding that differences of temperature between two objects—which are at the origin of life and complexity—have a spontaneous tendency to level out.

The idea of the heat death of the universe was suggested in the nineteenth century by the German physicist Rudolf Clausius, who wrote: 'The closer the universe comes to the state of maximum entropy, the fewer become the opportunities for internal change. If we suppose that this state is finally reached, then no further change can take place and the universe will be in a state of permanent death.'

These ideas, which were widely debated in the second half of the nineteenth century, had a considerable impact on the way people viewed the world, which is not unconnected with the dominant romantic mood of that period. However, nineteenth-century physicists could not determine the date of the heat death of the universe because they knew neither the energy source of the stars, nor the principle of galactic evolution.

In the twentieth century, scientists were able to provide answers to these questions. The stars derive their energy and their luminosity from the nuclear reactions that convert part of their mass into energy. Although this source of energy is considerable, it is not inexhaustible. Even the most parsimonious of stars (a tenth of the size of our sun) will have exhausted their fuel after several trillion years.

In addition, the stars are continually formed from the gas in the galaxies deriving from the Big Bang. Given that the reserves of gas have considerably diminished since then, it is obvious that the new stars generated over the coming billions of years will not be sufficient to make good the loss of dead stars. In this connection, I should like to quote from a remarkable book, written forty years ago by Arthur C. Clarke and entitled *Profiles of the Future,* which describes, more poetically than I could, the future of the stars and galaxies:

> Our galaxy is now in the brief springtime of its life—a springtime made glorious by such brilliant blue-white stars as Vega and Sirius, and, on a more humble scale, our own sun. Not until all these have flamed through their incandescent youth, in a few billions of years, will the real history of the universe begin. It will be a history illuminated only by the reds and infra-reds of dully glowing stars that would be almost invisible to our eyes; yet the sombre hues of that all-but-eternal universe may be full of colour and beauty to whatever strange beings have adapted to it. They will know that before them lie, not millions of years in which we measure the eras of geology, nor the billions

of years which span the lives of the stars, but years to be counted in trillions. They will have time enough, in those endless aeons, to attempt all things, and to gather all knowledge. They will not be gods, because no god imagined by our minds has ever possessed the power they will command. But for all that, they may envy us, basking in the bright afterglow of creation; for we knew the universe when it was young.[1]

When the stars go out

Having been in existence for 15 billion years, the universe is relatively young. In the long term, the starry sky that we see will cease to exist. The force of gravitation, which is at the root of most major phenomena in the macrocosm, will over trillions of years destructure this complexity by hurling some component parts into the gulf of black holes and by propelling others into intergalactic space. In 10^{27} years, there will be only isolated objects retreating from each other (in the case of an open universe), all the stars having long become extinct.

In the longer term still, microscopic effects will contribute to the destructuring of matter. As Stephen Hawking said in 1974, the black holes will evaporate. In addition, according to the current theories of microphysics, it would seem that protons are not eternal either and would have to change into lighter particles (electrons, positrons, gamma photons, etc.). Material structures will thus be impossible in the very long term.

The time-scales of the universe defy all understanding, and in this connection I should like to refer to a Nordic myth. 'In a distant country stands an enormous rock in the shape of a cube, each of its sides measuring 100 kilometres. Once every thousand years a small bird flies over the rock and for a few moments rubs its beak on it. When the rock has disappeared, completely worn away by the rubbing of the beak, one day in eternity will have been completed'. Similar myths are found in other civilizations. If one takes this myth literally, it would take about 10^{30} years to make this rock disappear; yet that is still nothing in comparison with eternity. It would take more than 10^{33} years for photons to disappear and over 10^{66} for black holes to evaporate.

Modern cosmology has revealed to us a future that is much longer, more complex and much more eventful than nineteenth-century physics suspected. Nevertheless, the final result of this long march of the cosmos is not so very different from the image of heat death. If the photon is unstable and if there is no source of energy, life and intelligence cannot survive eternally. Virtually the whole of matter will be converted

---

1. Arthur C. Clarke, *Profiles of the Future*, London, Gollancz, 1962.

into a cold and diluted radiation. The rare surviving particles will be increasingly dispersed into the vastness of an expanding universe.

Humanity's place in the universe

In these circumstances, it is hard to avoid pessimistic conclusions about the fate of intelligence. They are summed up in the following well-known passage by the philosopher Bertrand Russell: 'All the labours of the ages, all the devotion, all the inspiration, all the noonday brightness of human genius, are destined to extinction in the vast death of the solar system, and the whole temple of man's achievement must inevitably be buried beneath the debris of a universe in ruins—all these things...are yet so nearly certain, that no philosophy which rejects them can hope to stand.'[2] He added: 'I am told that this view of the world is a depressing one and that, if people believed it, they could not bear to go on living. In reality, however, nobody is bothered by what is going to happen in millions of years. Consequently, even if this view is a gloomy one, it is not so gloomy as to make life unbearable. Quite simply, it forces us to turn our attention to other things'.

Russell is indeed one of the best representatives of the positivist school. Others, however, find it hard to accept this resigned pessimism. In his autobiography, Charles Darwin, the originator of evolutionary theory, expressed his dismay at this failure of evolution in the following words: 'Believing as I do that man in the distant future will be a far more perfect creature than he now is, it is an intolerable thought that he and all other sentient beings are doomed to complete annihilation after such long-continued, slow progress.'[3]

H.G. Wells, the father of modern science fiction, author of *The Time Machine*, stated his faith in the future of the human race at a conference held by the Royal Institution in London in 1902:

> There is the reasonable certainty that this sun of ours must radiate itself towards extinction until some day this earth of ours will be dead and frozen, and all that has lived upon it will be frozen out and done with. There surely man must end. That, of all such nightmares, is the most insistently convincing. And yet one doesn't believe it. At least I do not. And I do not believe in these things because I have come to believe in certain other things—in the coherency and purpose in the world and in the greatness of human destiny. Worlds may

---

2. Bertrand Russell, 'A Free Man's Worship' (1903), in *Mysticism and Logic, and Other Essays*, London, George Allen and Unwin, 1917.

3. At that time, Darwin did not possess the image of the future provided by modern cosmology but that of heat death suggested by nineteenth-century physics. See Charles Darwin, *The Autobiography of Charles Darwin 1809–1882*, ed. Nora Barlow, London/New York, W. W. Norton & Co., 1963.

freeze and suns may perish, but there stirs something within us now that can never die again.

It is clear that everyone, depending on their philosophical beliefs, has a different view of the implications of physics and of cosmology for the future of the universe. That being so, some physicists who have not accepted the death of life and of intelligence have sought alternatives to prolong life indefinitely within the universe of the future.

One of these is Freeman Dyson, a famous physicist at Princeton, who twenty or so years ago wrote an article that founded *scientific eschatology*. He imagined the transplantation of intelligence onto a cloud of particles, electrons and positrons, which are in theory eternal. He also suggested that these ectoplasmic beings would have to adjust their temperature downwards, according to the pace of expansion and cooling of the universe, and adopt longer and longer periods of hibernation in order to survive eternally. He ended his article with the words: 'No matter how far we go into the future, there will always be new things happening, new information coming in, new worlds to explore, a constantly expanding domain of life, consciousness, and memory....a universe growing without limit in richness and complexity, a universe of life surviving for ever.'[4]

There is no guarantee that this optimism is justified. Recent work that takes the mathematical possibilities offered by quantum mechanics as its framework has shown that it is not possible to prolong life and intelligence *ad infinitum* in an expanding universe.

Will the marvellous complexity around us continue to exist forever? Is it just a sublime but temporary state destined to vanish? Today, no one knows the answer; but one day the answer will certainly be known.

An uncertain future

To conclude, I should like to quote from the preface of a work by Olaf Stapledon, a professor of philosophy in England in the 1930s, who attempted in his *Last and First Men* to imagine a history of the future of humankind up to the extinguishing of the sun:

> This is a work of fiction. I have tried to invent a story which may seem a possible, or at least not wholly impossible, account of the future of man; and I have tried to make that story relevant to the change that is taking place today in man's outlook. To romance of the future may seem to be an indulgence in ungoverned speculation for the sake of the marvellous. Yet

---

4. Freeman Dyson, 'Time Without End: Physics and Biology in an Open Universe', in *James Arthur Lectures on Time and Its Mysteries*, New York, New York University Press, 1978.

controlled imagination in this sphere can be a very valuable exercise for minds bewildered about the present and its potentialities. Today we should welcome, and even study, every serious attempt to grasp the very diverse and often tragic possibilities that confront us, but also that we may familiarize ourselves with the certainty that many of our cherished ideals would seem puerile to more developed minds. To romance of the far future, then, is to attempt to see the human race in its cosmic setting, and to mould our hearts to entertain new values.[5]

It should be remembered that, at the start of the twentieth century, scientists were ignorant of the two principles on which present-day physics is based, namely the theory of relativity and quantum mechanics. In the near future, new theories will perhaps radically modify our idea of the universe. Aware, therefore, that the history of humankind in the future was written on the basis of the knowledge of the physics of his time, Stapledon wrote again: 'If ever this book should happen to be discovered by some future individual, […] it will certainly raise a smile; for very much is bound to happen of which no hint is yet discoverable. And indeed even in our generation circumstances may well change so unexpectedly and so radically that this book may very soon look ridiculous. But no matter. We of today must conceive our relation to the rest of the universe as best we can.'[6]

I share this view completely. I have used Stapleton's preface as the conclusion of my own book entitled *Our Cosmic Future*. It is clear that a debate about the future of the universe and our place in it is an essential part of our reflections on the twenty-first century.

---

5. Olaf Stapledon, *Last and First Men*, Dover Publications, New York, 1968.
6. Ibid.

André Brahic

Scientific Enquiry: Doubts and Certainties

After millennia of trial and error, we have finally succeeded as a species in developing the tools that should enable us to begin answering the large questions we have always asked ourselves about our place in the universe. Who are we? Where are we going? Where do we come from? The spectacular progress of science has revealed to us a world governed by a handful of laws that are simple and universal in scope but very complex in their applications. The explosion of knowledge, particularly in astronomy and biology, has been so great in recent decades that we do not yet have the necessary distance to measure all the consequences in either human or practical terms. The history of scientific ideas is an excellent school of doubt, humility, rigour, honesty and the critical spirit, which are prime virtues in the service of a passion for knowledge.

Far removed from the certainties of those who refuse to think, from the 'truths' of the fanatics, scientific culture needs to be much more widespread among all citizens. They would learn in this way that a scientist can denounce what is false. He cannot in any case claim to possess the truth since any scientific proposition is formulated for critical scrutiny. The example of astronomy, the most ancient and most modern of the sciences, illustrates the point.

The twin pillars of the scientific method: observation and theory

Many people have a need of certainties, within a party, a religion or a tribe. To understand the scientific method, one has to realize that progress comes from a continuous process of calling into question. A proposition is only scientific if it is falsifiable, in other words if anyone can verify or invalidate it. The statement that a body held at arm's length falls if I release it can be verified at any moment by anyone—it is a scientific statement. The proposition is true on the Earth or on the Moon, but it is false in a space probe in space. The statement that I saw a ghost or a divine apparition last July is not a scientific proposition.

The scientific method is based on the twin pillars of observation and theory. Observing the world without interpreting it is of no great interest. Imagining the world as we would wish it to be without subjecting it to observations and without taking account of the real world is dangerous. It is in this way that, from the Inquisition to the Nazi or Siberian camps, human beings have been massacred down the centuries.

The rational approach was handed down to us from Ancient Greece. We know that every cause has an effect and every effect has a cause. Unfortunately, imagining the world to be imperfect, many at this time neglected observation in favour of pure thought. It was not until the Middle Ages that observation was rehabilitated. From the end of the sixteenth century, the scientific renaissance unified these two approaches to lay down the foundations of modern science. From this point onwards, the divorce between science and religion became definitive. The story of the meeting between Napoleon and Laplace, outlining his new theory of the formation of the planets, neatly sums up this situation: 'Monsieur le Marquis, God does not figure very much in your theories', the Emperor remarked to him; 'Sire, God is a hypothesis of which I have no need', replied the astronomer.

It must be clearly understood that a theoretical interpretation is only a tool, a model making it possible to imagine new observations to test that interpretation. For example, Ptolemy in 150 AD devised a model consisting of circles superposed around the Earth (epicycles) to describe the movement of the planets. Johan de Sarobosco, a professor at the University of Paris in the thirteenth century, even imagined some thirty circles to improve the model. This epicycle model makes it possible to ascertain the future position of Jupiter, yet it happens to be wrong!

A clear distinction must be made between the model and the truth we are seeking. Astrophysicists spend their time trying to demolish models or theories and thus, through successive approximations, they eliminate the blind alleys and circumscribe more closely the 'reality of the world'. A model that stands up to scrutiny does no more than confirm us in the view that we are moving in the right direction.

The astronomical revolution of the twentieth century

Astronomy is the most ancient of sciences, corresponding as it does to two age-old human concerns: the need for a calendar for agricultural purposes and the metaphysical idea that the sky was peopled with gods. Nowadays, the development of astronomy is essential for at least three reasons of a cultural, practical and economic nature.

- Knowing that the universe in which we live is a cultural ingredient no less important than history, geography, music and painting. How can a philosopher talk of our place in the universe if he is familiar with neither astrophysics nor biology? Understanding the history of our origins from the appearance of the first atoms, then the first stars and finally the Earth should form part of our cultural heritage. Knowing that the key mechanisms governing the evolution of the Earth should help us to work to safeguard our future. Grasping the nature of the scientific approach is a school of rigour, patience and intellectual honesty. Unfortunately, current scientific issues find very little echo in the classroom and the media despite the rapid development of knowledge in recent years. Today, isolated snippets of information, presented largely out of context, are all that reach the general public.

- The universe in general and the solar system in particular are magnificent laboratories offering extreme conditions of temperature, pressure, density and so on not achievable in laboratories on earth. Astronomical observations enable us to better understand the behaviour of matter and thus to control and utilize it more effectively.

- Space activity plays a key role in the economic competition between the major world powers—Europe, the United States and Japan. The launching of a space probe calls for total reliability since there is no 'vehicle repairer' en route to put matters right if a breakdown occurs. Being the dominant force in space research today guarantees supremacy in the economic world of tomorrow.

The emergence of new techniques and the development of space research have led to truly radical changes in our knowledge since the end of the 1960s.

Space exploration

Sending craft beyond the limits of the Earth's atmosphere has given us access to the radiation emitted by stars. Whereas until recent times we could only detect 'visible' light, we can today detect radio, infrarouge, ultra violet, X- and gamma rays. The atmosphere that protects us from harmful radiation prevents us from observing the whole of the universe. By going beyond, we have discovered that the universe is much richer, much more diverse and much more active than we initially imagined. Moreover, the dispatch of space probes in the vicinity of planets and their satellites has enabled us to discover new worlds that were previously no more than points of light in the sky. We have thus repeated in a sense the voyage of Christopher Columbus, but at less risk for human beings. These space craft are our eyes and ears projected at a distance. The fact of journeying in space has totally changed our vision of the world.

I was lucky enough to participate in the exploration of the solar system with the *Voyager* space probe. Through the probe, we were able to visit new and previously unknown worlds. The exploration of the solar system revealed a much richer and more diverse world than the astronomers had imagined. The cliffs of Miranda rising to over 27 kilometres, the geysers of Triton more than 8 kilometres high, the volcanoes of Mars over 25 kilometres in height, the fissures of Europe extending from one end of the satellite to the other, the plumes of smoke over 300 kilometres high emitted by the volcanoes of Io, and many other marvels testifying to the variety of landscapes in the solar system.

The adventure is continuing at the present time for my colleagues and myself thanks to the *Cassini-Huygens* probe, financed jointly by the United States and Europe. Launched on 15 October 1997, it flew past Jupiter on the night of 31 December 2000 and will arrive in the region of Saturn on 1 July 2004. This voyage will enable us to compare the world of Titan with its nitrogen atmosphere—making it a kind of 'refrigerated' Earth—with our own Earth and have a better understanding of the role of temperature in the evolution of our planet. Until 2011, it will revolve around the world of Saturn, its satellites and its rings, continually sending us information about this fascinating world.

Reason or unreason?

The impressive advances in our knowledge in the last part of the twentieth century should not however blind us to reality by making us believe that the irrational approach to the world belongs to a bygone age. Science remains a frequent target of attack, and such attacks do not come simply from a few fanatical and myopic religious fundamentalists. All those who do not understand the nature of its approach have a cavalier attitude towards science and tend to reject it. This includes those who think that science is the source of all our ills, those who are receptive to the irrational and those who hold forth about the world without knowing it.

To believe that science is responsible for all our misfortunes and at the same time travel by air or car, watch television, telephone, demand the best hospital treatment, make use of electrical heating and lighting, and so on is most paradoxical. It is to refuse to understand that it is the use we make of science, as citizens, that is at issue and not science itself. When someone is shot, it is the person who fired the gun who is guilty, not the laws of ballistics. One must not confuse science, which is aimed at knowledge, and technology, which is directed towards applications. While they are both essential, they are not of the same nature.

The fear of radioactivity is another example of an irrational attitude. It is thanks to radiation that the surface of the Earth attained a temperature enabling life to emerge. The medical applications of science have saved a great many human lives. Yet it is science that has been made to carry the can for the horror of nuclear bombs, or the failures of the Soviet administration that led to the Chernobyl catastrophe, rather than those who should bear responsibility for their acts. The invisible, odourless and flavourless character of radiation is so frightening to some that it gave rise in 1977 to a protest movement, encouraged by a sensationalist and unscrupulous press, which campaigned against the launching of the *Cassini-Huygens* probe to Saturn on the grounds that this robot craft contains a small amount of plutonium to supply the necessary energy at a distance of 1.5 billion kilometres from the sun. I was stupefied to witness the fearful reaction to this probe, which will enable human beings to progress further in their quest for knowledge, in a country at the cutting edge of technology. On this particular issue, the Europeans showed themselves more cultivated.

Again in the United States, a noisy minority rejects any scientific approach and considers that the Earth and humankind were created a few thousand years ago. These hard-line anti-Darwinian groups move heaven and earth to try and impose creationist education in schools. A few courageous teachers' organizations pursue a lone battle against these religious fanatics. Such a movement shows that a technologically advanced country such as the United States is not immune from obscurantism and that education is of key importance. In Europe, these creationists have a very restricted audience, but we must take care that these ideas do not cross the Atlantic. We should remember Berthold Brecht's warning: 'the belly that beget the foul beast is still fertile....'[1]

Primitive gropings after the truth dating from the time when the planets were a great mystery, and were hence endowed with supernatural powers, survive in beliefs that seem to us highly ridiculous, such as astrology and 'flying saucers'. It is obvious that the position of the planets at the moment of an individual's birth has strictly no influence on his or her future, and we may be thankful for that. Similarly, the thousands of astronomers who scrutinize the heavens with more and more sophisticated telescopes, to the extent of detecting in a few instants the appearance of any new star among the tens of millions of known stars of the same magnitude, have never observed a single landing by extra-terrestrials. Yet they are the first to be convinced of their probable existence among the infinite number of stars and to conduct a serious

---

1. Epilogue to *The Resistible Rise of Arturo Ui*.

search for signs of their presence and prepare the bottles of champagne to welcome them.

There are other more subtle but no less dangerous irrational attitudes. For example, certain philosophers claim that we cannot distinguish the true from the false, that the world about us is a mere illusion and that all theories are equally valid. The history of the scientific adventure proves the contrary. Other more congenial philosophers or social scientists, whose ideas are often fruitful, do not do science any service when they employ, frequently out of context, scientific terms whose meaning they do not understand. Recent examples[2] show that words cannot be used casually and that one cannot be too rigorous in this respect.

Some scientists, who may have made important contributions to their field of research, occasionally give themselves over to speculation reminiscent of primitive myth. We are impressed to observe on an everyday basis how ordered systems are born from an original chaos, whether it be the planets, the galaxies or life. Does this entitle us to see this order as purposive in any way? There are no grounds for affirming so at the present time. I am tempted in this connection to quote the words of Cyrano de Bergerac back in the eighteenth century in his *Journey to the Moon*: 'Add to that the unbearable pride of human beings, who are persuaded that nature was made for them alone, as if it were likely that the Sun [...] was lit simply to ripen his medlar fruit and plump out his cabbages.'

The fact of wishing to ascribe a purpose to the universe at any cost shows that some contemporary scientists have not learned the lessons of the history of geocentrism and the persecutions to which it gave rise. In their own way, they restore Man to the centre of the Universe. In the 'entropie/anthropie' debate, they argue for a process of growing complexity from the star to the planet, and then from the planet to human beings, in order to suggest that we are the ultimate goal of the universe. What megalomania! How can one believe that human beings who appeared on the Earth some 2 million years ago are part of the grand design of the universe? If that were true, it could wryly be observed that the universe is not a very efficient or very rapid machine. Let us settle for quoting Diderot here: 'One never knows what the heavens want or do not want, and perhaps they themselves have no idea.'[3]

Enthusiasm for the power of rational thought should not lead one to think that the physical sciences should run the world. Each discipline should invent its own techniques, while never departing from the rigour, the critical spirit and the absolute respect for the facts that characterizes the scientific approach.

To be fascinated by the universe revealed to us by twentieth-century astronomers and to marvel at the power of rational thought does not mean

---

2. Alan Sokal et Jean Bricmont, *Impostures intellectuelles*, Paris, Odile Jacob, 1997.
3. Denis Diderot in *Jacques le Fataliste*.

either that we must drop everything and undertake an anti-religious crusade. Science and religions are currently pursuing paths that are very far apart. To try and demonstrate the existence of God by scientific means is no more reasonable than the opposite attitude. Only religious fanaticism, over-zealous evangelism, fundamentalism and rejection of the other are intolerable. The key word in this connection is tolerance. We must accept the culture and originality of the other even if our ideas do not coincide in all respects. Diversity is what constitutes the world's richness. At the dawn of modern science, religions and primitive myths played a great role in enabling scientists to criticize written texts and refine their analytical methods. Since then, the questions posed in the two domains and the ends pursued have not been the same.

I was surprised one evening, at the end of a lecture I had just given on the origins of the solar system and exploration of the planets, by two members of the audience who, on hearing the same speech delivered at the same time by the same lecturer, drew from it two totally opposite conclusions. The first, very agreeable, person came up to me at the end to say that my lecture had finally convinced him of the existence of God, since only God was capable in his view of creating such a beautiful universe. The second, no less agreeable, approached me a few minutes later to say that my lecture had proved that there was no reason to appeal to the idea of God to explain the world. Their remarks at least showed me that my speech had not been partisan and that the essential virtue of tolerance had been on display that evening; but I must confess that I was puzzled by these differing reactions.

The scientific approach was not invented in the twentieth century; and I shall not resist the pleasure of quoting Seneca, who over 2,000 years ago contrasted his logical approach with the superstitions of his contemporaries concerning comets:

> The same thing holds in regard to comets. When one of these infrequent fires of unusual shape makes its appearance [...], there are people who seek to inspire terror by forecasting its grave import. [...] Comets move regularly along routes prescribed by nature. [...] Why be surprised that comets, which so rarely reveal themselves to the world, should not yet be subject to our rigid laws, and that we know neither the origins nor the destinations of these bodies, whose passages are separated by such immense intervals? [...]The day will yet come when the progress of research through long ages will reveal to sight the mysteries of nature that are now concealed. [...]The man will come one day who will explain in what regions the comets move, why they diverge so much from the other stars, what is their size and their nature.[4]

I find that science appears somewhat austere and complicated to young uninformed students. Given the increasingly important role of

---

4. Seneca, *Natural Questions*, Book VII.

science in our society, we need to develop a scientific culture, to make it known that science is simple, beautiful, useful and fascinating. Our future lies in science and, above all, in a balance between literary and scientific knowledge. A scientist without any literary knowledge is impoverished. A legal or literary specialist lacking scientific knowledge is handicapped. To be sure, the mastery of technique—as for an opera singer or a dancer—requires a great deal of work. But scientific results are within the reach of all. For a better understanding of our future, there is need in my view for greater public awareness of the importance of the scientific approach.

The debate on our origins: Creation or eternity?

The question of our origins has always obsessed the human mind. It has engendered a host of mythical accounts of the origins of the world, of the gods and of the tribes, and it is nowadays central to much scientific research. Since the dawn of time, men have argued over whether our world is the result of incessant changes or whether it was created 'out of the blue'. But how? From what? The past was said by the sceptics to be unpredictable, but discoveries in the twentieth century have given the lie to this view by finally lifting a corner of the veil.

We have spent millennia inventing imaginary worlds. Recently, we have changed and have acquired powerful observational tools to discover the real world. The first lesson of this adventure is that nature has far more imagination than all human beings put together. The second lesson is that we now know, as a result of the many observation-derived constraints, what did *not* happen. Did our ancestors waste their time in harbouring illusions? No, because their gropings prepared the ground and helped us to develop new concepts. The criticism of ideas and dogmas by our predecessors gave rise to modern science.

Have the Earth, the sky and the sun always existed? Are they eternal or were they created one day? We have asked these questions for millennia and on all continents. The idea of an eternal world, with neither beginning nor end, was set out and forcefully defended by Aristotle. It opposed the very strong message of Christianity, which believed in a god-created world. This debate on the existence or otherwise of a beginning raged for centuries and was at the centre of an extremely bitter controversy in the thirteenth century within the university in Paris, a world centre of knowledge and learning at the time. This quarrel was as lively as that surrounding the theories of Copernicus or Darwin some centuries later.

The quest for our origins is a pre-eminently scientific subject, and yet metaphysics got hold of it well before physics. All the religions and world systems that have claimed to be universal have proposed a history of creation. The target of all kinds of fanaticism and intolerance down the ages, this research is at the same time a marvellous illustration of human genius. But this wish to explain everything was not confined to religions. Throughout history, we frequently find conflicts between socioeconomic systems expressing themselves as ideological quarrels on human origins. For over 150 years, when France and England enjoyed primacy in the world, the French and English schools took opposing views on the formation of the planets. Between 1945 and 1990, the debate was focused on two theories, that of the American and Soviet schools respectively!

Although the study of our origins is mainly the concern of astronomers, physicists, chemists, mathematicians, mineralogists, geophysicists and many others, its philosophical and sociological implications are such that it continues to generate passions and sometimes polemics. Even between scientists, the disputes abound. The possible paths of exploration are so varied that many authors deliberately disregard one another. Examining the texts devoted to the question of our origins, one finds more 'philosophers' than 'engineers', and on occasion more metaphysics than physics, but the situation is in the process of changing. Space research and the development of observational and analytical capabilities have provided us with such powerful tools that we are living through a revolution in the history of knowledge acquisition, and it is no longer possible to disregard the constraints inherent in observations and models.

It now seems obvious to us that the Earth, the moon, the sun, the stars and other heavenly bodies were formed at some point in time and have evolved. Whatever our prejudices and preferences, we have no choice but to bow to the observed facts. In this respect, science offers us a good lesson in humility, whether we be politicians, leaders or those who carry out orders! Pure thought, *a priori* ideas and the great sacred texts have not proved of much use, and the blind determination to ignore an evident truth in defence of a founding myth has often been a stumbling block. Conversely, critical analysis of those *a priori* notions and above all cross-checking them against observations have shown themselves to be fruitful.

The whole history of enquiry into our origins is a centuries-long succession of preconceived ideas, hesitations and impasses, often cruelly lacking in observational constraints, together with some impressive advances. As Paul Valéry said, 'the more metaphysics there is, the less physics there is, and vice versa.'

The problem of our origins is comparable to that of assembling a huge jigsaw puzzle. Having patiently pieced together a mass of data on the first moments of the solar system, deriving in particular from space exploration in the latter part of the twentieth century, scientists have managed to retrace the five main steps in the formation of the Earth. Starting life as a molecular cloud, the very hot young sun collapsed upon itself, leaving a gaseous disk at its periphery. This was followed by a dust disk, then by planetesimals (objects about 1 kilometre in size) coming together to form a disk of embryos (bodies of several hundred kilometres). A disk of planets, resembling the present solar system, appeared at a fifth stage. If there is broad agreement among scientists on these five stages in the formation of the planets, the details of their evolution and the links between the different stages continue to be keenly debated.

It must be clearly understood that this description of our origins is not an unshakeable dogma. It is an instrument placed in the service of critical enquiry based on scientific observations. The role of scientists is to make instruments available and to challenge them. They must never impose an opinion or believe that they possess the truth.

One of these instruments is the knowledge we now have that the Earth and the planets owe their existence to generations of stars that produced a sufficient number of atoms. A few billion years ago, hydrogen and helium would not have been present in the quantities necessary for the appearance of these planets. Time was therefore required to enable the planets and life on Earth to appear and evolve, remembering that the solar system is some 4.56 billion years old. When an official asks me my age, I reply 'somewhere between 6 and 12 billion years—the time it took to produce my atoms. The rest is part of my private life'. We are the children of time!

Exploring the planets to improve our knowledge of the Earth

One of the ultimate goals is to improve our knowledge of the Earth. An astronomer cannot perform experiments on our planet in the manner of a physicist in the laboratory. There can be no question of cutting it in two, heating it, bombarding it or changing its composition to see how it behaves. By observing larger or smaller planets, hotter or colder ones, etc., we can come to understand the role of each physical factor.

Planetary exploration, which has been the great adventure of the last part of the twentieth century, has enabled us to understand by comparison the mechanisms that govern the evolution of the Earth. We can study what happens on Mars, where the greenhouse effect did not occur, and on Venus, which has experienced a runaway greenhouse effect, to gain a better understanding of the greenhouse effect on Earth. The surface of satellites and planets is littered with volcanoes, which by comparison enable us to understand more fully the evolution of the terrestrial volcanoes as particular cases of a more general phenomenon. The comparison of atmospheres should help to advance meteorology and climatology here on Earth.

We have the good fortune to be the first generation to witness the exploration of the solar system. The first lesson we have learnt is the diversity of landscapes and phenomena. Nature is richer than the most gifted theoretician ever imagined! We do not have space here to begin a journey through the mountains, canyons, volcanoes, fractures, depressions, plains, cliffs, geysers, craters and the immense variety of landscapes that our celestial neighbours have revealed to us in recent years. We can now admire tens of thousands of photographs and work on millions of observations.

I want to end with a little story imagined by a cartoonist. It shows two prehistoric ladies gazing at the moon. The first says to the second: 'One day, you know, men will go to the Moon'. 'Do you think so?' replies the other. 'And while this is going on', the first adds, 'we will take over'. This is exactly what has occurred at the close of the twentieth century: men have gone to the moon and, in the developed countries, woman has finally gained her rightful place. It is a remarkable fact that in the countries where astronomical research lags behind, the social situation of woman is unworthy. This little anecdote serves simply to remind us that scientific culture plays an essential role in the proper functioning of a society.[5]

---

5. A much fuller exposition of the ideas set out here can be found in the publication *Enfants du Soleil*, Paris, Odile Jacob, 1999. Some parts of the above text are taken from this work.

Jérôme Bindé

Conclusion: In Search of Lost Time— towards an Ethics of the Future?

This volume has posed the question of the 'future of values'. In the course of their reflections, our contributors have sketched the profiles of futures that, while possible, are not in every case desirable. The desirable future—the desirable *futures* for human societies in their diversity—are those that offer humanity the prospect of a human future. In an enquiry into the future of values, we cannot elude the question of what we are going to make of values. Preparing for the future requires a future-oriented ethic, an ethic of time.

Human societies are currently suffering from a dysfunction in their relationship with time. We are troubled by a major contradiction. To survive and prosper, we are increasingly obliged to project ourselves into the future. Yet we increasingly lack a project. Some have spoken of a divorce between projection and project. This divorce is becoming more marked, partly because wide-ranging thought and long-term thinking seem to have collapsed, and partly because globalization and the emergence of new technologies subordinate societies to the logic of 'real time' and short-term thinking, meaning that the logic of the financial and media worlds predominates, political decision-making in democratic societies is adjusted to the time-frame of the next election, and supreme importance is given to humanitarian action at a time when development aid is in decline. The tyranny of the immediate, which serves as an excuse for irresponsible short-termism, is matched by the tyranny of urgency. This is accompanied by the increasing eclipse of any reference to the idea of a collective project. We are no longer capable of projecting ourselves into a long-term future. From this standpoint, urgency destructures time and delegitimizes utopia. Time seems abolished by the present instant. Everywhere present generations are appropriating the rights of future generations, threatening their well-being, equilibrium and in some cases existence.

Far from being a transitory provision, the logic of urgency is becoming permanent: it is permeating all social processes, elevating the demand for immediate results into an absolute principle of collective action. Yet can it be said that the introduction of emergency measures has led to the long-term solution of problems? The failures of humanitarian action and the poor record of the international community in the multilateral management of global problems seems to point in the opposite direction.

How are we to reconstruct time in the age of globalization? How can we rehabilitate the long-term? As pointed out by the Belgian philosopher François Ost, two obstacles stand in the way of our making proper allowance for the future. The first has to do with the dominance of the ethical model of the social contract, which conceives of obligations only in terms of relations between approximately equal parties engaged in exchanges based on reciprocal clauses, whereas the point of the ethic of the future is to 'extend the ethical community to future parties with whom we are in a wholly asymmetric relationship'. The second obstacle is the 'temporal short-sightedness' of the age, 'which is reflected in amnesia in relation to the past, even the recent past, and in an inability to see ourselves as part of a reasoned future'. We need to reflect on ways of overcoming these two obstacles, by preparing the ground for an ethic of the future.[1]

The reconstruction of time also presupposes that social actors and decision-makers stop 'adjusting' and 'adapting' and start to anticipate and be proactive. The twenty-first century will be forward-looking or it will not be: the aim is to foresee in order to forestall. For the time lapse between the formulation of an idea and its translation into practice is often very great. One or more generations are often the minimum time required for a policy to become effective. Given that short and medium-term actions are to a greater or lesser extent already under way, the fate of future generations will increasingly depend on our ability to make the link between long-term vision and present policy-making. Strengthening forecasting and forward-thinking capacities is thus a priority for governments, international organizations, scientific institutions, the private sector, social actors and each and every one of us.

As Hugues de Jouvenal has noted, there is a growing tendency in the West to claim that the accelerating pace of change and the increasing factors of discontinuity are making the future more and more unpredictable and to deduce from this that the only thing that matters is flexibility. 'The "just-in-time" culture is thus increasingly set in opposition to [...] the culture of the long term, which nevertheless remains the only framework within which genuine development strategies can be pursued'.[2] Constructing an ethic of the future thus

---

1. Jérôme Bindé, 'Ethique du futur. Pourquoi faut-il retrouver le temps perdu?', *Futuribles*, December 1997.
2. Hugues de Jouvenal, 'Dimension du long terme et décisions publiques', *Futuribles*, January 1997.

requires that we call into question modes of management based on flexibility as an absolute principle and on the rejection of forward thinking.

But we must go further: if we do not act in time, future generations will not have the time to act at all; they risk becoming prisoners of processes that have become uncontrollable, such as population growth, the degradation of the global environment, disparities between North and South as well as within societies, social apartheid and the growing influence of the Mafia. Tomorrow is always too late. By way of example, nine years after the Earth Summit, Agenda 21 has remained essentially a dead letter, setting aside the timid progress at the Kyoto Summit and ensuing conferences on the reduction of greenhouse gases. How long can we afford to offer ourselves the luxury of inaction? Has anyone calculated the price of inertia and of the absence of an ethic of the future?

The construction of an ethic of the future requires that we start to think about values in a forward-looking way. For values, far from being a fixed heritage, are a 'heritage preceded by no testament' (Rene Char), and thus in movement, future-oriented. As noted by Paul Ricoeur, 'values are situated halfway between the lasting convictions of a historic community and the incessant re-evaluations called for by changes of epoch and circumstance with the emergence of new problems'.

Three developments are crucial here: the first is a temporal shift of responsibility: according to Ricoeur,

> hitherto someone has been considered responsible only for his or her past acts. [...] Hans Jonas, in his *Principle of Responsibility*, conceives on the contrary of a responsibility geared to a distant future. We have been entrusted with something that is essentially fragile and perishable: life, the planet or the city. For the city is perishable. Its survival depends on us (Hannah Arendt). No institutional system survives without being sustained by a will to live together... When this will collapses, all political organization falls apart, very quickly.[3]

The emergence internationally of the precautionary principle, predicated on uncertainty, constitutes a second major development: all forward thinking involves the management of the unpredictable and uncertainty, hence of risk. For François Ewald, the new paradigm of precaution attests to a radically new relationship with science, which is questioned less for the knowledge it offers than for the doubts that it prompts. Moral obligations here assume the form of ethics.[4]

The third development is this: through the continual increase in its scope of application, the heritage has established the responsibility of human beings to future generations. Previously, it was simply a legacy

---

3. Paul Ricoeur, 'La Cité est fondamentalement périssable', talk with Roger-Pol Droit published in *Le Monde*, 29 October 1991.
4. François Ewald, 'Philosophie de la précaution', *L'Année sociologique* 46, n° 2, 1996.

from the past; now it ultimately encompasses all culture and all nature. It does not end with rocks but also embraces the intangible, symbolic, ethical, ecological and genetic heritage. It becomes the defining element in our relationship with the Other: an other in space because the heritage belongs to humanity as a whole; and an other in time since humanity is transhistorical and encompasses future generations. According to Martine Rémond Guilloud,

> the function of the heritage is therefore not so much to transmit and perpetuate objects and values as to create a momentum for transmission, a dynamic sense of the solidarity between generations, that is to say, to give a meaning to the perpetuation of the human species, a reason to human beings to live.[5]

The construction of an ethic of the twenty-first century calls for the 'reform of thinking' referred to by Edgar Morin. Pascal was forward-looking and perceptive when he wrote: 'let us strive to think correctly, that is the principle of morality'.[6] Such a reform also presupposes a reform of the links between thought and action, based for example on an evolution towards a 'common law' of humanity (Mireille Delmas-Marty). According to François Ost, 'in the absence of any living link between past and future, any reference to tradition is bound to appear as an ideological reaction, even as regressive fundamentalism, whereas the formulation of projects for the future is today systematically decried as utopianism'.[7]

Yet, as Paul Ricoeur reminds us, 'we must resist the temptation of purely utopian expectations, which can only discourage action. Expectations must be determinate, thus finite and relatively modest if they are to encourage *responsible* commitment'. Edouard Portella found the words to draft the testament of utopia.[8] But again, as Paul Ricoeur suggests, 'we must prevent the horizon of our expectations from receding; we must bring it closer to the present through a series of intermediary projects that are within the compass of action'.

The political crisis has largely coincided, in the West, the East and the South, with the 'crisis of the future' and its increasing indecipherability.[9] The time has come to remember that politics consists first and foremost in *structuring time*, 'the specific concern of the politician' being 'the future and responsibility for the future' (Max Weber). There is a need then to reforge the link between what Reinhart Koselleck called 'experiential space' and the 'horizon of expectation'.

---

5. Martine Rémond-Gouilloud, 'L'avenir du patrimoine', *Esprit*, n° 216, November 1995.

6. Blaise Pascal, *Pensées*, VI, 'Les philosophes', 347 [63].

7. François Ost, 'Du contrat à la transmission: le simultané et le successif', in *L'environnement au XXIe siècle* (Actes du colloque de Fontevraud), Paris.

8. See *Keys to the 21st Century*, the first anthology of '21st-Century Talks' organized by UNESCO's Division of Foresight, Philosophy and Human Sciences, New York and Oxford, UNESCO Publishing/Berghahn Books, 2001.

9. See, on this last point, Marcel Gauchet, *Le désenchantement du monde*, Paris, Gallimard, 1985.

So are there any grounds for thinking in terms of a contradiction between solidarity with present generations and solidarity with future generations? Generosity is indivisible. Lack of concern with the excluded of the Third and Fourth Worlds is one side of the coin and disregard for future generations is the other. The ethic of the future is fundamentally an ethic of time that rehabilitates the future, but also the present and the past. The ethic *of* the future is not to be equated with an ethics *in* the future, perpetually deferred! It is an ethics of the *here and now* so that that there will continue to be a here and now.

As pointed out by Ricoeur, 'we have so many unaccomplished projects behind us, so many promises still not kept that we would have the means to build a future by reviving these multiple heritages'.[10] In the global city under construction, we shall only allow time the necessary time by establishing close links between forward thinking, political will and civic participation in the framing and implementation of long-term projects. For, according to Max Weber,[11] 'the possible will not be achieved unless the impossible is attempted over and over again in the world'.

If we wish to bring about a radical change in our relationship with time at the dawn of the twenty-first century, we should heed the poets and the prophets. What was it Henri Michaux said? 'To slow down is to take the pulse of things... We are, we have the time, we are the experience of slowing down'.[12] In this way, we shall perhaps succeed in rediscovering an ancient wisdom: that of living within time and, as the author of *In Search of Lost Time*[13] enjoins us, of regaining lost time.

---

10. Paul Ricoeur, 'La Cité est fondamentalement périssable.'
11. In the essays 'Science as a Vocation' and 'Politics as a Vocation'.
12. Henri Michaux, 'A la Ralentie', *Oeuvres complètes*, vol. 2, Bibliothèque de la Pléiade, Gallimard, 1990.
13. Marcel Proust, *In Search of Lost Time*, London, Chatto and Windus, 1992.

Select Bibliography

Annas, George J. 1975. *The Rights of Patients*. Illinois: Southern Illinois University Press.
———. 1998. *Some Choice: Law, Medicine, and The Market*. Oxford: Oxford University Press.
———. 1999. *Health and Human Rights*. New York: Routledge.
Appadurai, Arjun. 1981. *Worship and Conflict under Colonial Rule*. Cambridge: Cambridge University Press.
———. 1996. *Modernity at Large: Cultural Dimensions of Globalization*. Minneapolis: University of Minnesota Press.
———. 2001. *Globalization*. Durham: Duke University Press.
Arkoun, Mohammed. 1994. *Rethinking Islam*. Boulder: Westview Press.
———. 2000. *The Unthought in Contemporary Islamic Thought*. Palgrave: Macmillan.
———. 2003. *De Manhattan à Bagdad. Au-delà du Bien et du Mal* (with Joseph Maïla). Bruges: Desclée de Brouwer.
Barreto, Adalberto. 1996. *L'Indien qui est en moi*. Paris: Descartes et Compagnie.
Bateson, Gregory. 1972. *Steps to an Ecology of Mind*. San Francisco: Chandler.
Baudrillard, Jean. 1993a. *Symbolic Exchange and Death*. London: Sage Publications.
———. 1993b. *The Transparency of Evil: Essays on Extreme Phenomena*. New York: W. W. Norton & Co.
———. 1994. *The Illusion of the End*. Cambridge: Polity Press.
———. 1996a. *The System of Objects*. London & New York: Verso.
———. 1996b. *The Perfect Crime*. London & New York: Verso.
———. 1998. *The Consumer Society: Myths and Structures*. London: Sage Publications.
———. 2001. *Impossible Exchange*. London & New York: Verso.
———. 2002. *The Spirit of Terrorism: And, Requiem for the Twin Towers*. London & New York: Verso.
———. 2003. *La violence du monde* (with Edgar Morin). Paris: Le Félin.
———. 2004. *Fragments: Interviews with Jean Baudrillard*. London: Roultledge.
Beauvoir, Simone de. 1952. *The Second Sex*. New York: Alfred A. Knopf.
Béji, Hélé. 1982. *Le Désenchantement national*. Paris: La Découverte.
———. 1992. *Itinéraire de Paris à Tunis*. Paris: Noël Blandin.
———. 1997. *L'Imposture culturelle*. Paris: Stock.

Bindé, Jérôme. 2000. 'Towards an Ethics of the Future', *Public Culture*, vol. 12, No. 1.

———. 2001. *The World Ahead: Our Future in the Making* (in collaboration with Federico Mayor). London: Zed Books.

———, ed. 2001. *Keys to the 21st Century*. New York & Oxford: UNESCO Publishing/Berghahn Books.

Bloom, Harold. 1992. *The American Religion: The Emergence of the Post-Christian Nation*. New York: Simon & Schuster.

Bombardier, Denise. 1985. *Une enfance à l'eau bénite*. Paris: Seuil.

———. 1988. *Le Mal de l'âme. Essais sur le mal de vivre au temps present* (with Claude Saint-Laurent). Paris: Robert Laffont.

———. 1993. *La Déroute des sexes*. Paris: Seuil.

———. 2002. *Ouf*. Paris: Albin Michel.

Brahic, André. 1999. *Enfants du soleil*. Paris: Odile Jacob.

Contini, Éliane. 1995. *Un psychiatre dans la favela*. Paris: Les Empêcheurs de penser en rond.

Canto-Sperber, Monique. 2001. *L'inquiétude morale et la vie humaine*. Paris: PUF.

———. 2003. *Les règles de la liberté*. Paris: Plon.

Derrida, Jacques. 1977. *Of Grammatology*. Baltimore: Johns Hopkins University Press.

———. 1978. *Writing and Difference*. Chicago: University of Chicago Press.

———. 1981. *Dissemination*. Chicago: University of Chicago Press.

———. 2000. *Of Hospitality*. Stanford: Stanford University Press.

———. 2002. *Who's Afraid of Philosophy? Right to Philosophy I*. Stanford: Stanford University Press.

Diagne, Souleymane Bachir. 1989. *Boole, l'oiseau de nuit en plein jour*. Paris: Belin.

———. 2001a. *Reconstruire le sens: textes et enjeux de prospectives africaines*. Dakar: Codesria.

———. 2001b. *Islam et société ouverte: La fidélité et le mouvement dans la pensée de Muhammad Iqbal*. Paris: Maisonneuve et Larose.

———. 2002. *100 mots pour dire l'Islam*. Paris: Maisonneuve et Larose.

Gauchet, Marcel. 1997. *The Disenchantment of the World: A Political History of Religion*. Princeton: Princeton University Press.

Gaudin, Thierry. 1993. *2100, Odyssée de l'espèce*. Paris: Payot.

———. 1997. *Introduction à l'économie cognitive*. La Tour d'Aigues: Editions de l'Aube.

———. 1998. *Préliminaires à une prospective des religions*. La Tour d'Aigues: Editions de l'Aube.

———, ed. 1993. *2100, Récit du prochain siècle*. Paris: Payot.

Gordimer, Nadine. 1958. *A World of Strangers*. New York: Simon & Schuster.

———. 1970. *A Guest of Honour*. New York: Viking Press.

———. 1987. *Sport of Nature*. New York: Alfred A. Knopf.

———. 1990. *My Son's Story*. New York: Farrar, Straus and Giroux.

———. 1998. *The House Gun*. Rockland: Compass Press.

———. 2001. *The Pickup*. New York: Farrar, Straus and Giroux.

Goux, Jean-Joseph. 1978. *Les Iconoclastes*. Paris: Seuil.

———. 1990. *Symbolic Economies: After Marx and Freud*. Ithaca, N.Y.: Cornell University Press.

———. 1994. *The Coiners of Language*. Norman: University of Oklahoma Press.

———. 2000. *Frivolité de la valeur*. Paris: Blusson.

Select Bibliography

Hagège, Claude. 1985. *L'homme de parole*. Paris: Fayard.
———. 1987. *Le Français et les siècles*. Paris: Seuil.
———. 1992. *Le Souffle de la langue*. Paris: Odile Jacob.
———. 2000. *Halte à la mort des langues*. Paris: Odile Jacob.
Huntington, Samuel. 1998. *The Clash of Civilisations and the Remaking of World Order*. New York: Simon & Schuster.
Jelev, Jeliou. 1998. *Bulgarie. Terre d'Europe*. Paris: Frison-Roche.
Kahn, Axel. 1996. *La Médecine du XXIème siècle: des gènes et des hommes*. Paris: Bayard.
———. 1998. *Copies conformes: le clonage en question* (with Fabrice Papillon). Paris: Nil.
———. 2000. *Et l'homme dans tout ça?* Paris: Nil.
———. 2001. *L'Avenir n'est pas écrit* (with Albert Jacquard). Paris: Bayard Culture.
Kennedy, Paul. 1983. *Strategy and Diplomacy, 1870–1945*. London: George Allen and Unwin.
———. 1987. *The Rise and Fall of the Great Powers*. New York: Random House.
———. 1993. *Preparing for the 21st Century*. New York: Random House.
Klein, Melanie. 1932. *The Psycho-Analysis of Children*. London: Hogarth.
Kristeva, Julia. 1995. *New Maladies of the Soul*. New York: Columbia University Press.
———. 2001. *Female Genius: Hannah Arendt*. New York: Columbia University Press.
———. 2002. *Melanie Klein*. New York: Columbia University Press.
———. 2004. *Colette*. New York: Columbia University Press.
Le Goff, Jacques. 1982. *Time, Work and Culture in the Middle Ages*. Trans. Arthur Goldhammer. Chicago: Chicago University Press.
Maffesoli, Michel. 1995. *The Time of the Tribes: The Decline of Individualism in Mass Societies*. London: Sage Publications.
———. 1990. *Au creux des apparences*. Paris: Plon.
———. 1992. *La Transfiguration du politique*. Paris: Grasset et Fasquelle.
———. 1996. *Eloge de la raison sensible*. Paris: Grasset et Fasquelle.
———. 1997. *Du nomadisme*. Paris: LGF.
———. 1998. *Le Mystère de la conjonction*. Paris: Fata Morgana.
———. 2000. *L'Instant éternel*. Paris: La Table Ronde.
———. 2002. *La Part du diable. Précis de subversion postmoderne*. Paris: Flammarion.
Martinet, André. 1986. *Des steppes aux océans. L'indo-européen et les 'Indo-Européens'*. Paris: Payot.
Massuh, Victor. 1956. *El diálogo de las culturas*. Universidad Nacional de Tucumán: Facultad de Filosofía y Letras.
———. 1965. *El rito y lo sagrado*. Buenos Aires: Editorial Columba.
———. 1968. *La libertad y la violencia*. Buenos Aires: Editorial Sudamericana.
———. 1969. *Nietzsche y el fin de la religion*. Buenos Aires: Editorial Sudamericana.
———. 1975. *Nihilismo y experiencia extrema*. Buenos Aires: Editorial Sudamericana.
———. 1994. *Agonía de la razón*. Buenos Aires: Editorial Sudamericana.
———. 1999. *Cara y contracara: una civilisación a la deriva?* Buenos Aires: Emecé Editores.
Mbembe, Achille. 1988. *Afriques indociles*. Paris: Khartala.
———. 2001. *On the Postcolony*. Berkeley: University of California Press.
M'Bokolo, Elikia. 1981. *Noirs et blancs en Afrique équatoriale*. Paris: EHESS.

———. 1992. *L'Afrique noire. Histoire et civilisations*. Paris: Hatier.
———, ed. 1997. *L'Afrique entre l'Europe et l'Amérique*. Paris: UNESCO Publishing.
Mendes, Candido. 1977. *Beyond Populism*. New York: State University of New York Press.
———. 1977. *Justice, faim de l'Eglise*. Bruges: Desclée de Brouwer.
———. 2003. *Lula et l'autre Brésil*. Paris: Editions de l'IHEAL.
Montagnier, Luc. 2000. *Virus*. New York: W. W. Norton & Co.
———. 2003. 'Où va la recherche biomédicale française?', in *Quel avenir pour la recherche?Cinquante savants s'engagent* (volume). Paris: Flammarion.
Morin, Edgar. 1992. *Method: Towards a Study of Humankind*. New York: Peter Lang Publishing.
———. 1999. *Introduction à une politique de l'homme*. Paris: Seuil.
———. 2001. *L'Humanité de l'humanité: l'identité humaine*. Paris: Seuil.
———. 2003. *La violence du monde* (with Jean Baudrillard). Paris: Le Félin.
Mufwene, Salikoko. 2001. *The Ecology of Language Evolution*. Cambridge: Cambridge University Press.
Prantzos, Nicolas. 1988. *Soleils éclatés* (with T. Montmerle). Paris: Presse du CNRS.
———. 1998. *Naissance, vie et mort des étoiles*. Paris: PUF, Que sais-je? Series.
———. 2000. *Sommes-nous seuls dans l'univers?* (volume). Paris: Fayard.
Reich, Robert. 1993. *L'Economie mondialisée*. Paris: Dunod.
Ricoeur, Paul. 1974. *The Conflict of Interpretations*. Evanston: Northwestern University Press.
———. 1986. *Fallible Man: Philosophy of the Will*. New York: Fordham University Press.
———. 1994. *Oneself as Another*. Chicago: University of Chicago Press.
———. 1997. *Critique and Conviction*. New York: Columbia University Press.
———. 2004. *Memory, History, Forgetting*. Chicago: University of Chicago Press.
Rifkin, Jeremy. 1995. *The End of Work. The Decline of the Global Labor Force and the Dawn of the Postmarket Era*. New York: G.P. Putnam's Sons.
———. 1998. *The Biotech Century*. Harnessing the Gene and Remaking the World. New York: J.P. Tarcher/Putnam.
———. 2000. *The Age of Access: The New Culture of Hypercapitalism where all of Life is a Paid-For Experience*. New York: J.P. Tarcher/Putnam.
———. 2002. *The Hydrogen Economy: The Creation of the Worldwide Energy Web and the Redistribution of Power on Earth*. New York: J.P. Tarcher/Putnam.
Sagasti, Francisco. 1994. *The Uncertain Quest: Science, Technology and Development* (co-author). Lanham: Bernan Associates.
Sen, Amartya. 2000. 'La raison, l'Orient et l'Occident', *Esprit* (December).
Serres, Michel. 1995a. *The Natural Contract*. Ann Arbor: University of Michigan Press.
———. 1995b. *Angels, A Modern Myth*. Paris: Flammarion.
———. 2000. *Le retour au contrat naturel*. Paris: Bibliothèque Nationale de France.
———. 2001. *Hominescence*. Paris: Le Pommier.
———. 2003a. *L'Incandescent*. Paris: Le Pommier.
———. 2003b. *Les référents: éléments d'histoire des sciences*. Paris: Bordas.
———. 2004. *Five Senses*. London & New York: Continuum International Publishing Group–Mansell.

Shayegan, Daryush. 1991. *Qu'est-ce qu'une révolution religieuse?* Paris: Albin Michel.
———. 1996. *Le Regard mutilé.* La Tour-d'Aigues: Editions de l'Aube.
———. 2003. *La lumière vient de l'Occident.* La Tour-d'Aigues: Editions de l'Aube.
Sloterdijk, Peter. 1987. *Critique of Cynical Reason.* Minneapolis: University of Minnesota Press.
———. 1989. *Thinker on Stage: Nietzsche's Materialism.* Minneapolis: University of Minnesota Press.
———. 1998. *Sphären I—Blasen,* Frankfurt am Main: Suhrkamp.
———. 1999a. *Regeln für den Menschenpark.* Frankfurt am Main: Suhrkamp.
———. 1999b. *Sphären II—Globen,* Frankfurt am Main: Suhrkamp.
——— 2003. *Sphären III—Schäume.* Frankfurt am Main: Suhrkamp.
Sormon, Guy. 1997. *Le Monde est ma tribu.* Paris: Fayard.
Sue, Roger. 1982. *Vers une société du temps libre.* Paris: PUF.
———. 1994. *Temps et ordre social.* Paris: PUF.
———. 1997a. *Vers une économie plurielle.* Paris: Syros.
———. 1997b. *La richesse des hommes. Vers l'économie quaternaire.* Paris: Odile Jacob.
———. 2001. *Renouer le lien social. Liberté, égalité, association.* Paris: Odile Jacob.
———. 2003. *La Société civile face au pouvoir.* Paris: Presses de Sciences-Po.
Testart, Jacques. 1994. *Le Désir du gène.* Paris: Flammarion.
———. 1997. *Pour une éthique planétaire.* Paris: Mille et une nuits.
———. 1999. *Des hommes probables: de la procréation aléatoire à la reproduction normative.* Paris: Seuil.
———. 2003. *Le Vivant manipulé.* Paris: Sand & Tchou.
Touraine, Alain. 1995. *Critique of Modernity.* Oxford: Blackwell Publishers.
———. 2000. *Can We Live Together? Equality and Difference.* Trans. David Macey. Stanford: Stanford University Press.
———. 2000. *La recherche de soi.* Paris: Fayard.
———. 2001. *Beyond Neoliberalism.* Trans. David Macey. Cambridge: Polity Press.
Trinh Xuan Thuan. 1993. *The Birth of the Universe: The Big Bang and After.* New York: Harry N. Abrams.
———. 1995. *Secret Melody.* Oxford: Oxford University Press.
———. 2000. *Chaos and Harmony.* Oxford: Oxford University Press.
———. 2001. *The Quantum and the Lotus: A Journey to the Frontiers Where Science and Buddhism Meet.* New York: Crown Publishing Group.
———. 2003. *Origines: la nostalgie des commencements.* Paris: Fayard.
UNDP. 1996. *Human Development Report.* New York: UNDP.
UNESCO. 2000. *World Education Report.* Paris: UNESCO.
Vattimo, Gianni. 1988. *The End of Modernity: Nihilism and Hermeneutics in Postmodern Culture.* Baltimore: Johns Hopkins University Press.
———. 1992. *The Transparent Society.* Baltimore: Johns Hopkins University Press.
———. 1997. *Beyond Interpretation: The Meaning of Hermeneutics for Philosophy.* Stanford: Stanford University Press.
———. 2000. *Belief.* Stanford: Stanford University Press.
———. 2001. *Dialogo con Nietzsche.* Milan: Garzanti.
Welsch, Wolfgang. 1987. *Unsere postmoderne Moderne.* Weinheim: VCH Acta humaniora.
———. 1990. *Ästhetisches Denken.* Stuttgart: Reclam.

———. 1995. *Vernunft*. Frankfurt am Main: Suhrkamp.
———. 1996. *Grenzgänge der Ästhetik*. Stuttgart: Reclam.
———. 1997. *Undoing Aesthetics*. London: Sage Publications.
———. 2002. *Aesthetics and Beyond*. Changohun, PR China: Jilin People's Publishing House.
Wilson, Edward O. 1975. *Sociobiology: The New Synthesis*. Cambridge & London: Harvard University Press.
———. 1978. *On Human Nature*. Cambridge & London: Harvard University Press.
———. 1998. *Consilience: The Unity of Knowledge*. New York: Alfred A. Knopf.
———. 2001. *The Future of Life*. New York: Knopf Publishing Group.

www.ingramcontent.com/pod-product-compliance
Lightning Source LLC
Chambersburg PA
CBHW052210090526
44584CB00019BA/2687